PEER·VIII

Physician's Evaluation and Educational Review in Emergency Medicine

Volume 8

ANSWERS

Mary Jo Wagner, MD, FACEP

Editor-in-Chief

Program Director, Synergy Medical Education Alliance
Emergency Medicine Residency Program, Saginaw, Michigan
Professor, Division of Emergency Medicine, Michigan State University
College of Human Medicine, East Lansing, Michigan

American College of
Emergency Physicians®

ADVANCING EMERGENCY CARE

Table of Contents

Publisher's Notice

ISBN 978-0-9834288-4-8
First printing, October 2011

About the Editor

Mary Jo Wagner, MD, FACEP, is in her third term as Editor-in-Chief of the *PEER* content review and self-assessment series.

Dr. Wagner is program director of the emergency medicine residency program for Synergy Medical Education Alliance in Saginaw, Michigan, and a full professor in the Division of Emergency Medicine at Michigan State University College of Human Medicine. Dr. Wagner also practices emergency medicine in two community hospitals. She earned her doctor of medicine degree from Boston University School of Medicine and completed her residency training at St. Vincent Medical Center/The Toledo Hospital Emergency Medicine Residency Program in Toledo, Ohio. She has been board certified by the American Board of Emergency Medicine since 1992.

In addition to the two previous editions of *PEER*, Dr. Wagner has edited *Last Minute Emergency Medicine, Emergency and Primary Care of the Hand, Foresight,* and *Critical Decisions in Emergency Medicine.* She is on the editorial board for AccessEmergency Medicine.com.

Dr. Wagner has chaired the national ACEP Education Committee, the Educational Meetings Subcommittee, and the Federal Government Affairs Committee and has also served on the Academic Affairs Committee, the Focused Meetings Task Force, and several other work groups both nationally and locally. She is a past president of the Council of Emergency Medicine Residency Directors.

In 2005, Dr. Wagner was among a group of emergency physicians who worked on Capitol Hill to secure new or extra funding for residency positions after Congress passed the residency redistribution provision. And in 2009, Dr. Wagner received one of the College's highest honors, the Outstanding Contribution in Education Award, in recognition of her work on behalf of excellence in emergency medicine clinical practice, teaching, and research.

PEER VIII Editorial Board

The American College of Emergency Physicians gratefully acknowledges the contributions of the PEER VIII *Editorial Board in the development and writing of the* PEER VIII *questions and answer explanations.*

Contributors

Dr. Wagner and the PEER VIII *Editorial Board gratefully acknowledge the following individuals and organizations who contributed to* PEER VIII *by donating images, participating in item testing, and providing and reviewing information.*

Joshua Broder, MD, FACEP
Esther H. Chen, MD
Antonio Cummings, MD
David Duong, MD
Mark A. Hostetler, MD, MPH, FACEP
Christian Jacobus, MD
Timothy H. Kaufman, MD
Tina Latimer, MD, MPH
Edwin Lopez, MD
Amal Mattu, MD, FACEP
Kelly P. O'Keefe, MD, FACEP
Rianne Page, MD
Robert A. Rosen, MD, FACEP
Christopher Ross, MD
Robert C. Satonik, MD, FACEP
Loren Yamamoto, MD, MPH, MBA, FAAP, FACEP

EMS Fellow from the University of Pittsburgh Department of Emergency Medicine

Adam Z. Tobias, MD

Resident from the Denver Health Medical Center Emergency Medicine Residency Program

Todd Guth, MD

Resident from the Johns Hopkins Medical Institutions Residency Program

Sneha Shah, MD

Resident from the Loma Linda University Medical Center Residency Program

Vi Am Dinh, MD

Resident from the Naval Medical Center (San Diego) Emergency Medicine Residency Program

Steve Tantama, MD

Resident from the Regions Hospital Emergency Medicine Residency Program

Autumn Erwin, MD

Resident from the University of Maryland Emergency Medicine Residency Program

Joshua Moskovitz, MD, MPH

Residents from the Cook County Emergency Medicine Residency Program

Tamara Espinoza, MD
Roderick Roxas, MD
Michael Nelson, MD
Rachel Weiselberg, MD

Residents from the Synergy Medical Education Alliance/ Michigan State University Emergency Medicine Residency Program

Edris Afzali, MD*
Abdulaziz Alburaih, MD
Adel Alghamdi, MD*
Khaled Alghamdi, MD
William A. Bishop, MD
Thomas Charlton, MD
Mathias Christianson, MD*
Stacey Clark, MD
Jonathon Deibel, MD
Angela Gregory, MD
Roman Hill, MD
Marisa Homer, MD*
Ervin Hunt, MD
Charles Keersmaekers, MD*
Corrine Kvamme, MD
Neil Malhotra, MD
Nicole McCadie, DO
Heather Merrill, MD
Eric Minnihan, MD*
James Mlejnek, MD
Adam Nofziger, MD
Dilnaz Panjwani, MD
Peri Penman, DO
Sameh Sejiney, MD
Saleem Sheikh, DO*
Philip Sloan, MD
Kristy Smith, MD*
Dalkeith Tucker, DO
Tiffany Weiss-Feldkamp, DO*
Diana Yandell, MD*

*Additionally developed Questions book index.

Residents from the University of Iowa Emergency Medicine Residency Program

Sara Burnham, DO
David Dierks, DO
Kathryn Szajna, DO
Amy Walsh, MD

Residents from the University of South Florida Emergency Medicine Residency Program

Nadia Abrahamsen, MD
James Bartlett, MD
Phillip Ryan Coker, MD
Matthew Daniel Fucarino, MD
Tamas Gaspar, MD
Nicholas Nathaniel Healy, DO
Melinda Henry, MD
Lindsay A. Lyon, MD
Molly McIntyre, MD
Raymond Lee Merritt, DO
Deborah Marie Luiken Repaskey, MD
John Elliott Reynolds IV, DO
Nathaniel Ronning, MD
Kant Shah, MD
Kristopher Ryan Sutherly, MD
Sarah Temple, MD
Kimberly Norman Thivierge, MD
Veronica Theresa Tucci, MD
Andrew Brent Wilson, MD

ACEP Educational Publications

Marta Foster, Director and Senior Editor
Mike C. Goodwin, Creative Services Manager
Jessica Hamilton, Publications Assistant
Mary Anne Mitchell, Editor
Lexi Schwartz, Publications Sales and Service Representative
Thomas S. Werlinich, Associate Executive Director, Educational Products
National Education Representative: Linda Robinson, MD, FACEP
Proofreading: Lori Cavanaugh, Allison Frank Esposito, Kathleen Wildasin, MA
Indexing: Hughes Analytics
Printing: United Book Press, Inc.

Disclosures

In accordance with Accreditation Council for Continuing Medical Education (ACCME) Standards and ACEP policy, all persons who were in a position to control the content of this enduring material must disclose to participants the existence of significant financial relationships with commercial interests that might have a direct interest in the subject matter. Dr. House disclosed that he received consulting fees from GlaxoSmithKline. Dr. Broder disclosed that his wife is a research organic chemist at GlaxoSmithKline. Dr. Abrahamian disclosed that he received consulting fees from Merck and ConvaTec, Inc., and fees for non-CME services directly from Merck. Dr. Yamamoto disclosed that he received royalties from AAP and ACEP and that he has an ownership interest with Alkermes, Inc. No other individuals in control of content have significant financial interests or relationships to disclose.

ACEP expects all Editorial Board members and contributors to present information in an objective, unbiased manner without endorsement or criticism of specific products or services. ACEP also expects that the relationships they disclose will not influence their contributions.

In *PEER VIII*, in most cases, drugs and devices are referred to by their generic names. In a few cases, however, brand names do appear for the sole purpose of clarification or easier recognition. Brand names were obtained from a variety of sources, including the National Center for Biotechnology Information of the U.S. National Library of Medicine (http://www.ncbi.nlm.nih.gov/). If more than one brand name was found, they are listed, up to three. In no instance is a drug or device listed by a brand name for a commercial purpose.

PEER VIII received no commercial support.

PEER VIII is not affiliated with the American Board of Emergency Medicine.

1. **The answer is C, Chest radiography and urinalysis.**

(Marco, 18-24; Marx, 83-86)

Fever is a sign of serious illness in geriatric patients. Eighty percent of febrile illnesses can be accounted for by respiratory, urinary, or skin infections. This patient's skin is intact without rash, so the source of her fever is most likely a respiratory tract infection or a urinary tract infection. A WBC count can be elevated, normal, or depressed in an elderly patient with a fever and is not diagnostic. Blood cultures do not provide a diagnosis in the emergency department, although they can help guide antibiotic choices for inpatient care. If a blood culture is to be ordered, samples should be drawn before antibiotics are administered. Computed tomography scanning of the abdomen and pelvis is indicated in an elderly patient with fever if there are specific signs or symptoms that localize to the abdomen or if the initial laboratory and radiology findings do not provide an adequate diagnosis. Physicians should have a low threshold for performing diagnostic abdominal CT in elderly patients because they are less likely to have diagnostic physical findings. For example, the lack of abdominal wall musculature makes it unlikely that an elderly patient will develop abdominal guarding and rigidity, even in the context of peritonitis. Head CT and lumbar puncture are indicated if a CNS infection is suspected or if other evaluations have not identified a source of infection. The most common causes of increased confusion in febrile elderly patients are usually respiratory or urinary tract infections. Plain radiographs of the abdomen are indicated for assessment of bowel obstruction and to evaluate for free air or a foreign body. They are very unlikely to provide a diagnosis in an elderly patient with a fever. A CT scan of the abdomen is more likely to provide a diagnostic answer.

2. **The answer is B, Dilated esophagus proximal to a beaklike lower esophageal sphincter.**

(Marx, 1150-1151; Tintinalli, 548-551; Wolfson, 544-546)

The patient in the question has the classic symptoms of achalasia. The expected findings of a barium swallow include a dilated esophagus proximal to a beaklike lower esophageal sphincter. Achalasia is the most common esophageal motility disorder. It results from impairment of the normal swallowing-induced relaxation of the lower esophageal sphincter. Most patients with achalasia are 20 to 40 years old and complain of chest pain and odynophagia. The symptoms occur with both solids and liquids, are made worse by lying flat, and are accompanied by regurgitation of undigested food, especially with exercising. A barium swallow quickly confirms the diagnosis and might be done in the emergency department, so the patient can then be referred to a gastroenterologist for esophageal manometry. Treatment options begin with calcium-channel blockers to relax the smooth muscle in the distal esophagus. Diltiazem and nifedipine are reported to be effective, but not verapamil. Treatment of persistent symptoms might include endoscopic botulism toxin injections, dilation, and surgical myotomy. Diffuse ST-segment elevation and PR-interval depression are found in pericarditis, which is suggested by the positional nature of the chest pain but less likely given the pattern of this patient's symptoms in relation to food. The regurgitation of undigested food might prompt family members to suspect an eating disorder in patients with undiagnosed achalasia. Gastric inflammatory changes noted on upper endoscopy suggest gastritis, but the patient's dysphagia suggests an esophageal disorder. White matter changes suggest multiple sclerosis, which would be more likely to cause transfer dysphagia with swallowing. Transfer dysphagia results in difficulty with starting to swallow, as the food moves from the mouth to the esophagus. Liquids cause more difficulty than solids in these patients.

3.   The answer is B, Esmolol.

(Marx, 1174; Tintinalli, 443, 444, 450-453)

In a patient with acute aortic dissection without shock, typically a $beta_1$-blocking agent such as esmolol is used initially to reduce shear force by reducing cardiac contractility and to prevent reflex tachycardia before a vasodilator is added to reduce blood pressure. The goals of emergency department treatment of acute aortic dissection, in addition to resuscitation, are to prevent extension of the dissection, obtain early cardiothoracic or vascular surgery consultation, and control pain. To prevent extension of an aortic dissection, the shear forces on the intimal flap of the aorta must be reduced. This is achieved by controlled reduction of blood pressure and heart rate, as shear pressure is related to the rate of rise of left ventricular pressure (expressed as dP/dt). The heart rate should be reduced to a goal of 60 beats/min, or the lowest tolerated by the patient. The blood pressure should be reduced to a mean arterial pressure of 60 or systolic blood pressure of 100 to 120, or the lowest tolerated by the patient. A beta-blocker is preferred to prevent a vasodilation-induced reflex tachycardia that would increase shear pressure. Esmolol infusion is commonly used because it is easily titrated and short acting, although metoprolol or labetalol might also be considered. Sodium nitroprusside is an effective vasodilator with a short half-life and is also easily titrated but should be used after initial medications are administered to reduce heart rate. It is more potent than nitroglycerin for arterial vasodilation. Labetalol reduces cardiac contractility, heart rate, and arterial blood pressure, but its immediate effects on blood pressure are not as potent or predictable as those of sodium nitroprusside. Diltiazem, a calcium-channel blocker, can be used to reduce blood pressure and contractility in patients in whom beta-blockers are contraindicated, but it is not the first choice for therapy.

4. The answer is D, Treatment for significant cases includes oral steroids.

(Auerbach, 1267-1275; Marx, 1543)

The patient in this question is suffering from an allergic phytocontact dermatitis, likely from one of the toxicodendron species such as poison ivy, poison oak, or sumac. Systemic steroids are often needed for significant cases, and a long, slow taper to prevent disease rebound is recommended. The plants have different geographic locations: poison ivy is found east of the Rockies, poison oak is found west of the Rockies, and poison sumac is found in the southeast. But all contain similar urashiols found in the colorless or slightly yellow sap that turns black on exposure to air. Previous sensitization does not prevent recurrence but does determine when the clinical manifestations occur after resin exposure (1-2 days for previous sensitization, 10-14 days otherwise). Dermatitis occurs only where the resin has contacted the skin, which explains why linear lesions are typical (as in other allergic contact dermatoses). The thickness of the stratum corneum determines the degree of resin penetration and subsequent manifestations; this explains why the palms are typically spared and why the eyelids can develop severe swelling. Pruritus can precede the rash, which can progress from initial well-demarcated patches of erythema to papules. Vesicles and bullae are also characteristic, as is crusting. The rash itself, including fluid from the bullae, does not contain the urashiols and is therefore not contagious to others and does not spread the rash. The urashiols can remain stable on inanimate objects such as clothes, making reexposure possible. But discarding the clothes is not necessary, as both washing and bleaching can inactivate the urashiols. Administration of antihistamines and topical steroids is helpful in the treatment of intense pruritus. Various topical agents such as calamine lotion, aluminum acetate, cool compresses, nonscalding hot water, and oatmeal baths can also be used for comfort.

5. The answer is D, Hypotension fails to respond to standard resuscitation.

(Marx, 1671-1675; Wolfson, 1030-1033)

Most adrenal crises occur in patients with chronic adrenal insufficiency who have an illness or stress that results in inadequate cortisol production; hypotension out of proportion to the severity of that underlying illness and hypotension refractory to standard resuscitation are important clinical clues to adrenal crisis. Appropriate management of adrenal insufficiency includes treating the precipitating illness, aggressive fluid and pressor resuscitation, and correction of inadequate cortisol by administration of hydrocortisone or dexamethasone. The adrenal gland is composed of the cortex (which produces aldosterone, androgens, and cortisol) and the medulla (which produces catecholamines) and is in a feedback loop with the hypothalamic-pituitary axis. Adrenal insufficiency can be both primary

(Addison disease) or secondary due to lack of ACTH production from the pituitary gland. In primary adrenal insufficiency, aldosterone production and release are affected, but in secondary adrenal deficiency, they are not. Aldosterone promotes sodium reabsorption and potassium excretion, and the lack of it in primary adrenal insufficiency contributes to both hyponatremia and hyperkalemia and a potentially greater degree of hypotension. Hyperkalemia is common in primary adrenal insufficiency and is not expected in secondary adrenal insufficiency. Worldwide, tuberculosis, not cytomegalovirus, is the most common cause of primary adrenal insufficiency. Most cases of primary adrenal insufficiency in the Western world are autoimmune related. Other etiologies of primary adrenal insufficiency include congenital conditions, hemorrhage (traumatic, anticoagulation, infections [Waterhouse-Friderichsen in meningococcemia], infiltrative conditions (amyloidosis, hemochromatosis, sarcoidosis), and metastatic cancer. Causes of secondary adrenal insufficiency include pituitary problems (postpartum pituitary necrosis) and, the most common, chronic glucocorticoid use. Initial signs and symptoms of adrenal insufficiency are often nonspecific and commonly include generalized weakness, fatigue, gastrointestinal symptoms, and fever.

6. **The answer is A, A symptom-free interval followed by the manifest illness phase.**

(Adams, 1481-1485; Marx, 1937-1938; Tintinalli, 56-61; Wolfson, 1619-1624)

Acute radiation syndrome (ARS) is a condition that results from whole-body irradiation from an internal or an external source over a short time period. The latent phase is the second of four phases (prodromal, latent, manifest illness, and recovery or death), during which the victim is symptom free for weeks (at lower doses) to just a few hours (in severe ARS). The prodromal phase is characterized by a transient period of self-limiting autonomic symptoms, which usually include anorexia, nausea, and vomiting. The manifest illness phase can be divided into three subsyndromes based on the dose of whole-body irradiation. The hematopoietic syndrome begins with a rapid decline in lymphocytes; for this reason, the absolute lymphocyte count (ALC) is one of the best early indicators of prognosis for ARS. Specifically, the ALC measured at 48 hours' postexposure is a useful prognostic indicator for the progression of the disease and chance for recovery. The decline in lymphocytes is followed by further declines in granulocytes and platelets with resulting pancytopenia. The gastrointestinal syndrome occurs at radiation doses above those required for the hematopoietic syndrome. It is characterized by severe vomiting, diarrhea, and abdominal pain, which leads to significant volume loss and electrolyte abnormalities and progresses to fulminant enterocolitis; it is uniformly fatal. The cardiovascular and CNS syndrome occurs at even higher doses of exposure and is characterized by all of the symptoms described plus refractory hypotension, altered mental status, lethargy, ataxia, tremors, and convulsions within hours of exposure.

Death occurs within 24 to 72 hours as a result of circulatory collapse. The final phase in ARS is recovery or death. This can be predicted based on the patient's ALC measured at 24 and 48 hours. A patient whose ALC measured at 24 hours is above 1,200/mcL requires no clinical support and has a good prognosis. An ALC below 500/mcL at 24 hours is predictive of a poor prognosis and the need for intense levels of support and treatment. An ALC that remains above 1,200/mcL at 48 hours indicates a good prognosis and minimal supportive therapy; an ALC below 300/mcL at 48 hours is uniformly predictive of death.

7. The answer is D, Topical antibiotics applied using an ear wick.

(Marx, 881; Tintinalli, 1552-1553)

In cases of severe otitis externa when the ear canal is swollen shut, topical antibiotics might not penetrate the length of the canal. Instead, an ear wick or a small piece of gauze can be inserted to create a track for the delivery of the topical antibiotics. In a pediatric patient, the end of the wick provides a convenient point of access for application of antibiotics by the parent. Organisms typically responsible for otitis externa are *Pseudomonas aeruginosa* and *Staphylococcus aureus*. Despite the common identification of *S. aureus* in otitis externa, reports of methicillin-resistant *S. aureus* otitis and treatment failures are rare. Oral corticosteroids are not indicated. The primary treatment for otitis externa is cortisporin otic, a combination agent containing neomycin, polymixin B, and hydrocortisone. If cortisporin is used, the suspension form is preferred because it is less ototoxic than the solution preparation. Skull-based osteomyelitis is a concern in patients with diabetes or other forms of immunosuppression. It is not expected in a 12-year-old.

8. The answer is B, Disseminated intravascular coagulation.

(Marx, 1588-1589; Tintinalli, 929-932, 1467-1468)

Disseminated intravascular coagulation (DIC) is an acquired bleeding disorder characterized by low platelets, prolonged coagulation times (especially factors V, VIII, and XIII), and low fibrinogen levels. The disease process causes fibrin formation and then breakdown, consuming clotting factors. The D-dimer level is elevated in DIC because of the microvascular clotting that occurs, and elevation of the D-dimer level is often diagnostic of DIC compared to other disorders with low platelet counts and prolonged PT and PTT. Fragmentation of red blood cells can also occur as they travel through fibrin strands. The etiology of DIC is wide in variety and includes infections, carcinomas, acute leukemia, trauma, liver disease, pregnancy, envenomations, and transfusions. Blast crisis can present with thrombocytopenia and easy bruising but might also include fever and malaise. It usually does not affect the PT or fibrinogen levels. Liver cirrhosis produces stable thrombocytopenia and coagulopathy prior to decompensation seen in DIC. Primary fibrinolysis can be difficult to distinguish from DIC, but because fibrinolysis occurs without thrombin, the D-dimer will be normal in primary fibrinolysis. Factors V and VIII and platelets are usually in the low normal range.

9. The answer is C, Start hand-warming and consider oral nifedipine.

(Marx, 1347, 1357, 1812-1817; Tintinalli, 459; Wolfson, 867)

The patient in this question has scleroderma and presents with complications caused by Raynaud phenomenon triggered by holding cold drinks. The appropriate next step is to start gentle rewarming combined with topical or oral calcium-channel blocker or nitrates. Raynaud phenomenon results in characteristic color changes of pallor, cyanosis, and rubor (white, blue, red) usually accompanied by numbness, tingling, or pain. This happens when normal vasoconstriction from an environmental trigger occurs in the setting of subintimal hyperplasia limiting blood flow. The diagnosis of scleroderma requires one of the major criteria or two minor criteria. Major criteria include proximal thickening, tightening, and induration of the skin of the fingers and toes. Minor criteria include sclerodactyly, digital pitting scars of the finger pads, and bibasilar pulmonary fibrosis. Scleroderma is a systemic disease that affects multiple organs, but it is most obvious in the skin. It is usually clinically silent; patients might present to the emergency department for treatment of painful vasoocclusion of the hands, renal crisis, malignant hypertension, or cor pulmonale secondary to pulmonary fibrosis. Unless thrombosis occurs with prolonged vasoocclusion, angioplasty and tPA are not indicated. Intra-arterial injection of an alpha-adrenergic blocker such as prazosin is reserved for severe cases refractory to gentle warming and topical or oral calcium-channel blocker or nitrates. In recurrent disease, chronic management can include surgical digital sympathectomy.

10. The answer is B, Diarrhea with occasional blood and mucus and intermittent fever with abdominal pain for 3 weeks.

(Marx, 1200, 1211, 1213, 1218-1219; Tintinalli, 531-534)

Entamoeba histolytica, the causative agent of amebiasis, results in an indolent infection; patients generally present after having symptoms for 2 to 3 weeks. It causes crampy abdominal pain, fever, and loose stools mixed with blood and mucus. It is more likely to infect long-term travelers, such as Peace Corps volunteers. Left untreated, *E. histolytica* infection might progress to liver abscess. A ruptured liver abscess presents with acute right upper quadrant pain and fever. Amebiasis is diagnosed using stool examination for cysts, antigen tests on stool, or serum serology. Treatment in a symptomatic patient is with metronidazole in addition to iodoquinol or paromomycin. Compared with amebiasis, traveler's diarrhea has a more abrupt onset and shorter course. It is usually caused by enterotoxigenic *Escherichia coli.* The presentation described as several episodes of nonbloody diarrhea for 3 days with nausea, vomiting, and low-grade fever is typical of traveler's diarrhea but can also be caused by food poisoning. Copious, severe watery diarrhea should prompt consideration of cholera, caused by *Vibrio cholerae*. Cholera is endemic to several areas of the world, including South Asia, parts of South America, and Africa. Another cause is ingestion of contaminated shellfish from the Gulf of Mexico, but these cases are sporadic. Treatment is generally supportive with rehydration and a single dose of either doxycycline or a fluoroquinolone. Grossly bloody stools accompanied by fever are dysentery, which can be caused by infection with *E. coli, Campylobacter jejuni, Shigella,* or *Salmonella.* Treatment is generally with a short course of fluoroquinolones. *Giardia* infection, like amebiasis, is associated with an indolent course. It characteristically causes significant foul-smelling flatulence and abdominal cramps. It can be diagnosed using serology or stool examination and is treated with metronidazole.

11. The answer is D, Urinary retention.

(Marx, 1391-1392; Wolfson, 728-729)

The most consistent finding present in patients with cauda equina syndrome is urinary retention (sensitivity 90%). The patient might also complain of urinary or fecal incontinence, but urinary retention (which can manifest as overflow "incontinence") is more common. Cauda equina syndrome is not a true cord syndrome. It is a syndrome that affects the cluster of lumbar and sacral nerve roots that continues distal to the cord known as the cauda equina, or "horse's tail." A patient complaint of low back pain and bilateral motor or sensory findings, especially in the saddle or perineal region, should raise suspicion for this condition. Cauda equina syndrome is by definition a lower motor neuron lesion, as it involves only the nerve roots, so hyporeflexia might be seen. An upper motor neuron lesion or a mix of upper and lower can be seen with involvement of the distal spinal cord, a condition referred to as conus medullaris syndrome. Another way to distinguish between the two is that the cauda equina syndrome has signs and symptoms consistent with lumbosacral radiculopathies, and the conus medullaris syndrome has signs and symptoms consistent with spinal cord compression. These symptoms and other forms of spinal cord compression are referred to collectively as the epidural compression syndromes, with the symptoms differing only by the level of compression. The sensory changes in cauda equina syndrome are dermatomal and correspond to the affected nerve roots. The classic finding is saddle anesthesia involving the buttocks, the backs of the thighs, and the perineum. Patients might not be aware of this deficit (hence the risk of skin breakdown) and should be asked specifically about sensation in the sacral region. Nondermatomal sensory loss is seen in conus medullaris syndrome, consistent with spinal cord compression and dysfunction. In both cauda equina and conus medullaris syndromes, the causes can be degenerative or traumatic or related to spinal tumors or infection. The most common cause is multilevel lumbar stenosis. A herniated nucleus pulposus accounts for less than 5% of cases. Urinary retention (and post-void incontinence) and fecal incontinence are signs of sphincter dysfunction that are common in both syndromes.

12. The answer is B, Ongoing seizure activity that persists after tonic-clonic movements end.

(American College of Emergency Physicians [seizures], 605-625; Marx, 1347-1348)

The patient in this question is in status epilepticus. Patients in status epilepticus can continue to have ongoing EEG-detected electrical discharge despite the absence of obvious tonic-clonic motor findings. This is known as subtle convulsive status. Patients in status epilepticus typically present with either tonic-clonic movements that have persisted for longer than 30 minutes or with recurrent seizure activity that occurs prior to return to a normal level of consciousness. Status epilepticus is more common at the extremes of age. Because more than one agent might be required to terminate the seizure activity, the mortality rate ranges from 5% to 20% in patients whose seizures are controlled with a single agent, and up to 65% in patients who need multiple agents. Typical first-line agents are benzodiazepines and phenytoin. Additional agents that can be used include phenobarbital and valproic acid, as well as infusions of benzodiazepines, pentobarbital, or propofol. Additional treatments include aggressive cooling, protecting the airway, and paralyzing the patient. Patients in whom persistent subtle convulsive status epilepticus or nonconvulsive status epilepticus is suspected or in whom paralysis is initiated should be monitored with an EEG.

13. The answer is A, Law enforcement presence.

(Marx, 814; Roberts, 1081)

In the interest of safety for hospital personnel and security for the alleged suspect, law enforcement officers should be present at all times during the examination of a sexual assault suspect. There are several issues that should be taken into consideration, such as when the examinations of the victim and suspect are conducted. Examination of the victim should occur first; the history from the victim as to injuries inflicted on the suspect (scratches, bites) should prompt confirmation during examination of the suspect. Efforts should be made to prevent contact between the victim and the suspect while they are in the emergency department. Local laws and protocols must be followed for evidence collection. In some states, the examination can proceed without the suspect's consent, but the suspect always has the right to remain silent. Any statements made by the suspect should be noted in the record, as should photographs of injuries or identifying marks on the suspect, such as tattoos. Collection of hairs, blood, and body fluids from the suspect should be completed in a manner similar to that used for the victim, although more reference samples can be taken from the suspect. For example, in a male suspect, samples should include swabs of the fingers, penis, and scrotum. Tests for sexually transmitted diseases and other serology are typical but not required, and the cost for this testing and treatment rendered might not be covered under state law.

14. The answer is B, Associated seizures are typically resistant to treatment with phenytoin.

(Marx, 2014-2016; Wolfson, 1526-1527)

The mainstay of treatment for phencyclidine (PCP) intoxication is intravenous benzodiazepines. Similarly, benzodiazepines are the first-line treatment for PCP-induced seizures, with phenobarbital as an alternative. Other agents are typically ineffective. Phenothiazines should also be avoided because they can reduce seizure threshold, exacerbate hyperthermia, and induce hypotension. Although PCP is secreted into the stomach, it is at such low levels that activated charcoal is ineffective; it is contraindicated unless the patient is intubated and sedated because the stimulation from the procedure can dramatically worsen the patient's behavior and response, and altered mental status can contribute to aspiration. Activated charcoal may be considered if the patient is intubated and body packing is suspected. Additional clearance modalities that do not work for PCP include urine acidification, hemodialysis, and hemoperfusion. Most routine hospital drug screens do not include PCP, and quantitative analysis is not useful from a time standpoint. False-positive immunoassays for PCP occur with ketamine and dextromethorphan use. Intracranial bleeding can be a result of the hypertensive response to PCP or other stimulant abuse, or due to trauma occurring as a result of the intoxication. The primary treatment for PCP intoxication is sedation as required in addition to a calm, quiet environment. Although benzodiazepines are first-line agents for sedation, haloperidol can also be used to chemically restrain these patients; beware of rare, catastrophic sudden death associated with butyrophenone medications.

15. The answer is D, *Staphylococcus epidermidis*.

(Barretti, 212; Brenner, 2025-2027; Marx, 1279-1280; Tintinalli, 629-630)

The predominant bacterial etiology in peritonitis associated with peritoneal dialysis is *Staphylococcus epidermidis* (approximately 40%), followed by *Streptococcus* species (15%-20%), gram-negative bacteria including *Escherichia coli* and *Proteus* (15%-20%), and then *Staphylococcus aureus* (10%). Anaerobic bacteria are the cause in about 5% of cases, and fungus less than that. Symptoms of peritonitis from dialysis are similar to those of other etiologies and include abdominal pain, fever, and rebound tenderness. Patients often report cloudy dialysate. A fungal etiology should be considered in repeated episodes of peritonitis that are not found to be culture positive for bacteria. Laboratory testing performed on the dialysate should include cell count, Gram stain, and culture; more than 100 WBCs/mm^3 is significant. Antibiotics are usually added to the dialysate and infused under the direction of a nephrologist. Empiric therapy should cover all common etiologies of peritonitis. For gram-positive cocci, a cephalosporin or vancomycin should be used. For coverage of gram-negative rods, a third-generation cephalosporin or gentamicin should be used.

16. The answer is A, Legionnaire disease.

(Marx, 928-940; Tintinalli, 482, 1075-1077)

Legionnaire disease is caused by *Legionella pneumophila,* a gram-negative bacillus that is often found in water systems such as air conditioners, spas, or shower heads. It more commonly affects men, smokers, and patients with underlying diseases. Signs and symptoms of Legionnaire disease include dry cough, relative bradycardia, gastrointestinal symptoms, and neurologic symptoms such as confusion, gait abnormalities, and seizures. The key to the diagnosis is a pneumonia accompanied by gastrointestinal symptoms. Hyponatremia and elevated levels on liver function testing in the setting of pneumonia are most commonly associated with *Legionella* infection. A patchy infiltrate or lobar consolidation with or without a pleural effusion can be found on radiograph. The diagnosis is made by testing the urine for antigens. *Legionella* infection does not respond to beta-lactam antibiotics or cephalosporins; macrolide antibiotics are the treatment of choice. Psittacosis is caused by *Chlamydia psittaci*, which is transmitted by birds. Patients present with severe headache and upper respiratory symptoms. A patchy perihilar appearance is seen on radiograph. Elevated liver enzymes and a classic malar facial rash (Horder spots) can also be found. The diagnosis is made by elevated complement fixation antibody titer, and it responds well to treatment with tetracycline or doxycycline. Q fever is caused by *Coxiella burnetii*, which is found in dried soil contaminated with the excrement from sheep, cattle, and goats. Signs and symptoms include high fever, headache, and nonproductive cough. Chest radiography reveals segmental densities or consolidation in the lower lobes. Elevated liver enzymes and proteinuria are seen. Serologic studies are used to confirm the diagnosis, and tetracycline is the treatment of choice. Tularemia is caused by *Francisella tularensis*, which is a gram-negative coccobacillus that is transmitted by ticks or by direct exposure to wild rabbits. Patients with tularemia present with high fever, dry cough, and a maculopapular rash. Chest radiography reveals bilateral patchy infiltrates, hilar adenopathy, and pleural effusions. Diagnosis is made using serologic studies. Streptomycin is the drug of choice.

17. The answer is C, Octreotide.

(Marx, 1638; Nelson, 722-724, 734-736; Wolfson, 1553)

Sulfonylureas such as glyburide cause the release of preformed insulin that can result in life-threatening, recurrent hypoglycemia. In a child, even a single pill can be life threatening. Octreotide is a synthetic somatostatin analogue that can antagonize the release of insulin. It has been demonstrated to decrease the incidence of hypoglycemic episodes in sulfonylurea poisonings and is the favored treatment after dextrose. Somatostatin is very short acting; octreotide, in contrast, was purposely synthesized as a longer-acting analogue. Octreotide is particularly attractive for use in sulfonylurea poisonings in pediatric patients. It can prevent problems related to frequent dextrose administrations, such as the need for central intravenous access (due to loss of peripheral intravenous access from repeated infusions into small veins) and rebound hypoglycemia (due to intrinsic insulin release in a patient with a normally functioning pancreas). Glucagon should certainly be considered in a patient with hypoglycemia of any etiology in whom intravenous access is delayed and oral administration is not feasible. However, its onset of action is delayed, and it might be ineffective. In a patient with severe hypoglycemia from a sulfonylurea, the intrinsic pathways to reverse hypoglycemia (including glucagon and epinephrine release) have already been maximized, making exogenous administration unlikely to be beneficial. Diazoxide is an infrequently used antihypertension medication that can also antagonize insulin release. It can be considered if octreotide is not available, but it is not as effective, and there are risks (although largely theoretical) of hypotension. The ideal dosing of octreotide remains unclear; it can be administered either intravenously or subcutaneously. Administration does not obviate the need for admission and serial glucose measurements.

18. The answer is D, Patients older than 55 years are at increased risk of death.

(Marx, 243-247; Wolfson, 126-127)

Several groups of patients are at higher risk when involved in a traumatic event. These groups include patients younger than 5 years old or older than 55 years; those with diabetes; patients with hepatic, cardiac, or respiratory disease; those who are morbidly obese, pregnant, or immunosuppressed; and those taking anticoagulant medications. These patients have an increased risk of death even when the traumatic injury is of moderate severity. Critically ill trauma patients benefit from being transported to a designated trauma facility even if it is not the closest facility because of the availability of operating rooms, surgeons, subspecialty care, and intensive care units accustomed to providing that level of care. In the care of trauma patients, it is better to overtriage to avoid missing serious injuries and "ramp down" the care as the patient is assessed than to undertriage and potentially miss injuries or delay diagnosis. Knowing the mechanism of injury allows the trauma team to anticipate different types of injuries and be more focused on timely detection and treatment. It can lead to considering a particular injury before the patient decompensates to the point of displaying vital sign abnormalities.

19. The answer is A, Cellulitis overlying the site of needle insertion.

(Roberts, 971; Tintinalli, 1927-1929)

Contraindications to arthrocentesis include cellulitis over the site of the needle insertion and suspected bacteremia, either of which can lead to seeding the joint and septic arthritis. If clinical indications require that a joint be aspirated through an area of cellulitis, hospitalization and intravenous antibiotics are recommended to help prevent intra-articular infection from the procedure. Coagulopathies can also be considered a contraindication because of the risk that the patient will develop a hemarthrosis, but aspirin use by itself should not be an issue. Arthrocentesis is indicated when there is a need to evaluate the fluid in a major joint to determine if there is an infection (septic arthritis), an arthropathy (gout or pseudogout), or an occult fracture. Laboratory tests that should be ordered to analyze synovial fluid include CBC count, glucose, uric acid, albumin, mucin viscosity, and identification of crystals. Laboratory and clinical findings of joint fluid infection include significant leukocytosis (>15,000/mcL); glucose lower than 40 mg/dL of serum glucose, and significantly low viscosity. In inflammatory disease (gout, pseudogout), findings include mild leukocytosis, slightly lower glucose, and moderately low viscosity, as well as traumatic effusion in which the fluid includes blood or fat and only mildly reduced viscosity.

20. The answer is C, Occurrence-based policy.

(Wood, 28-44)

Some general professional liability policies are occurrence based, meaning the policy provides coverage if the event that caused injury occurred during the policy period, regardless of when the claim is filed. For insurance underwriters, occurrence-based policies are problematic because of the long period of coverage (the "tail," or the period of time after the coverage expires when patients can still file claims) that can extend well beyond the actual policy expiration date. Occurrence-based policies tend to be expensive because they must be based on worst-case scenarios that take into account many unpredictable factors, such as inflation, changes in law and tort reform, and rising jury rewards. Many insurers, as a result, offer claims-made policies, which simply provide coverage for claims made against the insured during their policy periods. A claim is defined as an assertion by a third party against the insured. Most insurers consider a claim to be made when a third party first files a lawsuit, regardless of when the insurer is notified. Claims-made insurance allows the insurer to better estimate the cost of a policy based on current liability exposure.

Claims that are made during the term of a claims-made policy but based on events that occurred before the policy was in effect are usually covered only if the insured party is unaware of any possible breach of professional duty that could give rise to a claim and no other policy covers the claim. Claims-made policies do not include tail coverage. There are some hybrid claims-made/reporting policies that provide coverage if a claim is made during the coverage period and if the insured notifies the insurer during the policy period. There are obvious gaps in coverage with this type of policy, so it is not ideal. Tail coverage, or extended discovery period coverage, can be purchased within a short period of time after a claims-made policy expires to extend coverage. Tail endorsements cover claims made after the expiration of the claims-made policy when the events occurred before expiration of the last claims-made policy. These policies generally extend coverage for another 3 years and are very expensive, averaging 150% to 200% of the price of a mature claims-made policy; a lump sum payment is usually required at the time of initiation. Prior acts, or "nose," coverage is purchased through a current insurer to cover claims made during the current policy period on events that occurred before the policy was in effect.

21. The answer is B, Immobility.

(Knoop, 608; Marx, 374)

Decubitus ulcers form in patients who have limited mobility, limited sensation, or limited mental acuity. These are more accurately called pressure ulcers because abnormal tissue pressure is a key component in their development. When patients with limited mobility (elderly, critically ill, and those with paralysis or altered mental status) are unable to reposition themselves, the pressure in the tissues increases, especially over bony prominences, and the skin is highly likely to break down. Nearly 70% of pressure ulcers occur over the sacrum, hips, and buttocks. The next most common location is the lower extremities, especially the heels of bedridden patients (around 25%). A pressure ulcer can develop in any location, provided there is sustained elevated tissue pressure. A pressure ulcer can develop in as little as 2 hours, which is why nursing protocols for critically ill patients include turning them at least every 2 hours, and why patients should be taken off backboards as soon as possible. In some vulnerable patient populations, such as those with malnutrition, systemic infections, and those with fecal or urinary incontinence, pressure ulcers can develop even more quickly. The development of a pressure ulcer over a bony prominence is not necessarily due to neglect. However, delay in recognition or failure to respond to the development of a pressure ulcer can be a sign of neglect. Infections of the skin, diabetes, and obesity are not specifically associated with the development of pressure ulcers. Patients with significant atrophic skin changes due to vascular disease are at increased risk of skin breakdown because their skin is less resilient to the stresses of increased tissue pressure.

22. The answer is B, 27-year-old man with chest pain and odynophagia who also has asthma and is HIV positive.

(Marx, 1140-1142; Tintinalli, 583-587; Wolfson, 928)

Fluconazole is used to treat infectious *Candida* esophagitis. Risk factors for infectious esophagitis include immunosuppression from AIDS and cancer and iatrogenic causes such as inhaled steroid use. The patient in the question is at risk for AIDS, and he might be using inhaled steroids for his asthma. In a previously healthy patient, a new diagnosis of infectious esophagitis requires an evaluation for an underlying immunosuppression. Endoscopy with biopsy and culture is required for a definitive diagnosis. Infectious esophagitis is most commonly caused by *Candida* species but can also be caused by herpes simplex, cytomegalovirus, mycobacteria, and several other pathogens. Pharyngoesophageal diverticulum, or Zenker diverticulum, classically presents after age 50 years with halitosis, transfer dysphagia, difficulty in swallowing from the mouth to the upper esophageal sphincter, and neck fullness. Eosinophilic esophagitis is likely in younger patients (and increasingly in adult patients) who have a history of allergic disorders and persistent dysphagia despite appropriate treatment for gastroesophageal reflux disease. Similar symptoms can occur with some medications, including doxycycline, a frequent cause of pill esophagitis, with symptoms lasting up to 6 weeks even after discontinuation. Esophageal cancer should be suspected in any patient who has a new progressive transport dysphagia, or difficulty swallowing solids from the upper to the lower esophageal sphincter. Expedited workup is essential: these patients typically survive less than 1 year.

23. The answer is B, CT angiogram.

(Marx, 1173-1174, 2165; Tintinalli, 450-453)

Computed tomography angiography of the chest has a sensitivity of 83% to 100% and a specificity of 87% to 100% for aortic dissection; of the tests listed, it will most quickly establish the diagnosis suggested by the nature of the patient's chest pain, the nausea and vomiting, and the chest radiography findings. The chest radiograph reveals a widened mediastinum (>8 cm) with an abnormal contour; 80% to 90% of patients with an aortic dissection have abnormal chest radiography findings, although the abnormalities are not specific and are rarely diagnostic. Other radiographic findings in aortic dissection include the calcium sign (calcifications pulled away from the aortic wall), pleural effusions, a pleural cap, an abnormal aortic contour, and deviation of the trachea, mainstem bronchi, or esophagus. Although MRI is more sensitive and specific, CT can be obtained more quickly due to availability and shorter scanning time. Transesophageal echocardiography (TEE) is highly sensitive but operator dependent; it also is not as quickly obtainable because of the need to sedate the patient and mobilize additional personnel. Expertise of personnel also limits the efficiency of obtaining TEE to diagnose a dissection. Angiography is the historic gold standard, but it is rarely used now as the initial diagnostic modality. It is an invasive study, and the time required to organize an angiography team limits its current use. Aortic dissection is the leading cause of death among patients with Marfan syndrome (a genetic connective tissue disorder). A younger patient such as the one in this question with acute severe chest pain should be evaluated for aortic dissection.

24. The answer is D, Permethrin.

(Marx, 1545-1546; Wolfson, 1317-1318)

Scabies is caused by the highly contagious human obligate parasite *Sarcoptes scabiei*, and the most appropriate treatment is with permethrin. Although not currently approved by the U.S. Food and Drug Administration for this indication, ivermectin (two doses orally separated by 1-2 weeks) is also an option. Transmission of scabies occurs by both skin-to-skin contact and (less commonly) fomites. The subsequent reaction (up to several weeks in those not previously exposed, within a day for those previously exposed) results from sensitization to the mite antigens. The most characteristic feature of the eruption is the linear or wavy 0.5- to 1-cm intraepidermal burrows that end with a small papule or vesicle. The rash can have various manifestations, and excoriations from scratching can obscure the burrows. Distribution is typically in locations of thin stratum corneum and sparse hair follicles such as the interdigitations of the hand and on the wrists. Involvement of the head, neck, palms, and soles can be seen in infants and children but is not typical in adults. The diagnosis is made clinically and should be considered in patients with intense pruritus (often worse at night) and when close contacts have pruritic rashes. Scrapings can be done to identify the mites/eggs/feces. Treatment with topical scabicides such as permethrin, lindane (less commonly used now because of potential convulsions), or benzyl benzoate is effective. Permethrin is applied to the entire body and left on overnight. Repeat application in 1 to 2 weeks is often done and indicated if symptoms continue. Topical and oral steroids can be used in severe cases but are not the primary treatment. The antifungal fluconazole has no role in the treatment of scabies, and bacterial antibiotics are indicated only for superinfection. All potential fomites such as clothing and bedding should be thoroughly washed in hot water, and all contacts should be treated.

25. The answer is C, Would be approximately 138 mEq/L in the absence of hyperglycemia.

(Marx, 1615; Wolfson, 1038)

Hyperglycemia causes a transcellular shift in water leading to true (not pseudo) hyponatremia. The sodium concentration falls by approximately 1.6 mEq/L for every increase of 100 mg/dL glucose concentration above 100 mg/dL. The resulting hyponatremia is not physiologically significant and will resolve when euglycemia is achieved. In this case, there is a 5-fold increase in glucose concentration above 100 mg/dL, which multiplied by 1.6 mEq/L = 8 mEq/L. Therefore, if there were not hyperglycemia present, the sodium concentration would be 138 mEq/L (normal). This calculation helps rapidly determine if a baseline sodium concentration problem is present that will remain even after the hyperglycemia is corrected. For example, if significant hypernatremia is present even after the correction is done, a very significant free water deficit is present. Pseudohyponatremia is a falsely low sodium measurement that is a technical artifact of certain instruments. It can occur in severe hyperproteinemia such as in multiple myeloma or hypertriglyceridemia (serum typically will appear lipemic).

26. **The answer is B, Caused by cardiac dysrhythmia on sudden contact with water much colder than core temperature.**

(Adams, 1473-1480; Marx, 1929-1932; Tintinalli, 1371-1374; Van Beeck, 853-856; Wolfson, 1612-1615)

Cold water immersion syndrome is described as syncope resulting from cardiac dysrhythmia on sudden contact with water that is at least 5°C lower than body temperature. There are several proposed mechanisms, but the most probable is vagal stimulation causing asystole and/or ventricular fibrillation secondary to QT-interval prolongation and massive release of catecholamines on contact with cold water. The cause of death is drowning secondary to loss of consciousness and submersion. It is thought that wetting the face and head before entering cold water might prevent the cascade of events leading to this syndrome. The risk of cold water immersion syndrome occurring is directly proportional to the difference between the temperature of the body and the temperature of the water. Ethanol consumption is a major risk factor in all types of submersion incidents. In the past, near drowning was referred to as survival greater than 24 hours after a submersion event, and drowning was defined as death within 24 hours as a result of a submersion incident. The World Health Organization (WHO) created a new policy defining drowning in 2005 to standardize the definition and improve accurate reporting of these events. The WHO now defines drowning as "the process of experiencing respiratory impairment from submersion/immersion in liquid," and "outcomes should be defined as death, morbidity, and no morbidity." As a result, the terms active, passive, silent, wet, dry, and secondary drowning and near-drowning should no longer be used.

27. **The answer is B, Difficulty with rapid alternating movements.**

(Marx, 94; Tintinalli, 1144-1146)

Difficulty with rapid alternating movements is a sign of cerebellar dysfunction, as is poor tracking with finger-to-nose movements or pronator drift. In a patient with vertigo, these findings suggest a central (CNS) rather than a peripheral (inner ear) cause. Central causes of vertigo include neoplasms and cerebrovascular disease. The other signs and symptoms listed are more associated with peripheral causes of vertigo, such as labyrinthitis, Ménière disease, and benign paroxysmal positional vertigo. Unilateral hearing loss with vertigo suggests Ménière disease or, if it has developed progressively, an acoustic neuroma tumor. The typical nystagmus of central causes is vertical, and peripheral vertigo usually results in a horizontal pattern. The fast component of this nystagmus is in the direction of the affected ear. Patients with peripheral vertigo typically suffer an intense, sickening degree of vertigo, while patients with central vertigo report vague, less incapacitating symptoms. The Dix-Hallpike test, performed by dropping a patient from a sitting to a supine position, elicits episodes of positional vertigo. Repeated testing in patients with peripheral vertigo leads to a reduction in symptoms, or a fatigue of the vertigo. Central vertigo is not fatigable or extinguishable.

28. The answer is D, Transfusion of packed red blood cells.

(Marx, 1568-1571; Tintinalli, 1480-1486)

The patient in this question has a low reticulocyte count, indicating aplastic crisis. This occurs more frequently in children but can occur in adults as a result of a reduction in red blood cell production. Aplastic crises can be seen in patients who have a reticulocyte count lower than 3%. It often is a self-limiting disease, but packed red blood cell transfusions might be required. Infection can be a source for aplastic crisis, but parvovirus is typical, and without other signs of infection in this patient, antibiotics are not indicated. Oxygen therapy has been a mainstay in treating patients with vasoocclusive crisis but has not been shown to be beneficial unless the patient is hypoxemia. It is the most common reason that persons with sickle cell disease seek medical care. Pain produced by vascular occlusion of sickled cells typically lasts less than 1 week. Hydroxyurea is used to treat sickle cell disease. It can increase the production of hemoglobin F and can decrease the episodes of pain crisis, as well as the occurrence of acute chest syndrome. Acute chest syndrome is defined as infiltrates on chest radiograph accompanied by chest pain and fever. Pain medication, oxygen, and antibiotics are the mainstays of treatment. Exchange transfusion is especially helpful in acute chest syndrome as it does not increase the hemoglobin concentration but decreases the number of sickled cells. Other complications of sickle cell disease including splenic sequestration can occur with vasoocclusion in the spleen, which can be resolved with splenectomy after the initial episode.

29. The answer is A, <50 cells/mcL.

(Tintinalli, 1036-1038; Venkat, 274-285)

This patient has symptoms consistent with disseminated *Mycobacterium avium* complex (dMAC) and cytomegalovirus (CMV) retinitis. These infections are unlikely with a CD4 level above 50 cells/mcL. Although the incidence of both CMV and dMAC has decreased as a result of advances with high-activity antiretroviral therapy, MAC has reemerged as a consequence of increased treatments. Weeks to months after treatment is started, a more invasive and localized form of MAC, along with lymphadenitis, pneumonitis, hepatosplenomegaly, and hypercalcemia, can develop as part of the immune reconstitution illness syndrome at sites of preexisting infection. Other opportunistic infections also vary by CD4 level. Patients with CD4 levels greater than 500 cells/mcL demonstrate similar infection as immunocompetent individuals. Increased incidences of bacterial respiratory infections and *Mycobacterium* tuberculosis occur below levels of 500 cells/mcL. As levels fall below 200 cells/mcL, prophylaxis for *Pneumocystis jirovecii* pneumonia, or PCP, should be initiated, and histoplasmosis should be considered in the differential diagnosis. Levels less than 100 cells/mcL indicate increased risk of oral thrush and candidal esophagitis as well as systemic infections, including CNS infections with *Cryptococcus neoformans* or *Toxoplasma gondii*. Diarrheal illness can have multiple causes, including bacteria, parasites, viruses, and fungi, with up to one-third of cases of unknown etiology. In end-stage disease, CMV and disseminated MAC are the most common causes but require biopsy for diagnosis.

30. The answer is D, Symptoms begin within 1 to 6 hours of ingestion.

(Marx, 1209-1211; Tintinalli, 1062-1067)

Staphylococcus in food, typically protein-based products such as ham, eggs, and mayonnaise, generates a preformed toxin. As such, symptom onset occurs soon after ingestion; colonization of the gastrointestinal tract is not required for the illness to begin. Violent, repeated vomiting dominates the clinical picture, which also includes abdominal cramps and a variable degree of watery diarrhea. Because the symptoms are caused by a preformed toxin and not growing bacteria, antibiotic therapy has no effect on the course of the illness; treatment is supportive. Unlike *Staphylococcus* toxin, which does not obviously alter the taste of the food, the histamine toxin found in the meat of scombroid fish causes a peppery taste, as described by patients, or a bitter or metallic taste. The scombroid toxin is heat stable and forms when the fish is caught. It immediately causes flushing, dizziness, dry mouth, urticaria, and vomiting, but this reaction is easily managed with histamine blockers such as diphenhydramine. Profuse, bloody diarrhea is the distinguishing characteristic of bacillary dysentery caused by *Shigella* and *Salmonella* species. Although bacillary dysentery is usually self-limited, treatment with quinolone antibiotics is appropriate and shortens the course of the illness. *Bacillus cereus* forms a toxin that results in vomiting and diarrhea 1 to 6 hours after ingestion, much like *Staphylococcus.* It is classically associated with eating reheated fried rice; treatment is supportive.

31.   The answer is C, Normal saline.

(Marx, 1650-1657; Wolfson, 1053-1058)

The patient in this question is in rhabdomyolysis and is at risk for developing renal failure. The primary treatment modality aimed at reducing the risk of renal failure is intravenous hydration with normal saline. Mannitol and sodium bicarbonate can both be used as adjuvant treatments but have not been proved effective in any controlled studies. Mannitol increases urine flow by diuresis and acts as a volume expander by drawing fluid out of interstitial spaces. It might also convert oliguric renal failure to nonoliguric renal failure, which has a better prognosis. Sodium bicarbonate is used to alkalinize the urine, which might increase the solubility of myoglobin and increase its clearance. The goal is to keep urine pH greater than 6.5. Loop diuretics such as furosemide can acidify the urine, which enhances precipitation of myoglobin and might decrease its clearance. Renal failure, which is a late complication of rhabdomyolysis, typically develops approximately 24 to 48 hours after the inciting event. In this case, crush injury to the muscle leads to release of myoglobin, which in combination with volume depletion and acidosis leads to acute intrinsic renal failure. Other etiologies of rhabdomyolysis include exertion, hyperthermia, drugs or toxins, electrocution injury, and infection.

32.   The answer is C, 3-year-old Chinese child with a family history of seizure disorder who is now acting normally.

(Hirtz, 618-623; Wolfson, 1171-1174)

Following an afebrile first-time seizure, a healthy child older than 12 months can be safely discharged without emergent imaging when there is no concern for an underlying structural, traumatic, or infectious etiology that might require intervention. In the emergency department, CT scanning or MRI can be obtained to evaluate for any of these findings. Nonemergent MRI is the indicated test for outpatient imaging. Neuroimaging is preferred in children younger than 12 months in the setting of first-time seizure. Patients who are at higher risk for a focal finding include those with recurrent or persistent seizures and those who are from areas endemic for cysticercosis, such as Mexico. Children who are immunocompromised, have hypercoagulable states such as sickle cell disease, or have sustained trauma should be imaged. Children with ventriculoperitoneal shunts or other conditions that put them at higher risk for having elevated intracerebral pressure should also be imaged. Other tests that might be indicated based on history and physical examination include serum glucose and electrolytes, urine toxicology, and lumbar puncture. In general, children with isolated first-time seizures without any identifiable etiology are not started on antiepileptic agents. Expeditious followup with a specialist for outpatient MRI and EEG is indicated.

33. The answer is C, Oral sex.

(Centers for Disease Control and Prevention [sexually transmitted diseases], 92-93; Marx, 812)

The risk of seroconversion is low in sexual assault, and transmission rates are even lower in oral sex. The use of postexposure HIV prophylaxis in cases where there is no sexual contact is unnecessary. But there are several factors associated with increased risk of HIV transmission, as follows: trauma or bleeding with vaginal, anal, or oral penetration; high-ejaculate viral load; presence of sexually transmitted disease/genital lesions on either victim or suspect; recent incarceration of the suspect; multiple suspects; sexual habits of the suspect (anal intercourse); and use of drugs by the suspect. If prophylaxis is recommended, the victim's consent should be obtained after discussion of the risks, side effects, and benefits of the medications. If the victim accepts treatment with antiretroviral medications, baseline blood testing (including CBC count and electrolytes) should be performed but should not delay administration. Close followup care should also be arranged, and enough medication should be prescribed to last until the followup appointment. Repeat HIV testing should be performed at 6 weeks, 3 months, and 6 months.

34. The answer is D, Naltrexone.

(Adams, 2081; Marx, 2392)

Naltrexone, a mu-receptor opioid antagonist, works by blocking alcohol-induced dopamine release in the brain. It is effective for reducing alcohol craving, use and relapse, and alcohol-induced euphoria. It is even more useful when combined with acamprosate, which might regulate glutamate and GABA neurotransmission, and is also effective as a single agent for reducing alcohol relapse. Disulfiram is also approved for the maintenance of alcohol abstinence, but it causes an unpleasant flushing (the disulfiram reaction) by increasing the production of acetaldehyde when alcohol is used, which limits patient compliance. Buprenorphine and methadone have no approved use in the prevention of alcohol use and instead are used to fight the craving for opiates. Both of these agents are mu-receptor agonists and function by providing long-term replacement therapy for the brain disorder associated with addiction. Buprenorphine and methadone have been compared to the use of prednisone in adrenal insufficiency or replacement therapy for hypothyroidism. Naltrexone must be taken daily as a pill. A long-acting depot formulation has been developed that provides the therapeutic effects for 30 to 40 days after a single injection. The role of medication in conjunction with a brief emergency department intervention is under study and worth considering.

35. The answer is A, Ceftriaxone once and ciprofloxacin for 14 days.

(Centers for Disease Control and Prevention [sexually transmitted diseases], 40-42; Chung, 295-298; Tintinalli, 630-636, 989-992)

In a young woman with recurring symptoms of urinary tract infection (UTI), additional coverage for gonorrhea and chlamydial infection should be considered. Fluoroquinolones (levofloxacin or ciprofloxacin) cover normal urinary pathogens and chlamydia but are no longer recommended by the Centers for Disease Control and Prevention for the treatment of gonorrhea because of resistance nationwide. Thus, the addition of ceftriaxone or another cephalosporin is necessary to cover for possible gonorrhea. When taking the history in such a patient, it is important to ask about new sexual partners, and especially whether the partner has a discharge. Trimethoprim-sulfamethoxazole, fluconazole, and cephalexin do not cover gonorrhea or chlamydia. Recurrent UTI is defined as three or more episodes in 12 months or two or more episodes in 6 months. Cultures of urine and vaginal discharge should be ordered. Patients with recurrent UTIs should be counseled to follow up for evaluation of urinary tract abnormality as well. Quinolones are recommended and used as second-line agents or used for complex UTI, although increased resistance in some communities might make them less effective. Amoxicillin-clavulanate may be used to treat a recurrent UTI, but amoxicillin alone should be used if the organism is susceptible. With the increase in bacterial resistance, local recommendations should guide empiric treatment, and cultures should be obtained for more complicated or recurrent infections.

36. The answer is D, Steroids and trimethoprim-sulfamethoxazole.

(Marx, 928-940; Stringer; Stringer, 891-896; Tintinalli, 1037-1038)

Pneumocystis pneumonia (PCP) is the most common opportunistic infection in HIV-positive patients. It is treated with trimethoprim-sulfamethoxazole (TMP-SMX). Scientists originally thought PCP was caused by a protozoan, *Pneumocystis carinii*; however, the organism was later identified as a fungus, *Pneumocystis jirovecii*. To prevent confusion, the original abbreviation, PCP, has been retained. It also can affect patients with immunosuppresion caused by chemotherapy or steroids. Patients at risk (with CD4 counts <200/mcL) should be on prophylactic therapy with TMP-SMX, which is also the preferred regimen for patients with active PCP. Patients with significant hypoxia (defined as PaO_2 <70), should be treated with steroids. Ceftriaxone plus azithromycin is the regimen of choice for community-acquired pneumonia. The majority of pneumonias in

HIV-positive patients are actually caused by pneumococcal infection, not PCP, but in this case the bilateral ground-glass appearance and the elevated LDH are highly suggestive of PCP pneumonia. The diagnosis is confirmed by induced sputum analysis. Endotracheal intubation is reserved for pneumonias complicated by respiratory failure. Isoniazid, rifampin, pyrazinamide, and ethambutol are used to treat tuberculosis, seen more frequently in HIV-positive patients with CD4 counts between 200 and 500/mcL.

37. The answer is B, Reduces the risk of delayed neurologic sequelae.

(Marx, 2037-2038; Nelson, 1661, 1663-1665; Wolfson, 1465-1466)

The best study to date examining the use of hyperbaric oxygen (HBO) therapy for carbon monoxide (CO) poisoning (randomized, double-blind, placebo ["sham HBO"] controlled) demonstrated that the incidence of delayed neurologic sequelae in CO poisoning was decreased (from 12% to 1% in one study) by the use of HBO therapy. The first steps in treatment of CO poisoning are removing the patient from the source and administering oxygen. Further treatment with HBO therapy remains controversial. Neurologic sequelae include abnormalities of memory and cognition that could be present at the time of presentation and remain (persistent) or develop 2 to 28 days after the exposure (delayed). One criticism of this study is that clinical outcomes were not examined, such as patients' ability to resume previous employment activities. Currently, there is no evidence that HBO therapy reduces mortality rates or decreases the risk of MI. Rhabdomyolysis has been described after CO poisoning; renal damage is a potential consequence, but there is no current evidence that HBO therapy lowers the risk. The neurologic benefit of HBO therapy seems to be from antagonism to a cascade of events initiated by CO poisoning. The potential benefits are not simply a result of more quickly removing CO or carboxyhemoglobin. Currently, the main, proven goal of HBO therapy and the predominant rationale for using it are to decrease the risk of delayed neurologic sequelae. One of the challenges is that it is currently not clear exactly who is at risk for these sequelae and therefore who would benefit from HBO therapy. Older age, prolonged exposure, loss of consciousness, and presence of cerebellar abnormalities at presentation might help predict adverse neurologic sequelae. A lower threshold for HBO therapy should probably be considered for pregnant patients given the particularly high risk of the effects of CO on the fetus. The time after exposure when benefits of HBO are no longer helpful and the optimal number of HBO treatments needed are currently unknown.

38. The answer is C, If present, the anterior placenta should be incised to improve access.

(Marx, 260; Roberts, 1058-1059; Wolfson, 332, 699)

The patient in this question is in cardiac arrest as a result of blunt trauma, and her prognosis is extremely poor. Although every attempt should be made to avoid iatrogenic injury, incision of the placenta is unlikely to cause harm to either the mother or the fetus and will improve access to the fetus during the emergent perimortem cesarean delivery. To perform this procedure, a vertical incision is made from the epigastrium to the pubic symphysis. A vertical incision should be made in the uterus as well, inferiorly to the level of the bladder reflection. A horizontal incision would not provide adequate access. To improve the chance of fetal survival, the procedure should be performed as quickly as possible, ideally within 5 minutes of maternal cardiac arrest. To optimize blood flow and oxygenation to the fetus, CPR should be continued throughout the procedure. Ideally, the most experienced physician should perform the procedure, but if an obstetrician or a surgeon is not available, the emergency physician should do it without delay. Perimortem cesarean delivery should be performed only to save a viable fetus. If the uterine fundus is below the level of the umbilicus, the fetus is likely to be less than 20 weeks' gestation and nonviable. Under some circumstances, the procedure can still be performed in an attempt to improve the effort to resuscitate the mother.

39. The answer is B, Epidural hematoma.

(Roberts, 1108-1117; Straus, 2013)

An epidural hematoma can develop as a result of lumbar puncture in a patient who is taking anticoagulant agents, even with minimal trauma. When lumbar puncture must be performed emergently prior to infusing clotting factor in a hemophiliac patient or before correcting the INR with fresh frozen plasma in an anticoagulated patient (like this one with chronic atrial fibrillation), the patient should be watched closely for weakness or numbness in the legs, incontinence, and worsening local pain. A spine abscess would not likely develop from the tap itself. If an unrecognized brain abscess exists, lumbar puncture can induce herniation. A brain abscess can also rupture, spill into the ventricular system, and cause ventriculitis and meningitis. If a lumbar puncture must be performed in a patient who is anticoagulated or has a coagulopathy, the most experienced clinician should perform the procedure and correct the coagulopathy if possible. In children with leukemia and low platelet counts, studies have shown that prophylactic platelet transfusions were not required when the platelet count was higher than 10,000/mcL. The incidence of spinal epidural hematoma is 0.1/100,000; it usually is related to lumbar puncture or epidural anesthesia but can rarely occur spontaneously. Spinal epidural abscess typically extends over four to five spinal vertebral segments. Symptoms include progressive back pain, focal tenderness to percussion, fever, sweats, and chills. Changes in bowel or bladder function and focal weakness are late symptoms and are unlikely to present immediately after lumbar puncture. Classic signs of peripheral diabetic neuropathy include tingling, numbness, nocturnal burning, and pain. A diabetic autonomic neuropathy can present with bladder dysfunction and paralysis but not with an acute presentation as described in this question. If lumbar puncture is performed in or near the correct vertebral space, damage to the spinal cord is unlikely. Minor nerve irritation can occur, which usually causes a tingling or an electric shock sensation, but nerve damage caused by direct needle trauma is not likely. Although the most common complication of lumbar puncture is a headache, occurring in up to 70% of patients, fever and stiff neck are not typical symptoms. The classic postspinal headache is much more severe when the patient is upright and improves or resolves when the patient lies down.

40. The answer is C, Emergency department visit level 4.

(Abraham, 20-21; Adams, 2215-2220; American College of Emergency Physicians [documentation guidelines])

The minimum billing requirements for the use of the emergency department visit level 4 Evaluation and Management (E/M) code are as follows: four to eight elements of the History of Present Illness (HPI) section; two to nine systems under Review of Systems (ROS); and two to seven body areas or organ systems on physical examination. In this case, only six systems were included in the ROS section, and a level 5 emergency department visit requires 10 elements, so this chart does not meet billing requirements for anything higher than an emergency department visit level 4. Medicare billing is a complicated process that is based on the coding of patient charts based on Current Procedural Terminology (CPT) codes developed and updated annually by the American Medical Association. There are five levels of E/M CPT codes for patient care in the emergency department, and they are based on varying degrees of cognitive performance required to care for each patient. Lower-level visits are those that generally require minimal diagnostic workup and less medical decision-making. Upper-level visits tend to be complicated, for example, those that involve critical care patients who require higher levels of medical decision-making. Elements of the history, physical examination, and medical decision-making are totaled per patient and compared to a list of minimum requirements for each level of service. Using the Centers for Medicare & Medicaid Services, or CMS, rules, minimum billing requirements for an emergency department visit level 1 include one to three elements of the HPI and one system on physical examination. Emergency department visit level 2 includes one to three elements of the HPI; one system under ROS; and two to seven limited organ systems on physical examination. Emergency department visit level 3 includes one to three elements of the HPI; two to nine systems under ROS; one of three areas under Past Medical, Family, and Social History (PMFSHx); and two to seven body areas or organ systems on physical examination. Emergency department visit level

4 includes four to eight elements of the HPI; two to nine systems under ROS; one of three areas under PMFSHx; and two to seven body areas or organ systems on physical examination. Emergency department visit level 5 includes four to eight elements of the HPI; at least 10 systems under ROS; two of three areas under PMFSHx; and eight or more organ systems on physical examination. Rather than specific history and physical examination requirements, medical decision-making is a consideration when billing for critical care time, which is a unique CPT code in addition to level 5 billing.

41. The answer is C, Gradual onset.

(Marx, 101-105; Tintinalli, 1940-1941)

A primary psychiatric disorder is most likely to be associated with a gradual onset of symptoms over weeks to months. In DSM IV, the previous terminology of organic brain syndrome has been removed because of the implication that functional mental disorders are not associated with biologic changes in the brain. The current terminology reflects both the symptom and the presumptive cause, for example, depression due to diabetes. Mental disorders directly caused by medical conditions are more likely to present with abnormal vital signs and a sudden onset of symptoms; they can occur in patients of any age and are associated with a fluctuating level of consciousness. These patients are usually disoriented and exhibit disturbances in attention and recent memory. Hallucinations are more likely to be visual or tactile than auditory in those with medical disorders. Primary psychiatric disorders are more likely in patients 12 to 40 years old. These patients are alert and oriented but often agitated and anxious. Immediate memory might be impaired, but recent memory and remote memory are usually intact. Hallucinations are most likely to be auditory. Delusions (a false belief, firmly sustained, not associated with cultural beliefs or ignorance or lack of information) are prominent. On physical examination, if the patient is not agitated, vital signs are typically normal.

42. The answer is C, Emergent surgical consultation.

(Marx, 2205-2206; Tintinalli, 581-587; Wolfson, 592-596)

Emergent surgical consultation is required for patients with strangulated hernias. Although inguinal hernias are more common in men, femoral hernias are more common in women and are more likely to incarcerate. By definition, an incarcerated hernia will not reduce and is at an increased risk for strangulation with vascular compromise and bowel necrosis. Strangulation should be suspected in patients with fever, erythema overlying the hernia, hypotension, and peritonitis. Appropriate treatment for a strangulated hernia includes broad-spectrum antibiotics, fluid resuscitation, and emergent surgical decompression. Attempts to reduce a strangulated hernia can worsen vascular compromise and introduce dead bowel into the abdomen. Barium enema or colonoscopy might help reduce a sigmoid volvulus but not a femoral hernia. Signs of abscess such as a hard, tender mass and overlying erythema can be present with a strangulated hernia, but incision and drainage would be disastrous. This radiograph shows a large intestinal obstruction, which can be seen with an incarcerated hernia. There is a subtle suggestion of bowel in the lower left portion of the film, below the pelvis, which should also suggest a possible hernia. There is contrast material in the bladder from another study. Small bowel obstruction also can frequently occur with incarcerated and strangulated hernias. Restricting oral intake, performing gastric decompression, and administering intravenous fluids are appropriate initial treatments for a small bowel obstruction, but in this case, the emergent underlying etiology must be addressed.

43. The answer is D, Vagal maneuvers.

(Mattu, 45-50; Neumar, S729-S767; Tintinalli, 136-141)

Vagal maneuvers (carotid massage, Valsalva maneuver, facial immersion in cold water) and adenosine are the preferred initial therapeutic choices for the termination of stable paroxysmal supraventricular tachycardia (PSVT). Vagal tone is increased when the carotid sinus is compressed. This maneuver should be done for 10 seconds at a time, only after a bruit is excluded, and only unilaterally. The Valsalva maneuver is performed with the patient in the supine position and with at least a 10-second strain phase. Twenty percent to 25% of reentry supraventricular tachycardias (SVTs) resolve after a vagal maneuver. The ECG for the patient in this question reveals a rapid, narrow-complex, regular tachycardia; the most common causes include sinus tachycardia, atrial flutter, and a reentry rhythm involving the AV node. If visible P waves precede the QRS complex and are upright in lead II and inverted in aVR, then the rhythm is likely sinus tachycardia. If there is a sawtooth P wave pattern, then the rhythm is likely atrial flutter. If the P wave follows the QRS complex and the P wave morphology is reversed (inverted in lead II and upright in aVR), then the rhythm is likely a reentry rhythm involving the AV node. When the P wave is not visible, as in this case, any of the above can be the cause. Although SVT is technically defined as any tachyarrhythmia originating from the atria or AV junction, the terms SVT and PSVT are commonly used to refer to reentry circuits involving the AV node. Reentry is the most common mechanism for tachyarrhythmias; others include automatic or triggered rhythms. Reentry tachycardias involve travel of an impulse down an anterograde pathway and back up a retrograde pathway. These can involve a single site, such as within the AV node itself (AV nodal reentry tachycardia, or AVNRT) or across sites, such as down an anterograde pathway in the AV node and back up an accessory AV tissue bridge as the retrograde pathway (AV reentry tachycardia, or AVRT). Even if the cause of a narrow regular tachycardia is unknown, it is safe to perform a trial of AV node blockade in a stable patient. If the mechanism is reentry through the AV node, as in this case, the arrhythmia will terminate. Adenosine is an ultra–short-acting, safe AV node blocking agent. Amiodarone is a longer-acting antiarrhythmic agent most often used to suppress wide-complex tachycardias or for refractory or destabilizing atrial flutter or fibrillation. It is rarely used for PSVT. Nondihydropyridine calcium-channel blockers (verapamil, diltiazem) and beta-blockers are therapeutic options if vagal maneuvers and adenosine are unsuccessful. Synchronized cardioversion is reserved for narrow-complex tachycardias in patients with unstable conditions. Signs include altered mentation, ongoing chest pain, hypotension, and other signs of shock.

44. The answer is D, Normal saline.

(Marx, 1624-1626; Wolfson, 1048-1049)

Severe hypercalcemia is usually associated with significant hypovolemia. Rapid treatment, the first step of which is rehydration with isotonic saline, is recommended for both symptomatic hypercalcemia and for all patients with calcium concentrations greater than 14 mg/dL. Primary hyperparathyroidism (most common cause in outpatients) and malignancy (most common cause in hospitalized patients) account for the vast majority of cases of hypercalcemia. Other causes include excess calcium ingestion, excess vitamin A or D use, medications such as thiazide diuretics and lithium, and granulomatous disorders such as sarcoidosis. Clinical manifestations of hypercalcemia are variable and nonspecific and include cardiovascular (shortened QT interval, bradycardia, ventricular dysrhythmias), gastrointestinal (anorexia, constipation, nausea, vomiting), neurologic (sedation, confusion, coma), and renal (nephrolithiasis, polyuria, polydipsia). Treatment of hypercalcemia can be divided into four stepwise approaches, as follows: restoration of intravascular volume; enhancement of renal calcium elimination; reduction of osteoclastic activity; and treatment of the primary disorder. Isotonic saline administration restores intravascular volume and begins to increase the renal clearance of calcium. Administration of loop diuretics such as furosemide is appropriate but only after intravascular volume has been restored. Thiazide diuretics such as hydrochlorothiazide are contraindicated because they increase calcium retention. A variety of drugs can be administered to reduce osteoclastic activity, typically in consultation with a specialist. They include the bisphosphonates (pamidronate, zoledronic acid), calcitonin, and hydrocortisone. Hemodialysis might be necessary in patients with renal failure or in those who cannot safely undergo aggressive hydration.

45. The answer is B, Discharge to home with outpatient plastic surgery consultation.

(Adams, 1451-1457; Marx, 1893-1902; Tintinalli, 1386-1391; Wolfson, 1615-1617)

The appropriate next step in the management of this patient is plastic surgery consultation for possible debridement and reconstructive surgery planning. The injury is cosmetic and will likely require reconstructive surgery for an ideal cosmetic outcome. There is also concern for injury to the labial artery with the initial bleeding, and the parents must be warned of the risk of delayed hemorrhage and rebleeding from the wound when the eschar sloughs off, usually around 5 days after the initial injury. Suturing this wound is not indicated because of the burned tissue. If the parents are able to watch the child closely and appropriate followup with consultants is arranged, the child could be safely discharged to home with the parents. Admission to a monitored bed for 12 to 24 hours would be unnecessary in this case. There has been no evidence that an isolated oral burn correlates with cardiac injury of any sort. On the opposite spectrum, discharge to home would be inappropriate without consulting plastic surgery first. Observation in the department would not be inappropriate, but discharge without appropriate consultation is not correct. At a minimum, a telephone consult with close followup arranged with plastic surgery in the next 1 to 2 days should be done. An oral challenge would be appropriate to make sure the child can tolerate pain medication, as are instructions for a soft diet initially.

46. The answer is D, Oral fluoroquinolones.

(Marx, 882; Tintinalli, 1553)

This question describes the typical presentation for malignant otitis externa, most commonly caused by *Pseudomonas aeruginosa* infection. Although this condition has been treated with admission and intravenous antipseudomonal antibiotics, most cases can be managed with oral fluoroquinolones given their high bioavailability. It is seen in immunocompromised patients, most often those with diabetes, but also in patients with HIV infection and the elderly. Persistent symptoms of otitis externa despite treatment should raise suspicion for this disease. It can invade the skull base and affect cranial nerves; the facial nerve is usually affected first. A chronic headache associated with a unilateral facial nerve dysfunction can also be caused by a neoplasm, such as invasive squamous cell cancer of the ear (treated with radiation), acoustic neuroma (treated with craniotomy and resection), or a granulomatous infection such as tuberculosis (treated with four-drug antitubercular therapy). These conditions are less common than malignant otitis externa and are less likely to be associated with persistent drainage. *Staphylococcus aureus* infection is a common cause of otitis externa, but a persistent methicillin-resistant infection after topical therapy is unusual.

47. The answer is A, 18-year-old man in respiratory distress with blood pressure 120/80, pulse 100, temperature 37°C (98.6°F), and $Paco_2$ 28 mm Hg.

(Marx, 1848; Tintinalli, 166)

The diagnosis of systemic inflammatory response syndrome (SIRS) is made when a patient has two of the following four criteria:
- Fever greater than 38°C (100.4°F) or less than 36°C (96.8°F)
- Heart rate greater than 90 beats/min

- Respirations greater than 20 breaths/min or a $PaCO_2$ level less than 32 mm Hg
- Abnormal WBC count (>12,000/mcL or <4,000/mcL or >10% bands)

Of the five presentations in the question, the patient in respiratory distress with an elevated pulse and low $PaCO_2$ level meets the criteria for SIRS, which is defined as a clinical response to a nonspecific insult of either infectious or noninfectious origin. This classification can alert clinicians to a potentially sick patient who might need early goal-directed therapy to address impending sepsis and shock. Early goal-directed therapy is a stepwise treatment approach that includes fluid boluses, empiric antibiotics, and close hemodynamic monitoring to avoid morbidity and mortality in septic patients. A patient who meets the criteria for SIRS and has an infection is defined to have sepsis. If that patient's condition progresses to hypotension despite adequate fluid resuscitation and the presence of perfusion abnormalities, he or she is said to have septic shock.

48. **The answer is B, Externally rotating the arm 10 degrees localizes tenderness over the bicipital groove.**

(Marx, 587-588; Roberts, 949-950)

Bicipital tendinitis is a local inflammatory process of the biceps tendon and its sheath that is often seen in persons who work with their arms over their heads, such as house painters. Tenderness, which is best localized with the arm in 10 degrees of external rotation, is usually present over the bicipital groove, which is typically located 3 inches below the anterior acromion. Flexion of the elbow against resistance aggravates the pain. Passive abduction of the arm in an arc might elicit pain that is typical of impingement syndrome, which has led to bicipital tendinitis. Two maneuvers can be performed to assist in diagnosis. First is the Yergason test; a positive result is that the patient complains of pain and tenderness over the bicipital groove with forearm supination against resistance, with the elbow flexed and the shoulder in abduction. The second is the Speed test; a positive result is that the patient complains of anterior shoulder pain with flexion of the shoulder against resistance, with the elbow extended and the forearm supinated. Both of these tests are positive in the setting of inflammation at the long head of the biceps tendon and are suggestive of bicipital tendinitis. They cannot differentiate between tendinitis caused by an impingement and that simply caused by isolated inflammation.

49. **The answer is C, Migraine without aura.**

(Marx, 1356-1359; Wolfson, 749-750)

Migraine without aura, or common migraine, is the most common type of migraine headache and represents about 80% of migraine-type headaches. Migraine with aura, or classic migraine, is less common. The only difference between the two types is the presence of a preceding aura. These auras are typically focal neurologic symptoms and are most commonly visual. They last for 10 to 20 minutes (rarely up to 1 hour) and then fully resolve. They are commonly characterized as a bright rim of light around an area where vision has been lost (scintillating scotomas); a "zigzagged" wall that moves slowly across the field of vision (fortification spectrums); a flash of light or brief spark (photopsias); or simply blurred vision. Patients typically develop headache symptoms after the aura has resolved. Migraine headaches are often described as unilateral, pulsating, and of moderate to severe intensity. Symptoms associated with migraine headaches include nausea, vomiting, photophobia, phonophobia, osmophobia, and lightheadedness. Cognitive impairment is rare and warrants evaluation for other more concerning etiologies of altered mental status and headache. Basilar-type migraines begin with an aura affecting neurologic functions of the brainstem. These patients can have vision disturbance, at times as severe as blindness, dysarthria, vertigo, tinnitus, paresis, and altered level of consciousness. Like other auras, these symptoms should completely resolve within 1 hour. Hemiplegic migraines begin with an aura that causes a hemiplegia, often associated with sensory changes. The motor findings march slowly while affecting additional muscle groups unlike a stroke, in which the motor function is affected at the same time. These symptoms resolve within 1 hour and are followed by a classic headache. Ophthalmoplegic migraines are rare and are characterized by unilateral headache and ocular nerve findings. The most commonly affected cranial nerve is the third nerve; motor deficits and pupillary findings can occur. Patients with focal neurologic findings should be evaluated for acute intracranial pathology.

50. The answer is D, Metronidazole 500 mg orally twice a day for 7 days.

(Marx, 1290-1294; Tintinalli, 711-715)

The presentation described in this question is consistent with bacterial vaginosis. Recommended treatment regimens are metronidazole 500 mg orally twice a day for 7 days; or clindamycin cream 2% every night for 7 days; or metronidazole gel 0.75% twice a day for 5 days. Alternative regimens, including single-dose metronidazole, are less efficacious. Bacterial vaginosis is caused by overgrowth of *Gardnerella vaginalis*, *Bacteroides*, *Mobiluncus*, and *Mycoplasma hominis*. These bacteria are normally found in the vagina, but the growth is controlled by *Lactobacillus*. Several factors can lead to the overgrowth, including recent change in sexual partners and douching. The discharge present in bacterial vaginosis is described as gray or white and copious with a fishy odor. Bacterial vaginosis during pregnancy can cause premature rupture of membranes and preterm labor. The discharge is described as mucopurulent, which is similar to chlamydial infections. Treatment is recommended for pregnant women who are at risk for preterm birth, but topical clindamycin should not be used in the latter half of the term. These are treated with azithromycin. Candidal vaginitis discharge is described as clumped, cottage cheese–like, and white. Pseudohyphae or yeast might be seen on wet mount. The treatment for candidal infection is with antifungal agents, including clotrimazole 1% vaginal cream. Atrophic vaginitis is seen typically in post-menopausal women as a result of the lack of estrogen stimulation of the vaginal lining. The vaginal lining is thin and smooth; accompanying symptoms include dryness, dyspareunia, pruritus, and occasionally discharge. Atrophic vaginitis is treated with estrogen replacement unless is the patient has a history of breast cancer.

51. **The answer is B, Clonidine can be administered by sustained-release patch for symptom relief.**

(Adams, 1622, 1624-1625; Marx, 2051)

The patient in this question is exhibiting the classic signs of narcotic withdrawal. Clonidine can help normalize vital signs and reduce withdrawal symptoms and can be used safely for outpatient treatment in a sustained-release patch. The onset of action can be delayed 24 hours, so patients might not have immediate relief of symptoms. The classic symptoms of narcotic withdrawal include excitation, restlessness, anxiety, seizures (rare), tachypnea, and adrenergic/sympathomimetic overdrive (lacrimation, piloerection, yawning, diaphoresis). Mydriasis and rhinorrhea are also typical. Hypertension and tachycardia can be present, although both blood pressure and pulse can be normal. Other classic symptoms are diarrhea, nausea and vomiting, sphincter relaxation, and drug craving. Administration of naloxone makes the narcotic withdrawal symptoms worse and is not indicated. Withdrawal typically occurs when a prescription dose has been missed after chronic use, when recreational use is decreased, or when methadone therapy is abruptly stopped. Antiemetic agents and benzodiazepines might reduce symptoms. Administration of a narcotic agent is probably the simplest way to provide symptom relief, but many physicians are reluctant to participate in the patient's addiction by treating them in this way. Inpatient treatment for narcotic withdrawal is otherwise not required; although uncomfortable, it is rarely as dangerous as alcohol or benzodiazepine withdrawal.

52. **The answer is B, 3 mL/kg/hr.**

(Bosch, 62-72; Tintinalli, 622-623)

The goal for urine output in rhabdomyolysis with acute renal injury is 3 mL/kg/hr, or about 200 mL/hr. The rate of volume replacement with saline is 400 mL/hr. Central venous pressure monitoring is needed. Hemodialysis might be necessary with symptomatic hyperkalemia, decreased urine output (<0.5 mL/kg/hr over 12 hours), anuria, fluid overload, or resistant metabolic acidosis (pH <7.1). Electrolyte abnormalities should be corrected if symptomatic. If mannitol is used to maintain urine output, it should be discontinued if adequate output is not maintained or the osmole gap is significantly abnormal. If the urine pH is acidic (<6.5), deposition of myoglobin is likely to occur. Theoretically, alkalinization of the urine might be considered in this case: this can be done by adding 2 amps of bicarbonate (44 mEq/amp) to 1 L of D5W and infusing at 100 mL/hr. But this is controversial, and more recent studies put this practice in question.

53. The answer is A, Admit with tuberculosis isolation.

(Marx, 1794-1815; Tintinalli, 494-500)

Pulmonary tuberculosis is common among immigrants and the elderly, as well as immunocompromised patients, the homeless, and prison inmates. Given the risk of spreading active pulmonary tuberculosis, the patient in this question should be admitted to a tuberculosis isolation area and undergo sputum analysis for acid-fast bacilli. The chest radiograph might also suggest lung cancer, which can be further evaluated with biopsy, CT scanning, or bronchoscopy. However, active pulmonary tuberculosis should be ruled out first. It is a public health issue, and discharging this patient with antibiotics could lead to the spread of the disease. Pulmonary tuberculosis is reactivation of primary infection that can be latent for many years. The primary infection usually occurs in the lower lungs and spreads to the hilar nodes, where it lives in the granulomas in the hilar lymph nodes for years. These calcified lymph nodes are known as Ghon complexes. The best way to screen for tuberculosis in asymptomatic patients is to use the purified protein derivative (PPD) test. Patients with positive PPD results might need to be treated to prevent reactivation later in life. Tuberculosis is spread by aerosolized droplets. Pulmonary tuberculosis tends to infect the upper lobes and can form cavitary lesions. Drugs used to treat tuberculosis are divided into first-line and second-line agents. Commonly used first-line agents include isoniazid, rifampin, pyrazinamide, and ethambutol. The most common standard regimen is a combination of three or four first-line agents for several months, followed by one to two drugs for an additional 6 to 8 months of treatment. Recently, multi–drug-resistant tuberculosis has emerged and can be very challenging to treat.

54. The answer is C, Calcium-channel blocker – insulin.

(Marx, 1946, 1987; Nelson, 39)

The only correct poisoning–antidote therapeutic pair listed is calcium-channel blocker–insulin. High-dose insulin therapy has become one of multiple accepted treatments for calcium-channel blocker poisoning. Calcium administration, glucagon, and/or vasopressor therapy is also used. In a severe overdose, multiple treatments might need to be started together. Insulin therapy, often referred to as hyperinsulinemia/euglycemia therapy, involves administering very high insulin doses (0.5-1 unit/kg/hour). Dextrose is often administered simultaneously, although not universally. Serial glucose measurements are done, but, despite the very high doses of insulin used, hypoglycemia is unusual until the poisoning begins to resolve.

This is attributed to the enormous insulin resistance that occurs with significant calcium-channel blocker poisonings. Improvement of myocardial carbohydrate metabolism is a theory as to how the therapy works, and it seems to improve hypotension much more than bradycardia. Poisoning–antidote therapeutic pairs are listed below. Supportive care is tantamount; there must not be more harm caused by the antidote than by the poison itself.

- Acetaminophen – *N*-acetylcysteine
- Anticholinergic – physostigmine
- Benzodiazepine – flumazenil
- Beta-blocker – glucagon
- Calcium-channel blocker – calcium, insulin
- Carbon monoxide – oxygen
- Cyanide – hydroxocobalamin; amyl nitrate or sodium nitrite, sodium thiosulfate
- Digoxin – digoxin-specific antibody fragments
- Ethylene glycol – fomepizole
- Heparin – protamine
- Iron – deferoxamine
- Isoniazid – pyridoxine
- Methemoglobinemia – methylene blue
- Methanol – fomepizole
- Opioids – naloxone
- Organophosphorous compounds – atropine
- Sulfonylurea – octreotide
- Tricyclic antidepressant – sodium bicarbonate
- Valproic acid – carnitine
- Warfarin/superwarfarin – vitamin K

55. The answer is D, Observation and cardiotocographic monitoring for 6 hours.

(Marx, 254-255; Wolfson, 332)

After blunt abdominal trauma, a pregnant patient of 20 to 24 weeks' gestation should undergo cardiotocographic observation for 4 to 6 hours to determine if there is any fetal distress or contractions even if she is asymptomatic. Even minor trauma can cause placental abruption, which can lead to fetal demise. During this period of monitoring, if the patient develops abdominal pain, contractions, vaginal bleeding, or leaking of fluid or if the fetus exhibits signs of distress, further monitoring or intervention is warranted. The patient in this question is relatively asymptomatic and has no vaginal bleeding or discharge and no contractions; no abdominal tenderness is present, and she has normal vital signs and a normal fetal heart rate. Therefore, cardiotocographic monitoring for 24 hours is unnecessary. Discharging this patient without cardiotocographic monitoring, however, creates a risk of missing a placental abruption. Ultrasonography is not sensitive enough to definitively exclude placental abruption.

56. The answer is C, Open the pericardium.

(Marx, 405; Roberts, 317-318)

It is difficult to rule out cardiac tamponade by visual inspection only, and if there is no apparent cardiac activity, incision of the pericardium should be done first. Compressions can be started next if there is still no cardiac activity, and the aorta can be cross-clamped in the presence of persistent hypotension. A nasogastric tube can help differentiate the esophagus from the aorta, but efforts should not be delayed simply to place the tube. The thoracotomy incision should begin just to the right of the sternum and extend to the stretcher or posterior axillary line in the fourth or fifth intercostal space. The procedure should not be delayed for counting rib spaces; in male patients, the incision should be made beneath the nipple line, and in female patients, at the inframammary fold. Next, the intercostal muscles should be cut with scissors just over the top of the rib to expose the thoracic cavity. The rib spreader should be placed and the space opened to allow visualization of the pericardium. Then, the pericardium should be opened, being careful to avoid the phrenic nerve, which will be posterior to the incised area. The right chest may be opened, if needed, to control hemorrhage from that side.

57. The answer is C, Meclizine.

(Marx, 94-100; Tintinalli, 530, 1146-1148)

Nausea and vomiting associated with vertigo are most likely to respond to anticholinergic and/or antihistaminergic agents. Antihistamine activity inhibits vestibular stimulation and vestibular-cerebellar pathways. Meclizine, dimenhydrinate, and prochlorperazine have significant H1 histamine antagonism activity (antihistamine) and are used as treatment for vertigo and as prophylaxis against motion sickness. Typically, antihistamines are more effective when given as prophylaxis against nausea than in treating active vomiting. Pharmacologic management of nausea is most likely to be effective when it is targeted toward a specific etiology. Phenothiazines such as promethazine and prochlorperazine also block the D2 dopamine receptor in the chemoreceptor trigger zone (CTZ) of the medulla. Dystonic reactions such as akathisia and dystonia are frequent complications of the use of phenothiazines and should be treated with an anticholinergic agent, such as diphenhydramine or benztropine. Butyrophenones such as haloperidol and droperidol are very effective as antiemetics, acting via D2 receptor blockade at the CTZ. Side effects and safety profile limit their routine use for nausea and vomiting. Benzodiazepines such as diazepam or lorazepam can also be very effective as antiemetics, especially if there is an anxiety component to be addressed. Benzodiazepines exert effects by GABA blockade. Sedation limits clinical use to patients who have not responded to traditional antiemetics. Ondansetron is a 5-HT3-receptor antagonist with a primary action in the area postrema and some secondary activity in the gastrointestinal tract. It is very effective against nausea and vomiting that involve a serotinergic pathway, including visceral distention and biliary disease, opiate use, and chemotherapy-induced nausea and vomiting, but less useful for vertigo. Ondansetron is safe for use in pediatric patients.

58.   The answer is B, Octreotide.

(Marx, 170-174; Tintinalli, 543-545; Wolfson, 550)

Octreotide has been proved to reduce hemorrhage in patients presenting with a massive upper gastrointestinal bleed (UGIB) secondary to suspected esophageal varices. Although most episodes of UGIB are caused by peptic ulcer disease, bleeding esophageal varices should be suspected in patients with end-stage alcoholic liver disease. Even with appropriate treatment, mortality rates are high, with up to two-thirds of patients experiencing recurrent episodes. Definitive diagnosis and bleeding control require emergent endoscopy. Both band ligation and sclerotherapy are effective in controlling bleeding, but band ligation results in less rebleeding and stricture formation. When endoscopy fails, surgery, interventional radiology, or balloon tamponade techniques must be considered. Octreotide is a useful adjunct to endoscopy because it reduces portal pressure and slows bleeding. Studies have recently shown octreotide to be as effective as sclerotherapy, with the combination being more effective than either is alone. Beta-blockers are commonly prescribed for outpatient treatment of esophageal varices. However, beta-blockade has no role in the acutely hemorrhaging patient. H2 antagonists like cimetidine are useful in treating peptic ulcer disease symptoms but have not been found effective in UGIB. Proton pump inhibitors are indicated for bleeding peptic ulcers but have no proven role in variceal hemorrhage. Vitamin K can help reverse warfarin toxicity over several hours but has no role in acute bleeding. Additionally, vitamin K has little effect in patients with end-stage liver disease who no longer produce vitamin K–dependent clotting factors.

59.   The answer is B, Adenosine 12 mg IV.

(Neumar, S750-S754; Tintinalli, 136-141)

Adenosine is an ultra–short-acting AV and sinus node blocking agent. It is the initial pharmacotherapy of choice for stable reentry supraventricular tachycardia (SVT) and is 90% successful in terminating AV node reentry arrhythmias. An initial dose of adenosine 6 mg IV should be rapidly pushed over 1 to 3 seconds through a large vein followed immediately by a saline flush and elevation of the extremity. If the arrhythmia does not terminate within 1 to 2 minutes, a 12-mg bolus of adenosine can be given. Failure of adenosine administration to terminate a regular, narrow-complex tachycardia might result from failure to deliver an adequate dose of adenosine to the heart or because the arrhythmia is adenosine unresponsive. This distinction can be made by observing whether there is temporary slowing of the ventricular rate, even for just a few beats. Reentry SVT can be thought of as an on-off switch. The rate will not slow: it will either remain unchanged or terminate. If despite ventricular rate slowing the rhythm fails to convert to sinus, then an adenosine-unresponsive rhythm is present, such as atrial flutter or atrial tachycardia from enhanced automaticity, a rhythm commonly associated with digoxin toxicity. Metoprolol is considered a second-line agent for stable reentry SVT. Synchronized cardioversion is indicated if this patient becomes unstable.

60. The answer is C, Intraocular pressure greater than 21 mm Hg.

(Mahmood, 52; Tintinalli, 1543-1544)

The likely diagnosis in this question is acute angle-closure glaucoma. The patient's intraocular pressure is probably far higher than 21 mm Hg; it is likely 30 or higher, with 20 or less being normal, as measured using tonometry. A typical presentation is the rapid onset of headache, eye pain, and vomiting. Most patients do not have a history of angle-closure glaucoma but present following their first attack. They have a shallow anterior chamber, which predisposes them to getting the angle closure. On examination, the patient has a fixed, midrange, steamy pupil with significant amounts of cell and flare when viewed using a slit lamp. The finding referred to as cell is the visualization of individual cells in the anterior chamber. It appears as light reflecting off specks of dust in the air in a movie theatre. Flare is light reflected off protein floating in the anterior chamber. It appears similar to light striking smoke. The emergency treatment of acute angle-closure glaucoma consists of emergent ophthalmology referral, pressure monitoring with a tonometry device, and administration of the following medications:

- Topical beta-blocker such as timolol 0.5% to decrease aqueous humor production by the ciliary body
- Topical alpha-agonist such as apraclonidine 0.1% to decrease aqueous humor production and increase trabecular outflow
- Topical steroid such as prednisolone 1% to decrease nerve injury from local inflammation
- Acetazolamide 500 mg IV or orally to further decrease aqueous humor production by acting on carbonic anhydrase
- Mannitol 1 to 2 g/kg IV to decrease intraocular pressure

61. The answer is B, Cefixime 400 mg and azithromycin 1,000 mg orally.

(Centers for Disease Control and Prevention [sexually transmitted disease], 40-42, 49-50; Marx, 1290)

The combination of penile discharge and dysuria in a sexually active man usually indicates urethritis. In the United States, the most common cause is infection with *Chlamydia trachomatis*, but in some patients the causative agent is *Neisseria gonorrhoeae*. Gonorrhea is typically associated with a more profuse discharge, but these organisms are essentially clinically indistinguishable, and co-infection is common. Either or both can also cause epididymitis. Therefore, the standard recommendation for a patient with these symptoms is to treat for both infections. The treatment for *C. trachomatis* infection is azithromycin 1 g orally at once or doxycycline 100 mg twice a day for 7 days. Since compliance with the azithromycin single-dose regimen is 100% (it can be given in the emergency department), this is the preferred regimen. Gonorrhea is treated with a single-dose regimen, either ceftriaxone 125 mg intramuscularly or cefixime 400 mg orally. Fluoroquinolones such as ofloxacin or levofloxacin had previously been used for the treatment of gonorrhea, but quinolone-resistant *N. gonorrhoeae* has rapidly spread in the United States and abroad. Since 2007, the Centers for Disease Control and Prevention no longer recommends the use of quinolones for the treatment of *N. gonorrhoeae* infection.

62. The answer is C, Tension headache.

(Marx, 1356-1366; Wolfson, 749-750)

Tension headaches, which have a lifetime prevalence as high as 78% of the general population, are the most common type of primary headache. Primary headaches are those that have no identifiable underlying cause. Secondary headaches, otherwise known as organic headaches, are those with an underlying structural etiology. Tension headaches typically consist of bilateral bandlike or squeezing pain that affects the head or neck or both. The pain is mild, often with focal points of tenderness, and is not usually associated with additional symptoms such as nausea, vomiting, or worsening with physical activity. Over-the-counter medications such as acetaminophen or ibuprofen, in conjunction with stress relief activities, often are successful. Cluster headache, the only headache that is more common in men, is typically seen in middle-aged smokers. The headaches tend to come in clusters and are recurrent, often with multiple episodes in 1 day. Patients complain of unilateral throbbing pain affecting the eye and surrounding area. Physical examination might reveal unilateral conjunctival injection, nasal congestion, lacrimation, or rhinorrhea. Thirty percent of patients can also have a partial Horner syndrome (miosis and ptosis). Cluster headaches can be successfully aborted with sumatriptan or high-flow oxygen. Additional therapies such as nerve blocks or steroids are more controversial and are not routinely recommended. Trigeminal neuralgia is pain located in the distribution of the trigeminal nerve. The pain is described as knifelike, lancinating, a sharp cutting or tearing sensation, or shocklike and severe. Episodes typically last 1 to 2 minutes and can be elicited by activities of daily living such as brushing teeth, chewing, or talking. Patients should be referred for outpatient evaluation to ensure there is no underlying mass lesion.

63. The answer is B, Placental abruption.

(Marx, 2285-2289, 2346; Roberts, 1047; Tintinalli, 697-702)

The hallmark sign of placental abruption is painful vaginal bleeding in later-term pregnancy. Placental abruption occurs in 1% of pregnancies but accounts for 15% of fetal deaths. Several factors are associated with abruption, including pre-eclampsia, hypertension, advanced maternal age, prior miscarriage, smoking, and prior abruption. The etiology is separation of the placenta from the uterine wall, which causes decreased blood flow to the fetus. It can be associated with disseminated intravascular coagulation from maternal hemorrhage or amniotic fluid embolus. The patient and fetus should be monitored closely and undergo emergent obstetrical consultation. Immediate resuscitation might include transfusions in addition to intravenous fluids and oxygen. Placental abruption can be misdiagnosed as early labor because of the uterine tenderness and bleeding that might resemble a bloody show. Ultrasonography can be beneficial in identifying the hematoma, although it can miss a small number of cases in which the hematoma is posterior. The use of ultrasonography in diagnosing abruption has limited sensitivity and a negative predictive value of 63% to 88%. Pre-eclampsia is associated with sudden weight gain in the last trimester, hypertension, proteinuria, and abdominal pain. Urinary tract infection does not typically present with decreased fetal movement or hypotension.

64. The answer is D, Tube thoracostomy.

(Marx, 393-396; Tintinalli, 500-504)

The radiograph shows a large right-sided pneumothorax without evidence of mediastinal shift. The treatment of choice for a large pneumothorax without signs of hemodynamic compromise suggesting a tension pneumothorax is tube thoracostomy. Spontaneous pneumothorax is more common in males, smokers, and patients with COPD and among patients 20 to 40 years old. It occurs when a subpleural bleb ruptures because of changes in intrathoracic pressures, such as would occur with a Valsalva maneuver, scuba diving, or positive-pressure ventilation. Small pneumothoraces have a variety of treatment options. The pneumothorax will reabsorb by about 1% a day. Administering oxygen will increase the rate of reabsorption. Not every pneumothorax requires a chest tube. Conservative treatment is possible for patients with a small pneumothorax without significant symptoms. If a repeat radiograph in 6 hours shows the pneumothorax is stable, conservative treatment with careful discharge instructions might be an option. Patients with a pneumothorax who are intubated or under positive pressure always require a chest tube. Needle decompression is reserved for tension pneumothorax. Tension pneumothorax occurs when pressure builds up inside the pleural space leading to shift of the mediastinal structures and impairment of venous return. Eventually, the pressure buildup compromises cardiac output and hemodynamic collapse. Needle decompression is performed by the insertion of a 14-gauge angiocatheter into the second intercostal space at the midclavicular line or the fourth intercostal space at the anterior axillary line.

65. The answer is A, Serum acetaminophen concentration.

(Marx, 1948, 1966, 1969-1970; Nelson, 81-83, 1053-1054; Wolfson, 1386, 1499)

In the scenario described in this question, of the choices listed, acetaminophen concentration is the only test result that can or should potentially change medical management. In acetaminophen overdose, signs and symptoms initially are nonspecific or absent; the decision to treat with N-acetylcysteine is guided by measurement of an acetaminophen concentration and determining the time of ingestion. Checking acetaminophen concentration is reasonable in all intentional self-poisonings: acetaminophen is commonly ingested in overdose; it is in multiple preparations; the test is easy and cheap; initial symptoms are nonspecific; fatal liver failure can occur; and the antidote is extremely effective in preventing liver failure if given early. Paroxetine (marketed in the United States as Paxil and Pexeva) is a selective serotonin reuptake inhibitor (SSRI), and in overdose, the clinical course is usually benign. Exceptions include massive overdoses and the SSRI citalopram (brand name Celexa), which unlike other SSRIs can potentially cause cardiac (QT-interval prolongation, bradycardia) and CNS (convulsions) complications. An asymptomatic patient, after an observation period, can be medically cleared. There is no known role for checking serum paroxetine concentrations, nor are they readily available. Quantitative serum ethanol concentrations can potentially be helpful by correlating the result with the clinical manifestations. In the patient described, however, who is asymptomatic with a normal physical examination, knowing the ethanol concentration will not change medical management. Urine drugs of abuse screens rarely affect management of patients who intentionally poison themselves. They are designed to detect exposure to certain drugs (not intoxication) and are plagued by false-positive results and misinterpretation. Signs and symptoms guide the management of most poisonings, not the mere detection of exposure. Although psychiatry consultants often ask for a urine drugs of abuse screen, in almost all cases the results do not and should not guide medical management. Some urine screens have a tricyclic antidepressant test, but false-positive results are common and only detect exposure. Instead, management should be guided by findings such as altered level of consciousness, convulsions, and QRS-interval prolongation.

66. The answer is D, Tympanic membrane.

(Tintinalli, 38-42; Wolfson, 323-325)

Detonation of high-order explosive agents causes a shock wave, which causes primary blast injury to gas-filled structures or those with air-fluid interfaces such as the brain, globe, lung, small bowel, and tympanic membrane. But the tympanic membrane is the most sensitive to the overpressure of the shock wave and therefore is the most commonly injured of those listed. The inferior pars tensa of the tympanic membrane is usually where the tear occurs. If severe, this can lead to injury to the ossicles or cochlea, causing tinnitus or hearing loss. The lung is the next most commonly injured organ, with injury resulting in pulmonary contusion, pulmonary edema and hemorrhage, pneumothorax, hemothorax, and lacerations of the lung parenchyma. Although these injuries are more severe, they are less common. The small bowel and brain are also susceptible to blast injury but are less frequently injured than the tympanic membrane and lung. Primary blast injury is the result of blast wave pressure on tissue, compared to the secondary injuries caused by damage from flying objects striking the body. Tertiary injuries are caused by the victim's body flying through the air and landing, and quaternary injuries are caused by associated problems such as smoke inhalation and nuclear or chemical exposure.

67. The answer is C, Proximal tibia.

(Marx, 267; Roberts, 436)

The proximal tibia is the preferred site for intraosseous infusion in this age group, followed by the distal tibia and the distal femur. Other sites have been used, but the humerus, clavicle, and calcaneus are held in less regard. The distal femur can be an alternative site for children but is hindered by the extra tissue in this area, which makes palpation of landmarks more difficult. The most common site for intraosseous infusion in adults is the distal tibia. Alternatively, the sternum may be used in adults, as it is large, flat, and easily accessed. Establishing intraosseous infusion access involves knowing the intraosseous infusion needle or apparatus; stabilizing the site (such as using a rolled towel under the knee/tibia area); prepping the site with an antiseptic agent such as chlorhexidine, betadine, or alcohol; anesthetizing the skin and bony surface if the patient is awake and alert; and using the proper force and direction of the needle. The sites of insertion vary depending on the bone, as follows:

- Proximal tibia – 1 to 3 cm below the tuberosity, over the flat medial aspect, in a slightly caudad direction to avoid the growth plate
- Distal tibia – On the medial surface at the junction of the medial malleolus and shaft of the tibia, just posterior to the greater saphenous vein, this time directed cephalad, away from the growth plate
- Distal femur – 2 to 3 cm above the external condyles in the midline in a cephalad direction, away from the growth plate

68. The answer is D, Eyes deviate toward stimulus, followed by nystagmus and return to midline.

(Marx, 106-112; Tintinalli, 1145)

If cortical responses are intact, the oculovestibular response to cold water irrigation is transient conjugate slow deviation of the gaze toward the side of the stimulus (mediated by the brainstem) followed by nystagmus with corrective efforts back to midline (mediated by the cortex). The oculovestibular reflex is used in formal brain death assessments and to exclude factitious coma. Cerumen impaction must be excluded before beginning the test, and the tympanic membrane must be intact. The patient's head is elevated to 30 degrees above supine, either by elevating the head of the bed or by reverse Trendelenburg positioning if cervical spine precautions are in place. This position isolates the horizontal semicircular canal. Ten to 30 mL of ice-cold water is then irrigated into the external auditory canal. If cortical responses are absent, there is sustained, tonic deviation toward the side of the stimulus. This indicates that the brainstem is intact and the patient is not brain dead. The opposite reaction will occur with warm water. A mnemonic for this test is COWS: cold opposite, warm same, indicating the direction of nystagmus. If there is no response to the stimulus and the eyes remain fixed, there is no brainstem response and the patient is likely brain dead. The responses to the irrigation of ice water are not under conscious control and cannot be resisted. If a normal response is elicited in a presumptively comatose patient, the patient likely has a factitious coma. The tonic deviation might be absent in an alert patient, with only nystagmus noted. During testing to confirm brain death, any movement of one or both eyes, whether conjugate or not, excludes a diagnosis of brain death and must mean that some brainstem function is intact. Only in brain death with complete cessation of brainstem function do the eyes remain completely fixed during oculovestibular testing.

69. The answer is C, Oral antibiotics.

(Marx, 1229-1232; Tintinalli, 578-581)

The appropriate emergency department management for suspected uncomplicated diverticulitis includes a thorough history and physical examination followed by oral antibiotics, a liquid diet for 48 hours, and close followup care. Diverticular disease occurs on the left side in 80% of patients older than 85 years in western countries, but on the right side in patients from Japan, and is virtually nonexistent in patients from countries with high-fiber diets. Middle-aged patients with typical clinical findings do not require extensive emergency department evaluation. Patients with atypical presentations, systemic symptoms, or significant tenderness should undergo laboratory testing and CT scanning to exclude other conditions and detect the complications of diverticulitis. Additionally, patients younger than 40 years, immunosuppressed patients, and elderly patients require a more extensive workup to detect often unsuspected complications such as abscess, fistula formation, perforation, and obstruction. Barium contrast studies and colonoscopy are not performed in the acute setting but are helpful after symptom resolution to exclude malignancy, which has been reported in up to 9% of patients with diverticulitis. Parenteral antibiotics are indicated for patients admitted for treatment of diverticulitis; oral antibiotics are initially administered in the emergency department to help establish whether a patient can tolerate outpatient antibiotic therapy. Admission is required for patients who cannot tolerate oral intake, elderly and immunosuppressed patients, those with complicated diverticulitis, and those with social issues that would hinder outpatient compliance with treatment or followup care.

70. The answer is D, 60-year-old woman with aortic valve replacement who fell and has an avulsed tooth and mucosal lacerations.

(Nishimura, 676-685; Tintinalli, 1046-1047)

The patient in this question, because of her recent aortic valve replacement and dental injury, is considered to be high risk for endocarditis and therefore requires antimicrobial prophylaxis. The 2008 revisions to the American Heart Association/American College of Cardiology guidelines for patients with valvular disease significantly narrowed the recommendations for which patient populations and which procedures warrant antimicrobial endocarditis prophylaxis to only those with the highest risks, which includes those with:

- Prosthetic material used for cardiac valve repair
- Previous infective endocarditis
- Congenital heart disease that is: unrepaired cyanotic; or repaired with prosthetic material for the first 6 months after repair; or repaired with prosthetic material and residual defects at the site or adjacent to the site
- Cardiac transplant recipients with valve regurgitation due to a structurally abnormal valve

The procedures for which prophylaxis is recommended include dental procedures that involve manipulation of either gingival tissue or the periapical region of teeth or perforation of oral mucosa. Prophylaxis is no longer recommended for nondental procedures that do not penetrate the mucosa, such as gastrointestinal (endoscopy) or genitourinary (Foley catheterization) procedures, in the absence of infection. Prophylaxis is not recommended for routine anesthetic injections through noninfected tissue or bleeding from trauma to the lips or oral mucosa. Bleeding from trauma to the lips or oral mucosa is not an indication for prophylaxis, and hypertrophic cardiomyopathy alone is not considered a high-risk condition for endocarditis. The rationale for these revisions comes from the knowledge that: infective endocarditis is more likely to result from frequent exposure to random bacteremias associated with daily activities than from bacteremia caused by a dental, gastrointestinal tract, or genitourinary procedure; prophylaxis might prevent an exceedingly small number of cases of infective endocarditis (if any) in individuals who undergo a dental, gastrointestinal tract, or genitourinary procedure; the risk of antibiotic-associated adverse effects exceeds the benefit (if any) from prophylactic antibiotic therapy; widespread prophylaxis might contribute to the emergence of multi–drug-resistant organisms; and selection of appropriate antibiotics is more challenging as multidrug resistance becomes more widespread.

71. The answer is B, Begin noninvasive ventilation.

(Marx, 904-912; Tintinalli, 511-517)

In a moderate to severe COPD exacerbation, noninvasive ventilation has been shown to improve acidosis and ease respiratory distress. The patient in this question has a long history of COPD and probably lives in a chronic state of hypoxia and hypercapnia. The ABG analysis shows a respiratory acidosis with some elements of compensation. For every increase in $PaCO_2$ of 10 mm Hg, the pH should change by 0.08. If this were a purely acute process, the expected pH would be closer to 7.2 (change in $PaCO_2$ [25 × 0.08 = 0.20]) If this were a chronic process, the kidneys would have time to compensate for this elevated CO_2 by increasing serum bicarbonate, leading to relatively normal pH. In this patient, the CO_2 level is rising faster than the kidneys can accommodate, leading to acidosis, which represents a more acute process. The patient is clinically exhibiting signs of respiratory distress, with ABG findings suggesting an acute respiratory acidosis. Some patients with COPD are accustomed to relative hypoxia, and high levels of oxygen might suppress respiratory drive. However, supplemental oxygen should not be withheld if the oxygen saturation level is below 90%. Steroids and antibiotics have a role in the management of acute COPD exacerbations, but improving respiratory status is a higher priority in this patient. D-dimer assay is used to screen patients with low pretest probability for pulmonary embolism, which would not be the first priority in this patient.

72. The answer is B, Measurement of compartment pressures.

(Marx, 477-479; Wolfson, 317-320)

This patient has a fractured tibia and fibula, as is evident in the radiograph. She is at risk for compartment syndrome because of the swelling and tissue edema associated with the fracture. Pain and paresthesias are early symptoms of compartment syndrome; pallor, neurologic deficit, and pulselessness are late findings. Measurement of compartment pressures can help make the diagnosis. Newer devices have been developed to ease the measurement of these pressures, and this can be done at the bedside by the emergency physician. Fasciotomy is indicated for pressures greater than 30 mm Hg. Given the mechanism of injury, a vascular injury is unlikely, so angiography is unnecessary. Ultrasonography is not the appropriate next step because a deep vein thrombosis is unlikely to develop so early in the course of the injury. A cast might further worsen the patient's condition by creating a constricting ring around the area of tissue swelling and edema. If the early diagnosis of compartment syndrome is not made, the risk of irreversible nerve and muscle injury is significantly increased.

73. The answer is B, Perform needle decompression of the chest.

(Roberts, 179; Wolfson, 82, 129)

Once the diagnosis of a tension pneumothorax with hypotension is suspected, immediate needle decompression should occur. One study found auscultation to be sensitive in 84% of patients and to have a diagnostic accuracy of only 89% despite a hemothorax or pneumothorax. It is possible for a patient to have a false-negative of symmetrical breath sounds despite having a tension pneumothorax. Insertion of a large-bore catheter is the immediate action. This procedure should not be delayed for a chest radiography or CT. Tube thoracostomy is time consuming and is done later as a followup intervention. Intravenous fluid administration can transiently improve the hypotension caused by a tension pneumothorax but will do nothing to address the tension pneumothorax. The emergency physician should immediately consider and treat without delay apnea, hypotension, or cardiac arrest in an injured patient. The diagnosis is confirmed when the vital signs improve after placement of the needle.

74. The answer is C, Solid needle.

(Centers for Disease Control and Prevention [occupational], 1-17; Marx, 1749; Tintinalli, 1041)

Less severe percutaneous exposures are associated with solid needles (suture needles) and superficial injuries. There is some evidence that blunt-tipped suture needles further reduce the risk to health care personnel. More severe percutaneous exposures are associated with deep punctures, large-bore hollow needles, visible blood on the device, and needles used in patients' arteries or veins. Similarly, smaller volume (a few drops) exposures are considered to be a lower risk than larger volume (major blood splash) exposures for mucous membrane and nonintact skin exposures. Most occupational exposures to HIV are not associated with transmission. Postexposure prophylaxis (PEP) is associated with significant side effects. Multinational studies suggest that many exposed health care workers do not complete the 4-week course because of these side effects. Each case must be evaluated individually using the current guidelines for reference. Broad categories to consider are exposure type and infection status of the source. Occupational exposure to HIV can be percutaneous, from mucous membrane, or through nonintact skin with blood, tissue, or other potentially infected body fluids. If a fluid, regardless of its bodily origin, is visibly bloody, then it is considered potentially infectious. Cerebrospinal, synovial, pleural, peritoneal, pericardial, and amniotic fluids are considered potentially infective. The risk for transmission of HIV infection from these fluids is unknown, and the potential risk to workers from occupational exposures is unknown. Feces, nasal secretions, saliva, sputum, sweat, tears, urine, and vomitus are not considered potentially infectious unless they are visibly bloody; the risk for transmission of HIV infection from these fluids and materials is low. Expert consultation for PEP is strongly recommended when initial presentation is delayed (>24 hours), the source patient is unknown, the exposed person is pregnant, the source patient is known to have virus resistant to antiviral medications, or the exposed person is experiencing significant symptoms on the initial PEP regimen.

75. The answer is D, Nuclear medicine scan.

(Adams, 432; Marx, 2179-2181; Strange, 70-80, 605-606)

A Meckel diverticulum classically presents as a large volume of painless rectal bleeding in an otherwise well-appearing infant without other sources of bleeding. The preferred diagnostic test is a radiolabeled nuclear medicine scan, also known as a Meckel scan. Diverticula arise from the incomplete closure of the vitelline duct during embryonic development. The majority contain ectopic tissue, most commonly gastric, with pancreatic tissue being a distant second. The acid secreted by ectopic gastric mucosa causes ulceration, bleeding, and perforation. Other complications include diverticulitis, obstruction, and intussusception. Many features of Meckel diverticulum follow the rule of 2's: 2% of those affected develop complications; men are affected 2 times as often as women; it is found within 2 feet of the ileocecal valve; it has a 2% prevalence; symptoms usually present by age 2; and it is usually 2 cm wide by 2 inches long. Other diagnostic possibilities must be considered, but none produces the large volume of rectal bleeding in an otherwise well-appearing infant or toddler. Ingestion of red-colored substances can cause stool to look bloody, but guaiac testing will be negative. The Apt test detects maternal blood swallowed during delivery or breastfeeding. The introduction of dairy or soy protein can result in blood-streaked stools with mucus as a result of a mild protein allergy. Abdominal ultrasonography is indicated for suspected intussusception or pyloric stenosis. However, pain or vomiting would be expected in both of these diagnoses.

76. The answer is A, Atrial fibrillation.

(Tekwani, 747-765; Tintinalli, 523, 546)

Embolism of a left atrial clot due to atrial fibrillation is a common factor in the development of mesenteric ischemia. Mesenteric ischemia is a life-threatening condition with a mortality rate as high as 60% to 80%. It occurs when the blood supply of the bowel is reduced below the metabolic demands. There are four pathophysiologic etiologies. Arterial embolism of the abdominal visceral vasculature accounts for about 50% of cases, usually originating from a mural cardiac thrombus in the setting of atrial fibrillation or after MI. Arterial thrombosis accounts for 25% of cases, usually from progressive atherosclerosis of the superior mesenteric artery. Nonocclusive mesenteric ischemia results from decreased cardiac output from heart failure, hypovolemia, or hypoperfusion due to hypotension and accounts for about 20% of cases. Venous thrombosis of the abdominal visceral veins is the least common cause (5%) and occurs in the setting of hypercoagulable states such as antithrombin III deficiency or protein C deficiency. *Campylobacter jejuni* is a gram-negative bacteria that causes enteritis characterized by abdominal pain, diarrhea, and fever, with symptoms usually lasting 1 day up to several days. Symptoms usually resolve by the time stool culture reveals the organism, but if necessary, the infection is commonly treated with fluoroquinolone antibiotics, erythromycin, or azithromycin. Celiac disease is a disorder of the small intestine caused by an autoimmune reaction to gluten, a component of wheat. It is characterized by chronic diarrhea with abdominal pain and bloating. It can present with more subtle symptoms such as fatigue and anemia or failure to thrive in children. Gastrointestinal bleeding and renal involvement might occur. von Willebrand disease is a hereditary bleeding disorder caused by a deficiency or derangement of von Willebrand factor, leading to impaired platelet adhesion.

77. **The answer is B, Continue albuterol and consider admission.**

(Marx, 894-902; Tintinalli, 504-511)

A normal PEFR for adults is between 400 and 550 L/min. A PEFR that is lower than 40% of normal or does not improve with treatment indicates severe bronchospasm and requires more aggressive intervention. The patient in this question, with a PEFR of 250 L/min, is in an intermediate group (40%-70% of normal); more treatment and possibly admission are needed. Measurements of PEFR are critical in the management of asthma patients and should be used to guide therapy. They are easier to perform at the bedside than other pulmonary function tests. Predicted peak flows are based on age, height, and sex. Ideally, treatment should be based on a patient's personal best PEFR rather than predicted norms. Patients who improve with treatment and those with PEFR greater than 70% can be discharged with good asthma teaching, albuterol, steroids, and close followup. First-line treatment for asthma exacerbations is inhaled beta-agonists such as albuterol and steroids. Anticholinergic agents such as ipratropium should be reserved for moderate to severe asthma. Subcutaneous beta-agonists such as terbutaline and epinephrine have not been shown to be efficacious and should be considered adjuvant therapies. Heliox is a mixture of 80% helium and 20% oxygen that might be helpful in patients with severe asthma who do not have hypoxia.

78. **The answer is D, Posterior dislocation.**

(Marx, 650-652; Wolfson, 302-303)

Posterior knee dislocation forces the tibia and fibula of the knee posteriorly into the neurovascular bundle in the popliteal fossa. This can directly lacerate or crush the popliteal artery or lead to intimal injury within the vessel. Knee dislocations are potentially limb threatening, whether anterior or posterior, given the possibility of vascular injury with both types. Even if the dislocation has already been reduced by the time the patient reaches the emergency department, vascular injury is still possible and should be considered. Anterior dislocations can stretch the vessels, but vascular injury is more common with posterior dislocations. An ankle-brachial index less than 0.90 is concerning for arterial injury. A value above 0.90 is reassuring. An intact distal pulse is also reassuring but does not rule out arterial injury. Reduction of knee dislocations is generally done with appropriate sedation and longitudinal traction. Joint effusions can occur with many different types of knee injuries, both bony and ligamentous, and are not specific for vascular injury.

79.   The answer is C, Palatal petechiae.

(Marx, 217-225; Tintinalli, 778-779, 848, 1583-1584)

Palatal petechiae are most commonly associated with group A beta-hemolytic *Streptococcus* (GABHS) infections. Less commonly, they can also be seen in infectious mononucleosis/Epstein-Barr virus (EBV) infections. A displaced uvula is associated with a peritonsillar or parapharyngeal abscess. Muffled voice is a sign in retropharyngeal abscess, peritonsillar cellulitis, and peritonsillar abscess. Abscesses are commonly polymicrobial, with a combination of gram-positive, gram-negative, and anaerobic flora from the mouth. Patients with epiglottitis are usually unable to phonate. A tender hyoid bone is associated with epiglottitis. The incidence of epiglottitis has changed dramatically since the introduction of the *Haemophilus influenzae* B (Hib) vaccine, although it is still the most common isolate in adult epiglottitis. Uvulitis, in contrast to classic streptococcal pharyngitis, has findings of uvular erythema and is most commonly caused by group A *Streptococcus* (*Streptococcus pyogenes*) in countries that provide widespread Hib vaccine administration.

80.   The answer is A, Give parenteral steroids.

(Marx, 1184-1188, 1213-1214, 1234-1237; Tintinalli, 534-536, 539-540)

The patient in the question has a prolonged ulcerative colitis flare with radiographic findings of toxic megacolon. Treatment includes parenteral fluids, antibiotics, and steroids. Toxic megacolon is suggested by large bowel dilation of greater than 6 cm on abdominal radiographs in a patient with systemic toxicity. Progressive inflammation weakens and finally dilates the bowel wall musculature. Early diagnosis is imperative, as prolonged dilatation leads to complications and death. With sigmoid volvulus, a barium enema can reveal the characteristic "bird's beak" appearance. A rectal tube or barium enema can help reduce sigmoid volvulus. *Clostridium difficile* infection causes pseudomembranous colitis characterized by bloody stools and abdominal cramping. However, this patient does not have a history of recent antibiotic use or hospitalization to support this diagnosis. Additionally, he would not be able to tolerate oral medications.

81. The answer is B, Pacemaker is set to fixed-rate mode.

(Mattu, 179-192; McMullan, 812-822)

A simplified approach to understanding pacemakers is to consider that they are designed to prevent bradycardia. When the sensing component detects appropriate native electrical activity, intrinsic firing by the pacemaker is suppressed. When it fails to sense a normal native beat, which might occur, for example, with a prolonged sinus pause, the pacemaker fires at its fixed backup rate. Placing a magnet over a pacemaker eliminates the sensing mode and causes the pacemaker to fire at its fixed backup rate without suppression by native beats (asynchronous mode). Although pacemaker sensing is temporarily disabled by the magnet, firing continues normally. This places the patient at a theoretical risk of a paced beat firing during the relative refractory segment of the cardiac electrical cycle (R-on-T phenomenom), which is vulnerable to induction of ventricular fibrillation but in practice rarely if ever occurs. The interrogation mode is not activated by a magnet, but rather through radiofrequency communication with the pacemaker by a wand device. Overdrive pacing is the delivery of a burst of pacing impulses at a rate faster than a tachyarrhythmia in order to terminate it by rendering cardiac tissue refractory. This can be an automatic function in an automated implantable cardioverter-defibrillator or a function that must be actively set with a pacemaker.

82. The answer is C, Obtain pulmonology or thoracic surgery consultation for bronchoscopy.

(Marx, 223-225; Tintinalli, 473-476)

Hemoptysis is classified as mild (<20 mL/24 hr), moderate (20-600 mL/24 hr), or massive (>600 mL/24 hr). This patient's condition would be classified as moderate hemoptysis, and given the abnormal chest radiograph finding, consultation for bronchoscopy is required. The treatment of massive hemoptysis focuses on stabilizing the patient and localizing the source of bleeding. Intubation might be required if respiratory compromise develops. Selective intubation of one bronchus might be needed but often requires specialized equipment, such as double-lumen endotracheal tubes. Left mainstem intubation is difficult because of the sharp angle of the bronchus. Chest CT can help identify and further characterize the mass, but it is not therapeutic. Bronchoscopy performed by a pulmonologist or thoracic surgeon can be both diagnostic and therapeutic in moderate hemoptyisis. If a source of bleeding is identified with bronchoscopy, it can be injected with epinephrine using the bronchoscope or treated with a bronchoscopic laser. Bronchial arterial embolization is another treatment option. Surgical resection can be used as a last resort. The etiology of hemoptysis includes tuberculosis, pneumonia, bronchitis, pulmonary embolism, bronchiectasis, immunologic disorders, cardiac causes, and cancers. Hemoptysis can be confused with hematemesis, and it is important to distinguish between the two. Hemoptysis is preceded by coughing and is not acidic.

83. The answer is D, Traumatic iritis.

(Marx, 230-232, 862-863, 866; Wolfson, 184)

This patient has blunt trauma to the globe resulting in contusion and spasm of the ciliary body and iris, called traumatic iritis or iridocyclitis. These findings are classic for this disorder. Traumatic iritis is characterized by a deep, aching eye pain, decreased visual acuity in the affected eye, injection of the limbus of the affected eye, both direct and consensual photophobia, and cells and flare in the anterior chamber. The presence of a sluggish pupil on the affected side is attributed to the ciliary spasm. In severe traumatic iritis, a hypopyon, or layering of white blood cells in the anterior chamber, can be visualized. Treatment consists of topical cycloplegic agents and oral pain medications. Tears or lacerations of these structures would lead to a hyphema, in which red blood cells layer in the anterior chamber, but in traumatic iritis, there is no such finding. Endophthalmitis is a severe infection of the deep structures of the eye that usually follows cataract or other eye surgery or penetrating trauma. Scleritis is an inflammatory disorder of the sclera; it presents with reddish or bluish discoloration of the white outer coating of the eye and severe boring pain.

84. The answer is C, Middle cerebral artery.

(Marx, 1335-1336; Tintinalli, 1128)

A stroke involving the middle cerebral artery presents with contralateral hemiparesis with hemisensory loss. The face and arm are usually affected more than the leg. If the dominant hemisphere is involved, aphasia is usually present. The more proximal the lesion in the middle cerebral artery, the more extensive the deficit is likely to be. If the nondominant hemisphere is affected, the patient has contralateral weakness and numbness, as does the patient in the question, but might also exhibit inattention, neglect, and constructional and dressing apraxias. Middle cerebral artery strokes are also associated with a homonymous hemianopsia and a gaze preference to the side of the infarct. Anterior cerebral artery strokes are associated with contralateral leg weakness and milder cortical sensory deficits. Any arm weakness is usually less significant than the leg weakness. Patients sometimes have perseveration on motor and speech testing. Occlusion of the basilar artery causes infarction of the ventral pons leading to quadriplegia; it also can result in the locked-in syndrome. There is preservation of cortical function. The upper brainstem and higher cranial nerves might also be intact, so the patient can usually see (CN II) and might be able to move the eyes and also blink (CN III). Strokes involving the posterior cerebral artery and vertebrobasilar system (posterior circulation stroke) produce a wide variety of symptoms and might not initially present as a stroke. These patients have cerebellar signs and extremity signs, including sensory deficits involving processing. They often have nausea, vomiting, dizziness, vertigo, and cranial nerve deficits, with or without extremity weakness. The posterior cerebral artery supplies portions of the parietal and occipital lobes, so vision and thought processing are impaired. The classic finding in a posterior circulation stroke is ipsilateral cranial nerve deficit and contralateral extremity deficit. Additionally, the motor deficits are on one side of the body and the sensory deficits on the other.

85. The answer is C, Endoscopic retrograde cholangiopancreatography.

(Adams, 418-421; Marx, 1170; Tintinalli, 562-566)

Patients presenting with acute cholangitis from choledocholithiasis require biliary decompression through endoscopic retrograde cholangiopancreatography (ERCP). Acute cholangitis is an emergency of the biliary tract requiring prompt recognition and treatment. Cholangitis is often caused by obstruction of the common bile duct from stone (80%), malignancy, or stricture. Obstruction causes an increase in the intraluminal pressures within the biliary tract, resulting in pain and nausea. If not relieved, continued obstruction leads to reflux of gastrointestinal bacteria into lymphatic vessels, portal vein circulation, and subsequently systemic circulation. Seen in less than one-third of patients, the classic presentation is the Charcot triad of fever, right upper quadrant pain, and jaundice. The triad becomes the Reynolds pentad with the development of hypotension and altered mental status. The WBC count and alkaline phosphatase and bilirubin levels help suggest the diagnosis in less clear-cut cases. Significant bilirubin elevations help distinguish bile duct obstruction from simple cholecystitis. Ductal dilation greater than 6 mm on ultrasound confirms the diagnosis. Neither a CT scan nor a hepatobiliary imino-diacetic acid (HIDA) scan is helpful in already-diagnosed cholangitis. Initial management includes aggressive fluid resuscitation and broad-spectrum antibiotics, but mortality rates approach 100% when obstruction is not relieved. The lowest mortality rates are achieved with ERCP, which is first-line treatment to decompress the biliary tract through removal of obstructing stones, sphincterotomy, or stent placement. If ERCP is unsuccessful, percutaneous transhepatic cholangiography with drainage should be considered. With a mortality rate of up to 40%, emergency surgery is performed only after less-invasive techniques fail.

86. The answer is C, Pacemaker oversensing is the most likely cause.

(Mattu, 179-192; McMullan, 812-822)

This patient's ECG does not suggest an abnormality or pacemaker malfunction. The most likely explanation for the syncope is oversensing of his pacemaker, which is suggested by the history: the electrical activity of the pectoralis muscle from the back-and-forth movement of painting was "oversensed," resulting in suppression of pacing, bradycardia, and then syncope. Sensing refers to the pacemaker function that detects appropriate cardiac electrical activity and results in suppression of pacemaker firing. When no appropriate cardiac electrical activity is sensed, it fires at its programmed rate. Oversensing occurs when an intracardiac or extracardiac signal is inappropriately sensed as inherent electrical cardiac activity, resulting in suppression of pacemaker firing. Electrical activity that might cause this phenomenom includes intracardiac signals such as T waves and P waves, myopotentials from muscular activity, electromagnetic interference, and external electrical sources such as transcutaneous nerve stimulation or electrocautery. Treatment involves pacemaker reprogramming. The ECG demonstrates appropriate ventricular pacing at 75 beats/min without other abnormalities. There is no evidence of undersensing, which would be seen as inappropriately occurring pacing spikes in the setting of appropriately occurring QRS complexes. Placement of a magnet over the pacemaker does not reveal undersensing, but rather tests its ability to fire and capture. Magnet placement mimics undersensing by suppressing sensing function and returning the pacemaker to an asynchronous mode of pacing. This ECG does not demonstrate pacemaker-mediated tachycardia, which is caused by a reentry dysrhythmia in dual-chamber pacemakers when the pacemaker itself acts as part of the reentry circuit. It should be suspected when a pacemaker is firing at an inappropriately fast rate (usually rates >100-110 beats/min). Applying a magnet interrupts the reentry circuit by inhibiting the atrial sensing of the retrograde P wave. Failure to capture refers to pacemaker impulses that fail to trigger myocardial depolarization. This would be seen on an ECG as pacer spikes without associated ventricular depolarization.

87. The answer is C, Inability to extend the knee.

(Marx, 658-659; Wolfson, 302-303)

Patellar fractures can require surgical repair or conservative management depending on the location, amount of comminution, and whether they are open or closed. If the extensor mechanism of the knee is disrupted, which is manifested by the patient not being able to fully extend the knee, surgical intervention is indicated. Hemarthrosis can occur in many different injuries, including ligament injury, and outpatient referral is appropriate unless there is another finding that mandates consultation. If there is radiographic evidence of a fluid-fluid level indicating a lipohemarthrosis, an occult fracture such as a tibial plateau fracture must be suspected. Patients who have contusions or sprains without radiographic findings who are unable to bear weight may be instructed to continue non–weight-bearing with crutches or a walker and treated with analgesics and outpatient orthopedic evaluation as followup. Patients with large effusions or with significant pain might be reluctant or unable to fully flex the knee; they can follow up with an orthopedist as outpatients. Patients with severe pain should receive adequate analgesia in the emergency department and may be discharged, and possibly instructed to continue non–weight-bearing, with timely outpatient orthopedic followup care.

88. The answer is D, She should undergo repeat ECG and biomarker testing.

(Anderson, e148-e304; Fesmire, 272-274)

Even though this patient has a normal ECG and a negative initial troponin (Tn) level, she should have another ECG and Tn measurement. Up to 10% of patients with acute coronary syndromes (ACS) have a completely normal initial ECG. Although cardiac marker (Tn or CK-MB) elevation might be detected early after symptom onset, American College of Emergency Physicians (ACEP) and American Heart Association/American College of Cardiology clinical policies currently recommend excluding MI with repeat marker testing at least 8 hours after the onset of most recent symptoms. If the most recent episode of symptoms began more than 8 hours prior to arrival, then a single cardiac marker test is acceptable. Another approach recommended in the ACEP Clinical Policy but not commonly used is the combination of a normal myoglobin, plus either CK-MB or Tn, at arrival and 90 minutes later. Finally, initially normal levels of CK-MB plus Tn, which do not rise on repeat testing in 2 hours, is a third approach recommended in the ACEP Clinical Policy to exclude MI. None of these three strategies excludes unstable angina, which requires some form of stress or imaging study. Relief of pain by administration of a GI cocktail (liquid antacid, viscous lidocaine, and anticholinergic agent) does not exclude ACS. Sublingual nitroglycerin relieves pain in approximately 35% of patients with active coronary artery disease (CAD) and 41% of patients without active CAD. Therefore, pain relief with nitroglycerin is not always predictive of ACS. When risk stratifying patients with active symptoms, traditional risk factors for CAD are less important than symptoms, ECG findings, and cardiac biomarkers. Risk factors for CAD are only weakly predictive of acute ischemia and should not be used to determine whether a patient should be admitted to the hospital.

89. The answer is D, Exploratory laparotomy.

(Marx, 419-425; Wolfson, 232-235)

This patient is hemodynamically compromised despite receiving initial crystalloid solution en route to the hospital. The ultrasound image reveals fluid in the Morison pouch, the hepatorenal recess. This finding most likely indicates hemoperitoneum secondary to the stab wound, with possible splenic laceration or vascular injury. Therefore, immediate exploratory laparotomy is indicated. This decision is appropriate because the patient has already had a crystalloid challenge; administering an additional 2 L would unnecessarily delay the indicated procedure and put the patient at risk of further bleeding and hemodynamic compromise. Computed tomography scanning of the abdomen and pelvis is time consuming and, in some centers, would take the patient away from the emergency department and put him in danger. Performing diagnostic peritoneal lavage would also delay needed care; it is not indicated in an unstable patient with penetrating abdominal trauma.

90. **The answer is D, Splinting or placing the arm in a sling with early range of motion.**

(Marx, 560-561; Wolfson, 268-269)

This patient presents with elbow pain and a positive posterior and anterior fat pad (with "sail sign") on radiograph. There is also a cortical break seen as the sharper stepoff of the normally smooth curve of the radius head transitioning to the neck. This presentation is consistent with radial head fracture. Radial head fracture is treated by splinting or placing the arm in a sling with early range of motion. It can be difficult to see on radiograph, so an injury with this mechanism (fall on an outstretched hand) accompanied by tenderness and radiographic evidence of positive fat pads should be treated as a nondisplaced radial head fracture. Computed tomography scanning is not indicated and would unnecessarily expose the patient to additional radiation. Nondisplaced fractures do not require surgical repair. Casting is unnecessary; it would lead to increased abnormality and could increase the need for rehabilitation due to stiffness. The radiograph shows both a positive posterior fat pad, which is always abnormal, and a large anterior fat pad with a sail sign indicating fracture or joint effusion. An AP view might help better identify the fracture line but might not demonstrate it in all cases.

91. **The answer is B, Diabetic mononeuropathy.**

(Marx, 1413-1416, 1646-1647, 1660-1661; Tintinalli, 1421, 1546)

Diabetic mononeuropathies of the third cranial nerve present with ptosis and the inability to adduct, depress, or elevate the eye with pupillary sparing. The patient often presents with diplopia. They are the most common cause of a unilateral oculomotor palsy. Pupillary function is presumptively spared because there is infarction of the central portion of the oculomotor nerve with sparing of the more peripherally situated fibers that mediate pupil constriction. However, pupil-sparing oculomotor palsies have a wide variety of causes, and CT or MRI is indicated. Imaging findings are normal in diabetic mononeuropathy, and the condition usually resolves in 4 to 6 weeks. Botulism causes bilateral binocular diplopia, most typically with fixed and dilated pupils. Adult patients experience diplopia, dysphagia, dysarthria, and blurred vision followed by a descending motor neuropathy with flaccid paralysis. Infants generally present with constipation, poor feeding, lethargy, and a weak cry. There are three main forms of clinical botulism. Infant botulism (about 75% of cases in the United States) occurs when botulism spores are ingested then produce toxin in the less-acidic stomach of infants. Wound botulism occurs almost exclusively in injecting drug users, and symptoms start 4 to 14 days after injection. Food-borne botulism occurs with ingestion of preformed toxin, typically from home-canned foods or inappropriately fermented foods. Symptoms occur 18 to 36 hours after ingestion. Myasthenia gravis results from antibodies directed against the nicotinic acetylcholine receptor at the neuromuscular junction. Pupillary responses are always normal, and the condition is bilateral. Myasthenia gravis eventually involves the ocular muscles in up to 90% of patients; more than 60% present with ocular muscle involvement. In thyroid ophthalmopathy, the patient typically complains of proptosis and exophthalmos; ptosis is extremely uncommon. Diplopia occurs when there is asymmetry in the edema of the extraocular muscles. The pupillary responses are intact.

92. The answer is C, Left lateral anal fissure.

(Adams, 386-388; Marx, 1245-1248; Tintinalli, 592)

Painful rectal bleeding is most often the result of an anal fissure, occurring almost universally in the posterior midline due to a relative lack of muscular support. Anal fissures in other locations are more likely to be a sign of underlying pathology, such as HIV infection, cancer, Crohn disease, syphilis, tuberculosis, or foreign body insertion. Postpartum women are also at increased risk for anterior midline fissures. Decreased structural support, likewise, can result in the formation of hemorrhoids. The dentate line separates internal and external hemorrhoids. Neither requires further workup for underlying disease, but both might require additional treatment in the emergency department. External hemorrhoids complicated by dark blue, tender, and firm thrombus can be treated by the emergency physician with a simple elliptical excision. Children, pregnant women, and patients with coagulopathies require specialty consultation. Internal hemorrhoids are classified into four groups based on the degree of prolapse and severity of symptoms. Irreducible internal hemorrhoids (fourth degree) can also develop thrombus and progress to necrosis that requires emergency surgical consultation. Fortunately, most fissures and hemorrhoids can be managed conservatively with sitz baths, a high-fiber diet, and stool softeners. For fissures, topical preparations of anesthetics, calcium-channel blockers, and nitroglycerin have been reported to provide additional symptomatic relief.

93.   The answer is C, Unstable atrial fibrillation.

(Neumar, S750-S752; Tintinalli, 133-147)

Synchronized cardioversion is indicated for treatment of unstable supraventricular tachycardia, unstable atrial fibrillation, and unstable atrial flutter. It is a shock that is timed for delivery with the QRS complex, avoiding the relative refractory segment of the cardiac electrical cycle, which is vulnerable to induction of ventricular fibrillation. Contraindications include an unidentifiable QRS complex (ventricular fibrillation) and when the delay to synchronize is a risk to the patient (pulselessness). Accelerated idioventricular rhythm (AIVR) is characterized by a ventricular rate between 40 and 120 beats/min. It is due to increased automaticity of a ventricular focus that is equal to or faster than the sinus atrial rate. It demonstrates gradual onset and offset, in contrast to ventricular tachycardia, which is sudden onset and offset. It is commonly seen with reperfusion of ST-segment elevation MI, digoxin toxicity, and cardiomyopathy. Accelerated idioventricular rhythm is a benign rhythm, usually self-limited, and rarely requires intervention. When treatment is required, atropine can be given to speed up the underlying sinus rate, which will inhibit the AIVR. Synchronized cardioversion is not effective for multifocal atrial tachycardia, characterized by multiple sites of increased automaticity. Cardioversion might actually increase the rate of an automatic focus. Only unsynchronized cardioversion (defibrillation) is indicated for treatment of ventricular fibrillation, pulseless ventricular tachycardia, and unstable polymorphic ventricular tachycardia.

94.   The answer is A, Clonidine.

(Nelson, 198, 753, 915, 1066, 1171-1172; Wolfson, 1450-1451)

Clonidine is an alpha$_2$-adrenergic agonist that, in overdose, can cause a depressed level of consciousness, hypoventilation (often responsive to tactile stimulation), and miosis. The presentation can closely mimic an opioid poisoning. Although initial hypertension and reflex bradycardia can occur and are attributed to nonspecific activation of peripheral alpha$_1$ receptors, sympatholytic hypotension and bradycardia are typical. Naloxone was likely first used in clonidine poisoning due to the similarity to opioid poisoning; occasionally, it reverses some of the effects of toxicity. Treatment of clonidine poisoning is supportive, and naloxone use can be considered. Poisoning with other alpha$_2$ agonists such as tetrahydrozyline (in eye drops) and xylazine (a veterinary anesthetic) present similar to clonidine. Poisoning with diphenhydramine, lysergic acid (LSD), and yohimbine typically result in mydriasis, not miosis. Diphenhydramine has antimuscarinic properties and can present with all of the typical signs of antimuscarinic (anticholinergic) poisoning such as tachycardia, mild hyperthermia, delirium, mydriasis, and dry skin. Diphenhydramine also has sodium-channel blocking activity, which can manifest as QRS complex prolongation and convulsions. Presentations related to LSD are uncommonbut mydriasis, tachycardia, and hallucinations are typical symptoms. Yohimbine is an alpha$_2$ antagonist (opposite of clonidine). Manifestations of poisoning include sympathomimetic symptoms and signs of tachycardia, hypertension, agitation, diaphoresis, and mydriasis.

95. The answer is B, Boarding increases left-without-being-seen rates.

(ACEP Task Force Report on Boarding, 8-10; Marx, 2547-2553)

Boarding is the practice of holding patients in the emergency department after they have been admitted to the hospital because no inpatient beds are available. According to a 2008 ACEP report, boarding and the resulting crowding increase the rate at which patients leave without being seen. Unfortunately, the percentage of people with serious illness is not that different between those who leave before being evaluated and those who wait to be seen. Boarding and crowding have been shown to increase the total hospital length-of-stay by as much as 1 day, and higher-acuity patients do wait longer to be seen. The Centers for Disease Control and Prevention found that, of patients labeled as critical in triage, up to 10% waited as long as 1 hour to be evaluated by a physician. Several studies have shown that the mortality rates for patients seeking emergency care during times of crowding are higher than those when crowding is not a problem, with a hazard ratio for death of approximately 1.3. Ambulance diversion is clearly caused by crowding and boarding of admitted patients in the emergency department. Crowding and boarding take up a finite number of telemetry monitors and bed space in the emergency department, and once there is no longer a place to put a monitored ambulance patient, the department could be forced to divert ambulance patients.

96. The answer is D, Reporting of suspected abuse.

(Fleisher, 1362-1363, 1656-1670; Marx, 792-795, 2255)

Nonaccidental causes of injury should be differentiated from accidental causes, and, if there is suspicion of abuse, the physician has a responsibility to report it to the authorities. In this case, the isolated diaphyseal fracture of the humerus is unlikely to be caused by rolling off a bed, and in a child younger than 3 years, abuse should be strongly considered. Child maltreatment is pervasive throughout all socioeconomic classes and is grossly underreported. There are more than 1 million cases annually. The physician's job is to care for the child. There are many types of child maltreatment. Descriptions differ among states, so physicians must be knowledgeable about the laws and reporting requirements where they practice. Common categories of maltreatment are as follows:

- Physical abuse is direct injury to a child's body. This includes bruising, burns, internal hemorrhage, internal organ damage, brain injury, and fractures.

- Emotional abuse is psychological injury that causes or is likely to cause serious impairment of the physical, social, mental, or emotional capacities of the child.
- Sexual abuse is inappropriate sexual exposure or touch by an adult to a child or of an older child to a younger child.

Neglect is further subdivided into general and medical. This is a very difficult area to define unless the neglect is grossly apparent or the child was abandoned. General neglect is failure to provide for the basic needs of a child. This designation requires the consideration of the family's cultural values, economic status, and societal standards of care, if there are any. Medical neglect is determined after analyzing the differences between medical neglect and noncompliance. As with general neglect, the economic status and cultural values must be considered, but, for example, if the caretaker is not administering a medication he or she already has and this causes further disease, medical neglect is present.

97. The answer is B, He has a known inherited immunodeficiency.

(Marx, 879; Spiro, 1235-1241)

Eighty percent of cases of acute otitis media resolve spontaneously, so watchful waiting for mild cases is a reasonable approach that reduces the use of antibiotics. In a randomized controlled trial of this approach in the emergency department setting, the presence of a known inherited immunodeficiency excluded patients from the study. Other exclusion criteria included suspicion of an additional bacterial infection such as pneumonia, toxic appearance, hospitalization, exposure to an antibiotic in the previous 7 days, presence of either myringotomy tubes or a perforated tympanic membrane, and uncertain access to medical care. The study enrolled 138 patients with a wait-and-see approach, and two-thirds (62%) never filled the prescription. These patients had good outcomes equal to those of the control group treated with amoxicillin. Although resistance to amoxicillin is high among patients with *Streptococcus pneumoniae* (the most common cause, along with *Haemophilus influenzae,* of otitis media) infection, amoxicillin remains the drug of choice. Patients with beta-lactam allergies may be treated with a trimethoprim-sulfamethoxazole and erythromycin combination, clindamycin, or azithromycin.

98. The answer is D, Thalassemia.

(Marx, 1561-1562; Tintinalli, 1457-1458, 1480-1488)

Thalassemic patients are sensitive to oxidative stress, such as that caused by nitrofurantoin. Oxidative stress is defined as a condition causing excessive free radicals. Nitrofurantoin is reduced by NADPH reductase into an anion radical, which causes membrane instability and eventual cellular destruction. Thalassemia is characterized by anemia, which varies depending on the erythropoiesis. It is common in persons of Mediterranean, Middle Eastern,

African, and Asian descent. Thalassemia is a decreased production of either the alpha- or beta-globin chains. In alpha thalassemia, beta tetramers form, which are soluble and lead to increased destruction; beta thalassemia produces alpha tetramers, which are insoluble and lead to increased destruction to erythroid precursors and early death of the cells. G6PD deficiency also increases destruction of red blood cells with oxidative stress, but it does not produce as profound an anemia in the common variant and is usually asymptomatic. Sickle cell disease and iron deficiency can present with anemia but do not increase destruction of cells with oxidative stress.

99. The answer is B, Measure forced vital capacity.

(Marx, 1413-1415; Wolfson, 790-793)

The patient in this question is exhibiting symptoms consistent with myasthenic crisis, which occurs in approximately 15% to 20% of patients with myasthenia gravis. She has no acute objective signs of respiratory failure, but her ventilatory status must be evaluated with either a forced vital capacity (FVC) or negative inspiratory force (NIF) measurement. The hallmark of myasthenic crisis is respiratory failure requiring mechanical ventilation, and the mainstay of treatment is airway management with monitoring of ventilatory status for worsening function. Myasthenic crisis can occur without any clear inciting factors, but it can be triggered by infection, fever, or stress or by the addition of a new medication such as muscle relaxants, anesthetics, and certain antibiotics such as the quinolones. Although this patient does not need emergent intubation, the clinical picture can change rapidly. Trending of the patient's FVC or NIF helps monitor ventilatory effort. Pyridostigmine, an acetylcholinesterase inhibitor, is used as an outpatient treatment for myasthenia gravis. By blocking the degradation of acetylcholine in the synapse, pyridostigmine prolongs acetylcholine activity. Use of pyridostigmine in the acute setting is not recommended because high doses can lead to muscle weakness. A patient in myasthenic crisis is at no higher risk for pulmonary embolism than any other person. Ocular symptoms are a common presentation in new-onset myasthenia and can manifest as diplopia or lid lag, which especially worsens with fatigue. Cold temperatures should improve these symptoms: placing an ice bag over the patient's eyes should result in a decrease in lid lag 2 minutes later.

100. The answer is A, Pathogens vary with patient age.

(Fleisher, 1564-1566; Marx, 1303-1306)

Urinary tract infections (UTIs) are a significant cause of illness in pediatric patients. They are the second most common bacterial infection after upper respiratory tract infections. *Escherichia coli* is the most common pathogen, but the bacteria vary depending on the age of the patient. During the neonatal period, *Klebsiella* is a more common pathogen. But older children and adults have similar pathogens and a similar mechanism of infection: fecal bacteria seed the surrounding skin of the urethra. In contrast, in the neonatal period, it is believed that a bacteremia first exist that then seeds into the urinary system. Initially, UTIs are identified more predominantly in male patients in the neonatal period but become more predominant in females during infancy (and into adulthood). From age 1 to 3 months, there is an incidence of up to 30% of UTI with sepsis, which decreases to 5% after 3 months. Signs and symptoms of UTI are less specific for children, especially neonates and infants. Poor feeding, vomiting, or other nonspecific symptoms can herald a UTI, while the presence of fever can actually indicate pyelonephritis. Older children can have more system-specific symptoms and indicate pain with urination. Accidental wetting can also occur in previously toilet-trained children. Diagnostic tests include urinalysis, which can be obtained many different ways: direct bladder catheterization (the most common), suprapubic aspiration, bag collection (the least reliable method because of the high contamination rates), and clean catch for the toilet-trained patient.

101. The answer is C, Using two drugs increases the risk of side effects that are seen with each drug individually.

(Godwin, 182-183; Miner, 182)

Opioids have been shown to pose a greater risk for respiratory depression than other medications (especially benzodiazepines), especially in higher doses and with rapid administration. This effect is greater when the opioid is given with a benzodiazepine. Because the opioid has the greater potential to cause respiratory depression, the suggested method is to administer narcotics first and titrate benzodiazepines. Opioids are associated with hypoxemia and a lowered ventilatory response to carbon dioxide. Propofol has been clearly shown as safe for use in the emergency department when appropriate guidelines are followed, which include monitoring for respiratory depression and careful preparation and administration of the agent. Pulse oximetry is routine for monitoring patients during procedural sedation; end-tidal carbon dioxide capnography might help detect respiratory changes before they are evident on pulse oximetry or in the patient's condition. Hypotension, not hypertension, is a common side effect of the rapid administration of sedative agents. Procedural sedation complications are related to the medications used and the dose and rate of administration. Opioids and benzodiazepines have been associated with hypotension regardless of route of administration, so intravenous access should be considered, as well as evaluation of the patient's intravascular volume status prior to beginning the procedure.

102. The answer is D, Nebulized albuterol.

(Marx, 895-901; Tintinalli, 506-510)

Beta-adrenergic agonists such as albuterol are the primary treatment for acute asthma exacerbations. Inhalation is the preferred route of administration because of its rapid onset of action and direct effect on the bronchi. There is a strong body of literature showing the equivalence of metered-dose inhalers to nebulizers. Intravenous or subcutaneous administration of beta-adrenergic agents is reserved for patients with severe asthma who might not have enough respiratory function to deliver sufficient amounts of the medication by inhalation. Anticholinergic agents such as ipratropium can and should be used in combination with inhaled beta-agonist agents to provide a synergistic effect. Steroids should be administered either intravenously or orally in most patients who present to the emergency department for an asthma exacerbation. Inhaled steroids are not helpful in the acute setting but have a role in long-term maintenance therapy. The effectiveness of ketamine has not been well studied. It is a potent bronchodilator but causes increased secretions. Ketamine might be helpful in severe asthma as an induction agent or before intubation. Magnesium might have a role in treating severe asthma as a smooth muscle relaxer, which could be particularly helpful when the first-line nebulized beta-adrenergic agonists are not able to reach peripheral airways.

103. The answer is C, Factor VIII therapy to 100% activity.

(Fleisher, 878-883; Marx, 1578-1587)

Head trauma can be life-threatening in hemophilia patients, and bleeds involving the CNS are the major cause of complications. With these injuries, treatment consists of replacement therapy to at least 50% activity before the child is sent for CT. If an injury is diagnosed, 100% activity should be achieved giving 50 units/kg of factor VIII. Lower percentages of activity are used for less severe injuries. Hemophilia is usually an X-linked recessive disorder causing a variation in factor VIII, which diminishes clot promotion in the clotting cascade. Emergency department treatment of bleeding events was once common, but most of the replacement therapy is now performed at the patient's home. Replacement therapy for hemophilia A includes cryoprecipitate or factor VIII:C concentrate. The infusion of 1 unit of factor VII/kg increases the level by approximately 2%. The screening for antihemophilia antibodies should be done in all hemophiliac patients, but especially in those who are not responding to factor repletion. Treatment for a bleeding issue depends on the specific location, but the emergency physician should institute therapy as soon as possible in patients with obvious signs of bleeding or those patients who indicate that they are bleeding. Hospitalization is likely after a head injury in a patient with hemophilia A, and observation alone is not enough therapy, as factor replacement is required. Communication with a hematologist is helpful to guide therapy further. Factor IX therapy is used for treatment of hemophilia B. Blood transfusion is often required for a patient suffering from hemorrhagic shock but not part of the management of hemophilia A.

104. The answer is B, It is superior to ultrasonography for diagnosing solid organ injury.

(Marx, 420-422; Wolfson, 227-231)

Computed tomography scanning of the abdomen and pelvis is the best diagnostic modality in the hemodynamically stable patient. When used with intravenous contrast, it is extremely sensitive for picking up solid organ injury, vascular injury, and retroperitoneal injury. It is also capable of determining the presence and amount of intraperitoneal blood and is therefore superior to ultrasound, which might miss small amounts of intraperitoneal hemorrhage. However, CT is not as sensitive at diagnosing pancreatic, hollow viscus, and mesenteric injuries, and it can also miss some diaphragmatic injuries. The use of oral contrast, while controversial, might improve the detection of hollow viscus and pancreatic injuries. In this case, obtaining a CT scan for this patient is appropriate because fluid administration stabilized his vital signs. If he were not stabilized, a FAST examination would be a more appropriate diagnostic approach because it can be done in the emergency department at the bedside. The FAST examination has a 60% to 90% sensitivity for detecting hemodynamically significant hemoperitoneum, but it is not accurate for finding solid organ injury that does not produce free blood in the abdomen.

105. The answer is C, Nausea.

(American College of Emergency Physicians [syncope], 431-434; Marx, 142-148; Tintinalli, 400)

Vasovagal (neurocardiogenic) or neurally mediated or reflex-mediated syncope is common and is usually associated with exposure to a noxious stimulus, prolonged standing, fatigue, or a combination of these factors. Nausea is very common in patients with vasovagal syncope and is often associated with vomiting. Vasovagal syncope is an uncommon cause of syncope in the supine position unless the patient is undergoing a medical procedure, such as placement of an intravenous line. An absent or brief prodrome is concerning for a cardiac dysrhythmia as a cause of syncope. The prodrome of neurocardiogenic syncope lasts 10 seconds to 1 minute and is associated with nausea, diaphoresis, graying of vision, and lightheadedness; bystanders often observe extreme pallor. Confusion lasting longer than a few moments after the syncope is not associated with neurocardiogenic syncope. A longer period of confusion (>30 seconds) suggests a postictal period, hypoglycemia, severe hypoxia, or another serious etiology. Orthostatic hypotension is defined as a drop in systolic blood pressure of more than 20 mm Hg when the patient goes from a horizontal to a vertical position. It is very common and commonly contributes to syncope. It should be suspected as the cause only if the patient has recurrence of syncope or presyncope when he or she stands up. The causes for orthostatic hypotension are multifactorial and include autonomic dysfunction, medications (particularly those with alpha- or beta-blockade), vasodilators, diuretics, and other causes of hypovolemia.

106. The answer is C, Aspartate aminotransferase and acetaminophen level testing.

(Marx, 1948-1952; Tintinalli, 1246-1252)

In patients with suspected chronic ingestions, the acetaminophen and the aspartate aminotransferase (AST) levels will determine the need for N-acetylcysteine (NAC) treatment. Acetaminophen is mainly metabolized in the liver through conjugation with glucuronide and sulfate. In toxic ingestions these pathways are saturated, which increases acetaminophen oxidation by cytochrome P-450 to the hepatotoxic metabolite N-acetyl-p-benzoquinone imine (NAPQI). Alcohol abuse, HIV infection, and isoniazid all increase the risk of chronic hepatotoxicity. The most sensitive indicator of hepatic injury in acetaminophen toxicity is the AST level. An AST two times greater than normal is significant for injury, whereas greater than 1,000 IU/L is considered hepatotoxic. Screening AST and acetaminophen levels are indicated when daily ingestions exceed 4 g/day in adults or 90 mg/kg in children. If both are elevated, immediate NAC treatment is recommended to replenish glutathione stores and inactivate NAPQI (acts as a free radical scavenger, limiting NAPQI effects). Intravenous NAC is the treatment of choice for chronic acetaminophen toxicity. The Rumack-Matthew nomogram for acute acetaminophen ingestions is not useful in this patient with possible chronic ingestion. Abdominal CT scanning and ultrasonography can confirm cirrhosis but not the underlying cause. Similarly, elevations in alkaline phosphatase and gamma glutamyltransferase levels suggest cholestasis but not the underlying etiology or treatment.

107. The answer is C, Pericardiocentesis.

(Marx, 1059, 1598; Roy, 1810-1818)

The patient's ECG shows sinus tachycardia and low voltage, along with electrical alternans, which suggests cardiac tamponade. Although initial treatment involves increasing the right ventricular filling pressure with intravenous fluids to overcome the pericardial constriction, pericardiocentesis is the definitive treatment in an unstable patient. Electrical alternans is present in 10% to 30% of patients with large pericardial effusions. This uncommon but classic pattern on ECG is thought to be caused by the "swinging" or changing position of the heart in the pericardial fluid relative to the electrodes on the chest wall. More commonly with pericardial effusion, the ECG is normal or shows only low voltage. Tamponade physiology develops when the effusion prevents adequate filling of the atria and ventricles, resulting in reduction of blood flow into the right ventricle and decreased stroke volume and cardiac output. Patients with chronic kidney disease, neoplastic disease, autoimmune diseases such as systemic lupus erythematosus, recent MI or cardiac surgery, and penetrating thoracic injury are at risk for developing pericardial effusions that progress to tamponade. The presentation can be insidious, with complaints of dyspnea on rest or exertion, or even cough. Symptoms of acute pericarditis such as chest pain are frequently absent. The classic Beck triad findings (hypotension, distended neck veins, muffled heart sounds) might be absent if symptoms progress rapidly. Kussmaul signs (muffled heart sounds, tachycardia, pulsus paradoxus, enlarged cardiac silhouette) are other findings for tamponade. Pulsus paradoxus is an exaggerated decrease in the systemic blood pressure during inspiration, which is normally less than 10 mm Hg. Bedside echocardiography confirms the diagnosis when a pericardial effusion and paradoxical systolic wall motion are seen. In the treatment of pericardial tamponade, enough fluid should be withdrawn during pericardiocentesis to stabilize the patient. A drainage catheter should be left in the pericardial space if the effusion is likely to reaccumulate. This patient does not have an ST-segment elevation MI requiring catheterization or thrombolytic therapy or signs of hyperkalemia requiring calcium gluconate, sodium bicarbonate, insulin, and glucose administration. Dobutamine is contraindicated and could contribute to hypotension. Although pulmonary embolism is a possibility, the likelihood of tamponade is significantly higher given the classic ECG findings. A bedside ultrasound examination can rapidly confirm a pericardial effusion.

108. The answer is A, Beta-hydroxybutyrate.

(Marx, 1641, 2386; Nelson, 1122-1123; Wolfson, 1019-1020)

Significant elevation of the ketone beta-hydroxybutyrate is the most specific test result to confirm the diagnosis of alcoholic ketoacidosis (AKA). Chronic ethanol use in the setting of starvation, the latter often occurring from an ethanol-induced disorder such as pancreatitis, can lead to AKA. The metabolic condition produced favors the production of beta-hydroxybutyrate, and significant elevation of it is the most specific (although not necessarily needed) laboratory confirmation. Ketone measurement in the blood and urine might also be helpful, but these tests are specific for acetone and acetoacetate, which are in much lower concentrations because of the metabolic state and NAD/NADH ratio present in AKA. The metabolic condition also favors the formation of lactic acid; however, a multitude of conditions can cause a lactic acidosis, so this finding is nonspecific. Alcoholic ketoacidosis can mimic a toxic alcohol (ethylene glycol or methanol) poisoning, particularly since alcoholics are often those who ingest a toxic alcohol. Oxalic acid and formic acid are toxic metabolites of ethylene glycol and methanol poisoning, respectively, are not routinely measured, and would not be elevated in the setting of AKA. Rapid correction of the acidosis in AKA with the administration of dextrose and food (the latter if the clinical condition allows for it) and intravenous fluid is characteristic. Searching for associated or precipitating illnesses, administration of thiamine, correcting electrolyte abnormalities such as hypokalemia and hypomagnesemia, and monitoring for ethanol withdrawal are all essential in managing AKA. Ethanol might or might not still be present in a patient presenting in AKA. Although it might yield some clinical information in a patient denying ethanol use, it does not confirm the diagnosis of AKA.

109. The answer is B, Parietal.

(Fleisher, 1428-1430; Marx, 2256)

Skull fractures occur in 2 per 1,000 infants annually and in 0.5 to 1 per 1,000 children and adolescents. In infants, the parietal bone is the most likely to be fractured, constituting up to 70% of all skull fractures. The next most likely areas of injury in infants are the occipital and temporal bones. The least likely to be injured is the frontal bone. The causes of skull fractures in infants include falls, motor vehicle or other blunt traumas, and nonaccidental injury. Abuse must be a consideration, as skull fractures are the second most common injury seen in these cases. In children and adolescents, the causes of skull fractures are likely from motor vehicle trauma or sports-related injury. Infants are at higher risk of fracture than older pediatric patients because of the immaturity of the bony skull, although this risk decreases after the first year of life. Falls from only 4 to 5 feet can cause significant injury: 50% of infants found to have a skull fracture fell from less than this height. A linear skull fracture is the most common manifestation, and plain radiographs of the skull might miss 25% or more of these injuries. Intracranial injury is obviously more likely in infants with a skull fracture, so CT is recommended if a fracture is found. Clinical findings often note overlying swelling, while palpable bony abnormalities are rare in the linear or minimally depressed skull fracture. The child should also be evaluated for clinical findings of head injury, including level of consciousness, vomiting, and seizures. Few infants require any specific treatment with just a simple skull fracture.

110. The answer is C, Cooling with fans and skin wetting from a spray bottle.

(Adams, 1437-1443; Marx, 1882-1892; Tintinalli, 1339-1344; Wolfson, 1603-1605)

A patient who presents with signs and symptoms of heatstroke requires immediate intervention with active cooling methods, the most effective of which are evaporative cooling and ice water immersion. Heatstroke and heat exhaustion can present with similar signs and symptoms, including weakness, fatigue, frontal headache, vertigo, and vomiting, but the hallmarks for the diagnosis of heatstroke include core temperature above 40.5°C (104.9°F) and profound CNS dysfunction, including disorientation, drowsiness, ataxia, and other signs of cerebellar dysfunction. If heatstroke cannot be excluded from the differential diagnosis, efforts to actively cool the patient should begin immediately. Evaporative cooling is performed by completely undressing the patient, placing standing fans close to the patient, and wetting the patient's skin with atomized tepid (40°C) water from a spray bottle. This is the ideal method because it is simple, readily available, noninvasive, and relatively effective. Ice water immersion can be used to rapidly reduce core temperature to less than 39°C in 10 to 40 minutes. This approach is noninvasive and relatively effective, but it is logistically difficult, cumbersome, and poorly tolerated by the patient and makes temperature monitoring more difficult. Cooling modalities other than evaporation and ice water immersion should be considered adjunctive therapies. Cardiopulmonary bypass with a heat exchanger has been used successfully in the treatment of malignant hyperthermia but is not the primary immediate treatment for heatstroke. Continuation of intravenous fluids and temperature monitoring is helpful for patients with heat exhaustion, many of whom improve with intravenous fluid replacement alone, but is not adequate in a patient with altered mental status and a core temperature of 41°C consistent with heatstroke. Acetaminophen and other antipyretic agents are ineffective in the treatment of heatstroke and should not be used to control environmental hyperthermia. Placing ice packs on the axillae and groin is another adjunctive therapy but is not the most effective immediate therapy.

111. The answer is A, He has been exposed to hepatitis B.

(Marx, 1153-1154; Wolfson, 567-570)

The hepatitis B virus has several immunogenic components. The viron envelope provides the surface antigen, designated by HBsAg; the antibody that develops against it is anti-HBs. The core of the virus has a separate antigen designated HBcAg, and actively infected patients demonstrate the hepatitis Be antigen, HBeAg, thought to be a degradation product of the core antigen. Patients who have been naturally exposed to hepatitis B develop antibodies to the surface (anti-HBs) and the core of the viron (anti-HBc). Patients immunized against hepatitis B virus develop a slightly different serologic picture. The hepatitis B vaccine contains only virus surface molecules (anti-HBs), and patients with immunity from the vaccine are anti-HBs positive yet core antibody (anti-HBc) negative. Patients who have immunity, either by natural infection or via the vaccine, should be core antigen (HBcAg) negative. Hepatitis C has much less complicated serology. Patients who have been exposed to hepatitis C are positive for the hepatitis C antibody (anti-HCV). There is no vaccine yet available for hepatitis C. Both hepatitis B and C are transmitted by body fluids and pose an occupational hazard for health care workers.

112. The answer is C, Head injury.

(Fleisher, 1233-1248; Marx, 262-265)

Trauma is the leading cause of death in children. In fact, 50% of all deaths of children 1 to 14 years old are because of trauma, with up to 22 million children injured annually. The most common single organ system injury associated with death in the injured child is head trauma. It is also the highest cause of injury among pediatric patients, although the injury pattern in children is different from that in adult trauma patients. Trauma deaths occur predominantly among males, with the highest frequency at age 8. Blunt trauma is the major mechanism of injury; motor vehicle crashes account for 90% of the injuries to children. Because children are smaller and more compact and lack musculature and adipose, and because of the more anterior location of the liver and spleen, multiorgan injury is the rule, not the exception. Heat loss also is a significant factor because of the higher surface area. A pediatric patient is more susceptible to secondary brain injury, which can lead to a worse neurologic outcome. Also, the younger child's brain is more prone to hyperemia and edema from the shearing effect after the trauma than an older child's is.

113. The answer is D, Rapid increase in serum creatinine.

(Bosch, 62-72; Marx, 1650-1657; Tintinalli, 622-624)

Acute kidney injury associated with rhabdomyolysis is associated with a more rapid increase in creatinine and a low fractional excretion of sodium. Urine findings of rhabdomyolysis include pigmented granular casts, dipstick urine tests positive for blood with no RBCs on microscopic examination, oliguria or anuria, and myoglobinuria. Blood testing might reveal an elevated CK level (although this does not correlate well with incidence of renal injury) and an elevated myoglobin (the causative agent of renal injury). Electrolyte abnormalities (hyperkalemia, elevated phosphate, elevated uric acid) and elevated anion gap with metabolic acidosis are characteristic findings as well. Neither of these laboratory findings correlates well with the level of acute renal injury. The mechanism of renal injury seems to be fluid sequestration in injured muscle, which releases mediators that cause renal vasoconstriction and lead to renal ischemia. Myoglobin can also form deposits by combining with Tamm-Horsfall proteins, which then cause tubular obstruction that leads to renal injury.

114. The answer is B, Pain on passive extension of the finger.

(Marx, 521-522; Wolfson, 724)

Of the four cardinal signs (Kanavel signs) of flexor tenosynovitis, pain on passive extension of the finger is most likely to be present early in the disease. The other three cardinal findings are flexed position of the finger at rest, symmetric swelling of the finger, and tenderness over the course of the flexor sheath. Dorsal hand swelling can develop as the infection progresses, but it is not a cardinal sign. Flexor tenosynovitis most commonly affects the right hand and digits 1 through 3. The most common etiology is a penetrating injury that seeds the tendon sheath. Without early recognition and treatment (intravenous antibiotics and possible surgical debridement), patients can suffer significant loss of range of movement.

115. The answer is D, Munchausen syndrome.

(Adams, 2070; Wolfson, 814-815)

Factitious disorders such as Munchausen syndrome and malingering have a combined prevalence of 1% to 5% of the population. Munchausen syndrome, or factitious illness with physical symptoms, describes the patient who creates stories about his or her medical illnesses to experience the adventure of a hospital admission and advanced medical care. These patients are often dramatic in their presentation and describe their symptoms exactly as if they had read textbooks on the subjects. They are typically young to middle-aged men, have a history of extensive travel, and report receiving care and undergoing procedures in many different cities. When pressed for specific details about their care, they might be vague or uncertain. A malingerer, in contrast, has clear secondary goals and external incentives other than just wanting to be admitted and have a procedure done. A conversion disorder should be considered if a loss of function, usually involving the neurologic system, appears to exist and a psychologic source seems to be the cause. This diagnosis must be considered with caution because patients have been subsequently found to have physical etiologies. A drug-seeker can present with multiple somatic complaints, multiple symptoms, and vague symptom complexes but typically stops short of undergoing significant procedures. Drug-seeking behavior often deteriorates into argumentative or manipulative behavior.

116. The answer is A, 100% oxygen by nonrebreather mask.

(Fleisher, 198-202, 699-701; Marx, 2138-2167)

Signs of cardiac disease in children can include poor weight gain and feeding issues and other nonspecific findings. The presentation in this question suggests cyanotic congenital heart disease. It can be difficult to distinguish from pulmonary disease, but the best way to differentiate the two is to provide high-flow oxygen and observe the patient's oxygen saturation and clinical status. In practice, any patient *in extremis* warrants 100% oxygen, and optimal delivery is by a nonrebreather mask. Cyanotic cardiac disease causes a right-to-left shunting, with a mixture of oxygenated and deoxygenated blood sent to the systemic circulation with subsequent cyanosis. In these children, administering 100% oxygen is not likely to change the patient's clinical status or coloration because the shunting of the blood remains unchanged. A mnemonic for the five cyanotic congenital cardiac diseases is as follows:

1 - Truncus arteriosus (1 trunk)
2 - Transposition of the great vessels (2 vessels)
3 - Tricuspid atresia (Tri = 3)
4 - Tetralogy of Fallot (Tet = 4, right ventricular hypertrophy, overriding aorta, pulmonic stenosis, and ventricular septal defect)
5 - Total anomalous pulmonary venous return (5 letters of "TAPVR")

Synchronized cardioversion is reserved for patients who are unstable with supraventricular tachycardia or ventricular tachycardia with pulses. Phenylephrine (correct dosing is 0.01-0.02 mg/kg IV) is given to increase systemic vascular resistance during an episode of shunting associated with tetralogy of Fallot, or a "tet spell." It can diminish the left-to-right shunting and improve overall circulation. Intravenous hydration is always an important component of resuscitation but is not the first priority. Clearing the airway and resuming breathing for the patient are critical: 80% of all pediatric arrests are respiratory. A full 20 mL/kg infusion can be deleterious if the pump delivering the fluid is not working efficiently (as can happen). If that is suspected, a 10 mL/kg infusion can be given and then repeated if the patient's clinical status does not worsen.

117. The answer is C, An early indicator of respiratory depression during procedural sedation.

(Marx, 24-26; Tintinalli, 285-287)

End-tidal carbon dioxide monitoring ($ETCO_2$), or capnometry, is a useful monitor of respiratory and metabolic status. It can detect apnea or hypoventilation before it is noted on clinical examination or by changes in pulse oximetry, including in patients with respiratory depression caused by procedural sedation. Exhaled carbon dioxide reflects the partial concentration of alveolar carbon dioxide, which correlates with arterial levels of carbon dioxide. There are two types of $ETCO_2$ monitoring devices: a colorimetric sensor and a quantitative capnometry that provides continuous measurement. Colorimetric sensors are used to confirm intubation and are good for only a short period of time. They turn from purple to yellow in the presence of $ETCO_2$. Capnometry can be used to monitor and even predict the response to resuscitation and CPR. In a pulseless patient without artificial ventilation and perfusion, the $ETCO_2$ level will be low, but this is related to poor perfusion, not to the accuracy of the monitor.

118. The answer is B, Hemodynamic instability.

(Marx, 446-450; Wolfson, 238-240)

Indications for the radiographic evaluation of renal injury include presence of blunt trauma with gross hematuria, blunt trauma with microscopic hematuria and hemodynamic instability, penetrating trauma, and high-energy deceleration mechanism. This patient has microscopic hematuria but does not have gross hematuria, penetrating trauma, or a deceleration mechanism of injury. Therefore, the combination of microscopic hematuria and hemodynamic instability should prompt further diagnostic evaluation for renal injury. Flank pain is likely given that he was hit with a baseball bat, but musculoskeletal injury can also cause pain and does not itself prompt radiographic evaluation. This patient's ultrasonography findings are normal and do not warrant further evaluation. A history of urinary tract infection and the presence of trace proteinuria do not contribute to the decision to evaluate for renal trauma in this setting.

119. **The answer is B, Midline and bilateral.**

(Marx, 159-162; Tintinalli, 519)

Visceral abdominal pain is felt in the midline and bilaterally around the midline. It follows the embryologic origin of the blood supply, as follows: pain from the foregut (stomach, duodenum, liver, pancreas) is felt in the epigastrium; pain from midgut structures (small bowel, proximal colon, including the appendix) is felt in the periumbilical region; and pain from hindgut structures (distal colon, genitourinary tract) is felt in the hypogastrium. Visceral pain does not lateralize because the sympathetic autonomic fibers (visceral afferents) that carry it are transmitted to both sides of the spinal cord. Visceral pain is often hard to describe and poorly localized; it is often colicky or crampy. Secondary autonomic processes include nausea, pallor, and diaphoresis. Somatic or parietal abdominal pain occurs when the parietal peritoneum is irritated. Somatic abdominal pain is transmitted by the fast A delta fibers of the somatic neurons to the dorsal root ganglions on the side of the irritation, and as a consequence the pain is sharp and well localized. This pain is typically intense and constant. A classic example of visceral and somatic abdominal pain is the textbook case of appendicitis. The appendix is a small tubular structure at the start of the colon (derived from midgut). When the lumen obstructs, mucus accumulates and produces distention. Visceral pain from distention is felt in the region of the midgut, so pain is felt in the midline periumbilical region. If the obstruction continues, ischemia of the wall of the appendix develops, leading to localized perforation and irritation of the parietal peritoneum in the right lower quadrant.

120. **The answer is B, Liver transplant.**

(Marx, 1160-1161; Tintinalli, 570-571)

Otherwise unexplained, worsening renal failure confirms a diagnosis of hepatorenal syndrome (HRS), for which the only effective treatment is liver transplantation. Cirrhosis results in portal hypertension, producing a chain reaction that begins with splanchnic arterial vasodilation. This decrease in effective circulatory volume activates the renin-angiotensin-aldosterone system. Ultimately, vasoconstriction and renal failure result. Hepatorenal syndrome should be considered when a patient's serum creatinine level is greater than 1.5 mg/dL, creatinine clearance is less than 40 mL/min, urine volume is less than 500 mL/day, and urine sodium is less than 10 mEq/L. Ultrasound examination demonstrates decreased Doppler flow. Prognosis is poor, with an average survival of only 21 days. Cirrhosis-induced hypoperfusion is the cause of this type of renal failure; kidneys remain histologically normal and can even function as transplant kidneys.

Appropriate management begins with correctly identifying and treating any other cause of renal hypoperfusion or underlying infection. Persistent renal failure in the absence of easily explained conditions confirms the diagnosis of HRS. Temporizing measures include vasoconstrictors, intravenous albumin, hemodialysis, and transjugular intrahepatic portosystemic shunt (the TIPS procedure). However, liver transplantation is the only treatment that disrupts the chain reaction at the start, restoring effective renal perfusion. Since the kidney is not the problem, renal transplant would not be effective. Fluids are used to treat other causes of renal failure, which should be considered in the cirrhotic patient but not HRS.

121. The answer is C, Primary angioplasty.

(Marx, 952; Tintinalli, 374-378, 385-389)

Primary angioplasty is the treatment of choice in a patient with MI and cardiogenic shock. The ECG in this question shows greater than or equal to 1 mm of ST-segment elevation in leads V_1 through V_3 and 0.5 mm in lead V_4, consistent with an acute anterior MI. In the setting of acute MI and a clinical presentation of cardiogenic shock, primary angioplasty has been shown to have significant mortality benefit over thrombolytic therapy, even after delays due to transfer. Cardiogenic shock is characterized by hypotension and end-organ hypoperfusion as a result of low cardiac output that is not responsive to restoration of adequate preload. An anterior location and associated cardiogenic shock are both predictors of higher mortality rates in patients with acute MI. Therapeutic adjuncts such as dobutamine and dopamine can provide vasopressor and inotropic support, but they also increase myocardial oxygen consumption. A fluid challenge is indicated in this hypotensive patient to increase preload, but it is not definitive therapy, and the potential for pulmonary edema should be anticipated. Other conditions that should be considered include cardiac tamponade, aortic dissection, pulmonary embolism, and ventricular free wall rupture.

122. The answer is B, Eversion of the lids.

(Fleisher, 1595-1602; Marx, 715-717)

Given this patient's history and examination findings, ocular foreign body is the most likely diagnosis. Corneal examination does not reveal imbedded foreign debris, so further examination under the eyelids is warranted. Any debris found can be removed using a cotton-tipped applicator or irrigation. Imbedded corneal foreign bodies may be removed using a sterile needle; rust rings from imbedded metal can be removed using an ophthalmic burr. Referral to an ophthalmologist is an option if corneal foreign bodies are noted. Fluorescein dye should be used to find corneal abrasions caused by the entry of debris. The Seidel test is used to determine if there is a globe injury; it is positive when diluted fluorescein is seen flowing from a globe rupture site. Slit lamp evaluation of an injured eye is crucial to help diagnose an anterior chamber injury or posterior chamber disease. It is part of a normal ophthalmologic examination, but it has a limited role, if any, in the evaluation for an ocular foreign body. A dilated examination is the best way to fully evaluate the components of the eye but, again, does not help in the examination of the patient in this question.

123. The answer is C, Separation of the epidermis from dermis from a lateral, shearing pressure with a finger.

(Marx, 1538, 1540; Wolfson, 825, 826, 830, 840)

Nikolsky sign refers to the separation of the epidermis from dermis as a result of a lateral, shearing pressure on the skin. It can be present in a variety of vesiculobullous dermatologic disorders, including bullous pemphigoid, pemphigous vulgaris, staphylococcal scalded skin syndrome, Stevens-Johnson syndrome, and toxic epidermal necrolysis. Blanching of an erythematous rash from applying pressure is found in a variety of rashes and signifies that the red blood cells responsible for the erythema are intravascular and hence mobile. Petechiae and purpura do not blanch, as red blood cells have extravasated into the skin and are not free to move. Punctate bleeding of a scaly lesion that has been scratched is typical of psoriasis and is referred to as the Auspitz sign. A whealing reaction after a stroke stimulus is referred to as dermatographism and is the most common form of physical urticaria.

124. The answer is B, Salter-Harris II.

(Fleisher, 1335-1337; Marx, 473-474, 2245)

The radiography reveals a fracture through the proximal metaphysis of the first metacarpal bone, an injury classified as a Salter-Harris II fracture. The Salter-Harris II is the most common physeal fracture in pediatric patients. Fractures in children are labeled according to the area of injury around the growth plate of a bone. The physis is the cartilaginous growth area of the bone that ultimately fuses to form the adult bone; it is bordered on each side by the metaphysis and the epiphysis. The Salter-Harris classification is used to describe the injury related to the open physis. Salter-Harris I describes a fracture involving only the physis. It can be seen as a widening or displacement of the physis on a radiograph, but sometimes the radiograph can appear normal. If there is pain in the area of an open growth plate, there is the potential for a Salter-Harris I injury that should be addressed with immobilization and close followup care. Salter-Harris II fractures involve the physis and the metaphysis. Salter-Harris III and IV fractures involve the growth plate. A Salter-Harris III affects the joint surface through the epiphyseal plate and epiphysis. Salter-Harris IV fractures extend from the metaphysis, through the physis, and into the epiphysis. Salter-Harris V is a crush injury at the physis that can affect the growth of the injured bone. It is often related to a compressive force and involves the knee and the ankle most commonly. In a torus fracture, the soft periosteum forms a bump or buckles so that the contour of the outer cortex is changed while the cortex remains intact. A pediatric bone has a softer periosteum and is more able to bow or bend with injury than an adult bone. This change can be obvious or very subtle on radiographs. In a greenstick fracture, the bony cortex is disrupted on only one side. This relatively common injury pattern in children accounts for up to 50% of all breaks in patients younger than 12 years. They often occur at the metaphyseal-diaphyseal junction and are related to the soft periosteum that accounts for the different fracture pattern in children. A complete fracture extends through both sides of the cortex. Plastic deformation is a bowing of the bone without discernible break in the cortex. It is important to look at the cortex for breaks in the cortex but also at the overall bone for its position and anatomic alignment. The force that causes this is likely longitudinal, and inadequate care can lead to poor functional and cosmetic outcomes.

125. The answer is D, Systemic lupus erythematosus.

(Marx, 928, 1206-1207, 1497-1503; Tintinalli, 1913)

This patient demonstrates signs of pericarditis along with arthritis, anemia, thrombocytopenia, and proteinuria, thus meeting the criteria for a diagnosis of systemic lupus erythematosus (SLE). The clinical diagnosis of SLE requires that the patient exhibit four of the following 11 signs:

- Antinuclear antibody
- Arthritis
- Discoid rash
- Hematologic disorder (hemolytic anemia, leukopenia, lymphopenia, thrombocytopenia)
- Immunologic disorder (anti-DNA Ab, anti-Sm Ab, antiphospholipid Ab)
- Malar rash
- Neurologic disorder (seizures, psychosis)
- Oral ulcers
- Photosensitivity
- Renal disorder (persistent proteinuria, cellular casts)
- Serositis (pleuritis, pericarditis)

Mycoplasma pneumoniae infection and coccidioidomycosis are associated with purulent pericarditis. This condition usually is an extension of local disease and is not consistent with this presentation. *Mycoplasma pneumonia* can lead to cold agglutinin disease, which is characterized by an autoimmune hemolytic anemia and hemoglobinuria that can worsen with exposure to cold weather, but this usually occurs acutely postinfection and is transient. Hemolytic uremic syndrome (HUS) is the most common cause of acute renal failure in children accompanied by microangiopathic hemolytic anemia and thrombocytopenia. Although microthrombi affect a wide distribution of organs, HUS rarely manifests clinically with lung or cardiac involvement. One-third of rheumatoid arthritis (RA) patients develop pericarditis within the first 3 years after diagnosis, but it rarely is of clinical significance. Additionally, proteinuria and thrombocytopenia are not typical presentations of RA.

126. The answer is B, Perforations caused by penetrating trauma can disrupt the middle ear bones and result in hearing loss.

(Marx, 878; Tintinalli, 1557)

Perforations of the tympanic membrane can occur as a result of barotrauma, very loud noises, expanding pressure from suppurative otitis media, and penetrating trauma. Of these, penetrating trauma is the most likely to be associated with disruption of the middle ear bones, and these patients should be referred to an otolaryngologist. In adults, penetrating trauma to the ear can result from using cotton-tipped swabs to clean inside the canal. In children, it can result from inserting foreign bodies into the ear and iatrogenically from physicians attempting to remove foreign bodies. Most cases of tympanic membrane rupture, even those caused by penetrating trauma, resolve spontaneously, so topical antibiotics are not routinely indicated. When looking at a tympanic membrane through the ear canal, two sheets of tissue separated by the handle and lateral process of the malleus can be seen through the thin membrane. The smaller, superior portion of the membrane is a relatively slack tissue called the pars flaccida. The larger, inferior portion is pulled tighter and is known as the pars tensa; this is the site of the vast majority of perforations. Following trauma from loud sounds, some patients experience tinnitus or vertigo. This is almost always transient.

127. The answer is D, MRI.

(Marik, 2025-2033; Marx, 1124-1127)

Magnetic resonance imaging for deep vein thrombosis (DVT) has a high sensitivity and specificity for the diagnosis of iliac vein thrombosis. Because it does not involve ionizing radiation exposure, it has the added benefit of not being harmful to the fetus. Compression ultrasonography has sensitivities and specificities above 90% for proximal DVT but is poor for imaging calf and iliac veins. A pulsed Doppler study assesses the velocity of blood flow and may be used for iliac vein thrombosis. When MRI is not available, a pulsed Doppler study or CT may be used to identify iliac vein thrombosis. Computed tomography scanning can also be of benefit but exposes the fetus and mother to unwanted ionizing radiation. Normal pregnancy can cause changes that increase the D-dimer level, although a negative test result in the first or second trimester has a 100% negative predictive value depending on the type of assay. In isolation, though, a negative D-dimer does not rule out venous thromboembolus. The management of saphenous, tibial, and peroneal vein occlusion has been debated. In about 25% of patients, occlusion progresses to more proximal thrombosis. Some authors recommend anticoagulation, and others recommend daily enteric-coated aspirin therapy with weekly serial ultrasound examinations. The incidence of DVT is highest in the first postpartum week. Treatment for the low-risk patient is early ambulation. Moderate-risk patients can be treated with low-molecular-weight heparin or compression stockings. High-risk patients are treated with low-molecular-weight heparin and compression stockings. Factors that place patients at moderate risk for developing pulmonary embolism (PE) following childbirth are as follows: age older than 35 years; obesity (BMI >30); parity greater than three; gross varicose veins; current infection; pre-eclampsia; immobility for more than 4 days prior to surgery; major current illness; and emergency cesarean delivery. A patient who has two or more of these moderate risk factors is considered high risk for PE.

128. The answer is C, Symptoms are often made worse by coughing or sneezing.

(Marx, 1601-1602; Wolfson, 728)

This patient has signs and symptoms of epidural cord compression. These symptoms are often worsened by activities that increase intraspinal pressure (Valsalva, coughing, sneezing). When caused by malignancy, epidural cord compression is most commonly associated with lymphoma and lung, breast, or prostate cancer. The most common site is the thoracic spine (68%). Patients usually present with back pain, which can be gradual or sudden onset, often located at the level of the tumor. Radicular symptoms might be present. Up to 75% of patients have motor weakness at the time of diagnosis, and up to half have sensory change. When epidural cord compression is diagnosed early, patients typically present with symmetric flaccid paralysis and hyporeflexia. When the condition is diagnosed late, patients might present with signs of upper motor neuron disease, including spasticity and hyperreflexia. Emergency department treatment is administration of corticosteroids and consultation with radiation oncology for possible emergent radiation treatment. Despite a normal or minimally abnormal examination, epidural cord compression can progress to irreversible neurologic functions in a few hours. For this reason, the request for radiation oncology must be emergent. In most patients, vertebral disease is noticeable on plain radiography; however, the gold standard for making the diagnosis is MRI. It should be obtained for all patients with abnormal radiographs, as well as for patients with normal radiographs who have abnormal neurologic findings.

129. The answer is D, Herpes simplex virus infection.

(Marx, 868; Roberts, 1172)

Slit lamp examination in this case reveals a corneal epithelial defect in the shape of a dendrite, the hallmark of herpes simplex virus (HSV) infection. Patients usually present with foreign body sensation, tearing, photophobia, clear drainage, and decreased vision. Fluorescein staining might show superficial punctate keratitis, an ulcer, or this dendritic pattern. None of the other disease processes listed produces this finding. Ocular HSV can present with vesicles on the skin of the eyelids along with conjunctiva involvement or as corneal disease alone. An HSV infection of the cornea, as in this question, is treated with topical trifluridine 1% drops. Oral acyclovir can be helpful when a patient has recently (within 3 or 4 days) developed skin lesions, but any corneal involvement requires topical ophthalmic therapy. Acute angle closure glaucoma presents as a visual field loss beginning at the periphery, and examination shows conjunctival injection and a dilated, sluggish-to-fixed cloudy cornea. Conjunctivitis presents with a foreign body sensation, pink eye, drainage, and crusting but lacks a focal specific fluorescein uptake. Anterior uveitis is diagnosed by visualizing the cell and flare in the anterior chamber; the cornea will be clear.

130. **The answer is D, Pleural fluid protein level-to-serum protein level ratio greater than 0.5.**

(Marx, 943-944; Tintinalli, 471-473)

Pleural effusions are either exudates or transudates. According to the Light criteria, pleural fluid is considered an exudate if one or more of these three criteria exist:

- The ratio of pleural fluid protein level to serum protein level is greater than 0.5;
- The ratio of pleural fluid LDH level to the serum LDH level is greater than 0.6; or
- The pleural fluid LDH level is greater than 2/3 × (upper limit of normal for serum LDH level).

The LDH level can be measured in exudates and should be elevated (>200), resulting in a high fluid-to-serum LDH level. A low level of LDH in pleural effusion is suggestive of a transudate. Exudates are the result of infection, malignancy, or some other inflammatory process. This results in damage to the capillaries or obstruction of lymphatic drainage, which allows fluid and proteins to accumulate in the pleural space. Transudates are the result of shifts in hydrostatic or oncotic pressures. Heart failure causes a transudate because of increased hydrostatic pressures, leading to leakage of water into the pleura. Low albumin states such as cirrhosis lead to decreased oncotic pressure, causing water to leak into the pleura. The pH level of pleural effusions should be 7.4 or higher. A pH less than 7.1 is suggestive of an empyema.

131. **The answer is A, Advanced age.**

(Marx, 319-320; Wolfson, 157-164)

The CT image demonstrates a subdural hematoma on the left. The cause of this condition is injury to the bridging veins in the subdural space. In this patient's case, the most likely cause is the traumatic injury she sustained when she hit her head when she fell. Patients with brain atrophy such as elderly persons and alcoholics have a higher risk of this injury than younger patients do because of the increased distance the bridging veins must traverse. The subdural hematoma depicted is left-sided, concave, and white, indicating that it is acute. Aneurysm rupture leads to subarachnoid hemorrhage, not subdural hematoma. Severe hypertension leads most often to basal ganglia and internal capsule bleeding. Middle meningeal artery injury leads to epidural hematoma, which is biconvex in appearance and does not cross suture lines. This patient might require surgical intervention, but at this point she is neurologically intact and stable.

132. The answer is A, Age.

(Fleisher, 564, 569-570; Marx, 2101)

Febrile seizure is the most common convulsive condition among pediatric patients. The National Institutes of Health defines febrile seizure as "a seizure occurring in patients aged 6 months to 5 years that is associated with a fever (temperature greater than 38°C) but without any signs of intracranial infection or other neurologic disease." Febrile seizures are classified into two basic categories: simple and complex. A simple febrile seizure is defined as follows: first episode with age between 6 months and 5 years, short duration less than 15 minutes, generalized without any focality, and single episode within a 24-hour period. A complex febrile seizure is defined as follows: first episode with age younger than 6 months and older than 5 years, duration greater than 15 minutes, focality of seizure or a Jacksonian march with the focal area then leading to a generalized seizure, and more than one seizure within a 24-hour period. An estimated 2% to 5% of the population has seizures related to fever, and although they are terrifying to watch, they are not typically life-threatening events. A prolonged seizure can lead to brain injury, and steps must be taken to stabilize the patient's airway, breathing, and circulation while also treating the seizure with benzodiazepines with or without the addition of antiepileptic agents. The patient should be placed in the recovery position during the episode so that, if emesis occurs, there will not be aspiration. An extensive diagnostic workup is not needed in the emergency department after a simple febrile seizure if the child has a normal-for-age neurologic examination (although the patient might have a short postictal stage and be initially hyperreflexic) and no signs of CNS infection. But in a patient who has had a complex febrile seizure, lumbar puncture is recommended to rule out meningitis. It is important to communicate to families that up to one-third of patients can have another seizure, and three-fourths will do so within the first year. The likelihood of repeated episodes is higher among younger patients with higher temperatures.

133. The answer is C, Facial swelling.

(Marx, 1592-1594; Tintinalli, 1510-1511)

Facial swelling that is prominent early in the morning and resolves over the first few hours the patient is up is an early sign of superior vena cava (SVC) syndrome. The patient might also have early morning periorbital edema, nasal congestion, and conjunctival suffusion. The SVC syndrome is caused by intrinsic or extrinsic obstruction of the SVC. The severity of the symptoms is related to the degree of obstruction, the rate of obstruction, and the location of the obstruction relative to the azygos vein. Obstruction of the SVC promotes the development of collateral venous return draining the upper body to the heart by four routes. If the obstruction of the SVC is above the azygos vein, then blood might drain through the azygos system to join the lower SVC. If the level of obstruction is below the azygos vein, then collateral vessels form between the internal mammary venous system and the superior and inferior epigastric veins and between the long thoracic veins and its connections to the femoral and vertebral veins. The SVC syndrome is rarely life threatening by itself; death is related to the underlying pathology. In adults, more than 80% of SVC syndromes are due to malignancy, of which the vast majority are lung cancer and lymphoma. Cyanosis, facial plethora (flushed face), and upper extremity swelling are all associated with more complete obstruction of the SVC. Shortness of breath is the most commonly reported symptom. In the emergency department, simple measures such as elevating the head of the bed, rest, and supplemental oxygen can provide significant relief. Definitive treatment is directed at the underlying cause.

134. The answer is C, Metronidazole 750 mg IV.

(Adams, 400-401; Marx, 1163-1165; Tintinalli, 1888-1889)

The patient in this question has an amebic liver abscess that has extended into his pleural cavity. Entamoeba histolytica infection is the only cause of amebic liver abscesses, and the treatment of choice is high-dose metronidazole. Amebiasis is contracted after ingestion of food contaminated with fecal matter containing cysts. In the intestines, the mebic cysts transform into trophozoites, invade the mucosal wall, and spread to the liver through the portal vein. Within the United States, there is a higher incidence of E. histolytica infection in men, among Hispanic persons, and in the southwest. Worldwide, the disease is endemic in Asia, Africa, and Latin America. Symptoms include right upper quadrant abdominal pain, fever, nausea, and vomiting following a diarrheal prodrome. Typically, only one amebic liver abscess exists at a time, as compared to the multiple lesions associated with pyogenic abscesses. Amebic liver abscesses appear as hypoechoic lesions with thick irregular walls on an ultrasound image. E. histolytica serum antibodies are 90% sensitive, which also helps differentiate it from pyogenic abscesses. High-dose metronidazole (750 mg) has a 90% cure rate and can be prescribed in the oral form for outpatient treatment of mild disease. Abscesses larger than 5 cm or complicated by extrahepatic extension require hospitalization for drainage. Extension into the lung can cause pleural effusion, lung consolidation, and production of an anchovy-like, dark, thick sputum. Triple antibiotic coverage with ampicillin, gentamicin, and metronidazole is indicated for pyogenic abscesses. Substituting ampicillin and gentamicin with ceftriaxone is an increasingly supported alternative for treating pyogenic abscesses, but treatment of amebic abscesses such as the one in this case requires high-dose metronidazole intravenously. Levofloxacin is appropriate for pneumonia but does not cover *E. histolytica*. Paromomycin is used to treat the intestinal phase of amebiasis after treatment with high-dose metronidazole.

135. The answer is A, Order CT angiography and obtain a vascular surgery consultation.

(Marx, 1103-1109; Tintinalli, 458-463)

Acute embolic limb ischemia requires emergent vascular surgery intervention. The ankle-brachial index is calculated by dividing the systolic pressure of the dorsalis pedis or posterior tibial artery by the systolic pressure of the arm. It is an objective measure the vascular surgeon needs, along with the history and physical examination findings, to initiate surgical management. An index (ratio) greater than 0.9 is normal, and less than 0.5 indicates severe impairment of flow. Although thrombotic occlusion is a significantly more common cause of acute limb ischemia, embolic occlusion of peripheral arteries accounts for about 20% of lower extremity cases and 33% of upper extremity cases. The most common location for an embolus in the leg is the bifurcation of the common femoral artery followed by the popliteal artery. Most emboli originate from the heart, most commonly due to a left atrial clot in the setting of atrial fibrillation, as in this case. Patients with acute limb ischemia present with one or more of the six Ps: pain, pallor, pulselessness, paresthesias, paralysis, and poikilothermia. Pain can be the earliest symptom. Hypesthesia or hyperesthesia due to ischemic neuropathy is typically an early finding. Although tissue loss generally occurs within 4 to 6 hours, irreversible limb dysfunction can occur with shorter occlusion times. The treatment is restoration of blood flow to preserve limb function. Definitive treatment is percutaneous mechanical thrombectomy or surgical embolectomy. Anticoagulation therapy with heparin is helpful in acute arterial occlusion and should be initiated in consultation with vascular surgery. Anticoagulation might be more helpful in thrombotic limb ischemia. Fibrinolytic therapy is controversial and generally used as intra-arterial, catheter-directed drip, so it is not appropriate for use in a patient, like the one in this question, who has an acute limb-threatening ischemic condition. Although imaging with CT angiography is often requested by the consultant, it should be ordered concurrently and should not delay consultation with a vascular surgeon when an acute arterial occlusion of the limb is highly suspected, similar to management of suspected acute bowel ischemia. Treatment with a beta-blocker to rate control of atrial fibrillation does not improve the acute management of limb salvage and raises the theoretical concern of unopposed alpha effect worsening ischemia by increasing vasoconstriction.

136. The answer is B, Lapse.

(Adams, 2161-2170; Kohn, 28, 55-56; Marx, 2547-2553; Wolfson, 1670-1674)

Errors in clinical practice have been categorized by the Institute of Medicine (IOM). Among these categories and types is the lapse, and the best example of it is the inability to recall something, such as the order in which medications are to be given. Error, as defined in the 2000 IOM report *To Err Is Human,* is the "failure of a planned action to be completed as intended or the use of a wrong plan to achieve an aim." These failures are either active or latent. An active failure, such as lapse, is an "error that occurs at the frontline and whose effects are felt immediately." A latent failure is defined as an "error in design, organization, training, or maintenance that is often caused by management or senior level decisions; when expressed, these errors result in operator errors but may have been hidden, dormant in the system for lengthy periods before their appearance." Overcrowding is an example of a latent failure. It is a systems-based problem not directly caused by any individual practitioner. Other examples of latent failure include poor communication systems, inadequate staffing, lack of supervision, and rapid organizational changes. Improving these failure types requires a multifactorial approach. Latent failures can lead to multiple types of active failure, posing the greatest threat to safety. Cognitive-based errors lead to active failures. Skill-based cognitive performance errors are known as slips and lapses. Slips arise when actions fail to proceed as planned, such as writing the wrong dosage for a medication. Lapses are memory based and are the result of not being able to recall something to execute a plan. Rule-based and knowledge-based cognitive errors are known as mistakes. In rule-based error, the wrong rule is applied to a situation. In knowledge-based error, incorrect knowledge is applied or a flawed analytic process is used. Anchoring is a type of violation-producing behavior that results in active failure. It happens when a physician commits early to a diagnosis and does not consider other possibilities in the differential strongly enough.

137. The answer is D, Hepatitis E.

(Marx, 1153-1154; Wolfson, 567-570)

Hepatitis A and E are the two forms of viral hepatitis that are transmitted by the fecal-oral route. Hepatitis E has a incubation period of 15 to 60 days and is most common in Asia and Africa. Hepatitis B and C are transmitted through body fluids, including blood and semen. The hepatitis delta virus is an "incomplete" virus and can only coexist in patients infected with hepatitis B. Four percent to 30% of patients with hepatitis B are coinfected with delta, which requires the hepatitis B surface antigen (HBsAg) for its viral coating.

A newly discovered hepatitis virus is hepatitis G, which is transmitted through body fluids, and usually by blood transfusions. It is not clear whether hepatitis G causes any significant disease, as it has so far been found as a coinfection with another, more active virus. Most hepatitis infections cause an indolent disease, with few or no symptoms. They can present with jaundice, right upper quadrant pain, or malaise and anorexia. One percent to 2% of infections produce a fulminant, life-threatening course. Coinfection with hepatitis B and D is most commonly associated with fulminant disease, but it can occur with any of the hepatitis viruses. Autoimmune hepatitis is not caused by a virus; it is immune-mediated liver inflammation with a clinical presentation similar to that caused by a hepatitis virus.

138. The answer is C, Diphenhydramine.

(Marx, 45-46; Tintinalli, 1494, 1497-1500)

Rash or pruritus in conjunction with a blood transfusion is a mild allergic reaction and rarely progresses to wheezing and anaphylaxis. These symptoms can resolve with the administration of diphenhydramine, and the transfusion may continue without further workup. Other transfusion reactions such as intravascular hemolysis and dyspnea, bronchospasm, hypotension, shock, tachycardia, and fever require that the transfusion be stopped. Hemolytic reactions are the most serious transfusion reaction. The most common cause is an error of ABO incompatibility, which can lead to destruction of red blood cells. Symptoms include fever, chills, headache, nausea, vomiting, chest restriction, joint or back pain, or burning at the transfusion site. The administration of saline infusion, maintaining urine output at 1 to 2 mL/kg per hour, and replacing all intravenous tubing are necessary. Febrile reactions are the most common and least serious. They are characterized by a 1-degree increase in temperature without any other identifiable source. Treatment depends on exposure to other blood products: if the patient has never had a transfusion, acetaminophen may be used and transfusion continued. If the patient has had a transfusion in the past, the reaction is likely hemolytic. Transfusion-related acute lung injury, or TRALI, has the highest mortality rate. Symptoms occur abruptly, usually within 6 hours of the transfusion, and include noncardiogenic pulmonary edema, dyspnea, hypoxia, and bilateral infiltrates on chest radiograph. Treatment is supportive. Delayed reactions such as graft versus host disease or extravascular hemolytic reactions (non–ABO-mediated immune reactions) are also possible. Any reaction to a transfusion should be reported to the blood bank.

139. The answer is B, Knee-to-chest positioning.

(Fleisher, 198-202, 699-701; Marx, 2148-2150)

In a patient with tetralogy of Fallot, a period of increased cardiac demand such as occurs with crying or feeding can result in cyanosis. The key to resolving this "tet spell" is to increase systemic vascular resistance (SVR), and the quickest way to do that is to bring the patient's knees to the chest. This position simulates the typical response of an older patient with tetralogy of Fallot, who will squat during a spell to increase SVR. Tetralogy of Fallot is a congenital heart disease that consists of four separate abnormalities: right ventricular hypertrophy, overriding aorta, pulmonic stenosis, and ventricular septal defect. Although tetralogy of Fallot is rare (only 0.5 per 1,000 live births), it is the most common form of cyanotic congenital cardiac disease. The patient becomes cyanotic as a result of the lack of oxygenated blood entering the systemic circulation because of a right-to-left shunting. Cyanosis might not be present at birth. The typical treatment for a patient with a ductal-dependent lesion is prostaglandin E_1, which can maintain the ductus. A bolus of 0.1 mcg/kg is followed by an infusion of 0.05 to 0.1 mcg/kg/min. There are significant side effects, including hypotension, bradycardia, seizures, and apnea. Phenylephrine (0.01-0.02 mg/kg IV), propranolol (0.01-0.2 mg/kg IV), and even morphine sulfate (0.05 mg/kg IV or IM) are other drugs used to mitigate a tet spell. Vagal maneuvers are relegated to the treatment of stable patients presenting with supraventricular tachycardia and have no role in patients with tetralogy of Fallot.

140. The answer is D, *Staphylococcus aureus.*

(Marx, 1477-1480; Wolfson, 733-738)

Staphylococcus aureus is the most commonly encountered organism in acute monoarticular septic arthritis. Gram-positive organisms, in particular *S. aureus,* account for 80% to 90% of these infections. Other etiologies, including gram-negative organisms and *Neisseria gonorrhoeae,* account for the rest. *N. gonorrhoeae* infection typically presents as polyarticular arthritis. Methicillin-resistant *S. aureus* (MRSA) is increasingly becoming a major cause of septic arthritis in prosthetic joint infections, and antibiotic treatment choices should take this into consideration. The classic presentation involves large joints, most commonly the knee, with joint pain with significant restriction of movement, effusion, and fever. Evaluation typically includes measurement of CBC count, ESR, and C-reactive protein level, blood cultures (which are positive about 50% of the time), and arthrocentesis. Arthrocentesis is the diagnostic test of choice. Synovial fluid analysis includes viscosity, crystal analysis, WBC count with differential, and Gram stain and culture. Synovial fluid in septic arthritis classically is cloudy with low viscosity. The WBC count is significantly elevated (>50,000 WBC/mm^3) with greater than 95% PMNs. Typically, antibiotic choice should be based on the Gram stain, which reveals the organism in up to 70% of cases. Gram-positive organisms should be treated with cephalosporins, with coverage for MRSA as appropriate. Treatment for infection with gram-negative organisms should cover *Pseudomonas* infection.

141. The answer is B, Impaired ability to learn new information.

(Adams, 1124; Marx, 1369-1375; Tintinalli, 1136-1139; Wolfson, 743-747)

Dementia is defined as the presence of multiple cognitive defects (memory impairment, aphasia, apraxia, agnosia, disturbed executive functioning) in a person whose consciousness is not necessarily clouded. Dementia is characteristically insidious and progressive; the patient's attention and speech remain intact, but cognitive function is impaired. This can include difficulty learning new information or difficulty recalling previously known information. Primary dementias, of which Alzheimer disease is the most common type, account for up to 80% of all dementias and are nonreversible degenerative conditions. Secondary dementias are potentially reversible; causes include secondary dementia include drugs or toxins, depression, infection, mass effect, hydrocephalus, and metabolic imbalance. Delirium, in contrast, is a disturbance in consciousness with a change in cognition. Both delirium and dementia can involve memory deficits, but delirium is more likely to be acute and abrupt, associated with a change in underlying medical status (such as an infection or other acute stress), and associated with physical findings such as fever and tachycardia. Causes of delirium include infection (such as urinary tract infection), medications, environmental agents, metabolic abnormalities, and the release of inflammatory mediators.

142. The answer is C, Elements of both heart failure and COPD.

(Marx, 24-26; Tintinalli, 186-190)

Noninvasive positive-pressure ventilation (NPPV) is used as an alternative to endotracheal intubation and mechanical ventilation. It reduces the work of breathing, improves cardiac output by reducing preload and afterload, maintains inflation of alveoli, and improves lung compliance. Use of NPPV in heart failure has been well studied but has not shown a mortality rate benefit. However, it has been shown to reduce the need for intubation. Noninvasive positive-pressure ventilation is particularly useful for rapidly reversible conditions like heart failure, COPD, and asthma and has even been used successfully in patients with pneumonia. However, it is contraindicated in the setting of acute MI. Patients need to be awake and cooperative in order to use NPPV. Other contraindications to NPPV include risk of aspiration, altered level of consciousness, vomiting, frequent coughing with sputum production, apnea, vomiting, and facial trauma or other factors that affect the use of tight-fitting face masks. Noninvasive positive-pressure ventilation does not provide any airway protection. Patients with severe respiratory acidosis such as pH of 7 are likely to fail NPPV, as these patients often have minimal respiratory effort and will not reverse hypercarbia as rapidly as it improves PaO_2.

143. The answer is C, Order additional diagnostic imaging.

(Marx, 604-609; Wolfson, 291-294)

This patient likely has injuries in addition to those revealed by the initial radiographs, so additional imaging is needed. She has bilateral symphyseal fractures that involve the left superior and left inferior pubic rami and the right superior pubic ramus. The fractures on the left side are displaced. Fractures of the superior and inferior pubic rami on the same side with displacement of the fractures are concern for an additional posterior pelvic fracture or another yet-undiagnosed fracture of the pelvic ring. Additional imaging such as CT scanning of the pelvis might demonstrate sacral or iliac fractures. This patient is unlikely to do well with crutches or a walker given that she has bilateral pelvic fractures. She will most likely require a period of total non–weight-bearing even if she has no additional injuries. Angiography would be indicated only if she has significant pelvic bleeding, which is unlikely with the pubic rami fractures shown here. Angiography with therapeutic embolization might be needed if additional studies reveal posterior pelvic injuries. Demanding that the orthopedic surgeon operate on a patient he or she deemed a nonsurgical case is unlikely to be helpful. If additional injuries are identified on CT scan, however, the consultant might re-evaluate the plan of care.

144. The answer is A, Benign paroxysmal positional vertigo.

(Marx, 93-100; Roberts, 1134-1135; Tintinalli, 1146-1151)

The Dix-Hallpike test is useful in the diagnosis of benign paroxysmal positional vertigo (BPPV). It is performed by having the patient sit up with legs extended then quickly lie down (with assistance) with the head turned 45 degrees to one side and with about 20 degrees of extension. The eyes are observed for 45 seconds. There can be a brief latent period before the onset of the nystagmus. If there is no nystagmus after 45 seconds, the test is negative and then is repeated on the other side, after a brief break. A positive Dix-Hallpike test is characterized by latency of onset (usually 5-10 seconds), fatiguability, reversal, and nystagmus that is most typically torsional/rotational. Following a positive Dix-Hallpike test, the Epley maneuver, also referred to as the particle repositioning or canalith repositioning procedure, can be performed to relieve the symptoms of BPPV (up to 80% resolution). To perform the Epley maneuver, the patient should be positioned seated with the head turned at a 45-degree angle toward the affected side, then lain down flat, hanging the head over the side of the bed. After the symptoms pass, the patient's head should be rotated to face the opposite shoulder. Then, the patient should be rolled onto the side, and the head rotated further face down. Then again, after symptoms pass, the patient should be returned to the seated position. Keeping the head upright for 24 hours is advised; some suggest that the procedure can be repeated until the patient's condition improves. Other forms of peripheral vertigo such as labyrinthitis (acute suppurative, serous, toxic), Ménière disease, and vestibular neuronitis do not produce a positive Dix-Hallpike test, which specifically identifies canaliths or particles within the semicircular canals. These conditions do not respond to the Epley maneuver; because the lesions are of the peripheral nerves, the symptoms are made significantly worse by changes in head position. There are not usually any associated neurologic symptoms. Vertebrobasilar insufficiency is a cause of central vertigo. It usually is associated with other neurologic findings and is more likely in elderly patients. If a patient with BPPV is being tested using the Dix-Hallpike method and develops new neurologic signs or symptoms during the test, the test should be stopped, and acute cerebral ischemia should be considered.

145. The answer is A, Administer intravenous fluids and antiemetic agents.

(Marx, 1209-1210; Tintinalli, 1062-1070)

The best management strategy for patients presenting with acute food poisoning includes intravenous hydration and antiemetics. The most common cause of food poisoning, acute staphylococcal gastroenteritis, is a toxin-induced illness occurring after the ingestion of preformed enterotoxin from protein-rich foods such as eggs, mayonnaise, potato salad, and ham left at ambient temperatures. Abdominal cramping, repeated vomiting, and a variable degree of diarrhea begin 1 to 6 hours after ingestion and typically resolve within 24 to 48 hours. Stool studies are not indicated because the diagnosis is confirmed by the short time of onset and often presentation of multiple patients with similar symptoms. Antibiotics are of no benefit because the illness is toxin mediated rather than bacterial. Laboratory testing and admission are indicated only for patients who are systemically ill or immunosuppressed. *Giardia* is an intestinal protozoa that causes illness after drinking from water sources contaminated with cyst-infested feces. Although usually asymptomatic, *Giardia* infection can result in a carrier state characterized by chronic relapsing diarrhea. Patients and their close contacts with suspected *Giardia* infection should be advised to seek medical attention even if they are asymptomatic. *Escherichia coli* O157:H7 is an important cause of bloody diarrhea in elderly persons and children. Treatment of *E. coli* O157:H7 infection is mainly supportive; antibiotics are contraindicated because eradication of normal bowel flora increases the risk for development of hemolytic uremic syndrome.

146. The answer is B, Atropine.

(Neumar, S729-S767; Tintinalli, 129-151)

The patient in this question has evidence of hypoperfusion (hypotension, weak pulses), which should be addressed immediately, and the ECG reveals AV node (junctional) bradycardia. Atropine and transcutaneous pacing are the initial treatments of choice in the emergency department management of symptomatic bradycardia. In the absence of known reversible causes, atropine should be given at a dose of 0.5 mg IV every 3 to 5 minutes until the desired response is achieved or until a cumulative dose of 3 mg is given. Additional doses are usually not effective. The administration of atropine should not delay transcutaneous pacing if it is available. Epinephrine (along with dopamine or glucagon) is considered a second-line agent for symptomatic bradycardia but can be used if atropine and transcutaneous pacing are not effective. Transvenous pacing is the definitive treatment for progressive or persistent symptomatic bradycardia, but it is not the initial intervention because of the time and preparation required to perform it. The challenges to performing this procedure might be even greater in a patient with low cardiac output. Aspirin is an appropriate treatment for MI, but it is not the initial intervention in a patient with hypoperfusion.

147. The answer is C, Manifestations can include focal neurologic deficits.

(Nelson, 719-720; Wolfson, 1014-1017)

Hypoglycemia can present with a wide variety of signs and symptoms, including focal neurologic deficits. Signs and symptoms can be divided into adrenergic and neuroglycopenic. The adrenergic symptoms result from the release of epinephrine that acts to counteract the hypoglycemia. Adrenergic signs and symptoms can include diaphoresis, hypertension, palpitations, tachycardia, and tremors. Importantly, these adrenergic symptoms are not universally present and should not be relied on when determining the index of suspicion for symptomatic hypoglycemia. Neuroglycopenic signs and symptoms are those manifesting from the brain not receiving adequate glucose. Signs and symptoms can include coma, convulsions, delirium, headache, and psychiatric-appearing disturbances. Focal neurologic deficits such as hemiplegia are uncommon but important-to-recognize manifestations of hypoglycemia. The differential diagnosis of symptomatic hypoglycemia is very large, but the vast majority of emergency department patients suffering from it are diabetic and being treated with either insulin or sulfonylureas. Metformin decreases insulin resistance; when taken alone, it is only very rarely associated with hypoglycemia, and in such cases typically in the setting of overdose and severe lactic acidosis. Rapid identification and treatment of hypoglycemia are essential, as is determining the cause and a management plan to help prevent future episodes. Alcoholic patients, who are at risk for Wernicke encephalopathy, should receive thiamine. Administration of 50 mL of 50% dextrose (D50W, the typical amp of D50) provides a total of only 100 kilocalories (50 mL × 50 g/100 mL × 4 kcal/1 g = 100 kcal), 1 tablespoon of peanut butter. This highlights the need to have a patient eat a meal after initial correction. Less concentrated dextrose solutions are used in neonatal patients (D10W) and children (D25W) to avoid sclerosing veins and causing significant osmotic shifts.

148. The answer is D, Hand.

(Marx, 741; Medeiros, 1469-1493; Tintinalli, 354-355)

The degree of vascularity and anatomic structure predict the tendency of that structure to become infected as a result of a bite. The higher the rate of infection for a given anatomic structure, the more likely a bite wound is to benefit from prophylactic antibiotic treatment. A mammal bite to the hand is a high-risk wound that is particularly prone to infection. The structure of the hand increases the risk of infection, and the tendon sheaths and fascial planes of the hand allow infections to spread rapidly. A Cochrane systematic review of eight published trials addressing the use of prophylactic antibiotics in the treatment of mammal bites demonstrated a significant reduction in the rate of infection in the subgroup analysis focusing on hand bites (OR = 0.10; 95% CI: 0.01 to 0.86). The pooled results of the review failed to demonstrate any benefit from the use of prophylactic antibiotics to prevent infection at other anatomic bite sites. The highly vascularized face and scalp and the moderately vascularized extremities tend to resist infections from mammal bites better than the hand and fingers do. Mammal bite wounds become infected at rates greater than nonbite lacerations; therefore, thorough wound cleansing and irrigation are mandatory for all bite wounds, with antibiotic prophylaxis reserved for high-risk patients and high-risk wounds such as hand bites.

149. The answer is B, Slipped capital femoral epiphysis.

(Fleisher, 1361-1362, 1575-1576; Marx, 642-644, 660, 2254-2255)

Slipped capital femoral epiphysis (SCFE) is a hip disorder in which the epiphysis of one or both femoral heads begins to slide off center. It occurs predominantly in males, with a 4:1 male-to-female ratio. There is a higher incidence among obese and African-American children and among patients 8 to 15 years old. A high index of suspicion for a hip injury is warranted in the examination of adolescent boys presenting with either hip or knee pain. In SCFE, physical examination elicits abnormal range of motion of the hip. The diagnosis can be verified with radiographs; AP views might not clearly show the SCFE, so frog-leg views should be obtained. Computed tomography, MRI, bone scintigraphy, or ultrasonography can be used if plain radiographs do not show the abnormality but clinical suspicion is high. In up to 10% to 25% of SCFE cases, the abnormality is bilateral, so both aspects of the femoral heads must be reviewed. This can be an issue if the clinician is using the "good" side as a comparison to the "bad." Treatment requires case discussion with an orthopedic specialist and surgical pinning. Some orthopedists pin both heads even if the condition is unilateral as a prophylactic measure. An anterior cruciate ligament rupture is unlikely in a young adolescent boy without a significant injury who has normal findings on examination, as most of these injuries cause severe pain, instability, and effusion of the knee joint. Septic arthritis generally presents as a limp in a child with hip pain and is most common in children 3 to 10 years old. The four predictor diagnostics for this malady include fever, refusal to bear weight, an elevated sedimentation rate (>40 mm/hr), and an elevated WBC count (>12,000/mm^3). Septic arthritis is difficult to distinguish from toxic synovitis (nonbacterial inflammation of the hip joint); in both conditions, ultrasonography reveals joint effusion. A tibial spiral fracture (known as a toddler's fracture) is a nondisplaced tibial spiral fracture that can be caused by minimal twisting trauma, which can occur when a toddler jumps down one stair. It is rarely seen in a child of this patient's age.

150. The answer is A, Chalazion.

(Marx, 868; Tintinalli, 1530)

A chalazion is a tender, red nodule under the eyelid caused by blockage of the meibomian oil glands. It is very similar to a sty (also known as a hordeolum), which is a pustule caused by staphylococcal infection of the hair follicles of the eyelash or the associated oil glands (Zeis glands). As compared to a chalazion, which is found beneath the lid, a sty can be seen on the lid itself. Both conditions are treated initially with warm compresses. A sty is likely to resolve with this conservative therapy alone, but a chalazion might require topical or oral antibiotics, such as doxycycline 100 mg twice daily for 14 to 21 days. Chalazions can become chronic nodules, occasionally flaring up and becoming more painful and swollen. Patients with chronic chalazions should be referred to an ophthalmologist for excision. A foreign body in the eye can get trapped under the eyelid. When this happens, the patient might have linear abrasions on the cornea from the material wiping across the eye with each blink. A foreign body should be distinguishable from the immobile, flesh-colored chalazion. Herpes simplex virus infection results in development of vesicles, not a nodule, and they are rarely solitary. Melanomas can also present on the eye or on the eyelids, but they usually appear as an irregularly shaped patch of hyperpigmented skin rather than as a palpable nodule.

151. The answer is A, Balanitis.

(Marx, 2201-2202; Vilke, 193-198)

Balanitis is an inflammatory condition involving the glans. It can be caused by infection, chemical exposure, trauma, or contact dermatitis. Treatment includes local cleansing, antimicrobial therapy for skin organisms (including *Staphylococcus*, *Streptococcus*, and fungal infections), and topical steroids to decrease inflammation. Paraphimosis and phimosis are disorders of the foreskin. Paraphimosis is the inability to pull the foreskin forward (distal), whereas phimosis is the inability to retract the foreskin backward (proximal). Although paraphimosis is a true emergency, phimosis requires treatment when the patient cannot void or when ischemia of the penis is evident. Phimosis is treated by making a dorsal slit in the foreskin. The typical treatment of paraphimosis is manual reduction of the foreskin over the glans, but in severe cases, a dorsal slit procedure might be indicated. In both cases, a urology consultation should be obtained.

152. The answer is B, Negative inspiratory force less than 30 cm H₂O.

(Marx, 1400-1401; Wolfson, 779-780)

The patient in this question has Guillain-Barré syndrome, a demyelinating polyneuropathy that often presents 1 to 2 weeks after an infectious illness. These patients are at risk for respiratory failure related to respiratory muscle weakness, which is best predicted by a negative inspiratory force less than 30 cm H_2O. An alternative measurement that can be used is forced vital capacity (FVC). An FVC less than 20 mL/kg is predictive of possible impending respiratory failure; intubation is not usually needed if FVC is greater than 40 mL/kg. Arterial blood gas measurements can be used to evaluate for respiratory function by measuring PCO_2. Elevations in PCO_2 are indicative of alveolar hypoventilation and are associated with respiratory failure. There is no absolute PO_2 that is predictive of respiratory failure. Peak flow measurements are typically used to evaluate patients with obstructive lung disease such as asthma. A PEFR of 100% predictive for age and sex would be a reassuring finding; however, there is no absolute measurement that is predictive of respiratory failure. On physical examination, patients with Guillain-Barré syndrome usually present with bilateral lower extremity weakness, greater distally than proximally, often with sparing of the anal sphincter. Deep tendon reflexes are often diminished or absent, and the sensory changes can vary. Recommended treatment includes plasma exchange or intravenous immunoglobulin. Steroids are no longer indicated.

153. The answer is D, Pain out of proportion to clinical findings is commonly the earliest finding of compartment syndrome.

(Marx, 477-479; Roberts, 989)

Pain out of proportion to clinical findings, also seen with early bacterial fasciitis, is an important early finding for compartment syndrome. The classic symptoms of compartment syndrome—pallor, pulse deficit, paresis/paralysis, paresthesias, and pain on passive stretching—are typically late findings and are often unreliable, especially in children. The lower extremities are the most frequently affected, with the anterior compartment most frequently involved and the posterior compartment most frequently missed. Strict sterile technique must be used to prevent infection when measuring compartment syndromes. This procedure can be so painful as to require procedural sedation or local anesthesia at a minimum. If local anesthesia is used, care should be taken to avoid injection into the compartment itself, as this can falsely elevate the pressure. A combination of clinical findings and pressure measurements should be used to determine the need for intervention. Normal compartment pressure is less than

12 mm Hg; clinically significant impairment of blood flow can occur at pressures greater than 20 mm Hg; and fasciotomy is recommended at values greater than 30 mm Hg. Actions to prevent falsely elevating the pressure in the compartment include providing adequate pain control to prevent movement, using ultrasound to guide the placement of the needle and decrease the number of attempts, and placing the extremity at the level of the heart in an appropriate position for insertion of the needle.

154. The answer is C, Observe the patient for a few hours.

(Marx, 933-934; Tintinalli, 487-489)

A person who inhales foreign material into the lungs is at risk for inflammation and the development of aspiration pneumonitis, then pneumonia. Most healthy patients, however, can be treated conservatively if significant symptoms do not develop after a few hours of observation in the emergency department. Aspiration pneumonitis is chemical injury to the respiratory tract that can lead to pneumonia. Symptoms develop immediately or over the first few hours and include cough, chest pain, shortness of breath, and bronchospasm. The severity of the injury depends on the pH level and the volume and type of materials inhaled. A pH level of less than 2.5 tends to cause a chemical burn to the lungs, and severe symptoms can develop over hours. Volumes as little as 20 to 30 mL can cause injury. The aspiration of viscous materials or particulate matter causes more problems. Normal gastric pH is very acidic, with a range between 1.5 and 3.5. Aspiration of gastric contents can cause a significant injury known as Mendelsohn syndrome, in which patients develop aspiration pneumonitis that rapidly progresses to pulmonary edema. The mortality rate is high. In some patients with severe symptoms, deep tracheal suctioning, bronchoalveolar lavage, or bronchoscopy might be helpful. Albuterol can be helpful to treat bronchospasm. Steroids have not been shown to be helpful and might increase the risk of infection. Antibiotics should not be administered unless signs of infection develop or symptoms persist for several days. If antibiotics are required, it is important to cover anaerobes (with clindamycin or metronidazole) in addition to common respiratory pathogens.

155. The answer is D, Tube thoracostomy.

(Marx, 392-397; Wolfson, 213-220)

This patient has right-sided rib fractures, a right hemopneumothorax, and pulmonary contusions, so chest tube placement is the appropriate intervention. Given the hemothorax, a larger tube, such as a 36 F tube, should be used and placed posteriorly. A chest radiograph should be obtained afterward to determine correct placement, confirm evacuation of the hemothorax, and assess re-expansion of the lung. High-flow oxygen should be started based on the associated pulmonary contusion. Prophylactic antibiotics are not indicated; the consolidation on the radiograph is caused by pulmonary contusion, not pneumonia. Intravenous furosemide is unlikely to help this patient acutely because his airspace disease is not caused by volume overload. Aspirin could make the bleeding worse, and the chest pain is the result of thoracic trauma, not an acute coronary syndrome. Aspirin would be indicated only if other test results indicated its use.

156. The answer is C, Sensory ataxia.

(Adams, 1009-1011; Tintinalli, 1143)

A positive Romberg test suggests a diagnosis of sensory ataxia. In a Romberg test, the patient is asked to stand with the feet together and the arms outstretched, initially with the eyes open. Presence of unsteadiness during this phase confirms the ataxia but does not suggest the type. When the eyes are closed, the visual input to balance is lost. If the ataxia worsens after the eyes are closed, the Romberg test is positive, and the ataxia is most likely sensory. Similarly, finger-to-nose testing with the eyes closed is a test of upper extremity posterior column (proprioception) function and indicates a sensory ataxia. Sensory ataxia is primarily due to loss of proprioception or disease of the dorsal/posterior columns of the spinal tracts. Ataxia is broadly divided into three groups: cerebellar (motor), sensory, and vestibular. There is often some overlap either because of location (as in a stroke that affects the vestibular input into the cerebellum) or because the disease process involves multiple pathways (such as loss of proprioception and cerebellar disease). Patients with cerebellar (motor) ataxia have a wide-based gait. When asked to stand with the feet together, even with the eyes open, such a patient is very unsteady and ataxic. With the eyes closed, the ataxia does not get worse (in reality, the patient is extremely unsteady with the eyes open and is unable to stand for more than a few seconds); this is therefore, technically, a negative Romberg test. It is often a point of some confusion: the Romberg test is not positive because of the presence of ataxia, but only if the unsteadiness worsens with loss of visual input. Vestibular ataxia is seen with disorders of the vestibular system. In acute dysfunction, it is often associated with nausea, vomiting, and vertigo. In more chronic conditions, only the ataxia might be present. Optic ataxia, which is a lack of coordination between eye movements and hand movements, is uncommon.

157. The answer is A, A definitive "clunk" with movement of the femoral head.

(Fleisher, 1004; Marx, 2257-2259)

In a patient with developmental dysplasia of the hip (DDH), a positive Ortolani sign is a definitive "clunk" when the dislocated femoral head reduces into the acetabulum with movement. Clinical findings of DDH can include asymmetric skin folds noted in the groin, along the thighs, or below the buttock; one-third of patients have skinfold asymmetry, but this finding is not specific for the disorder. Shortening of the leg on the affected side with a reduced range of motion can also be noted. There is ultimately atrophy of the gluteal muscles on the affected side. To perform the Ortolani maneuver, the physician slightly abducts the patient's hip and, with the index and middle fingers over the greater trochanter, pulls up on the thigh to reduce the hip dislocation. The abnormal finding is the perceptible relocation/dislocation by either feel or sound. The Barlow test is another diagnostic approach. The physician places a thumb on the patient's inner thigh near the lesser trochanter and adducts the hip, applying downward pressure on the thigh with the thumb. This test is also called provocative: any abnormal movement of the femoral head and acetabulum is a positive finding. The Barlow and Ortolani tests are less effective in detecting instability of the hips in older pediatric patients. Radiography is not useful in a patient younger than 6 months because of the lack of ossification and the difficulty of interpreting the findings. Ultrasonography is best delayed in a newborn, as some conditions (such as laxity without dislocation) can be seen early in life and resolve without intervention by the time the infant is 4 to 6 weeks old.

158. The answer is A, Antibiotics.

(Marx, 1144-1147; Tintinalli, 554-557)

The approach to preventing recurrence of this patient's uncomplicated gastritis includes antibiotic therapy to eradicate *Helicobacter pylori* infection. The most common causes of gastritis and peptic ulcer disease are *H. pylori* infection and NSAID use. Other important causes include aspirin, iron, toxic ingestions, Crohn disease, radiation, and autoimmune disorders. The exact diagnosis of gastritis requires endoscopic visualization of acute or chronic inflammation of the gastric mucosa, but a clinical diagnosis is often made in the emergency department. Outpatient management begins with the patient avoiding known inciting factors, specifically NSAIDs, aspirin, and alcohol. Treatment with H2 receptor antagonists and proton pump inhibitors suppresses acid production, which reduces pain and complications, but does not prevent recurrence. The addition of two distinct antibiotics, typically clarithromycin and amoxicillin or metronidazole, yields 80% to 90% cure rates for *H. pylori* infection. There is significant clinical overlap between the clinical presentations of gastritis and other gastrointestinal tract processes such as esophagitis, pancreatitis, cholelithiasis, and hepatitis. Oral analgesia with NSAIDs, weight loss, restriction of fatty foods, and cholecystectomy are effective therapies for biliary stone disease.

159. The answer is A, Activation of the cardiac catheterization laboratory is warranted.

(Anderson, e41-e43; O'Connor, S792-S794; Tintinalli, 373-378)

The 2010 guidelines from the American Heart Association provide a class I recommendation (level of evidence B) for early invasive therapy (diagnostic angiography with revascularization) for patients with unstable angina/non–ST-segment elevation MI (UA/NSTEMI) who have refractory angina. The patient in this question presents with UA/NSTEMI based on his symptoms and ECG findings of inferolateral ST-segment depression (leads II, III, aVF, I, aVL, and V_4 through V_6). If serial troponin levels remain negative, especially if the ST-segment changes resolve with anti-ischemic therapy, then the diagnosis of UA can be made. If a troponin elevation occurs, then NSTEMI can be diagnosed. Appropriate treatment of UA/NSTEMI includes either a conservative approach with medical therapy and early risk stratification or an immediate invasive strategy. Therefore, activation of the cardiac catheterization laboratory is an acceptable approach, especially in a patient like the one in this question who has persistent pain despite medical management. An NSAID should not be used in the setting of acute coronary syndrome because of the associated increased risk of death, reinfarction, hypertension, heart failure, and myocardial rupture. Nitroglycerin is of theoretic benefit for cardiac ischemia given that it reduces myocardial oxygen demand while enhancing myocardial oxygen delivery; however, reduced mortality rates from treatment have not been shown. This patient, however, has an absolute contraindication to treatment with nitroglycerin therapy: nitrate use within 24 hours after sildenafil or vardenafil use, or within 48 hours of tadalafil use, has been associated with profound, refractory hypotension, MI, and even death. This patient lacks indications for thrombolytic therapy, which include 1 mm of ST-segment elevation due to MI in two contiguous leads or presumed new left bundle branch block and ongoing symptoms of less than 12 hours' duration.

160. The answer is C, Topical antibiotic therapy alone is the standard treatment.

(Marx, 1841-1842; Wolfson, 1325-1326)

Impetigo is a highly contagious superficial skin infection most common in children and often occurs on exposed areas such as the face, as shown in this case. Topical antibiotic therapy alone with an agent such as mupirocin is considered standard therapy. The classic appearance is a honey-colored crusting. Causative organisms include both *Staphylococcus aureus* and *Streptococcus pyogenes*. Both a nonbullous and less common bullous form can occur. The bullous form can mimic thermal burns such as from a cigarette and be mistaken for child abuse. Although the diagnosis is typically made clinically, Gram stain of the exudative part of the rash likely demonstrates the causative organism. Topical treatments such as soaks, washes, and application of povidone-iodine solution do not seem to be helpful and can in fact cause satellite lesions. Oral antibiotic therapy can be considered for extensive local disease and in patients unable to tolerate topical therapy. Using an agent that covers for MRSA should be considered given its increasing prevalence. Combination therapy with topical and oral antibiotics is not typically necessary. Postinfective glomerulonephritis is a potential complication, but antibiotics have not been demonstrated to decrease the risk of its development.

161. The answer is D, Vascular permeability.

(Hall, 1615-1626; Marx, 1521-1525, 2546-2550; Nabel, 1259-1270; Tintinalli, 177-181)

Third spacing from increased vascular permeability can result in a rapid and sustained fluid shift into the extravascular space. The combination of third spacing and loss of vasomotor tone can produce significant hypotension within minutes of the inciting event. For this reason, aggressive crystalloid resuscitation should be instituted early in the treatment regimen of any patient presenting with anaphylaxis regardless of the degree of hypotension. Anaphylaxis is an IgE-mediated response to a trigger resulting in mast cell and basophil degranulation with release of immune modulators such as histamine, prostaglandins, and leukotrienes. The standard treatment of anaphylaxis is separated into the first- and second-line approaches. First-line treatment includes addressing airway, breathing, and circulation; removing exposure to the causative agent; and administering epinephrine and crystalloids. Second-line treatment includes H1-receptor antagonists such as diphenhydramine, H2-receptor antagonists such as ranitidine, and glucocorticoids, which have a slow onset of action and target the delayed phase of hypersensitivity reactions. Patients with profound anaphylactic shock can develop hypothermia (not hyperthermia) secondary to cardiovascular collapse and severe third spacing, but this is not a universal finding. Hypoxia might develop from airway obstruction but is less likely in an intubated patient. When hypoxia is present, the patient exhibits a change in mental status and might appear obtunded, agitated, or combative. Hypoxia in an intubated patient warrants evaluation for DOPE: dislodged tube, obstructed tube, pneumothorax, equipment failure. Although the surge in immune modulators can cause myocardial depression, this is not a consistent finding in all patients with anaphylaxis. Increased vascular permeability is more likely. Systemic vasodilation with loss of vasomotor tone is the predominant finding in anaphylactic shock.

162. The answer is C, Intraosseous line in the anterior tibia.

(Fleisher, 17-19, 1761-1762; Roberts, 431-442)

During a resuscitation, establishing intraosseous (IO) access can be faster than establishing intravascular access in both pediatric and adult patients. Typical placement of an IO line is in the anterior-superior aspect of the proximal tibia, approximately 1 cm distal and 1 cm medial of the tibial tuberosity. Contraindications to IO line placement include prior attempt at IO placement or fracture in the extremity, overlying cellulitis, and past medical history of osteogenesis imperfecta or osteopenia. Besides the tibia, other sites for IO line placement include the distal femur, the medial malleolus, the distal humerus, and the anterior-superior aspect of the iliac crest. Complications of IO line placement include osteomyelitis, compartment syndrome, fracture of the bone the line is placed in, and necrosis of the underlying skin. Any medication except for sodium bicarbonate can be infused using an IO line. When a patient is in cardiopulmonary arrest, attempts to establish peripheral intravenous access, especially in children, are not likely to be successful and should not be attempted. Establishing central intravenous access is a step that should wait until after the patient's condition has been stabilized; that time is better spent on resuscitation efforts. The preferred site for central intravenous access in the pediatric patient is in the femoral vein. Subclavian vein cannulation is not ideal in younger patients because of a higher rate of complications with pneumothorax.

163. The answer is D, *Mycobacterium tuberculosis.*

(Marx, 1798; Tintinalli, 494-499; Wolfson, 926)

This is a typical case of pulmonary tuberculosis (TB). Reactivation of disease classically involves the apices and is usually associated with hilar lymphadenopathy, as shown in the image. Primary TB, however, can result in infiltrates in any lobe. Miliary TB, the most contagious form, is demonstrated by multiple small (1-3 mm) nodules throughout the lung. Tuberculosis is more common in persons not born in the United States and those with a history of incarceration. Because TB can infect most organs in the body, patients can present with a variety of syndromes; however, pulmonary TB most commonly presents with cough, fever, night sweats, weight loss, and bloody sputum. Coccidiomycosis, caused by *Coccidioides immitis*, is associated with soil exposure in the southwestern United States, including Arizona. It results in a chronic infection with cough, fever, weight loss, and diffuse pulmonary infiltrates. A localized lobar infection is possible but unusual. *Histoplasma capsulatum*, the cause of histoplasmosis, is clinically very similar to coccidiomycosis but is associated with the soils of the Mississippi and Ohio River valleys. A history of incarceration is a major risk factor for MRSA infection. Pulmonary MRSA can present with a lobar infiltrate or abscess anywhere in the lung, but the right lower lobe is the most common because aspiration is a factor in the infection. *Bacillus anthracis* is the cause of anthrax. Pulmonary anthrax is associated with fever, infiltrates, and hilar adenopathy, but the clinical course is much more abrupt; a patient with pulmonary anthrax would not likely survive for 2 weeks without treatment, as the patient in this question did.

164. The answer is B, Incision with no pus obtained.

(Marx, 1284-1285; Roberts, 674-677)

In the evaluation of a patient who presents with swelling in the vaginal area and pain with walking, examination is likely to reveal glandular swelling characteristic of a Bartholin gland abscess. The goal of treating an abscess within the Bartholin gland is to allow drainage either by fistulization or marsupialization. When drainage is attempted, failure to obtain pus or note the release of pressure indicates failure of the drainage procedure. At times, the abscesses can be deep and a practitioner can miss the abscess, resulting in an incision with no pus obtained. Standard incision and drainage of the abscess also is associated with risk of recurrence but can be performed if fistulization cannot be. If this is the management approach, the patient should be instructed to change the packing in 24 to 48 hours and continue Sitz baths after 24 hours; a referral for fistulization should be made if only standard incision and drainage is performed. Placement of a Word catheter produces a fistula, which helps decrease the incidence of recurrence. Once the catheter is placed, Sitz baths can be started after 24 hours. The catheter is left in place for 4 to 6 weeks, and if it falls out, it should be reinserted. Marsupialization is reserved for patients who have recurrent abscesses. This should be completed in the operating room, as it requires suturing the edges of the gland open. If cellulitis is the only presenting symptom and no abscess is present, antibiotics can be used. The choice of antibiotic is dependent on assessment of risk for sexually transmitted diseases.

165.   The answer is A, Avascular necrosis.

(Aguilar, 929-941; Marx, 1828)

The patient in this question has a common complication of sickle cell disease (Hgb SS) known as avascular necrosis (AVN). The areas of radiolucency alternating with areas of focal sclerosis in the humeral head on this patient's radiograph are a classic appearance of AVN. The most common location for this process to occur in patients with sickle cell disease is in the femoral head (lifetime prevalence of 50%); however, up to 20% of patients also have AVN in the humeral head (as this patient does). The pathophysiology of osteonecrosis involves a progressive occlusion of microcirculation, which leads to increased intraosseous pressure and cell death. Subsequent bone resorption occurs, and collapse of the bone can occur. Bone collapse is more common in the femoral head than in the humeral head, likely related to weight-bearing stresses. Avascular necrosis also occurs in other patient populations; AVN of the hip has been noted as a post-traumatic complication when the injury disrupts the blood supply to the bone. Femoral neck fractures (up to 20% complication of AVN) and hip dislocations (40% complication of AVN) are the common mechanisms of injury. Other patients at risk include those on long-term corticosteroid therapy and those with alcoholism or chronic pancreatitis. Patients with osteomyelitis typically present with fever and pain over the affected bone. There can be skin changes or an obvious portal of entry (ulceration, post-surgery). Patients with sickle cell disease are at higher risk for developing osteomyelitis, and the most common causative agents are *Staphylococcus aureus* and *Salmonella* species. Although AVN does put patients at higher risk for bone collapse, there is no evidence of a fracture or dislocation on this radiograph. There is no increased risk of primary bony tumors in this patient population. Bone lesions are still most commonly metastatic lesions.

166. The answer is A, Administer haloperidol 5 mg IM and lorazepam 2 mg IM, and apply four-point restraints.

(Adams, 2050-2053; Wolfson, 812-813)

The patient in this question requires both chemical and physical restraint methods until both he and the condition are under control and the medication has a calming effect. Using physical restraints alone in an aggressively resistant patient creates risk of injury to both patient and staff. Some have suggested initially restraining patients in the prone position to reduce their ability to generate enough force to overturn a gurney; however, the prone position, especially when combined with the restriction of the patient's ability to expand the chest by moving the upper arms, has been associated with impairment of cardiopulmonary function and should be avoided. If a patient presents to the emergency department in a prone or hobbled position, he or she should be repositioned on his or her side and closely monitored for complications such as rhabdomyolysis, metabolic acidosis, arrhythmia, and respiratory compromise. When a patient's violent behavior is related to pain, morphine can be a helpful treatment adjunct. But in the scenario described, however, morphine is not an appropriate medication for the rapid control of a violent patient. The combination of lorazepam and haloperidol for rapid sedation of an agitated psychotic patient has been found to be superior to either agent alone. Finally, an approach that involves leaving a combative, out-of-control patient unrestrained and alone with a nurse puts both patient and staff at risk of injury and is not appropriate.

167. The answer is D, Myasthenia gravis.

(Marx, 13-14; Tintinalli, 204)

Succinylcholine is a noncompetitive, depolarizing neuromuscular blocking agent, and its administration can lead to life-threatening hyperkalemia. Patients with large amounts of denervated muscle due to neuromuscular disease are particularly at risk. In these patients, there is upregulation of acetylcholine receptors at the neuromuscular junction due to the lack of acetylcholine. When succinylcholine is given, it triggers an exaggerated release of potassium. In acute injuries such as spinal cord injuries, burns, or crush injuries, it takes hours to days for this upregulation to occur, so succinylcholine may be safely administered at the time of the initial injury. Succinylcholine is associated with malignant hyperthermia but not neuroleptic malignant syndrome. It raises intraocular pressure and causes fasciculations. The correct dose is 1 to 1.5 mg/kg IV. Other complications of succinylcholine use include masseter muscle spasm.

168. The answer is B, Emergency department thoracotomy.

(Marx, 396-406; Wolfson, 224-226)

This patient is suffering from pericardial tamponade; the ultrasound image reveals a pericardial effusion. When a patient has penetrating trauma to the chest with hypotension, the emergency physician must presume that the patient has pericardial tamponade until proved otherwise. In this patient, emergency department thoracotomy would relieve the cardiac tamponade and also provide exposure for great vessel or laceration repair or myocardial repair and allow for clamping of significant arterial bleeds. Internal cardiac massage may also be performed. Pericardiocentesis is not necessary given the ultrasound findings; it is more temporizing than definitive in thoracic trauma. Tube thoracostomy would not resolve pericardial tamponade. The patient has cardiac activity on the ultrasound; the tachycardia is caused by the inability of the heart to fill and perhaps volume depletion, not an arrhythmia, so amiodarone would not be helpful. Although epinephrine is the medication of choice to use in a patient such as this one with pulseless electrical activity, treating the cause (that is, relieving the pericardial tamponade) is the intervention most likely to improve the patient's prognosis.

169. The answer is D, Treatment includes therapies that can help clear mucus, such as *N*-acetylcysteine aerosols.

(Fleisher, 1091-1097; Marx, 2135-2136)

Respiratory compromise is a typical presentation for patients with cystic fibrosis (CF). Management consists of early and aggressive treatment of any respiratory symptoms with mobilization of the mucus using a flutter device or oscillating vest, beta-agonist therapy, mucolytic agents such as *N*-acetylcysteine, and treatment with steroids and antibiotics. The common bacterial pathogens are *Haemophilus influenzae*, *Staphylococcus aureus*, MRSA, *Pseudomonas aeruginosa*, and *Burkholderia cepacia* (which has been associated with increased mortality rates). Resistance is a common issue, and appropriate antibiotic coverage is best individualized based on prior infection and pulmonary cultures. Chest radiograph findings vary but can include emphysema, thickening of the bronchi, focal infiltrates, and bronchiectasis, which is dilation of the bronchial tree because of the chronic inflammation and infections related to the disease. Cystic fibrosis is an autosomal recessive disease that comes from a mutation of the long arm of chromosome 7, and there is no sex difference in incidence. By the time they are 18 years old, 80% of patients with CF are colonized with *P. aeruginosa*. Up to 15% of patients have a hypersensitivity reaction to *Aspergillus fumigatus* that results in chronic wheezing and cough most successfully treated with high-dose oral steroids. Pancreatitis is a common manifestation of CF, but the levels of amylase and lipase, although initially elevated with flares, progressively fall as the patient gets older; this is the result of the destruction of the exocrine tissue, which eventually becomes completely nonfunctioning. At that point, the patient does not become symptomatic. Hyponatremic hypochloremic dehydration in CF is related to the excessive loss of sodium chloride from sweat.

170. **The answer is C, Sclerosing cholangitis.**

(Marx, 187-190; Tintinalli, 562-565)

Sclerosing cholangitis produces a conjugated hyperbilirubinemia by extrahepatic biliary ductal obstruction. Jaundice is typically classified using two broad categories: conjugated/direct and unconjugated/indirect. Jaundice is clinically evident at levels of bilirubin around 3 mg/dL. Unconjugated/indirect jaundice is usually caused by an increased rate of red blood cell destruction (as in hemolytic anemia, sickle cell disease, absorption of hematoma) or, less commonly, by decreased hepatic uptake (sepsis, some drugs) or abnormal conjugation that can be congenital (Gilbert syndrome) or acquired (advanced hepatocellular disease). In unconjugated hyperbilirubinemia, the transaminase and alkaline phosphatase levels are likely normal. In conjugated/direct jaundice, hyperbilirubinemia results from impaired excretion by the hepatocyte of conjugated bilirubin into the bile cannaliculi or from obstructed bile flow into the intrahepatic or extrahepatic ducts. Impaired hepatocyte excretion or intrahepatic obstruction (cholestasis) can be congenital or acquired. Extrahepatic obstruction can also be classified as intrinsic or extrinsic depending on the anatomic location of the obstruction. Clinical evaluation is greatly assisted by ultrasound imaging, which reveals dilated bile ducts in extrahepatic biliary obstruction. Transaminases are often markedly elevated, and alkaline phosphatase is near normal in hepatocellular processes with cholestasis. In an extrahepatic obstruction, transaminases are near normal, and alkaline phosphatase is markedly elevated.

171. **The answer is A, Bedside esophagogastroduodenoscopy.**

(Tintinalli, 544-545; Wolfson, 548-558)

Emergent esophagogastroduodenoscopy (EGD) is the treatment of choice to control upper gastrointestinal tract bleeding in peptic ulcer disease (PUD). Hemorrhage is the most common complication of PUD, occurring in 15% of cases. Most bleeding is self-limited, with a mortality rate of 2% to 3% in patients whose conditions are stable but rises to 20% for patients who rebleed during hospitalization. Historically, a barium esophagram was used to identify the source of upper gastrointestinal tract bleeding. Today, direct visualization with EGD allows both accurate diagnosis and lifesaving therapeutic maneuvers to be performed at the bedside. Bleeding ulcers visualized during endoscopy are treated with epinephrine injection, electrical coagulation, or laser treatment. Interventional radiology-guided embolization or surgery is indicated when treatment with EGD fails or for rebleeding refractory to further EGD management. Nasogastric tube placement is indicated in patients with active gastrointestinal tract hemorrhage to help decompress and clear the stomach but does not stop bleeding. Current consensus guidelines recommend starting a high-dose omeprazole infusion prior to endoscopy to lower the risk of rebleeding, transfusion requirements, and the need for surgery. Octreotide has been shown to reduce bleeding in PUD; vasopressin, however, a similar medication, is not used because of its serious side effects, including vasoconstriction causing ischemia and dysrhythmias. Although the patient in this question had bloody stools, in any unstable patient, brisk upper gastrointestinal tract bleeding must be ruled out in any patient whose condition is unstable prior to investigating the lower gastrointestinal tract. A colonoscopy is warranted if an upper gastrointestinal tract source cannot be identified. The Sengstaken-Blakemore tube is a tamponade device used in active variceal bleeding when procedural endoscopy coupled with pharmacologic therapy fails to achieve hemostasis. The device is not recommended for hemorrhagic PUD because of increased risk of perforation.

172. **The answer is C, Hemorrhagic stroke 6 months earlier.**

(Marx, 977-979; Tintinalli, 376-377)

In this patient, a history of hemorrhagic stroke would prevent treating his STEMI with a thrombolytic agent. The other conditions are either relative contraindications or not contraindications. Absolute contraindications to thrombolytic therapy are as follows:
- Strong suspicion for aortic dissection or pericardial tamponade
- Active gastrointestinal or other internal bleeding (other than menses)
- Known structural cerebrovascular lesion such as arteriovenous malformation or aneurysm
- Known malignant intracranial neoplasm
- Ischemic stroke within 3 months
- Previous intracranial hemorrhage
- Intracranial procedure or head injury within the past 3 weeks
- Known severe bleeding disorder such as a coagulation abnormality (hemophilia, von Willebrand disease) or severe thrombocytopenia

Relative contraindications include:
- Traumatic or prolonged (>10 min) CPR or recent (<3 weeks) major surgery such as coronary artery bypass graft, obstetric delivery, organ biopsy, previous puncture of noncompressible vessels
- Gastrointestinal or genitourinary bleeding within the past 10 days
- Older than 75 years
- Severe uncontrolled hypertension (systolic >180 mm Hg, diastolic >110 mm Hg)
- Hemostatic defects from systemic disease such as hepatic cirrhosis, severe renal insufficiency, malignancy
- Current use of anticoagulant medications with INR above 1.7 or PT longer than 15 seconds
- Pregnancy

- High likelihood of left heart thrombus or subacute bacterial endocarditis
- Diabetic hemorrhagic retinopathy or other hemorrhagic ophthalmic condition

173. The answer is D, Sodium bicarbonate.

(Marx, 1962, 1964-1968; Nelson, 1051-1055)

The ECG in this case demonstrates tachycardia, QRS-complex prolongation, and a terminal rightward axis (prominent S in lead I and R in aVR), all characteristic of tricyclic antidepressant (TCA) poisoning. Sodium bicarbonate administration to narrow the QRS interval and prevent dysrhythmias is indicated. Both QRS prolongation and the amplitude of the R wave can be helpful in predicting who will develop convulsions and ventricular dysrhythmias. Convulsions are initially treated with benzodiazepines, and dysrhythmias can ideally be prevented and also treated with sodium bicarbonate. Various properties manifest in TCA overdose. Sodium-channel blocking activity leads to delayed inward sodium currents, leading to QRS prolongation and dysrhythmias. Both increasing extracellular sodium and serum alkalinization are beneficial in reversing the sodium channel blockade. Tricyclic antidepressant agents also cause potassium channel blockade that contributes to QT-segment prolongation. The antimuscarinic property of TCAs contributes to tachycardia and effectively narrows the corrected QT interval, helping explain why torsade de pointes is uncommon in acute TCA poisoning. If it were to develop, magnesium sulfate administration would be indicated. Potassium administration is not indicated for QT-interval prolongation and does not have any specific role in the initial management of TCA poisoning. Due to the QT-interval prolongation that TCAs can induce, it is prudent to avoid administering any agent that can further prolong the QT interval. Calcium administration also does not have any specific role in treating TCA poisoning, but it can be considered as initial empiric therapy in suspected hyperkalemia.

174. The answer is A, Combined public-private.

(MacFarlane, 188-191; Marx, 2461-2463; Tintinalli, 1-4; Wolfson, 1653-1661)

In the combined public-private model of EMS systems, a public fire department provides the first responder team that is later met by a private ambulance service that transports the patient to the hospital. Advantages of this approach include the ability for faster extrication of patients from scenes. In the public utility model, there is a government contract between a city and a private company that provides ALS or BLS services to the area for a fee. The third-service model of EMS is one in which the municipal department itself operates the ambulances and provides personnel to respond to medical calls. The station-based model of EMS uses fire departments to respond to all EMS calls. The fire personnel are usually EMT-B, EMT-I, or EMT-P trained. Other designations for EMS responses include single-tiered and multitiered systems. Single-tiered services use only BLS personnel or ALS personnel. Multitiered services have both ALS and BLS personnel. The multitiered service approach is becoming more commonly used because it is less expensive to pay for EMT-B level personnel than EMT-P personnel. Therefore, instead of staffing an ambulance crew with two EMT-Ps, an EMT-P and an EMT-B could work together as an ambulance crew. In the volunteer model, volunteers respond, often from their own homes to scenes of accidents and medical incidents, and usually without government funding. This is the typical service used in rural environments.

175. The answer is A, Corneal perforation.

(Marx, 231; Tintinalli, 1533-1536)

The patient in this question has a corneal ulcer with an associated collection of white blood cells in the anterior chamber, which is known as a hypopyon. Left untreated, the infection can rapidly erode the cornea and cause perforation of the eye. This disruption of the visual axis can be restored only with a cornea transplant. Extension of the corneal infection can also lead to endophthalmitis and loss of the eye. Corneal ulcers can occur secondary to trauma or to incomplete eye closing in facial nerve paralysis. They are most commonly associated with soft contact lens use, especially in persons who wear them for an extended period of time. A corneal ulcer is a medical emergency that will not resolve spontaneously. It should be treated aggressively with topical antibiotics every hour and no patching. Chronically elevated blood sugar from diabetes mellitus and long-term corticosteroid use are risk factors for premature cataracts, an opacification of the lens. The infectious process in this case would not likely lead to cataract formation. Corneal ulcers, unless they are associated with endophthalmitis, do not lead to increased intraocular pressure. Patients with prolonged, poorly controlled glaucoma, either acute or chronic, develop optic nerve damage as evidenced by an increased cup-to-disc ratio on retinal examination.

176. The answer is D, 1,600 U.

(Marx, 1585-1587; Tintinalli, 941-945)

The standard formula to calculate the amount of factor to administer is as follows: patient's weight (kg) × 0.5 × percentage change in factor. In emergency therapy, the assumption should be that a bleeding hemophiliac is at 0% activity. Depending on the site of bleeding, differing levels of activity are needed. In this case, the etiology of the shoulder pain is hemarthrosis. Hemarthrosis activity levels should be 30% to 50%. Gastrointestinal tract and CNS bleeding require 100% activity, so the calculation is 80 kg × 0.5 × 40% = 1,600 U. Several doses of the same number of units are needed over 1 to 2 days to control bleeding, as the half-life of factor is only 12 to 24 hours. The patient's hematologist should be consulted after the initial treatment to help guide further therapy. Hospitalization might be required for patients who have bleeding at sites that have potential life-threatening complications. Several factor VIII products are available, and the choice of product depends on availability, cost, and past reactions.

177. The answer is B, Cerebellar hemorrhage with intraventricular extension.

(Marx, 1338-1345, 1362-1363; Wolfson, 769-771)

The patient in this question has sustained a cerebellar hemorrhage. The head CT shows a large cerebellar hemorrhage with surrounding edema. There is extension of blood into the ventricular system, resulting in the development of an obstructive hydrocephalus. There seems to be compression of the pons anteriorly, which is likely causing her pinpoint pupils. Intracerebral hemorrhage (ICH), or bleeding directly into the brain parenchyma, occurs in 10% to 15% of stroke patients. The cerebellum is the second most common location. The most common location is the subcortical white matter (lobar hemorrhage). These typically present with unilateral symptoms similar to an ischemic stroke, although the severity of symptoms is related to the size of hemorrhage. In patients with cerebellar hemorrhage, ataxia with headache is often a presenting complaint, but clinical symptoms can deteriorate rapidly. Extension of blood into the ventricular system is more common and can lead to obstructive hydrocephalus and a resultant abrupt increase in intracranial pressure (ICP). The classic presentation for a pontine hemorrhage is a severe headache with rapid neurologic decline to coma, hyperthermia, pinpoint pupils, and loss of corneal reflexes with abnormal caloric response. Carotid artery dissection classically causes a headache with Horner syndrome and contralateral stroke symptoms. Patients often are significantly hypertensive with hemorrhagic strokes, as this is a major risk factor for the development of the disease. Patients with ICH often require aggressive blood pressure management. Despite controversy in this area, consensus recommendations exist for patients with systolic blood pressure greater than 180 mm Hg. Modest reductions can be made in patients with systolic blood pressure between 180 and 200; more aggressive approaches should be made for systolic blood pressure over 200. Medications should be administered parenterally. Historically, nitroprusside has been the agent of choice because of its rapid onset and ease of titration; however, concerns have been raised about the risk for worsening hemorrhage as a result of vasodilation. Labetalol is another acceptable option. Nicardipine, a calcium-channel blocker that decreases peripheral vascular resistance, is the newest drug used for this indication. Frequent blood pressure monitoring is needed; if there is concern for increased ICP (specifically in patients with intraventricular extension), intracerebral monitoring is recommended. In this patient, emergent neurosurgical consultation for potential decompression of the ICH is needed. Cerebellar hemorrhages are the most common surgically managed ICH; cortical ICH is less likely to require surgical intervention.

178.   The answer is A, Aspiration and intravenous antibiotics.

(Marx, 920; Roberts, 1181-1187)

The patient in this question has a peritonsillar abscess with the classic findings of sore throat, odynophagia, fever, rancid breath, and occasional trismus. Needle aspiration performed by the emergency physician or by an otolaryngologist is safe, cost and time effective, diagnostic, and curative. Antibiotics are needed to treat associated cellulitis, and at least one dose of intravenous antibiotics should be given to any patient who is having difficulty swallowing or appears systemically ill. Antibiotics alone do not successfully treat a peritonsillar abscess. Cancers are occasionally associated with peritonsillar abscess, but treatment of the infection should take priority. Computed tomography is not required when the diagnosis is clear but can be used if trismus prevents a clear view of the posterior pharynx or if there is a concern for extension of the infection. Surgical drainage is not required if the area can be aspirated or incised intraorally. The patient should be prepared for the procedure by careful positioning and adequate analgesia, sedation, or both. The area can be locally anesthetized using a topical anesthetic gel or lidocaine spray or primarily infiltrated with 1 to 2 mL of 1% lidocaine with epinephrine. For aspiration, the needle should protrude only 1 cm beyond the needle cover; for incision, the No. 11 or No. 15 blade should be taped over, allowing only the distal 0.5 cm to penetrate. It is very important to advance the needle or blade only in the sagittal plane, never to the side, as the carotid artery is 2.5 cm behind and lateral to the tonsil. The differential diagnosis for peritonsillar abscess includes unilateral tonsillitis, cellulitis, abscess, mononucleosis, neoplasm, foreign body, and rarely, internal carotid artery aneurysm. Testing for diseases such as mononucleosis should be considered, but antibiotics and drainage are still required.

179.   The answer is D, Start intravenous administration of clindamycin.

(Marx, 931-932; Tintinalli, 491-494)

The CT scan demonstrates a left lung abscess seen as a thick-walled intraparenchymal consolidation with a definite air/fluid level present. Abscesses often are a complication of aspiration but are also associated with lung cancers. Most lung abscesses are polymicrobial with either pure anaerobes or a combination of anaerobic and aerobic organisms. Clindamycin is an ideal treatment choice given its efficacy against both aerobes and anaerobes. Other rare causes of lung abscess include tuberculosis and fungi. Abscesses develop over time, and symptoms tend to develop over 1 to 2 weeks. Risk factors for lung abscess are similar to the risk factors for aspiration, which include poor dentition, neurologic conditions or depressed mental status that impairs swallowing and gag, chronic alcoholism, and reflux disease. Signs and symptoms of lung abscess are fever, shortness of breath, cough, and chest pain. Most cases of lung abscess respond to antibiotics treatment. If antibiotic therapy fails, surgical debridement is required. Bronchoscopy might be helpful in the management of aspiration or to obtain a biopsy but does not reach the abscess. A chest tube does not drain an abscess in the lung parenchyma but is helpful in treating empyema. Computed tomography-guided drainage might be helpful to drain a deep abscess or obtain a biopsy if necessary. Patients such as the one in this question might have an underlying cancer that requires biopsy, but treatment should be directed at the abscess first.

180. The answer is B, Alkaline.

(Adams, 225-226; Marx, 860-861; Wolfson, 182-183)

Strong alkaline burns cause a liquefactive necrosis of the ocular tissues. Alkaline agents continue to penetrate until removed, which is why prompt and copious irrigation is necessary when a patient presents with a chemical injury to the eye. Ideally, irrigation is started at the scene; it should not be delayed for a measurement of visual acuity. Particles should be identified and removed as well. Irrigation should continue until the pH of the tear film is neutral. If it continues to be alkaline, more irrigation is required. Alkaline burns have a high potential to cause corneal injury, perforation, scarring, and neovascularization. Injuries caused by acid burns tend to be milder because they produce a coagulation necrosis with precipitation of proteins, which limits penetration. Infrared radiation can produce a superficial keratitis but can also lead to cataract formation or macular injury. When thermal injury to the cornea occurs, it is treated as a corneal abrasion. Ultraviolet burns occur in high-altitude environments and in tanning beds. They cause a superficial keratitis and are also treated as a corneal abrasion. Treatment of an uncomplicated corneal abrasion is supportive and commonly includes topical antibiotic ointment or drops and cycloplegic drops to reduce ciliary spasm, although the evidence supporting the use of either is not strong.

181. The answer is D, Require a surgical procedure.

(Marx, 2348-2352; Tintinalli, 526)

Abdominal pain in elderly patients is more likely to reflect a serious abdominal pathology, with up to 60% of elderly patients having a surgical pathology. Nearly 20% of elderly patients with abdominal pain go directly to the operating room. The mortality rate for abdominal pain pathology in older patients is significantly elevated when compared with that for younger patients. For example, the mortality rate associated with appendicitis is about 0.02% in younger patients. In the elderly, it ranges from 3% to 8%. The presentation of an elderly patient with serious abdominal pathology might not initially reflect the magnitude of the pathology. Elderly patients are less likely to develop a fever in response to a serious intraabdominal pathology than are younger patients. Elderly patients are often not able to localize the pain and complain only of vague abdominal pain. They usually present later in the course of the illness, and they rarely present with peritoneal signs, as they lack the abdominal musculature to produce guarding and rebound. The prevalence of atherosclerosis makes the development of necrotic complications of otherwise simple pathologies such as cholecystitis more likely.

182. The answer is C, Perforation.

(Chiu, 320-327; Levine, 731-735; Tintinalli, 557; Wolfson, 554-558)

In an elderly patient with prior peptic ulcer disease who presents with protracted abdominal and back pain and laboratory findings consistent with pancreatitis, a posterior perforation is the most likely diagnosis despite normal radiographs. Classically, perforation presents as a sudden change from the patient's typical abdominal pain, rapidly becoming more severe and diffuse, with signs of peritonitis on physical examination. More prolonged symptoms with less abdominal tenderness are more often seen in elderly patients as well as those with partially occluded or posterior perforations. Pancreatitis can result from posterior perforation with leakage of gastric contents into the retroperitoneum. Plain radiographs can miss 20% to 50% of cases, as with this radiograph. Instilling 200 mL of air through a nasogastric tube has been suggested to improve visualization but might result in the opening of a partially occluded lesion, increasing spillage, and worsening clinical status. An abdominal CT scan is more sensitive for the detection of free air. Emergency department management includes initial resuscitation, broad-spectrum antibiotics for enteric pathogens, and preparation for emergent surgical exploration. An abdominal aortic aneurysm is unlikely when no pulsatile mass is noted on a thin, elderly patient. With normal alkaline phosphatase and bilirubin levels, cholangitis is very unlikely. Mesenteric ischemia is always a consideration in an elderly patient but is typically a rapidly fatal disease and less likely associated with pancreatitis.

183. The answer is A, Air enema.

(Fleisher, 1520-1522; Marx, 2176-2178)

Intussusception is defined as a telescoping of a proximal section of bowel (intussusceptum) into the more distal bowel (intussuscipiens). This can lead to a small bowel obstruction with ischemia of the involved bowel. Clinically, the patient presents with a history of intermittent abdominal pain, classically represented by the child pulling his or her legs into the chest or entering the fetal position. The air enema has supplanted the contrast enema in the diagnosis and treatment of intussusception because it has a better success rate for reduction (90% compared to 79% for hydrostatic). Either method can lead to a perforation, so involvement of a pediatric surgeon is suggested before performing the procedure. There is less radiation associated with air enema, and data indicate shortened lengths of stay and decreased morbidity rates. Because the success rate is high with a relatively low recurrence rate, most patients can be discharged after they demonstrate feeding tolerance. Intussusception can be caused by an infectious process (Henoch-Schönlein purpura, cystic fibrosis, upper respiratory tract illness, diarrheal disease) or a mechanical lead point (polyp, oncologic process, indwelling gastrointestinal catheter, hemangiomas), or both. During the initial onset, the patient might appear well between episodes of pain. This can transition into lethargy later in the course of bowel invagination. In the later phase of intussusception, the patient can have diarrheal stools that become bloody as the bowel ischemia worsens. The classic triad of symptoms (colicky abdominal pain, vomiting, red currant-jelly stools) occurs in less than one-third of cases. The abdomen can be normal in the early phase and become progressively more distended; a palpable mass in the right upper quadrant is possible. Currant-jelly stool or heme positive stool or both are seen in only half of cases and are often a late finding. Plain abdominal radiographs are often not diagnostic initially, although the classic finding is a right upper quadrant soft tissue mass with focal dilation of the bowel, indicating obstruction.

184. The answer is C, Normal intraventricular conduction on a prior ECG.

(Antman, 588-636; O'Connor, S787-S817; Sgarbossa, 481-487; Tabas, 329-336)

A new left-bundle branch block (LBBB) in a patient with active chest pain should be managed as ST-segment elevation MI: emergent reperfusion with percutaneous coronary intervention (PCI), if available, or otherwise thrombolysis. It is challenging to reliably diagnose ischemia in the presence of LBBB. The three ECG criteria with the highest specificity for diagnosing acute MI, based on the Sgarbossa criteria, are as follows:

- ST-segment elevation of greater than 1 mm in the same direction as the QRS complex (5 points)
- ST-segment depression of greater than 1 mm in lead V_1, V_2, or V_3 (3 points)
- ST-segment elevation greater than 5 mm in the opposite direction of the QRS complex (2 points)

An accurate diagnosis of ischemia requires a minimum score of 3. The best strategy for detecting acute MI includes comparison with old ECGs, examination of serial ECGs, understanding the ST-segment changes of LBBB, and, if the patient has a history or presentation that suggests acute coronary syndrome, consideration of a cardiology consultation. The ECG criteria for LBBB are: QRS complex longer than 0.12 seconds; abnormal QRS morphology in the left precordial leads (V_5, V_6) and left limb leads (I, aVL); and QS or rS pattern in the right precordial leads (V_1, V_2). Known history of LBBB, contrast dye allergy, lack of current symptoms, and recent normal catheterization are relative contraindications to emergent PCI.

185. The answer is A, Vitamin A.

(Nelson, 609-618; Marx, 1363, 1624)

Toxicity from excessive vitamin A ingestion can present with a variety of findings, including intracranial hypertension, hepatotoxicity, and hypercalcemia. Vitamins can be divided into two major classes: those that are fat soluble and those that are water soluble. All of the fat-soluble vitamins except vitamin K are associated with toxicity in overdose. Toxicity from vitamin A most commonly results from excess ingestion of supplements but has also occurred from eating the livers of various animals, such as polar bear. Intracranial hypertension is a recognized complication and can cause headache, psychosis, visual field deficits, and sixth cranial nerve palsies. Hepatotoxicity including cirrhosis and hypercalcemia are well-described complications. Various hair (loss, thinning) and dermatologic (xerosis) manifestations have also been described. Vitamin D toxicity predominantly manifests with hypercalcemia. Water-soluble vitamins are not stored in the body and are less likely to be associated with toxicity in excess than are fat-soluble vitamins, which can bioaccumulate. Water-soluble vitamins such as folic acid, vitamin B_1 (thiamine), and vitamin B_{12} (cyanocobalamin) are not associated with any excess syndrome. Nicotinic acid (niacin), vitamin B_6 (pyridoxine), and vitamin C (ascorbic acid), although water soluble, have been associated with toxicity in excess. Adverse effects of niacin ingestion (even at therapeutic dosing for hyperlipidemia) can cause cutaneous flushing and pruritus. Vitamin B_6 excess has been associated with peripheral neuropathies. Oxalate nephrolithiasis has been described after overdose of vitamin C but only with intravenous dosing or large ingestions in patients with renal failure. Here are the key signs and symptoms of vitamin deficiency and excess:

- Vitamin A deficiency – night blindness
- Vitamin A excess – hepatotoxicity, hypercalcemia, intracranial hypertension, xerosis
- Vitamin B_1 (thiamine) deficiency – Wernicke-Korsakoff syndrome
- Vitamin B_3 (niacin) excess – flushing
- Vitamin B_3 (niacin) deficiency – pellagra (three Ds: diarrhea, dementia, dermatitis)
- Vitamin B_6 (pyridoxine) excess – peripheral neuropathies
- Vitamin C deficiency – scurvy (bleeding, gingivitis, poor wound healing)
- Vitamin D excess – hypercalcemia

186. The answer is B, Recompression therapy is the only definitive treatment.

(Marx, 1909-1915; Tintinalli, 1370-1371)

The diagnosis of arterial gas embolism (AGE) should be presumed in any diver who surfaces unconscious or loses consciousness within 10 minutes of surfacing and had been breathing compressed air. Treatment includes 100% oxygen and hyperbaric oxygen (HBO) as soon as possible, as recompression therapy is the only definitive treatment. Resubmersion for recompression on site is risky, time consuming, and difficult to monitor and therefore not recommended. If initiated early, HBO therapy has been shown to improve outcome. The most common symptoms of AGE result from emboli in the brain, leading to headache, loss of consciousness, dizziness, seizures, or other stroke symptoms. Coronary artery air emboli can cause ischemia or cardiac dysrhythmias. Even if the patient's symptoms resolve, HBO treatment is recommended for AGE because of delayed recurrent symptoms; peripheral and capillary edema and microbubbles can remain in the central and cerebral circulation. The patient should be monitored in the flat position, as Trendelenburg positioning has been shown to increase intracranial pressure and promote coronary gas embolization. Before starting HBO therapy, all endotracheal tubes and urinary catheter balloons should be inflated with saline solution instead of air to prevent changes in volume occurring with recompression therapy.

187. The answer is C, *Staphylococcus aureus*.

(Marx, 1696; Tintinalli, 911, 999-1003, 1071, 1082)

This patient is suffering from toxic shock syndrome (TSS), a secondary syndrome caused by staphylococcal colonization of the foreign bodies in his nostrils. The case definition for TSS includes the following criteria: fever ($\geq$38.9°C); diffuse macular erythroderma; desquamation 1 to 2 weeks after the illness; hypotension ($\leq$90 mm Hg); and multisystem involvement (including vomiting or diarrhea, mucous membrane hyperemia, renal failure, elevated transaminases, thrombocytopenia, or altered mental status). Toxic shock syndrome was originally recognized on a large scale in 1981 among women with long-term tampon use. Changes in tampon formulation and public education about the importance of changing tampons frequently have led to a dramatic decline in the prevalence of TSS, but cases still occur. Tampon use is not the only cause of this disease. Any patient treated with nasal packing can be affected and should also be treated with antistaphylococcal antibiotics for prevention. Dengue fever, a viral infection transmitted by *Aedes* mosquitoes, occurs throughout Central and South America, South Asia, and some of Africa. It causes a high fever, severe myalgias and arthralgias, and a faint, diffuse, erythrodermal rash. *Rickettsia prowazekii* is the causative organism in epidemic typhus, a disease transmitted by the body louse, which is rarely seen today due to modern hygiene. The rash is characterized by nonblanching petechiae and purpura; it starts on the trunk and spreads peripherally. Plague, caused by *Yersinia pestis*, still occurs sporadically in the western and southwestern United States. It presents with regional suppurative lymphadenopathy and sepsis. Some patients have an eschar at the site of inoculation, which leads to buboes in that limb. In the late stages of the disease, petechiae and purpura can develop. The pneumonic form is highly contagious and poses a risk to health care workers.

188. The answer is C, Peptic ulcer disease.

(Adams, 316-317; Marx, 1076-1079, 1145-1147, 1521)

The most common emergency department complication of Zollinger-Ellison syndrome (ZES) is peptic ulcer disease, which occurs in 90% of patients. Zollinger-Ellison syndrome is caused by gastrin-secreting tumors (gastrinomas) within the gastrointestinal tract, resulting in hypersecretion of gastric acid. Although ZES is very rare, the development of peptic ulcer disease in a patient who does not have *Helicobacter pylori* infection or significant NSAID use should heighten suspicion for this disease. Symptoms include epigastric pain, abdominal fullness, nausea, vomiting, and diarrhea. Without appropriate therapy, peptic ulcers often develop in atypical locations such as the jejunum or distal duodenum. Initial management consists of conservative therapy with H2 blockers or proton-pump inhibitors. Surgical antrectomy and resection of metastatic tumors are indicated in severe cases. Despite aggressive surgical treatment, lesions often recur. Hypertension, especially in young, otherwise healthy individuals, is a common complication of pheochromocytoma, a rare neuroendocrine tumor of the adrenal medulla. Tricuspid and pulmonary valve abnormalities are common in patients with carcinoid syndrome. Other symptoms include flushing, bronchoconstriction, and severe diarrhea. Carcinoid syndome is caused by the release of serotonin from carcinoid tumors within the gut. Cholelithiasis is not a common complication of neuroendocrine tumors.

189. The answer is A, Perform a digital nerve block and make a single lateral incision around the ulnar aspect of the finger.

(Marx, 521; Roberts, 682-687)

The patient in this question has a felon, which is an infection of the distal digital pulp. Simple felons are managed with a single lateral incision on the ulnar aspect of digits 2, 3, or 4 and on the radial aspect of digits 1 and 5. The incision should be approximately 0.5 cm distal to the distal interphalangeal crease to avoid injury to the flexor tendons. The incision should be extended to the end of the nail. Blunt dissection usually is needed for complete drainage given the multiple septa in the finger. These septa have an important part in the progression and spread of infection; proper drainage is the main reason simple infections such as felons are not associated with a high incidence of tendon sheath or joint infections. Following incision and drainage, the next steps are to culture, irrigate, pack, and splint the finger. Packing is removed in 48 to 72 hours. Felons are usually the result of penetrating trauma, although often patients cannot recall an inciting event. Given that felons often start as cellulitis, oral antibiotics are indicated. Extensive or recurrent felons should be managed surgically. Intravenous antibiotics and consultation with a surgeon for closed tendon sheath irrigation are appropriate in the treatment of flexor tenosynovitis. A felon is generally confined to the distal pulp space; with flexor tenosynovitis, in comparison, the pain and swelling extend along the length of the flexor tendon on the palmar aspect of the digit. Surgical management is crucial because these infections can easily spread proximally to other compartments in the hand. A paronychia is an infection around the lateral nail fold. A simple paronychia can be treated by performing a digital nerve block then elevating the eponychial fold with a No. 11 blade. The incision might have to be extended to remove the lateral or proximal nail bed if the infection has spread underneath. Packing is needed for large abscesses, with removal in 48 hours. Antibiotics are not necessary unless there is overlying cellulitis. Herpetic whitlow is an infection of the distal phalanx caused by the herpes simplex virus. It is associated with prodromal fever, pain, and swelling followed by clear vesicles; the digital pulp spaces remain soft. It is important to differentiate herpetic whitlow from other hand infections because in the treatment of whitlow, incision and drainage are contraindicated because of viral dissemination and secondary contamination. Management of herpetic whitlow is supportive and includes wrapping the finger with a dry occlusive dressing, prescribing an antiviral medication against herpes if the infection is caught early, splinting, and elevation.

190. The answer is B, Eating disorder.

(Adams, 2086-2087; Tintinalli, 1959-1962)

These ECG findings are classic for the presentation of a patient with an eating disorder, specifically, bulimia. Not all patients with an eating disorder present with these obvious symptoms, so careful questioning might be necessary. The typical patient is in mid-to-late adolescence. The dental findings are the result of forced vomiting, and the calluses result from manual induction of emesis (Russell sign). The ECG shows a prolonged QT interval with a U wave seen after the T wave (normally best seen in leads V_2 and V_3). Both a prolonged QT interval and U wave are seen in patients with hypokalemia, a common finding in patients with chronic vomiting. Other laboratory findings common in patients with chronic vomiting include hypochloremia and metabolic alkalosis. Arrhythmia is the most common life threat to these patients, resulting from severe electrolyte abnormalities. Other complications include dehydration and renal insufficiency, starvation and vitamin deficiency, osteopenia, esophageal trauma (including Mallory-Weiss tears), rectal prolapse from laxative abuse, and physical changes to the gray and white matter of the brain, resulting in inattention and mental status changes with chronic disease. A predominance of diarrhea from laxative abuse results in acidosis rather than the alkalosis seen with excessive vomiting. Associated comorbidities include anxiety disorders, depression, and substance abuse, not acute psychosis. Catabolic states associated with increased caloric consumption (infections, hypermetabolism) should be considered in the differential diagnosis but should be relatively easy to distinguish from inadequate caloric intake or purging.

191. The answer is C, Increase the positive end-expiratory pressure.

(Marx, 27-28; Tintinalli, 1004-1005)

Adult respiratory distress syndrome, also known as acute lung injury, is characterized by inflammation of the lung parenchyma leading to increased permeability of the capillaries. The lungs become heavy and noncompliant, leading to impaired gas exchange, which results in hypoxia. Patients with ARDS can develop severe hypoxemia, which does not improve with oxygen. Once hypoxemia develops, increasing positive end-expiratory pressure has been shown to be helpful. Adult respiratory distress syndrome develops as a complication of another process such as sepsis, pneumonia, aspiration, or trauma. It is essentially organ failure of the lungs that often occurs as part of multisystem organ failure. Adult respiratory distress syndrome has a high mortality rate. There is evidence to suggest that lower tidal volumes (6 mL/kg) have been shown to decrease development of ARDS. Increasing the respiratory rate or tidal volumes improves ventilation but does not correct hypoxia. Steroids have not been shown to be helpful. In patients with heart failure, chest radiographs reveal cardiomegaly in addition to interstitial and alveolar infiltrates. In ARDS, the heart size is normal to enlarged. Although furosemide is helpful in treating cardiogenic causes of pulmonary edema, it is not helpful in ARDS. It is more likely that the patient will need fluid resuscitation.

192. The answer is B, Definitive treatment is lateral canthotomy to release the globe.

(Marx, 230-235; Wolfson, 185)

The patient in this question has a retrobulbar hematoma as a result of orbital trauma. This is a true ocular emergency: the retina can withstand complete ischemia for only 90 minutes without suffering permanent damage. The presence of the hematoma places a stretch on the retinal artery, which limits blood flow and results in ischemia. Definitive treatment of the orbital compartment syndrome caused by a retrobulbar hematoma consists of lateral canthotomy to release the globe. This procedure should be performed by the emergency physician and should not be delayed unless the ophthalmologist is readily available. Administration of mannitol and acetazolamide is a temporizing measure, not definitive treatment. Orbital emphysema can lead to a similar presentation, and needle aspiration of the air by an ophthalmologist might spare the patient a canthotomy, but because of the proximity of the globe, aspiration is generally not performed by an emergency physician. In addition, needle aspiration of a hematoma is not likely to be successful. When performing a lateral canthotomy, the lateral canthus, not the medial canthus, should be incised to avoid injury to the lacrimal duct.

193. The answer is C, Hypoactive delirium is more common than hyperactive delirium.

(Han, 193-200; Hustey, 338-341; Marx, 101-103; Tintinalli, 1136-1139)

Of all patients with delirium seen in the emergency department, about 70% have hypoactive delirium, and about 30% have hyperactive delirium. Hyperactive delirium is easier to identify because the behavioral changes are more dramatic and distressing to others. Screening for delirium includes assessment of orientation and recall. A simple method of testing for delirium is the confusion assessment method scale. It assesses acute onset and/or fluctuating symptoms, inattention, and either disorganized thinking or altered level of consciousness. The Mini-Mental State Exam is most useful for assessment of patients with cognitive impairment such as dementia. It is less helpful in patients with delirium because they must pay attention to the tasks involved. A very brief method of assessing cognitive impairment is the Mini-Cog test, which consists of a three-item recall with a clock-face drawing. Attention is not typically affected in dementia until the disease is significantly advanced. The incidence of delirium in elderly emergency department patients is not known, but the prevalence has been reported to be 8% to 10%. In a recent study, about 25% of elderly patients in the emergency department had either delirium or were newly found to have baseline cognitive impairment, and the diagnosis was identified in only 30% of these patients. The mortality effects of delirium persist well beyond the acute episode, with up to a 30% mortality rate in the first 3 months and a significant 1-year mortality rate or admission to a nursing home.

194. The answer is D, Discharge home with next-day followup.

(Marx, 726-728, 1139; Tintinalli, 552-553)

Once a button battery has passed into the stomach, an asymptomatic patient may be safely discharged home with reliable parents and close followup care. In contrast, a button battery lodged in the esophagus represents a true emergency that requires immediate gastrointestinal consultation for endoscopic removal. Alkaline injury to the esophageal mucosa can occur within 4 hours and perforation within 6 hours of ingestion. Lithium batteries are associated with the worst outcomes, especially with larger-sized batteries that are more likely to be lodged in the esophagus. Mercury batteries can split, but toxic heavy metal poisoning is very uncommon. In this case, because the radiograph reveals that the button battery is within the stomach, the patient can be safely discharged home. Prior to discharge, the parents should be instructed to get a reassessment and repeat radiographs in 24 hours to confirm passage through the pylorus. Batteries are typically expelled within 3 to 4 days. Indications for emergent surgical removal include the development of abdominal symptoms, failure to pass the pylorus within 48 hours, and radiographic signs of perforation, impaction, or battery rupture.

195. **The answer is B, Hydrochlorothiazide administered orally and discharge with instructions to follow up with primary care physician within 1 week.**

(Jones, 1-3; Slovis, S7-S9)

The asymptomatic patient with severely elevated blood pressure may be treated either immediately with an oral hypertensive agent or referred to a primary care physician for repeat blood pressure measurement within 1 week. An emergency medicine consensus panel could find no literature to demonstrate that patients, without the presence of acute end-organ damage, who received pharmacologic intervention in the emergency department had better outcomes than those referred for repeat blood pressure measurements, subsequent screening for end-organ damage, and treatment. The panel recommended that emergency physicians initiate outpatient antihypertensive therapy in asymptomatic patients with blood pressure measurements persistently greater than 200 mm Hg systolic or 120 mm Hg diastolic. It is acceptable but not required to obtain a basic metabolic profile before initiating or restarting antihypertensives to guide selection of the most appropriate antihypertensive agent. Patients should be referred for outpatient followup care within 1 week, at which time they normally undergo blood testing (electrolytes, glucose, renal function, lipid profile), a 12-lead ECG, and urinalysis. Calcium-channel blockers, ACE inhibitors, alpha$_1$ blockers, angiotensin receptor blockers, diuretics, and beta-blockers are equally efficacious in treating hypertension. But ACE inhibitors are contraindicated in pregnancy; hydralazine or labetalol is the preferred agent. Hypertensive emergencies are characterized by severe hypertension with evidence of end-organ damage. These include hypertensive encephalopathy, intracerebral hemorrhage, acute myocardial ischemia, acute pulmonary edema, aortic dissection, glomerulonephritis, and eclampsia. An uncomplicated headache is not considered evidence of end-organ damage. Hypertensive emergencies require immediate blood pressure reduction with parenteral agents, with a goal of therapy to reduce the mean arterial blood pressure by 25% within 1 hour and then to 160/110 within the next 6 hours. Excessively rapid blood pressure reduction can precipitate renal, cerebral, or coronary ischemia.

196. **The answer is A, Chance of survival is excellent with early detection and excision.**

(Wolff, 310; Wolfson, 828)

A patient's chance to survive melanoma is excellent with early detection and excision. Hence, recognition and appropriate referral of patients with identified concerning lesions are essential, even for emergency department patients who present for entirely different reasons. Although melanoma is a far less common form of skin cancer than both basal cell (the most common) and squamous cell, it accounts for the majority of deaths from skin cancer. Amelanotic melanomas are an uncommon form and, because of a lack of the typical pigmentation, are very challenging to diagnose. The ABCDE rule refers to six characteristics of melanoma that can be helpful in identification, as follows:

- A – Asymmetry in shape of the lesion
- B – Border, which is typically irregular
- C – Color, which is typically not uniform
- D – Diameter greater than 6 mm (the head of a pencil eraser)
- E – Elevation/enlargement, surface distortion, and increasing size

197. The answer is D, Intubation.

(Marx, 1526-1527; Nabel, 1259-1270; Tintinalli, 181)

The patient in this question is manifesting signs of ongoing airway obstruction and impending suffocation, as evidenced by stridor and the inability to tolerate secretions. The appropriate first step is to secure the airway without delay. Fiberoptic intubation might facilitate intubation in these difficult patients, but preparation for an emergent surgical airway should also occur. Hereditary angioedema (HAE) is an inherited disease that results in a decrease of C1-inhibitor (C1-esterase) activity that normally suppresses the complement cascade. C1-inhibitor deficiency results in increased production of inflammatory mediators such as kallikrein and bradykinin, resulting in vasodilation and capillary leakage. This manifests clinically as recurrent episodes of edema predominantly affecting the upper respiratory and gastrointestinal systems. Airway obstruction remains the leading concern. Treatment of angioedema is usually empirical, although history can guide management. Purified C1 inhibitor has recently been approved by the U.S. Food and Drug Administration for prophylaxis and for the treatment of acute abdominal and facial angioedema in adolescent and adult patients with HAE. It neutralizes the proteases that activate complement. But it is not the appropriate first step in this case because its administration would delay addressing the immediate airway concern. When available, it can be administered after intubation or in patients with less severe cases. Although HAE is relatively refractory to epinephrine, it remains the cornerstone of treating anaphylaxis and angioedema secondary to a hypersensitivity reaction. In many cases in which the etiology is uncertain and the airway is patent or secured, epinephrine might be administered. In this case, however, the cause is known to be HAE. Fresh frozen plasma contains complement factors, including C1 inhibitor, but is not recommended for the treatment of acute attacks. Current recommendations include prophylactic use prior to airway procedures or surgery. Hereditary angioedema is relatively refractory to parenteral glucocorticoids such as methylprednisolone. Its use in angioedema is indicated primarily when the cause is allergic or unknown, targeting the delayed phase of hypersensitivity reactions.

198. The answer is A, Bleeding can occur spontaneously in patients with sickle cell disease.

(Marx, 862-863; Tintinalli, 1539)

A collection of red blood cells in the anterior chamber of the eye is a hyphema. Direct trauma to the eye is the typical etiology, but patients with sickle cell disease might also experience spontaneous bleeding and development of a hyphema. Treatment focuses on promoting natural drainage of the anterior chamber, which can be obstructed by red blood cells. This results in an increase in intraocular pressure. The patient should sit at a 30-degree angle, and the pupil should be fully dilated; topical beta-blockers are a useful first-line agent for pressure control. If the patient has sickle cell disease, carbonic anhydrase inhibitors such as acetazolamide are contraindicated. Lowering the pH level of the aqueous humor causes the cells to sickle further, thereby impeding drainage. Even after successful management, rebleeding occurs in up to 30% of cases, usually 3 to 5 days following the initial event. A hyphema that extends to less than one-third of the cornea is not likely to rebleed and may be managed with outpatient treatment if preferred by the ophthalmologist.

199. The answer is D, Retropharyngeal abscess.

(Fleisher, 898-900, 905-912, 1554; Marx, 913-914, 921-923, 2107)

The retropharyngeal space extends from the base of the skull to the top of the mediastinum. A retropharyngeal abscess is an infection in this space resulting from lymphatic emptying, direct trauma, or spread of an upper respiratory tract infection. Physical examination reveals signs of posterior pharyngeal bulging in more than half of patients, but this area should not be palpated in children. There are numerous causative organisms, which can be different in pediatric and adult patients. They include gram-positive organisms (such as *Staphylococcus*, MRSA, group A beta-hemolytic *Streptococcus* [GABHS]) and gram-negative or even anaerobic species. Significant sequelae from abscess include sepsis, mediastinitis, complete airway obstruction, thrombosis of the jugular vein, extension leading to formation of an epidural abscess, and even hemorrhage from carotid artery erosion. Epstein-Barr viral pharyngitis (mononucleosis) is often associated with fatigue. An enlarged spleen can be palpable, with enlarged tonsils, cervical adenopathy, and significant pharyngeal exudate. Laryngotracheobronchitis, or croup, is not associated with torticollis but can present with respiratory distress, erythema of the pharynx, and anterior cervical chain adenopathy. A pediatric patient might also have a history of a recent upper respiratory tract illness, but the clinical examination is almost always associated with either stridor or hoarseness and the presence of a cough described as barking or seal-like.

200.   The answer is C, Contact vulvovaginitis.

(Marx, 1283, 1293-1294; Tintinalli, 711-715, 995-996)

Contact vulvovaginitis is one of many conditions that causes vulvovaginal discomfort. It typically is a response to a chemical agent but can result from an allergen. Soaps and other scented products, as well as toilet paper, topical antibiotic products, even articles of clothing can cause the irritation, burning, and swelling that patients describe. Findings on examination include a swollen, erythematous vulvovaginal area; at times, ulcerations can also be present if concentrations of the irritant are strong. Symptoms usually resolve with removal of the causative irritant. Topical corticosteroids are sometimes necessary, but in most cases, even without their use, symptoms resolve within a few days after removal of the irritant. Sitz baths and wet compresses of dilute boric acid can also provide relief. Oral antihistamines can be used if an allergic reaction is present. Infectious causes should be ruled out, as is the case with a normal wet mount. Genital herpes produces lesions that begin as painful, fluid-filled vesicles. Bacterial vaginosis also presents with a fishy odor to the discharge and clue cells on wet mount. Hyphae or yeast elements noted on wet mount are present with *Candida* infections.

201.   The answer is D, Sensory symptoms are common presenting complaints.

(Marx, 1386-1388; Wolfson, 794-797)

Sensory findings (numbness, tingling, pins and needles effect) are some of the most common presenting symptoms of multiple sclerosis (MS). The classic definition of MS involves multiple neurologic complaints separated by time and space. Multiple sclerosis is an autoimmune inflammatory disease that results in demyelination and disruption of normal neurologic pathways. Because demyelination can occur anywhere, the findings can include both sensory and motor findings. The motor findings can include one limb or multiple limbs or affect one side of the body (hemiparesis). Paresis is often associated with upper motor neuron dysfunction (spasticity, hyperreflexia). Symptoms often remit, either partially or completely, but relapses are unfortunately a part of the disease. New symptoms can also occur. Ocular symptoms are common, with diplopia and blurred vision among the initial presentation symptoms. Internuclear ophthalmoplegia, a finding in which movement of the eye toward midline is limited and the abducting eye has nystagmus, is very suggestive of MS. This finding is a result of plaque in the medial longitudinal fasciculus in the brainstem. Optic neuritis is present in up to 40% of patients who have MS, and about half of patients who have optic neuritis develop MS. Optic neuritis typically presents as monocular vision loss with associated pain. Findings can include cells and flare on slit lamp examination, a swollen optic disc, and an afferent pupillary defect. Warm temperatures have been noted to worsen symptoms. This phenomenon, known as the Uhthoff sign, is caused by worsened nerve conduction in already partially demyelinated axons.

202. The answer is B, Can be relieved by placing the mother in an extreme lithotomy position.

(Marx, 2340-2342; Roberts, 1051-1052)

When shoulder dystocia occurs in a vertex delivery, placing the mother in an extreme lithotomy position (knees to chest) can free the shoulder and allow delivery. This is known as the McRoberts maneuver. It flattens the lordosis of the pelvis and rotates the pelvis. If this maneuver fails to free the shoulder, an assistant can apply moderate pressure to the suprapubic area while the physician gently applies traction to the head. Additional maneuvers include the Ruben or reverse corkscrew procedure, in which the fingers are placed into the vagina, and, by pushing on the scapula, the posterior shoulder is rotated 180 degrees. Another delivery method is to insert the hand along the patient's sacrum, exerting pressure on the posterior arm of the fetus, moving the flexed arm across the chest, then extending to deliver the arm and shoulder. Shoulder dystocia is unusual, occurring in 1% or less of vertex deliveries. Risk factors for shoulder dystocia include macrosomia, maternal diabetes, multiparity, and late-term delivery. Complications are serious and include brachial plexus injury, fractures of the humerus and clavicle, and fetal death. Fetal respiratory and circulatory compromise can occur, and controlled clavicle fracture by the physician might be needed if simple maneuvers to free the shoulder fail. Time is of the essence to avoid respiratory compromise and hypoxic injury to the fetus, so a slow, relaxed approach is not appropriate.

203. The answer is D, Tube thoracostomy.

(Marx, 943-946; Tintinalli, 471-473, 491-492)

This patient's chest radiograph shows a large pleural effusion. Pus has accumulated in the pleural space, so it is referred to as an empyema. Given the presence of fever, the size of the effusion, and the mild respiratory compromise, inserting a chest tube is the appropriate choice. Pus in the pleural space always requires drainage using a large chest tube; the purulent material cannot be successfully drained using a small chest tube or needle thoracentesis. Pleural effusions are caused by a wide variety of illnesses, including heart failure, cancer, and pneumonias. Parapneumonic effusions sometimes respond to antibiotics and treatment of the underlying pneumonia. Signs and symptoms of an empyema include fever, pleuritic chest pain, shortness of breath, and night sweats. Patients can appear very ill or toxic. Emergent drainage can significantly improve respiratory status. Thoracentesis can help confirm the diagnosis. Gross pus or fluid that cultures out an organism is considered an empyema. A pH level of less than 7.1 or glucose level less than 50 mg/dL is highly suggestive of empyema. There are three stages to empyema formation. In the exudative stage, the fluid is free flowing and easily drained by chest tube. The fibrinopurulent stage is characterized by the development of fibrin strands that can lead to loculations, which make chest tube drainage more complicated. The final stage is fibrosis, in which dense scar tissue forms, which might require thoracotomy. Decubitus radiographs or a chest CT scan can help identify loculations. Large or symptomatic effusions must be drained. Needle decompression is used to treat tension pneumothorax in a patient who is hemodynamically unstable. Bronchoscopy is not helpful in the treatment of effusion but can be helpful in diagnosing underlying conditions such as lung cancer. Furosemide is used to treat heart failure, which is unlikely in this patient. Pleural effusions resulting from heart failure tend to be bilateral.

204. The answer is C, The tooth should not be replanted.

(Marx, 335-336; Wolfson, 172-178)

Dental avulsions are a time-sensitive emergency. However, only adult teeth should be replanted. Replantation of primary teeth can lead to fusion of tooth to alveolar bone and can interfere with normal eruption of secondary adult teeth. The use of antibiotics for dental fractures is controversial. Some dental practitioners believe that antibiotic administration decreases inflammatory root resorption. The base of an avulsed permanent tooth should be gently rinsed (but not wiped) to avoid removing the periodontal ligament cells, which are necessary for successful replantation. There is a greater chance of successful replantation if the tooth is replanted as soon as possible, but preferably in less than 60 minutes from the time of avulsion. After 60 minutes, the viability of the periodontal ligament cells decreases dramatically. Milk or a commercially available preservative solution is preferable to water as a tooth transport medium.

205. The answer is D, Supraclavicular.

(Marx, 886-887; Tintinalli, 724, 787-788, 932-933, 1588-1589)

Supraclavicular lymph nodes drain the lymphatics from the mediastinum, including the lungs and the esophagus. On the left side, the supraclavicular nodes also drain the abdomen through the thoracic duct. The finding of a hardened, enlarged left supraclavicular lymph node with an abdominal malignancy was first described by Rudolf Virchow and Charles Emile Troisier and is thus referred to as both a Virchow node and a Troisier node. In both adults and children, the presence of an enlarged supraclavicular lymph node on either the left or the right side of the body is concerning for malignancy and should be aggressively evaluated, including making arrangements for urgent lymph node biopsy. Lymphadenopathy is frequently found in pediatric patients because they come in contact with a large variety of new antigens. Lymphadenopathy is common in children younger than 12 years, with lymph nodes often felt in the axillary, inguinal, and cervical regions (including the jugulodigastric and parotid locations). The size of the lymph node that is considered to be normal varies by anatomic location. Inguinal lymph nodes can be as large as 1.5 cm in diameter, axillary lymph nodes 1 cm in diameter, and anterior cervical lymph nodes as large as 2 cm in diameter. Because lymphadenopathy is typically inflammatory, a patient with an enlarged lymph node with a focus of infection or inflammation can be reexamined in 1 to 2 weeks. In most anatomic locations, a lymph node larger than 3 cm is more likely to be associated with malignancy. However, an epitrochlear node (at the elbow) or a supraclavicular node larger than 0.5 cm is more likely to be associated with malignancy and should be promptly investigated.

206. The answer is B, Cytomegalovirus.

(Marx, 2371-2372; Tintinalli, 1030, 1999-2005; Wolfson, 576-581)

The most common cause of infection 1 to 6 months after liver transplantation is cytomegalovirus (CMV). Infection most commonly results in a mononucleosis-like illness but can cause further immunosuppression and secondary opportunistic infection, or rarely, allograft rejection. Hepatitis, CMV pneumonitis, and chorioretinitis can also occur. Another common virus to consider, especially in children, is the Epstein-Barr virus. A mononucleosis-like illness is again common, but a diffuse B-cell lymphoproliferative syndrome with a high mortality rate can result as well. Overall, infection is the most common complication of liver transplantation, occurring in over 60% of cases; rejection is a close second, occurring in over 50% of cases. Immunosuppression reduces the risk of rejection but increases the risk of infection, often times with overlapping subtle presentations. In the first 30 days after transplantation, infection is mainly due to nosocomial bacteria or fungal species similar to other surgical patients. Gram-negative organisms, often *Pseudomonas aeruginosa,* are the most common, but gram-positive organisms such as *Streptococcus pneumoniae* and anaerobic infections can occur as well. Fungal infections, typically as a result of *Candida* species, are less common.

207. The answer is B, Obtain diagnostic echocardiography.

(Marx, 959; Mattu, 79)

The ECG shows ST-segment elevation in leads V_2 through V_5 and Q waves in leads V_1 through V_5. This is consistent with either an ST-segment elevation MI (STEMI) or a left ventricular aneurysm from a prior anterior wall MI. Reciprocal ST-segment depression, which is absent on this ECG, increases the likelihood of acute anterior wall MI. Echocardiography is an accurate, rapid bedside diagnostic test to detect a left ventricular aneurysm (LVA). An LVA is not a true aneurysm, but rather a dyskinetic area of myocardium, typically in the apex, that on cardiac imaging seems to balloon during systole. It is most commonly found in the setting of a previous anterior wall MI with a characteristic ECG pattern of Q waves in the anterior leads (V_1 through V_4) with persistent ST-segment elevation. A definitive diagnosis can be made by the presence of similar findings on a previous ECG or by characteristic wall motion abnormality on transthoracic or transesophageal echocardiography. Given this patient's atypical presentation, currently asymptomatic condition, and known recent STEMI, additional information such as a previous ECG or immediate imaging should be sought if it can be rapidly obtained. Even if the history of LVA is not known, other findings are suggestive, including the lack of reciprocal ST-segment depression and his current treatment with warfarin in the setting of a prior MI. If echocardiography is not available and the diagnostic picture is uncertain, emergent cardiac catheterization with ventriculogram can be diagnostic. Only in a symptomatic patient for whom there are no confirmatory data and when cardiac catheterization is not available should immediate thrombolytic therapy be considered. Complications associated with anterior wall MI include ventricular rupture, heart failure, and ventricular arrhythmias. One of the most feared complications of ventricular aneurysm is embolic disease such as stroke. Patients commonly require prolonged anticoagulation given the risk of thrombosis in the akinetic myocardial region. Nonsteroidal anti-inflammatory drugs are helpful in patients with pericarditis, but this patient does not have clinical findings of pericarditis or evidence on ECG such as diffuse, upsloping ST-segment elevation or PR interval depression. Finally, antiarrhythmia drugs are not indicated for LVA in the absence of an arrhythmia.

208. The answer is D, Headache.

(Marx, 2036-2038; Nelson, 1660-1661; Wolfson, 1464-1466)

Carbon monoxide (CO) poisoning can manifest with a variety of nonspecific signs and symptoms. Of those listed, headache is by far the most common. In developed nations, CO remains the most common cause of acute poison-related deaths. It is formed by incomplete combustion of any carbonaceous fuel, and its danger partly owes to the fact it is invisible, odorless, and nonirritating. The adverse effect of CO is ultimately due to its binding to iron found in hemoglobin, myoglobin, and intracellular cytochrome. It binds to hemoglobin with a much higher affinity (250 times) than does oxygen, and it shifts the oxygen dissociation curve so that at a given partial pressure of oxygen the bound oxygen (oxyhemoglobin) is held tighter. By binding to myoglobin, the normal function of myoglobin to store and transfer oxygen in muscle (such as the heart) is disrupted. Additionally, dissolved CO binds to intracellular cytochromes and leads to inhibition of oxidative phosphorylation similar to cyanide. Hence, CO can prevent both cellular oxygen delivery and intracellular oxygen utilization. The most adversely affected organs are those with high oxygen utilization such as the brain and the heart. Poisoning can manifest with a variety of nonspecific signs and symptoms depending on the length, quantity of exposure, and patient age and underlying disease processes. Symptoms are various, nonspecific, and often attributed to other diseases such as viral illness; they include headache, nausea, vomiting, angina, depressed level of consciousness, hypotension, convulsions, coma, dysrhythmias, and death. Cherry red skin owing to the color of carboxyhemoglobin is an autopsy finding and almost never clinically present. Headache is a very common symptom and far more common than the others listed. Physicians must be aware of the nonspecific presenting symptoms to ensure the correct diagnosis and avoid sending a patient back into a potentially lethal environment.

209. The answer is C, EMT-P.

(Marx, 2461-2468; National Highway Traffic Safety Administration, 19-21; Tintinalli, 1-4; Wolfson, 1653-1661)

EMT-Paramedics, or EMT-Ps, are trained in advanced airway techniques that encompass cricothyrotomy, endotracheal intubation and associated adjunct devices, needle decompression, and transthoracic pacing. Whether these skills are used by a system's paramedics is determined by the individual medical director. EMT-Ps are credentialed through the National Standard Curriculum, which requires 1,000 to 1,200 hours of education. EMT-P is the highest level of EMT providers. Other EMT levels include EMT-Intermediate (EMT-I) and EMT-Basic (EMT-B). EMT-I encompasses a variety of skills that might include endotracheal intubation, intravenous access, and defibrillation, as well as administering selected medications. EMT-I requires 300 to 400 hours of training. EMT-B is the minimal level of training needed to operate an ambulance and involves 110 hours of training. EMT-Bs are trained in basic CPR and defibrillation skills as well as simple triage assessments. First responders are trained to respond first to a medical/traumatic incident while awaiting higher level of care personnel and are trained in basic skills including CPR, control of bleeding, and spine immobilization. Sixteen to 36 hours of education are required to be a first responder.

210. The answer is D, Tetanus, diphtheria toxoid, and acellular pertussis.

(Centers for Disease Control and Prevention [tetanus], 1-34; Marx, 1682)

Patients with any breaks in their skin are at risk for developing tetanus. Emergency physicians should take these opportunities to ask patients about their vaccine status and provide boosters for not just tetanus but all three diseases: tetanus, diphtheria, and pertussis. If a patient has had the primary vaccine series within the past 10 years or has had a booster within the past 10 years, no treatment is required. If the wound is high risk for tetanus (more than 6 hours old, contaminated, ischemic, or infected) and the patient's last booster was more than 5 years earlier, updating the vaccine should be considered. For patients 11 to 64 years old requiring the vaccine, the tetanus, diphtheria toxoid, and acellular pertussis (Tdap), formulation should be given at least once. This vaccine updates the diphtheria and the pertussis vaccination status. Following this one-time update, the standard diphtheria and tetanus toxoid vaccine (Td) can be used. The diphtheria, tetanus, and whole-cell pertussis or DTP vaccine, discontinued in 2002, carried a small but significant risk of neurologic adverse effects, including encephalitis and prolonged seizures. It was replaced with the diphtheria, tetanus, and acellular pertussis or DTaP formulation for children younger than 7 years. The adolescent and adult version, Tdap, has a reduced diphtheria toxoid component. Patients who have never received the primary vaccine series should be treated with human tetanus immune globulin (HTIG); HTIG prophylaxis (250 units IM) is recommended for unimmunized and underimmunized patients with high-risk wounds. These patients should also receive the Td vaccine, but it should be given in opposite limbs.

211. The answer is B, Aspirin 81 mg.

(Goldman, 1248-1252; Marx, 1571-1573; Wolfson, 988-989)

Complications of polycythemia are related to hyperviscosity, especially noted when the Hct is greater than 60%. Aside from thrombosis, hemorrhage and reduced blood flow to the tissues are also complications. Treatment is phlebotomy and volume replacement with saline, with a goal of reducing the Hct level to less than 55%. This should be done slowly, 1 to 1.5 L over 24 hours, although in the case of emergencies such as a thrombotic stroke, up to 500 mL can be phlebotomized rapidly in otherwise healthy patients. Low-dose aspirin should also be started. Patients who are known to have polycythemia can receive outpatient care, but for newly diagnosed cases, hospitalization is required for further workup, which might include bone marrow aspiration and determination of erythropoietin level. Polycythemia vera is a myeloproliferative disorder. Aside from the increase in red blood cells, leukocytosis, thrombocytosis, and splenomegaly can be present. The most common cause of death is vascular thrombosis. There is some debate as to the etiology of the thrombosis. Increased platelet collisions with red blood cells and decreased blood flow to organs can lead to thrombosis. The polycythemia conditions are classified as apparent (plasma loss) or true (congenital or acquired). True cases include conditions that produce chronic hypoxia, polycythemia vera, or tumors.

212. The answer is D, Spinal stenosis.

(Marx, 594-598; Tintinalli, 1889-1893)

The classic features of spinal stenosis include bilateral leg pain that is worse with prolonged standing or walking (termed pseudoclaudication) and back extension. The pain is ameliorated by rest and lumbar flexion, which help decrease spinal cord tension by opening up the spinal canal. The diagnosis is confirmed by CT or MRI. Peripheral vascular disease can present similarly, but in this patient with intact peripheral pulses, it is unlikely to be the etiology. It is important to differentiate pseudoclaudication due to spinal stenosis (pain caused by neurologic compression) from vascular claudication due to peripheral vascular disease (pain caused by arterial compromise). This is done by checking ankle-brachial indices and peripheral pedal pulses, which are normal in spinal stenosis. In addition, vascular claudication does not improve with lumbar flexion and might even get worse. Although cancer is always in the differential diagnosis for low back pain, there are no other signs to indicate malignancy in this patient. Red flags include known history of malignancy (especially breast, lung, prostate), unintentional weight loss, and continuous pain, including nighttime pain. Ankylosing spondylitis is a spondyloarthropathy, an autoimmune condition that causes inflammatory changes of mostly the pelvis and vertebral column. It is more commonly diagnosed in men younger than 40 and is characterized by low back pain that improves with activity.

213. The answer is D, Panic disorder.

(Adams, 2064-2065; Wolfson, 806-807)

Panic attacks are characterized by discrete episodes of intense fear or discomfort in the absence of real danger and are manifested by distinct somatic and cognitive symptoms. A feeling of impending doom might be present. Chest tightness, shortness of breath with hyperventilation, loose stools, and symptoms of irritable bowel are just a few of the common symptoms associated with anxiety and panic disorder. Agoraphobia might be accompanied by panic disorder but is commonly triggered by fear of being in a specific place or situation that the patient fears he or she cannot escape from or avoid. Obsessive-compulsive disorder is characterized by obsessions that cause marked anxiety and compulsions that serve to reduce this anxiety. Although medical conditions should always be considered before assuming that a patient's symptoms are caused by a mental health disorder, the patient in this question has undergone evaluation for cardiac disease. Initial emergency department management of panic disorder includes educating the patient about the fight-or-flight response experienced during a panic attack and the sensations they cause. The patient should be advised to avoid smoking, caffeine, some over-the-counter cold medicines, and other stimulants and counseled about methods to control breathing, simple relaxation techniques, regular exercise, adequate sleep, and regular meals. Medications that can be used include selective serotonin reuptake inhibitors (SSRIs), serotonin-norepinephrine reuptake inhibitors (SNRIs), and other antidepressants. Benzodiazepines can be used but with caution regarding potential dependence; clonazepam is thought to be less likely to cause dependence because of its longer onset of action, and so it is often used to treat panic attacks on a short-term outpatient basis. Ideally, these drugs should be used only temporarily. Patients should be referred for cognitive and behavioral therapy and for management of pharmacotherapy, generally an SSRI on a long-term basis.

214. The answer is D, Patient was sleeping on his stomach.

(Fleisher, 160-161; Marx, 71-73)

Although there is no clear cause of sudden infant death syndrome (SIDS), one of the associated risk factors is a prone sleeping position. The definition of SIDS is the sudden death of an infant younger than 1 year that remains unexplained after a thorough case investigation, including performance of a complete autopsy, examination of the death scene, and review of the clinical history. In the United States, SIDS occurs in approximately 2 of 1,000 live births. There is no significant history of apnea or prior acute life-threatening event (ALTE) in patients who present as a result of SIDS. Maternal age exclusive of other risk factors and recent immunization have not been found to be associated with an increased incidence of SIDS. The literature indicates that the following factors might increase the likelihood of SIDS:
- African-American ethnicity
- Smoking exposure in the home
- Maternal smoking or heroin or cocaine use during pregnancy
- A brief period of time between pregnancies
- Premature birth; pregnancy during teenaged years
- Sleeping prone
- Sleeping on a soft mattress
- The presence of blankets or other coverings in the crib

The following actions have been recommended to reduce the likelihood of SIDS:
- Supine sleeping, which prompted the popular and effective "back to sleep" campaign
- Keeping the infant's crib in the caregiver's bedroom
- Breastfeeding

215. The answer is C, Lateral soft tissue radiographs of the neck.

(Marx, 917-919; Tintinalli, 1583-1587)

A presentation of fever, stridor, and muffled voice should raise suspicion for epiglottitis, a diagnosis that can be confirmed with lateral soft tissue radiographs of the neck. Although the incidence of epiglottitis among pediatric patients has been on the decline since the introduction of the *Haemophilus influenzae* vaccine, children are at high risk for obstruction with stimulation; they should undergo early airway management with surgical backup options, including needle cricothyrotomy and tracheostomy. Epiglottitis in adults (which is on the rise) can still progress to airway obstruction, but it is less common than in children. In adults, fibrotic laryngoscopy can also be used to visualize the epiglottis. Epiglottitis is predominantly bacterial, and antibiotics with ceftriaxone should be initiated. Albuterol is more helpful in bronchospasm than it is for upper airway problems. Racemic epinephrine might be helpful for patients with upper airway swelling. Steroids are routinely used in the treatment of croup, not epiglottitis.

216. The answer is D, Orbital roof fracture.

(Marx, 334; Wolfson, 182)

Orbital roof fractures are caused by high-force injury and lead to violation of the cranial vault, which can lead to concomitant brain injury. Any patient with an orbital roof fracture should undergo brain imaging and then neurosurgery consultation if brain injury exists. Consideration should be given to obtaining specialist consultation with either ophthalmology or a facial trauma surgeon emergently. The lamina papyracea is the very thin, smooth, lateral portion of the ethmoid bone that makes up a portion of the medial orbital wall. Medial orbital fractures that involve the ethmoid can cause nasolacrimal duct injuries as well, but these are not emergent surgical conditions. Fractures that cause muscle entrapment, leading to restriction of extraocular movement, or fractures that cause enophthalmos, require surgical repair, but this can usually be accomplished in the outpatient setting. In any patient with orbital fracture, the eye should be carefully examined for traumatic iritis, hyphema, and cornea or retinal injury.

217. The answer is A, Dilated cardiomyopathy.

(Marx, 211-216; Tintinalli, 470-471, 820-825)

Peripheral cyanosis without associated central cyanosis is caused by five main events: low cardiac output states (including dilated cardiomyopathy), environmental exposure to cold with vasoconstriction, arterial or venous occlusion, and redistribution of blood flow. Peripheral cyanosis is seen in the peripheral vasculature (such as in the nail beds) when there is slowed flow of normally oxygenated blood, when more oxygen is extracted from the red blood cells with a resultant increase in the concentration of deoxyhemoglobin. In anemic patients, the concentrations of both oxyhemoglobin and deoxyhemoglobin are lowered, and it can be difficult to appreciate peripheral cyanosis. Central cyanosis is primarily a result of low arterial oxygen levels, anatomic shunts, or abnormal Hgb. Tetralogy of Fallot and tricuspid atresia are forms of cyanotic congenital heart disease and present with central cyanosis. Primary pulmonary hypertension causes ventilation-perfusion mismatch, leading to low arterial oxygen levels and central cyanosis.

218. The answer is A, Crohn disease involves the entire bowel wall, resulting in abscess and fistula formation.

(Marx, 1236-1239; Tintinalli, 536-540)

Lesions involving the entire bowel wall distinguish Crohn disease from ulcerative colitis. Crohn disease is defined by large ulcerations that extend through the entire thickness of the gastrointestinal wall and into mesenteric lymph nodes. It is complicated by relapsing abscess and fistula formation, strictures, and bowel obstruction. Skip lesions and a mucosal cobblestone appearance are characteristic endoscopic findings. Lesions can occur anywhere in the gastrointestinal tract but are most commonly found in the small bowel (30%), colon (20%), or both (50%). Surgery is required in 75% of patients within 20 years of diagnosis, although recurrence rates approach 100% even after surgical management. Unlike Crohn disease, ulcerative colitis involves only the mucosa and submucosal layers of the large bowel. Nearly all patients have rectal disease, characterized by cryptogenic lesions that progress continuously to the more proximal colon, most often with sparing of the small bowel. However, up to 15% of patients develop pancolitis. Bloody diarrhea is a hallmark feature. Fistula and abscess formation are less common, with the exception of perirectal involvement. Surgical management is curative for severe disease. Persons who have ulcerative colitis have a 10- to 30-fold increased risk of developing colon cancer, mandating early preventive screening. The incidence of carcinoma in Crohn disease is 3 to 5 times higher than it is in the general population but less significant than in ulcerative colitis. Toxic megacolon is a serious complication of inflammatory bowel disease and is seen equally in Crohn disease and ulcerative colitis. Patients present with severe abdominal pain, fever, increased diarrhea, and toxemia. Mortality rates approach 50% without prompt recognition and surgical management. Chronic relapsing diarrhea, anorexia, weight loss, and abdominal pain are common clinical features of both Crohn disease and ulcerative colitis. The pathophysiology of both types of inflammatory bowel disease is unknown. A combination of hereditary, environmental, autoimmune, and host factors likely has a role. Extraintestinal complications occur in 20% to 30% of patients with Crohn disease and ulcerative colitis.

219. The answer is D, Vasodilators will decrease her preload and worsen her symptoms.

(Bonow, e530-e534, e539-e547, e576-e579; Marx, 1041, 1073-1074)

Acute valvular dysfunction is the third leading cause of heart failure, usually involving the aortic or mitral valves. In patients with decompensated heart failure caused by aortic stenosis, administration of vasodilator agents that cause preload reduction can result in decreased flow across a fixed obstruction, potentially leading to hypotension, syncope, and worsening heart failure. Aggressive diuresis also decreases preload with similar results.

In contrast to those with aortic stenosis, patients with mitral regurgitation respond well to vasodilators because the afterload reduction improves antegrade blood flow. Clinically, an aortic stenosis murmur is classically described as a systolic ejection murmur heard best at the right sternal border of the second intercostal space that radiates into the carotids, as described in this question. In comparison, a mitral regurgitation murmur is described as a midsystolic harsh murmur heard best at the apex of the heart that radiates into the axilla. In patients with aortic stenosis, symptoms such as chest pain, near syncope, syncope, or heart failure generally appear in patients when the valve area is severely narrowed (<1 cm^2 compared to normal = 3-4 cm^2). The severity of symptoms and echocardiography findings are used to determine whether valve replacement is necessary. Valve replacement is generally recommended when patients develop symptoms attributable to the aortic stenosis. In addition to clinical presentation findings, echocardiography findings are evaluated to determine the degree of aortic valve stenosis and the degree of systolic and/or diastolic dysfunction; the decision regarding surgical repair is then made based on this information. In contrast, repair for patients with mitral regurgitation might be indicated before symptoms develop. Patients with aortic stenosis are more likely to have diastolic heart failure than systolic heart failure because of the associated left ventricular hypertrophy due to the increased resistance associated with a fixed obstruction.

220. The answer is A, Characterized by paroxysms of hypertension.

(Marx, 1078, 1447; Wolfson, 1035-1036)

Pheochromocytomas are catecholamine-producing tumors that characteristically cause paroxysms of hypertension. They are the responsible etiology of hypertension in only a small minority (<1%) of patients. A high level of suspicion is necessary in appropriate situations. Early diagnosis, appropriate management, and potentially definitive surgical treatment can prevent significant complications and death. The tumors are often referred to as the ten percent tumor: 10% are bilateral (both adrenals), 10% are extraadrenal, 10% are familial, and 10% are malignant. Patients with neurofibromatosis (von Recklinghausen disease) have an increased incidence. Pheochromocytomas are also present in the syndromes of multiple endocrine neoplasia (2A and 2B). The presentation of pheochromocytomas can be quite variable, and the resolution of symptoms by the time the patient reaches the emergency department can make the diagnosis challenging. Signs and symptoms can be precipitated by a variety of stimuli, including various medications and even emotional stress. Paroxysms of hypertension can be associated with abdominal pain, anxiety, diaphoresis, headache, hyperglycemia, and palpitations. Pheochromocytoma should be at least considered in a patient who presents with recurrent panic attacks. Patients with persistent, difficult-to-treat hypertension should also be tested. Blood pressure might require emergent control in the emergency department, and sodium nitroprusside and/or phentolamine is favored. Beta-blockers alone such as metoprolol should be avoided as unopposed alpha vasoconstriction can occur and cause worsening hypertension. Diagnosis is made by serum and urine measurement of catecholamine and catecholamine metabolite (such as metanephrine) concentrations. Imaging is used for tumor location.

221. The answer is D, 45-year-old man with inability to urinate.

(Marx, 1908-1916; Tintinalli, 1369-1370)

Decompression sickness (DCS) results from the formation of small bubbles of nitrogen gas that accumulate in the blood and tissues during ascent. Nitrogen is highly fat soluble with a proclivity for the white matter of the CNS. There are two types of DCS: type I, which affects the skin, lymphatic system, and musculoskeletal system, and type II, the more common and serious entity, which predominantly affects the CNS, inner ear, and lungs. Spinal DCS usually involves limb weakness or paralysis and paresthesias but can also include urinary symptoms, fecal incontinence, and priapism. Symptoms of spinal DCS can have an atypical distribution of sensory and motor findings, unlike traumatic spinal cord injury. A diver who surfaces unconscious or loses consciousness within 10 minutes of surfacing must be presumed to be suffering from an arterial gas embolism (AGE), not DCS. Symptoms of AGE present suddenly; it is a life-threatening condition caused by air bubbles being forced across the alveolar-capillary membrane and entering the arterial circulation. Emboli can reach any organ. The most common presentation is alteration in consciousness, headache, dizziness, convulsions, and vision changes. Barotrauma occurs when a diver fails to adequately expire gas during ascent; this results in unequal pressures in air-filled spaces, which then causes pneumothorax, pneumomediastinum, subcutaneous emphysema, and alveolar hemorrhage. Barotrauma can also occur from negative pressure exerted on a diver's mask, resulting in facial and conjunctival edema, facial petechiae, and subconjunctival hemorrhages.

222. The answer is D, *Staphylococcus aureus.*

(Marx, 1837-1838; Tintinalli, 1528-1529)

This patient has developed periorbital, or preseptal, cellulitis. Most cases of orbital and periorbital cellulitis are caused by *Staphylococcus aureus* and *Streptococcus* species. *Haemophilus influenzae* was an important cause at one time but has decreased in incidence since the advent of the *H. influenzae* vaccine. If present, *H. influenzae* is a hallmark of bacteremia, and other sources of serious bacterial infection should be considered. Orbital cellulitis can be distinguished from periorbital cellulitis by the presence of proptosis, impaired pupillary muscle response, decreased visual acuity, and pain with extraocular movements. The distinction can be made definitively with a CT scan of the orbits. Both are predominantly seen in children and are frequently associated with sinus infections. In the case presented here, the patient should probably be treated with a broad-spectrum antistaphylococcal antibiotic for bacterial infection. Spontaneous angioedema of the eyes and mouth can develop from a hereditary deficiency of C1 complement inhibitor. Without this inhibitor, the complement system activates more easily and inappropriately. Angioedema can manifest as redness and swelling, but it is not usually tender or associated with a fever, and it is often bilateral. The patient in this question might have touched a plant that secretes a noxious oil, such as poison ivy. If she then rubbed her eye, a contact dermatitis could have developed around the eye that is difficult to distinguish from periorbital cellulitis.

223. The answer is D, Tamsulosin 0.4 mg orally.

(Singh, 552-563; Tintinalli, 655-656)

The use of alpha-antagonists and calcium-channel blockers has been recently studied in the treatment of moderately sized ureteral calculi. One meta-analysis reported a reduction in the mean number of days to stone expulsion by using either medication. The reason these medications work seems to stem from their action on the ureteral smooth muscle contractions, decreasing peristalsis of the ureter. Tamsulosin was the most commonly studied alpha-antagonist. Nifedipine was the calcium-channel blocker studied. Currently, there are no good studies evaluating beta-blockers and other calcium-channel blockers. Both medications were well tolerated with few side effects. Antibiotics have no role in improving expulsion and are used only if the urine is infected. Cyclobenzaprine is a muscle relaxant, but it does not help with expulsion of renal stones.

224. The answer is A, Clozapine.

(Marx, 2043-2044; Wolfson, 1501-1503)

The patient in this question is having a dystonic reaction. Dystonic and akathetic reactions are most commonly associated with antiemetic and antipsychotic medications. Of the medications listed, clozapine, an antipsychotic medication, is known to cause both dystonic and akathetic reactions. Dystonic reactions involve muscular contortions, which can induce both physical and psychological discomfort. Any muscle group can be affected, but the more common locations include the neck (torticollis, retrocollis, anterocollis), eyelids (blepharospasm), and the lower jaw, mandible, and tongue (mandibular or lingual dystonia). Dystonic reactions are believed to be linked to alterations in neurotransmitter function (in particular dopamine and acetylcholine) in the basal ganglia. Akathisia is a condition that involves a component of restlessness as well as mental unrest and agitation. Both of these conditions can occur acutely after a single dose of a drug, as well as with chronic use. Treatment of either of these reactions involves use of an antimuscarinic agent such as diphenhydramine or benztropine mesylate. Intravenous administration is preferred because it is more reliable and allows rapid onset, but intramuscular and oral routes are acceptable. Typical resolution of symptoms occurs within about 2 minutes. For patients on chronic outpatient therapy, the agents should be discontinued. Sumatriptan and tramadol have all been implicated in the development of serotonin syndrome, a potentially life-threatening condition characterized by an excess of serotonin. It produces a hyperadrenergic state (fever, sweating, tremors, agitation) as well as myoclonus, hyperreflexia, and altered mental status. Ephedrine, which is currently banned in the United States, can cause sympathomimetic symptoms such as tachycardia, hypertension, and fever. The effects of ephedrine can be difficult to distinguish from serotonin syndrome.

225. The answer is C, Normal or nonspecific genital findings.

(Marx, 796-798; Roberts, 1080-1081)

One study has demonstrated that most children display normal or nonspecific genital findings despite known sexual abuse. Genital findings believed to signify evidence of sexual assault include areas of hymenal absence when the child is examined in the knee-chest position, hymenal transection, and anal lacerations. Findings suspicious for assault include less than 1 mm narrow hymen, acute abrasions or lacerations of the labia or vagina, or more than 15 mm anal dilatation without stool in the vault. Nonspecific findings include redness, increased vascularity, and labial adhesions. Some other medical conditions can mimic findings of sexual abuse. Urethral prolapse can present as a painful, erythematous swelling in the perineal region. Lichen sclerosus et atrophicus can affect prepubertal children, manifesting as perianal or perihymenal atrophic skin, which can display blisters, petechiae, or, alternatively, hypopigmentation. The report of sexual assault history remains a primary indicator of assault and should merit an investigation by a sexual assault expert.

226. The answer is A, Administer albuterol.

(Tintinalli, 476-479; Wenzel, 2125-2130)

Patients like the one in this question most commonly have acute bronchitis and will benefit from the symptom relief provided by albuterol. Acute bronchitis is caused by inflammation of the large and medium airways as a result of bacterial or viral infection. Bacteria are implicated in a small minority of cases. The symptoms are similar to pneumonia or upper respiratory tract infection, but cough predominates and can last for months. Antibiotics and steroids are generally not indicated for healthy adults; however, they might be useful in acute exacerbations of chronic bronchitis. Although many clinicians use antibiotics in the treatment of acute bronchitis in smokers, there is little evidence to support the practice. Arterial blood gas analysis is not helpful in uncomplicated acute bronchitis when the patient has no signs of other illness.

227. **The answer is B, *Pseudomonas aeruginosa.***

(Laughlin, 126-128; Marx, 712; Wolfson, 155)

Pseudomonas aeruginosa causes approximately 90% of cases of osteomyelitis of the foot due to puncture wounds. Patients often sustain the injury through a shoe; tennis shoes most frequently provide the suitable environment for the organism to grow. *Staphylococcus aureus* is the second most common pathogen in this injury and resulting infection. *Clostridium perfringens* infection is a common cause of gas gangrene, or myonecrosis, and can cause food poisoning, but it is not a common cause of osteomyelitis from puncture wounds of the foot. *Streptococcus pyogenes* causes pharyngitis, cellulitis, and in some cases necrotizing fasciitis. *P. aeruginosa* osteomyelitis of the foot is treated with intravenous antipseudomonal antibiotics.

228. **The answer is C, 65-year-old woman with new-onset seizure but no focal neurologic findings.**

(American College of Emergency Physicians [headache], 407-436; Tintinalli, 403, 1118-1119, 1129-1130, 1155, 1699)

Emergent neuroimaging is required for those patients who have a time-dependent and treatable condition and who require a diagnosis in the emergency department. Other patients who require emergent neuroimaging include those with headache accompanied by focal neurologic signs, acute mental status change, or altered cognitive function. New-onset seizures, especially in older patients, are an indication for emergent neuroimaging. Urgent neuroimaging is suggested for patients who might have an acute intracranial pathology but have normal neurologic examinations; outpatient imaging is acceptable, or it can be done in the emergency department if convenient or if close followup cannot be assured. This is especially true of patients older than 50 with new headaches. Patients with pre-eclampsia or eclampsia require management of hypertension; they do not require emergent neuroimaging. Neuroimaging is often performed for evaluation of syncope and near syncope. The yield is extremely low unless there are new neurologic signs. Healthy young adults without focal neurologic findings who have tension-type headaches do not require emergent or urgent neuroimaging.

229. **The answer is B, Begin intravenous antibiotics and arrange for surgical drainage.**

(Marx, 1236-1239; Tintinalli, 536-539)

This patient has developed a retroperitoneal abscess requiring intravenous antibiotics and surgical drainage. Abscess and fistula formation occur in 20% to 30% of patients with Crohn disease. Retroperitoneal abscessess do not present with the classic signs of focal tenderness overlying a palpable mass. Patients instead present with diffuse mild abdominal pain and focal hip or low back pain that worsens with ambulation, and often fever. Abdominal

CT is the imaging modality of choice. Definitive treatment includes open surgical drainage or interventional radiology-guided percutaneous drainage. Other common gastointestinal complications of Crohn disease are obstruction, intraperitoneal and extraperitoneal fistula, and toxic megacolon. Recurrence rates are extremely high, even for those requiring surgical intervention. Steroids are first-line treatment of acute exacerbations of gastrointestinal symptoms but can cause further complications in a patient with an acute infectious abscess. Bowel decompression is not indicated.

230. The answer is C, Echocardiography.

(Fleisher, 690-699; Marx, 2151-2152)

The presentation of heart failure in pediatric patients is similar to that of adult patients, but children do not present with distended neck veins or peripheral edema as often. For the patient in this question, the best initial test is an echocardiogram, which can be done at the bedside. The echocardiogram yields the most information about the underlying clinical abnormality and allows the patient to remain in the emergency department for close monitoring. Chest radiography has not been shown to be reliable for the interpretation of cardiomegaly and does not provide specific anatomic information. Although MRI has become an exceptional diagnostic test to elucidate cardiac abnormalities, it is not as readily available or fast as bedside echocardiography. The causes of cardiac failure in this age group are often related to large ventricular septal defects or other congenital anomalies that cause a left-to-right shunt. Immediate care consists of supporting the airway, breathing, and circulation, which includes elevating the head and chest, adding diuretics or morphine for the pulmonary edema, and adding inotropic support, with consideration given to decreasing afterload.

231. The answer is C, Percutaneous coronary intervention is the treatment of choice.

(James, 1564-1571; Marx, 2302-2303)

Percutaneous coronary intervention is the treatment of choice for acute MI (AMI) in pregnancy despite the risk of radiation exposure to the fetus. Coronary artery disease is rare in pregnant women, with a higher risk in patients with advanced maternal age, hypertension, diabetes, and tobacco use. Pregnancy increases the risk of MI by 3- to 4-fold. Pregnancy-associated AMI peaks during the third trimester and peripartum period. The risk of death is higher during the intrapartum period because of the high cardiac output during labor and delivery. Up to 29% of pregnant women with AMI have normal coronary arteries. Pregnancy is a relative contraindication for thrombolytic therapy, although neither tPA nor streptokinase crosses the placenta. Thrombolytic therapy has been associated with maternal hemorrhage and death, placental abruption, preterm delivery, fetal death, and fetal intracranial hemorrhage. Although low-molecular-weight heparin is safe in pregnancy, unfractionated heparin is the preferred anticoagulant during the third trimester: its infusion can be stopped quickly, and it has a more predictable reversal response to protamine sulfate if labor begins.

232. The answer is D, Target lesion presence.

(Marx, 1543-1544; Wolfson, 825)

Erythema multiforme (EM) is a cutaneous reaction to a variety of antigenic stimuli, and target lesions are characteristic. The lesion has a target appearance because it has three zones of color. The center, often a dark papule or vesicle, is surrounded by an area of blanching that itself is surrounded by a halo of erythema. The rash also is typically symmetrical, involves both the palms and soles, and as the name implies, has a variety of erythematous forms, including macular, papular, vesicular, and bullous. The degree of mucosal involvement, if any, distinguishes milder forms of EM from the more severe forms. The most common precipitating factors of EM include certain drug exposures (penicillin, phenytoin, sulfonamides) and herpes simplex virus (HSV). Other less common precipitants include a variety of fungal and viral infections. When the etiology cannot be determined, the condition is classified as idiopathic, although HSV might be responsible. Stevens-Johnson syndrome is a severe form of EM that is indistinguishable from toxic epidermal necrolysis and is often precipitated by a drug exposure. Fortunately, most individuals with EM spontaneously recover. Any potential drug precipitant should be identified and stopped. Recurrent EM, if precipitated by HSV, can be prevented with use of anti-HSV medications. Admission, aggressive supportive care, and consideration of steroids (controversial) are required for severe forms of EM.

233. The answer is C, Sarcoidosis.

(Marx, 1068, 1625; Statement on sarcoidosis, 736-755; Tintinalli, 490)

This patient has sarcoidosis. The triad of erythema nodosum, bilateral hilar adenopathy, and arthralgia, as seen in this patient, is called Löfgren syndrome and is typically associated with a good prognosis. Sarcoidosis is a chronic systemic inflammatory disease characterized by diffuse noncaseating granulomas of unknown etiology. It commonly presents with clinical manifestations of the pulmonary (90%) and lymphatic (33%) systems, although it can affect multiple organ systems. Other clinically relevant manifestations include uveitis, cardiac conduction blocks, anemia, and hypercalcemia. Death is most commonly secondary to cardiopulmonary involvement, including hypoxic respiratory failure and cor pulmonale from extensive pulmonary fibrosis. Laboratory findings can include leukocytosis, elevated ESR, elevated ACE levels (75% of cases), and hypercalcemia. Definitive diagnosis is made using biopsy. Differentiating sarcoidosis from lymphoma is challenging and often requires multiple biopsies given their very similar presentations.

However, erythema nodosum is less common in lymphoma. Other causes to exclude include infections such as coccidioidomycosis, in which 25% of cases present as valley fever with a classic triad of fever, erythema nodosum, and arthralgia. Transmission usually is through inhalation of arthrospores and rarely systemic. Radiographs might demonstrate findings that tend to be unilateral, such as hilar adenopathy, infiltrate, or pulmonary nodules. Tuberculosis is also a granulomatous disease but is caseating and not as strongly associated with arthralgias or erythema nodosum. Of note, skin anergy with PPD is common in patients with sarcoidosis.

234. The answer is D, Start oral trimethoprim-sulfamethoxazole with routine local wound care.

(Liu, 1-38; Marx, 753, 1837; Moran, 666-674)

This patient likely has an abscess with surrounding cellulitis from MRSA infection rather than a spider bite. Complicated abscesses and cellulitis can be managed with oral trimethoprim-sulfamethoxazole or clindamycin and close followup care. For more severe infections or when close observation is not possible, admission for intravenous vancomycin treatment is indicated. Simple abscesses, even those caused by MRSA, can be adequately treated with incision and drainage alone. Many patients with MRSA skin infections assume that they have been bitten by spiders. In fact, in a multivariate logistic regression analysis of 422 patients with MRSA skin infection, the three historical factors most strongly associated with positive cultures for MRSA were close contact with a person with a similar infection, history of MRSA infection, and reported spider bite. A history of incarceration or participation on a sports team is considered a risk factor for MRSA infections as well. The ulcerating, progressive abscess common in MRSA skin infections can resemble the necrotic, volcanic ulcer caused by the bite of the brown recluse spider (*Loxosceles reclusa*). But skin infections with MRSA are far more common than brown recluse spider bites and tend to be associated with multiple small furuncles near the main lesion, whereas a brown recluse spider bite is almost always solitary. True brown recluse spider bites pose a management challenge. There are several suggested regimens available, but immediate wide surgical excision is not recommended. Routine wound care with close followup care is a reasonable initial approach. Dapsone has been shown to reduce systemic symptoms of the bite and limit the size of the lesion at the bite location. An antivenin for *Loxosceles* is produced in Brazil but is not available in the United States.

235. The answer is C, Gestational sac.

(Ma, 295-298; Tintinalli, 690-694)

The earliest sign of pregnancy detected using ultrasonography is the gestational sac. It can be detected with the transvaginal approach at 4 to 5 weeks and by 6 weeks using the transabdominal view. The gestational sac is a fluid-filled structure containing the developing embryo. It is a discrete hypoechoic structure located within the uterine cavity. The next finding is referred to as the double decidual sac sign. This is a useful sign to help distinguish between early intrauterine pregnancy and pseudogestational sac. It appears as two distinct hyperechoic areas consisting of the lining of the uterus (decidua vera) and the lining of the gestational sac (decidua capsularis). The yolk sac appears after the double decidual sac sign as a small hyperechoic ring within the gestational sac. The fetal pole can be seen adjacent to the yolk sac at 6 weeks. The yolk sac functions as the circulatory system until the heart becomes functional. Finally, cardiac activity is seen also at about 6 weeks. If no intrauterine structures are noted, the ultrasound examination should be repeated in 1 week. If the patient is having abdominal pain, ectopic pregnancy should be considered.

236. The answer is B, Clostridial myonecrosis is most commonly caused by wound contamination.

(Cainzos, 433-439; Marx, 1845-1847) .

Clostridial myonecrosis most commonly occurs from contaminated postsurgical or traumatic wounds. It does not affect healthy tissue, but rather is a superinfection of already infected or traumatized tissue. Clostridial myonecrosis is commonly referred to as gas gangrene and spreads in tissues through intrafascial planes. This type of infection (monomicrobial) accounts for only 20% of necrotizing soft tissue infections. Other common pathogens include group A streptococci and anaerobic staphylococci. Type I infections (polymicrobial) are more common and account for up to 80% of necrotizing soft tissue infections. Both aerobic and anaerobic organisms are present. Broad-spectrum antibiotics are indicated as soon as the diagnosis is suspected and might include monotherapy with imipenem-cilastatin, meropenem, ertapenem, or piperacillin-tazobactam. Empiric treatment must include coverage for gram-positive, gram-negative, and anaerobic organisms. Other organisms to consider, which might require a change in antibiotic choice, include *Clostridium, Pseudomonas,* and MRSA. Because of the high morbidity and mortality rates associated with these infections, early recognition is essential so that the definitive treatment with excision and surgical debridement can be arranged. Disease can progress rapidly; deep tissue necrosis can spread with minimal superficial changes in appearance. A good history is crucial. Pain out of proportion to clinical findings is common. Crepitus and gas noted on imaging (plain radiography, CT, ultrasonography) are late findings and thus not helpful in detecting the disease early.

237. The answer is A, Acquiescence to invasive diagnostic testing.

(Adams, 2070-2071; Tintinalli, 1951; Wolfson, 814-815)

Somatization is the process by which a patient's psychological issues manifest as physical symptoms. Such patients are chronically and persistently sick, with vague and multiple symptoms (the entire review of systems might be positive) and a very strong conviction that they are sick. They will generally acquiesce to invasive diagnostic tests because they are convinced that there is a medical cause of their symptoms. In contrast, patients with deliberate factitious disorders or malingering feign significant disability for secondary gain. They are more likely to have an antisocial personality, to be involved in a lawsuit against someone else, and because they do not really have anything significantly wrong, are more likely to be noncompliant. Malingering is specifically associated with a clear, definable goal, and the symptoms usually resolve when the goal is achieved. Munchausen syndrome, a form of factitious disorder, is a specific diagnosis reserved for "chronic or career medical imposters," some of who have undergone a variety of painful procedures or diagnostic tests. In Munchausen syndrome, the symptoms are often textbook and out of proportion to physical findings or appearance.

238. The answer is C, Obtain ENT consultation.

(Marx, 2399-2400; Tintinalli, 1594-1595)

In patients with stable conditions who present with complications of a recent tracheostomy, urgent ENT consultation should be obtained before the airway is further manipulated. Tracheostomy tubes are placed into the trachea through an opening called a stoma. If the tracheostomy was performed within 7 days, the layers of the stoma have not had time to mature and might separate if manipulated, creating a false passage when the tracheostomy tube is changed. Often times, tracheostomy tubes are sutured in place for the first week to prevent accidental extubation and help the stoma mature. Suctioning can actually cause trauma and lead to bleeding. Any manipulation of a new tracheostomy can dislodge a clot and lead to a worsening in bleeding. Inflating the cuff might help tamponade bleeding. Tracheostomy tubes are used to facilitate long-term mechanical ventilation or bypass upper airway obstructions. They come in all shapes and sizes and are made of metal or plastic; they often have removable inner cannulas to facilitate cleaning. Tracheostomy tubes can be uncuffed or cuffed. Cuffed tracheostomy tubes are used for mechanical ventilation and prevent air leaks. Tracheostomy tubes can be fenestrated to allow air to pass through the hole in the curvature of the tube to improve speech. If the stoma is mature, tracheostomy tubes can often be easily changed. A mature stoma will not instantly collapse or shrink. Changing a tracheostomy tube can be facilitated by the use of an obturator. An obturator is solid cannula with a blunt end that protrudes for the tube. Tracheal suctioning, which can be facilitated by placing 2 to 3 mL of sterile saline into the tracheal tube, is used to loosen secretions and unblock the tube in a mature tracheostomy.

239. **The answer is C, Delayed primary closure or healing by secondary intention is appropriate.**

(Marx, 739-741; Wolfson, 155, 1650)

Clenched-fist injuries should be presumed to be human bite wounds until proved otherwise. For this reason, these wounds should be treated by delayed primary closure or secondary intention if at all possible to avoid the increased risk of infection with closure. If the wound is gaping, it can be loosely approximated to allow for drainage of secretions. Patients with tendon or joint involvement should be admitted and treated with intravenous antibiotics, and a hand surgeon should be consulted. If the wound is closed, nonabsorbable monofilament sutures should be used. Braided sutures provide an additional nidus for infection, as do absorbable sutures. There is a high incidence of infection in these wounds, so antibiotic prophylaxis is recommended. Amoxicillin-clavulanic acid is the current drug of choice. It covers *Streptococcus, Staphylococcus* (methicillin sensitive), *Pasteurella, Bacteroides,* and *Eikenella,* which can commonly infect bite wounds. *Eikenella* is commonly found in human bite wounds, and *Pasteurella* is more commonly found in cat bite wounds. *Pasteurella* is not commonly found in human bite wounds. First-generation cephalosporins might be used to cover skin flora but they do not provide adequate monotherapy for all typical pathogens in human bite wounds.

240. **The answer is C, Proximal muscle and limb girdle weakness with muscle tenderness and normal reflexes.**

(Marx, 87-92, 1415-1416; Simon, 125-151; Wolfson, 115-121)

Myopathies are diseases of the skeletal muscles. In myositis, patients typically present with muscle pain, which they might also describe as weakness. Weakness of the proximal musculature and hip and shoulder girdles is prominent, and patients classically describe difficulty getting up out of a chair. The degree of weakness is variable. The muscles are often tender to palpation. Reflexes and sensation are normal. Some patients have an associated rash (dermatomyositis) that classically presents as erythema and swelling over the extensor surfaces and around the eyes. The creatine kinase level is elevated, although rhabdomyolysis is uncommon. Management involves corticosteroids and supportive care. Examination of the deep tendon reflexes can be very helpful in determining the level of the lesion. Intermittent weakness that is relieved by rest with normal reflexes and normal sensation is a description of myasthenia gravis, a condition in which the number of functioning acetylcholine receptors within the neuromuscular junction is decreased, resulting in disordered neurotransmission. Symmetrical ascending weakness with decreased or absent reflexes with minimal sensory involvement is a classic description of Guillain-Barré syndrome, an immune-mediated lower motor neuron neuropathy. Tick paralysis might present in a very similar manner. Distal muscle weakness with abnormal sensation and loss of control of the bladder or bowel is a feature of an upper motor neuron neuropathy such as transverse myelitis. Initially, the reflexes are diminished but also typically improve over time.

241. The answer is C, Intussusception.

(Marx, 1184-1188, 2172-2178; Tintinalli, 838-839, 841-843)

Intussusception is the most common cause of small bowel obstruction in the pediatric population. It occurs when a proximal lead point telescopes into a more distal segment of the bowel. In children, the lead point is most commonly caused by inflammation of Peyer patches after a viral infection. Other causes include Henoch-Schönlein purpura (HSP), vasculitis, Meckel diverticulum, cystic fibrosis, and mechanical obstruction. The ileocolic junction is the most common location for childhood intussusception. However, HSP is classically associated with ileoileal intussusception. Less than 5% of intussusception cases occur in adults, and they typically involve the small bowel. Manifestations range from nonspecific indolent abdominal pain to acute partial bowel obstruction. About 90% of adult patients, unlike pediatric patients, develop intussusception as a result of a pathologic lesion and ultimately require surgical exploration. Midgut volvulus is an important etiology of neonatal small bowel obstruction but is less common than intussusception. Malrotation develops from incomplete rotation of the mesentery during embryologic development. Patients classically present within the first month of life with bilious emesis and abdominal distention. Seventy-five percent of neonatal patients with malrotation develop volvulus, with mortality rates of 3% to 15%. Surgical adhesions are the leading cause of small bowel obstruction in adults, accounting for greater than 50% of cases, but are less common in children. Hernias and small bowel masses are also less common etiologies, although single juvenile polyps can prolapse and cause obstipation or painless hematochezia.

242. The answer is B, Echocardiography.

(Marx, 1065-1067; Mattu, 167-170)

The clinical picture and ECG in this question are suggestive of hypertrophic cardiomyopathy. The highest yield diagnostic test to assess the severity of obstruction in suspected hypertrophic cardiomyopathy is echocardiography. The abnormal findings on this ECG include high QRS voltage, early R-wave transition in the anterior leads (both due to thickened ventricular wall myocardium), abnormal T-wave inversions in the anterior leads (due to abnormal repolarization), and deep, narrow Q waves in the lateral leads (due to septal hypertrophy). The pathophysiology of hypertrophic cardiomyopathy is complex and heterogeneous, including left ventricular hypertrophy, diastolic dysfunction, mitral regurgitation, left ventricular outflow obstruction (especially during exertion), and arrhythmias. In some patients, the initial event is sudden death, and other patients can remain asymptomatic throughout life. Increases in heart rate (exertion, beta-agonists) decrease the diastolic filling period, compromising left ventricular filling and worsening function. A classic presentation is that of a young patient who develops syncope associated with exertion. The murmur is a crescendo-decrescendo, midsystolic murmur that decreases in intensity when the patient changes from standing to squatting, a maneuver that increases venous return. Beta-blockers are the most efficacious pharmacologic therapy because they decrease myocardial contractility and heart rate, thereby increasing the diastolic filling period. Computed tomography of the chest does not help evaluate the severity of disease. Exercise stress testing can assess for coronary perfusion defects or exertional dysrhythmia as a potential cause of his symptoms but does not assess the severity of his cardiomyopathy. A Holter monitor might show the presence of dysrhythmias but does not predict sudden death any better than clinical factors.

243. The answer is C, Gamma-hydroxybutyric acid.

(Nelson, 1153; Wolfson, 1405-1407, 1409-1410, 1413, 1521-1522, 1529)

Intermittent bouts of agitation and quick return to coma are unique to GHB (gamma-hydroxybutyric acid) compared with other sedative-hypnotic agents, as is the rapid, full return of consciousness from a comatose state. Use of GHB is illegal in the United States except in the treatment of narcolepsy (brand name Xyrem [sodium oxybate]). Two precursors of GHB, namely 1,4-butanediol (1,4-BD) and gamma-butyrolactone have industrial uses and remain available. When ingested, the precursors are metabolized to GHB, and the presentations are identical. Use of the drugs might induce euphoria, but excessive ingestion is associated with a depressed level of consciousness and coma. Hypothermia and significant bradycardia, typically without hemodynamic compromise, are common. Treatment is supportive; some patients require intubation for airway control. Carisoprodol (marketed in the United States as Soma, Soprodal, Vanadom) is a sedative-hypnotic agent; the active metabolite is the sedative agent meprobamate. It is known to be abused, and excessive use is associated with a characteristic myoclonic encephalopathy (coma with myoclonic jerking movements). Flunitrazepam (Rohypnol) is a potent benzodiazepine often referred to by abusers as a "roofie," and like GHB, has been used in date rape. Neither drug is detected on routine drugs of abuse panels. In excess, like other benzodiazepines and sedative-hypnotic agents, it can certainly induce coma, but rapid return of consciousness is not expected. Additionally, prolonged coma has been described. Ecstasy (MDMA) is a methamphetamine derivative, and its toxicity is associated with a sympathomimetic presentation.

244. **The answer is B, 35-year-old woman with respirations 6/min with blue coloration who is able to talk in one-word sentences.**

(Koenig, 174-183; Marx, 2486-2489; Tintinalli, 27-33; Wolfson, 1667-1670)

The purpose of a triage system is to determine priority of patient care. Most EMS systems in the United States use the START method (Simple Triage and Rapid Treatment), in which patients are color coded according to transport and triage decisions. Red patients are given first priority: they have life-threatening shock or hypoxia but a good chance of survival if stabilized quickly. The red patient in this question is the woman who is cyanotic with respiratory distress. She has a high likelihood of stabilization with intervention. Yellow patients are second in priority: they have injuries that are not yet life threatening, but systemic decline can occur. These patients have an estimated 45- to 60-minute window before they are at immediate risk of decompensation. The woman who has third-degree burns is an example of a yellow patient who could quickly decompensate. Green patients represent nonurgent transports that involve minimal care and are unlikely to decompensate. The man with the amputation is in the green START category, but because he is at risk of losing a limb, he should be given priority in triage over other green patients. Black patients are those who are dead. No effort is made to transport these patients in mass-casualty incidents, as resources are better spent caring for others. The pulseless victim is an example of a black patient, as there is no chance that he can be quickly resuscitated and stabilized.

245. **The answer is B, Retinal detachment.**

(Marx, 864; Tintinalli, 1543-1545)

This case describes a patient with a likely retinal detachment, as suggested by the presence of flashing lights, floaters, and filmy or cloudy vision, leading to decreased visual acuity. Detachments occur by one of three mechanisms. The most common is rhegmatogenous, which is the tearing of the retinal neuronal layer as the vitreous humor contracts centrally in an age-related change. The average age for this vitreous contraction is 55 years. The vitreous humor can contract without tearing the retina, causing floaters, or it can lead to a detachment. Detachments can also occur as a result of trauma or of exudative processes that result in blood or fluid leaking into the vitreous. Severe hypertension, toxemia of pregnancy, and central retinal venous occlusion lead to exudative detachments. Ocular migraines can cause floaters and flashing lights, but they are less likely to cause persistent vision loss and are bilateral. Optic neuritis is inflammation of the optic nerve, which presents with vision loss and severe eye pain with movement. It is not usually associated with floaters. Temporal arteritis is a concern in this patient's age group, and it can present with vision loss and minimal headache symptoms, but a tender temple or decreased temple pulse is expected. Vitreous hemorrhage, most common in patients with diabetes, results in painless vision loss and a cloudy vitreous humor.

246. **The answer is C, Dry, stimulate, and provide warmth.**

(Fleisher, 35-44; Marx, 77-82)

Neonatal resuscitation follows a clear algorithm, which begins with warming, drying, and stimulating the baby and initially clearing all parts of the airway component. If the baby does not have a pulse greater than 100 beats/min, oxygen should be provided. If bradycardia persists or if there is cyanosis, positive-pressure ventilation should be started. If the pulse is below 60 beats/min after this intervention, chest compressions should be started. The C-clamp technique is performed by placing two thumbs on the lower third of the infant's sternum while encircling the rest of the chest and supporting the back with the other fingers. This technique has been shown to provide higher peak systolic and coronary perfusion pressure than the two-finger technique. Compressions are then given using the thumbs, with a rate of 3:1 compressions to respirations. Definitive intravenous access can be obtained using the umbilical vein but is not indicated in this clinical scenario. The Apgar score is an objective measure of five physical signs: heart rate, respirations, muscle tone, reflex irritability, and color. Each category gives 0, 1, or 2 points, respectively, with a maximum score of 10, as follows:
- Heart rate – absent, slow, less than 100 beats/min
- Respirations – absent, slow/irregular, good cry
- Muscle tone – limp, some, good active flexion
- Reflex irritability – none, grimace, cough and sneeze
- Color – blue/pale, blue extremities, pink

The score is applied at 1 and 5 minutes. If the score is greater than 7 at 5 minutes, it can be reassessed every 5 minutes afterward until the baby is 20 minutes old. The scores at 5 minutes and longer have mild predictive value for neurologic status and survival. The calculation of an Apgar score should never delay resuscitation efforts.

247. **The answer is B, Gas in the scrotal wall.**

(Marx, 1845-1846; Santora; Tintinalli, 647, 1020-1021)

Although Fournier gangrene occurs more frequently in men, it can affect women as well. Pain in the urogenital area is a common complaint. Imaging studies, if obtained, show air within the soft tissue planes. Gas in the scrotal wall is the hallmark sign of Fournier gangrene. Other sonographic signs include air in the perineal area, scrotal wall edema, normal testes, and epididymitis. If the patient's condition allows time for imaging, CT scanning is the best option. Elevation of the base of the bladder is seen in an enlarged prostate. Epididymitis produces hyperemia of the testis on the affected side. Patients with compromised immunity (particularly those with diabetes) are affected. Intravenous fluid resuscitation, blood testing for sepsis, antibiotics, and emergent surgical consultation are the mainstays of emergency department treatment. Due to fibrinoid coagulation, a hypoxic environment is created, allowing anaerobic and facultative anaerobic bacteria to thrive. When the diagnosis is uncertain but the examination and other findings are consistent with a necrotizing infection, the patient should be taken to the operating room for exploration.

248. The answer is A, High risk: symptoms occurred while he was taking a prophylactic antiplatelet agent.

(Cucchiara, S27-S39; Wolfson, 761-763)

The patient in this question had a transient ischemic attack (TIA), the development of an acute ischemic neurologic deficit lasting less than 24 hours. A recently proposed change to the definition alters the time frame to less than 1 hour. Transient ischemic attacks that occur in patients while they are taking high-dose antiplatelet agents (325 mg aspirin or dipyridamole) indicate high risk for consequent stroke. Patients who experience TIA symptoms more than three times in a 72-hour period (crescendo TIAs) whose symptoms last longer than 10 minutes and who have symptoms of posterior circulation ischemia (vertebrobasilar system) or symptoms that suggest varied territories are being affected and would raise concern for a cardioembolic etiology are also at high risk. The ABCD score has been validated to predict the risk of future stroke in patients who have presented with a TIA. The score ranges from 0 to 6; patients with scores of 5 or 6 have an 8-fold increase in stroke risk for the immediate 30-day period compared with patients with scores of less than 5. The ABCD scoring system is as follows:

- A – Age 60 years or older, 1 point
- B – Systolic blood pressure greater than 140 mm Hg and/or diastolic blood pressure greater than 90 mm Hg, 1 point
- C – Clinical features of unilateral weakness, 2 points, or speech disturbance without weakness, 1 point
- D – Duration of symptoms 10 to 59 minutes, 1 point, or 60 minutes or longer, 2 points

Patients with TIA symptoms that reflect a deficit in the anterior circulation should undergo carotid Doppler testing to evaluate for stenosis of greater than 50%, as well as CT or magnetic resonance angiography and echocardiogram, if it is indicated. The timing of these studies, whether inpatient, outpatient, or during an observation stay, should be based on the severity of the patient's symptoms, ability to obtain these studies in an expeditious manner, and resources available to the provider. Patients with anterior circulation TIA symptoms and carotid stenosis of greater than 50% should be referred for carotid endarterectomy, which decreases the risk of subsequent stroke.

249. The answer is A, Blood remains fluid up to 36 hours after the injury.

(Marx, 516-517; Roberts, 687-690)

This patient has a subungual hematoma—the presence of blood under the nail, usually from localized trauma. Subungual blood remains liquid enough to be removed using some gentle expression up to 36 hours post injury. Trephination (placing a small hole in the nail to drain the blood underneath) without nail removal is fully adequate for most injuries, including nails with hematoma over essentially 100% of the nail surface. Nail removal is necessary only if there is significant nail bed injury and an unstable fingertip. Subungual hematomas covering more than half of the nail bed have been associated with a 60% chance of nail bed laceration. This increases to 95% if there is an associated distal phalanx fracture. Various studies have shown mixed responses with removal of the nail for full evaluation and treatment of underlying nail bed lacerations, so current recommendations are to remove the nail and repair the nail bed only if there is a broken nail or if the nail edges are disrupted. Although, technically, trephination converts a closed fracture into an open one, there is no significant complication from this, and studies have indicated that antibiotics are not needed. Antibiotics are recommended if there is an open fracture of the phalanx that is not covered by the nail. Anesthesia is not needed to complete this procedure, and relief is immediate.

250. The answer is B, Inhalation anthrax.

(Centers for Disease Control and Prevention [anthrax]; Marx, 2498-2500; Tintinalli, 364)

Inhalation anthrax causes a flulike illness that progresses to respiratory failure. Widened mediastinum is a classic finding on chest radiography, and hilar adenopathy with possible pleural effusions and consolidation are seen using chest CT. Inhalation anthrax infection is caused by *Bacillus anthracis*, a gram-positive spore-forming bacterium, but the disease is caused by the spores rather than by the bacterium. The spores have been found in the hides of sheep, cattle, and horses. Anthrax is uncommon in the United States because of animal vaccination programs but is still seen in sub-Saharan Africa and Middle Eastern countries. Anthrax has been weaponized and used as a bioterrorism agent. In addition to the respiratory tract infection, anthrax also causes cutaneous and gastrointestinal tract infections. Cutaneous anthrax is more commonly seen and appears initially like a vesicle surrounded by edema, followed by formation of an eschar. Antibiotics are given to prevent systemic infection. The mortality rate from inhalational anthrax is 50% to 90%. The initial diagnosis is made based on symptoms of flulike illness, history of potential exposure, and chest radiography or CT with mediastinal widening from adenopathy. The treatment of choice is intravenous ciprofloxacin. Esophageal rupture presents with sharp chest pain, often after vomiting, and the patient's condition can rapidly deteriorate as well. Chest radiography might reveal pleural effusion (left more than right), pneumomediastinum, or subcutaneous emphysema. Fever and sepsis can occur in the setting of mediastinitis, but this is unlikely without a history of vomiting or esophageal instrumentation. Lung cancer presents in a more indolent manner. Signs and symptoms include weight loss, hemoptysis, dyspnea, and chest pain. Lung cancer can cause hilar adenopathy, but a mass would likely be visible in the parenchyma. Pneumonia can present with fever and respiratory distress. A chest radiograph would most likely demonstrate an infiltrate, although pleural effusions and mediastinal lymphadenopathy can be seen as well in patients with pneumonia.

251. The answer is C, Large myocardial contusions can present with hemodynamically significant cardiogenic shock.

(Marx, 399-403; Wolfson, 219)

Myocardial contusion results from a direct blow to the chest, producing cellular damage to the myocardium. In severe cases, myocardial necrosis can occur in a localized area. Patients with large contusions might present with hemodynamically significant cardiogenic shock because a large amount of heart muscle is involved: the muscle can be stunned or undergo cellular death. There is no real gold standard for identifying myocardial contusion. Neither ECGs nor cardiac biomarkers are completely reliable indicators for this disease process. Although most patients with myocardial contusion have external signs of thoracic trauma such as rib fractures, crepitus, subcutaneous emphysema, contusions, and abrasions, it is possible for the contusion to occur from a direct blow to the chest, causing the heart to strike the sternum, without leaving external signs of trauma. Commotio cordis, also called myocardial concussion, leads to a stunning of the myocardium and can cause both fatal and benign dysrhythmias. Few patients with myocardial contusion suffer from complications that require intervention, and there is some controversy as to how aggressive to be in working up all patients with blunt chest trauma for this disorder. Traumatic myocardial contusion can occur from either direct blunt injury of the coronary arteries or severe contusion of the myocardium leading to myocardial necrosis, which is more common than direct injury to the coronary arteries.

252. The answer is A, Altered mental status.

(Marx, 113-117; Tintinalli, 1153-1159)

Altered mental status is the hallmark clinical sign of a generalized seizure disorder. True seizures have a sudden onset, are not associated with emotional provocation, rarely last longer than 2 minutes, and are associated with nonpurposeful movements. Additionally, generalized seizures are followed by an acute state of confusion referred to as the postictal period. The duration of the postictal period is usually proportional to the duration of the seizure itself. Transient altered mental status is also seen with many other disorders, hence the classic syncope-versus-seizure or fit-versus-faint dichotomy. Seizure activity can be confirmed only by EEG, although the history and physical examination findings are highly suggestive of the diagnosis. The differential diagnosis for seizure includes syncope, breath-holding attacks, hyperventilation syndrome, hypoglycemia, alcohol intoxication or withdrawal, movement disorders, and psychiatric disorders. Pseudoseizures are functional disorders that occur most typically in patients who also have a true seizure disorder.

253. The answer is D, Hypokalemia.

(Marx, 1184-1188, 1619-1620; Tintinalli, 541-542, 581-583, 609)

Hypokalemia is a common cause of adynamic (paralytic) small bowel ileus. It affects membrane polarity and smooth muscle activity within the bowel wall. Once serum potassium levels fall below 2.5 mEq/L, peristaltic function is decreased or absent, resulting in dilatation and a functional obstruction or ileus. Symptoms include diffuse abdominal pain and distention leading to an inability to pass stool. Other causes include laparotomy, abdominal trauma, abdominal infection, renal colic, skeletal injury, and medications, particularly narcotics. Abdominal radiograph findings appear similar to those in mechanical small bowel obstruction; however, the entire lower gastrointestinal tract is involved, including the colon. Additionally, air-fluid levels with small bowel dilatation are not as pronounced. Findings of stool and air within the rectal vault suggest adynamic ileus but are not diagnostic and do not rule out a proximal mechanical obstruction. Treatment of ileus is mainly conservative, with intravenous fluids, nasogastric tube placement for gastric decompression, and admission for observation. Underlying causes should be evaluated and treated appropriately. Hypernatremia results from a total body-free water deficit and primarily causes neurologic manifestations. Hypocalcemia primarily affects the neuromuscular and cardiac systems and causes paresthesias, weakness, muscle spasms, tetany, cardiovascular depression, and dysrhythmias. Hypermagnesemia does not generally cause gastrointestinal symptoms; severe toxicity can cause nausea, somnolence, and decreased reflexes. Hypomagnesemia appears clinically similar to hypocalcemia but can cause chronic constipation. Deficits in calcium and potassium often cannot be corrected until magnesium levels are restored.

254. The answer is D, Sensitivity is improved with venous phase CT venography of the lower extremities.

(Stein, 2317-2327; Tintinalli, 430-441)

Computed tomography pulmonary angiography (CTPA) has become the standard radiologic test for diagnosis of pulmonary embolism. Generally, CTPA scanning should be avoided in the low-risk patient (less than 15% probability) if the patient has been screened negative by the PERC rule (Pulmonary Embolism Rule-out Criteria) or has had a negative D-dimer test result. If the patient is low probability with a positive D-dimer test or shows moderate to high pretest probability (more than 15%), then a CTPA should be performed. The PIOPED II investigators found a sensitivity of 83% for detection of pulmonary emboli when they studied 4-, 8-, and 16-slice multidetector CTPA in aggregate. The same study found that multidetector CTPA plus venous phase CT venography of the lower extremities improves sensitivity to approximately 90% for pulmonary embolism, with a specificity of 95%. Causes of a false-negative CTPA result in detecting pulmonary emboli include inadequate contrast opacification of the pulmonary vasculature, inadequate CT scanning equipment to image smaller pulmonary vessels, failure to reconstruct images, and failure to use indirect venography phase. Motion artifact generally produces a false-positive or indeterminate result.

255. The answer is B, Potassium chloride.

(Marx, 1631, 1641-1643; Wolfson, 1007-1008)

Diabetic ketoacidosis (DKA) is characterized by significant deficits in water and various electrolytes, including potassium. The patient in this question has a potassium concentration of 5 mEq/L, which reflects transcellular shifting as a result of acidosis, despite likely severe total body store depletion. As appropriate treatment with intravenous fluids and insulin is initiated, acidosis improvement, potassium excretion, and transcellular potassium shifting can lead to precipitous hypokalemia and predispose to life-threatening dysrhythmias. In patients with DKA who do not have initial significant hyperkalemia and who are not in renal failure (this patient had a normal creatinine and could urinate), potassium administration and monitoring should be done early in the course of treatment. Exogenous glucose (such as in the form of D5 in half normal saline) can be considered later to avoid hypoglycemia from exogenous insulin (generally initiated when the blood glucose level is below 250 mg/dL). The hyponatremia in this patient reflects expected dilution from transcellular water shifting to the intravascular space. Appropriate management of this dilutional hyponatremia is to treat the underlying process, the DKA. Sodium bicarbonate administration has not been demonstrated to be of benefit in DKA and has no role in most patients who have it. Administration of sodium bicarbonate remains controversial even in those with extreme acidemia, which this patient does not have. Although patients with DKA might have phosphate deficits, trials have not demonstrated benefit of administration. Monitoring for severe hypophosphatemia is reasonable, and in those cases (<1 mg/dL) administration is appropriate. Due to coincident potassium depletion in DKA, using potassium phosphate in those situations is appropriate.

256. **The answer is C, Synchronized vesicular eruption with highest concentration on the face and limbs.**

(Marx, 2501-2502; Tintinalli, 50-54)

Smallpox, caused by the variola virus, is a severe febrile illness characterized by a vesicular eruption. These vesicles tend to all be in the same stage of development (synchronized) and begin primarily on the limbs and face. From the limbs, they spread centrally (centrifugal). This character of the rash distinguishes it from chickenpox. In varicella infection (chickenpox), the rash erupts in "crops," so many of the vesicles are in a variety of stages of development, and the rash spreads from the trunk to the limbs (centripetally). Although smallpox was eradicated as a natural disease by 1980, samples of the virus remain in Atlanta and Moscow. It is now apparent that the former Soviet Union produced smallpox as a biologic weapon, and it is not known if all of the stockpile of weapons remains accounted for. Diplopia, blurry vision, difficulty swallowing, and dysarthria associated with a purulent wound on an extremity are symptoms of wound botulism. Botulinum toxin as a biologic weapon has been studied but not used. Large, painful, regional lymphadenopathy with purulent drainage is a description of bubonic plague, a disease that was used as a weapon by Japan in World War II.

257. **The answer is A, Elevate the presenting fetal part.**

(Lin, 269-277; Roberts, 1045; Tintinalli, 708)

Umbilical cord prolapse is a rare obstetric emergency, and prompt delivery of the fetus is required, but the most appropriate initial action is to elevate the presenting fetal part to reduce compression on the cord. To do this, the examiner must leave his or her hand in place in the patient's vagina, even during transport to the operating room. Umbilical cord emergencies require emergent interventions to prevent complications in the fetus because the cord supplies oxygen. Long cord length increases the risk for cord emergencies (prolapse, knots, nuchal wrapping). The patient can be placed in the knee-chest or deep Trendelenburg position to further relieve compression. Obstetrics should be consulted immediately for cesarean delivery. Before cesarean delivery was routinely available, umbilical cord prolapse was treated with cord reduction and vaginal delivery. However, there is no current evidence recommending reducing the cord. Emergent bedside cesarean delivery in the emergency department is reserved for a situation in which death of the mother is imminent. Pushing the fetus back can harm both fetus and mother and should not be attempted in the emergency department.

258. **The answer is D, Place a volar splint, prescribe ibuprofen, and follow up with primary care physician.**

(Marx, 1406-1407; Tintinalli, 1162)

Although this patient presents with bilateral symptoms, examination reveals a median mononeuropathy with impingement at the carpal tunnel level, along with visible thenar atrophy (carpal tunnel syndrome). Volar splints (especially used at night) and regularly scheduled NSAIDs are often attempted first for a period of 4 to 6 weeks. Sensory symptoms such as pain, burning, paresthesias, and numbness are most common in carpal tunnel syndrome. Motor symptoms are less common and affect the median intrinsics, weakening thumb opposition and abduction. Both types of symptoms are present in a median nerve distribution (palmar aspect of thumb, index finger, middle finger, and radial half of ring finger). Sometimes patients have poorly localized symptoms extending to the forearm or arm. Exacerbation of symptoms occurs at night and with handshaking, driving, and repetitive activities such as typing or knitting. Diabetes, hypothyroidism, and pregnancy are associated with carpal tunnel syndrome. The symptoms are often reproducible in a median nerve distribution by flexion of the wrist for 1 minute (Phalen sign) and tapping the volar aspect of the wrist crease over the median nerve (Tinel sign). If symptoms fail to improve, then consulting a hand surgeon for corticosteroid injections, nerve conduction studies, and surgical carpal tunnel release is recommended. Although this patient would benefit from better control of blood glucose level, diabetic neuropathy (for which carbamazepine is sometimes prescribed) is not the etiology of her hand pain. It often presents in a classic stocking-and-glove distribution, a bilateral, symmetrical sensory loss in hands and feet, and with loss of deep tendon reflexes and vibratory sense. Injecting a corticosteroid into the carpal tunnel is not recommended in the emergency department because of the risks of direct injection into the median nerve, which can cause significant complications by permanent loss of motor and sensory median nerve function. It should be performed by experienced and credentialed providers such as orthopedists and hand surgeons. Magnetic resonance imaging has good sensitivity but poor specificity for diagnosis. It would be appropriate in a patient with symptoms suggestive of carpal tunnel syndrome with normal nerve conduction studies.

259. **The answer is C, Loss of rational thinking as a result of psychosis.**

(Adams, 2060-2061; Tintinalli, 1944-1945; Wolfson, 804-805)

The SAD PERSONS scale is a screening tool to help assess depression and suicide risk. One of the 10 factors is rational thinking loss, as would be a concern in a person with psychosis. Frankly psychotic patients and those who have previously attempted suicide are at greater risk, as are persons under psychiatric care, those who use alcohol excessively, and those who lack social support. Men are more likely to commit suicide than are women, with those older than 45 years being at greatest risk. Other persons who are at greater risk are those who are widowed, divorced, or separated, and those who describe themselves as feeling hopeless, helpless, or exhausted. Individuals who are capable of rational thinking are less likely to kill themselves, but those who have made significant suicide attempts before, have a well-thought-out and organized plan, or say that they will try again score higher on the SAD PERSONS scale and are therefore at increased risk.

260. The answer is D, Undressing the infant completely.

(Fleisher, 203-205; Strange, 91-95; Wolfson, 1137-1139)

The physical examination of a completely undressed infant has been shown to yield information leading to a diagnosis in over half of infants who present with acute, unexplained, excessive crying. There are many causes of excessive crying that range in severity from benign to life threatening. Admittedly, there are numerous instances in which excessive crying spontaneously resolves and the etiologies are never definitively identified. When the crying persists and an etiology can (eventually) be found, the physical examination seems to be the most helpful part of the evaluation. The examination should specifically cover signs of injury (including nonaccidental), hair tourniquets, signs of infection (rash, umphoelitis), signs of cardiovascular distress, testicular torsion, and intussusception. This is particularly true when, as in this case, the histories of these conditions are similar. Supraventricular tachycardia is a recognized cause of excessive crying and can be identified on a cardiac monitor. Urinary tract infections are one cause of excessive crying but can present with fever. Corneal abrasions are a cause of crying; fluorescein staining reveals the diagnosis, but corneal abrasion is the cause of excessive crying in only a small minority of afebrile infants.

261. The answer is C, Provide calm reassurance.

(Marx, 124-131; Tintinalli, 112, 962-967)

The patient in this question is most likely suffering from hyperventilation based on her symptoms and is best treated with calm reassurance to slow her breathing. Some have advocated breathing into a paper bag or into a nonrebreather mask (not connected to an oxygen source) to allow the patient to rebreathe the exhaled carbon dioxide. However, this approach can lead to hypoxia or hypercarbia. Hyperventilation occurs when a patient's minute ventilation increases, leading to a decrease in $PaCO_2$ and respiratory alkalosis. Attacks are often triggered by stress or anxiety. As the pH falls, changes in the nervous system and cerebral blood flow occur, leading to paresthesias, vision changes, and even syncope. Administering supplemental oxygen can lead to a lower $PaCO_2$ and worsening symptoms. The diagnosis of hyperventilation is one of exclusion, and other more serious pathologies must be ruled out. Aspirin toxicity is a more serious cause of hyperventilation and respiratory alkalosis. Acetaminophen does not cause changes in respiratory rate as might be seen with salicylate toxicity. Cardiac problems can certainly lead to dyspnea and syncope, but emergent echocardiography is not the first step in the workup. Cardiac auscultation for a murmur, an ECG, and chest radiography would be important first steps.

262. The answer is B, Placement of a nasogastric tube.

(Eren, 467-477; Marx, 398-399; Shah, 1444-1449)

Blunt abdominal trauma can result in rupture of the diaphragm. In many cases, this diagnosis can be made initially using chest radiography: visualization of a soft tissue density with gas in the thorax is pathognomonic for rupture of the diaphragm with herniation of abdominal contents into the hemithorax. Other findings that are more subtle include irregularity of the diaphragm, an elevated hemidiaphragm, the presence of inferior atelectasis or pleural effusion, and mediastinal shift without evidence of another cause. If gas is not present in the thorax, placement of a nasogastric tube might be helpful, as it can demonstrate herniation of the stomach into the thorax. There is a high incidence (up to 20%) of false-negative results when using diagnostic peritoneal lavage in suspected diaphragmatic rupture, so it is not recommended. Left-sided ruptures are more common than right-sided ruptures. This is thought to be secondary to the right hemidiaphragm being protected by the liver; also, the left diaphragm is thought to be weaker than the right. Magnetic resonance imaging can be used to diagnose diaphragmatic rupture in patients who are hemodynamically stable, but these injuries can be diagnosed by radiography and CT more easily and expeditiously. Rupture of the diaphragm requires prompt surgical repair because of high morbidity and mortality rates.

263. The answer is C, Oral rehydration and symptomatic outpatient therapy.

(Marx, 176-181; Tintinalli, 531-535)

Diarrhea is very common, and most people experience multiple episodes of it over their lifetimes. Most of these episodes are caused by viral pathogens and are self-limited. In a well-appearing adult, management consists primarily of careful examination to exclude other causes, reassurance, oral rehydration therapy, and consideration of options for symptom relief (such as loperamide) after the patient is discharged. Laboratory tests are of limited value in mild, self-limited cases, except to evaluate the degree of dehydration or to determine whether the patient has metabolic acidosis from tissue hypoperfusion or metabolic alkalosis from profuse diarrhea. If the patient has been taking antibiotics, testing for the *Clostridium difficile* toxin might be useful. Intravenous fluid resuscitation should be reserved for patients who exhibit signs of severe dehydration or are unable to tolerate oral intake. Empiric antibiotic treatment should be started when there is a high clinical suspicion of invasive bacterial illness with systemic symptoms, profuse diarrhea, bloody stools, fever, and abdominal pain and tenderness. The current recommendation for nonpregnant adult patients is a fluoroquinolone, typically ciprofloxacin or levofloxacin for 3 days. Diagnostic imaging studies should be used when there is a concern about a noninfectious etiology for the symptoms or a surgical pathology.

264. The answer is C, Intersphincteric abscess.

(Marx, 1248-1250; Tintinalli, 593-597)

Intersphincteric abscesses are the most common cause of anal fistulae. Obstruction of the anal glands results in polymicrobial infection and abscess formation. With persistent obstruction, an abnormal epithelium-lined tract, or fistula, often develops between the anal canal and the skin. Ulcerative colitis, Crohn disease, rectal infections (chlamydial, for example), and malignancy all increase the risk of fistula formation. However, uncomplicated ischiorectal abscess is still the most common cause of anal fistulae. Patients typically present with pain that occurs when the fistula occludes, resulting in recurrent abscess formation. Prior to abscess formation, patients might report only chronic, blood-tinged, foul drainage from the open fistula. Careful bidigital rectal examination is essential to properly identify the fistula. Anterior fistulae follow a direct route, but a more complicated route to the anal canal often occurs with posterior fistulae. Ultrasound examination and MRI can help confirm the diagnosis and identify more complicated fistulae tracts. Initial management includes antibiotics. Other medications, including infliximab and cyclosporine, are helpful in patients with Crohn disease. However, definitive surgical intervention is often required to prevent sphincter damage and eventual fecal incontinence. The four common types of anorectal abscesses based on anatomic location are perianal, ischiorectal, intersphincteric, and supralevator. Perianal and superficial ischiorectal abscesses in otherwise-healthy adults are often easily managed by the emergency physician. Deeper, more complicated abscesses require surgical evaluation and drainage. Pilonidal cysts, distinctly separate from anal fistulas, develop over the sacrum and coccyx 5 cm from the anus. They are thought to form when ingrown hair causes a localized abscess and reaction, leading to fistula or sinus formation.

265. The answer is D, Up to 10% to 15% of calf vein thrombi result in pulmonary embolism.

(Bates, 268-277; Tintinalli, 430-441)

Most calf vein thrombi break up spontaneously; only 20% to 25% of them actually extend into the proximal veins. If there is extension of a deep calf thrombus into the proximal thigh veins, it usually occurs within a week of presentation. Half of the thrombi that extend to the proximal veins cause pulmonary embolism. The highest risks of deep vein thrombosis (DVT) are associated with major surgery or trauma, prolonged immobilization, malignancy, acquired hypercoagulable states, and prior thromboembolic disease. Suspicion of DVT by symptoms alone may be sufficient to initiate the diagnostic workup of DVT despite a negative physical examination. The physical examination is not perfectly sensitive to detect DVT. The sensitivity of unilateral leg swelling is 35% to 97%; calf tenderness is 56% to 82%, and the constellation of pain, redness, swelling, warmth, and tenderness is present in less than half of patients with confirmed DVT. The Wells criteria are used to assess the risk of DVT. Each criterion is valued at 1 point, with low (0 points), moderate (1-2 points), and high risk ($\geq$3 points) defined as pretest probability of 5%, 33%, and 85%, respectively. If there is an alternative diagnosis as likely or more likely than that of DVT, negative 2 (–2) points are given. The Wells criteria include the following:

- Active cancer
- Paralysis, paresis, or recent plaster immobilization of lower extremities
- Recently bedridden for more than 3 days or major surgery within 4 weeks
- Localized tenderness along the distribution of the deep venous system
- Swelling of the entire leg
- Calf swelling greater than 3 cm (10 cm below the tibial tuberosity)
- Pitting edema confined to the symptomatic leg
- Collateral superficial veins (nonvaricose)

266. The answer is A, Admit to the burn ICU.

(Marx, 1538-1539; Wolff, 173-176; Wolfson, 823)

Toxic epidermal necrolysis (TEN) is a disorder with significant morbidity and mortality rates that requires aggressive inpatient supportive care. The first step is to stop taking the offending agent. Patients are then best served by being treated in a manner similar to that of a major burn victim, including admission to a burn unit, with a high priority on fluid resuscitation and infection control. Toxic epidermal necrolysis usually occurs in adults, and various drugs (anticonvulsants, NSAIDs, penicillins, sulfonamides) are the precipitants in the vast majority of cases. It can be considered a severe form (more body surface involvement) of the otherwise similar Stevens-Johnson syndrome. The pathophysiology of both is not completely understood but is considered a cytotoxic immune reaction. Onset of symptoms after exposure typically occurs within 1 to 3 weeks. Prodromal symptoms consist of arthralgias, fever, malaise, and sore throat, and they often precede any rash presence. When skin lesions begin to occur, there is typically a rapid confluence of the erythematous rash. Mucous membrane involvement is universal. Sheetlike loss of the epidermis and a positive Nikolsky sign (separation of the epidermis from dermis due to a lateral, shearing pressure with a finger) are typical. Treatment with intravenous steroids or intravenous immunoglobulin remains controversial. Early administration might be helpful in certain cases but might also predispose to infections.

267. The answer is C, Renal artery thrombosis.

(Marx, 2365, 2372-2373; Tintinalli, 2006-2008; Venkat, 330-341)

Acute renal artery thrombosis is a serious but potentially treatable surgical complication after renal transplant. Patients can present with oligoanuria, acute kidney failure, and uncontrollable hypertension days to weeks after surgery. Pain might also be present over the graft. In the setting of kidney transplant, acute renal failure (ARF) is defined as a 20% increase from baseline serum creatinine. This differs from the standard 50% increase for nontransplant patients. These symptoms might also be seen in the setting of acute rejection, making them exceedingly difficult to differentiate clinically and without biopsy. It is important to identify renal artery thrombosis early to maximize the likelihood of salvaging the graft. Doppler ultrasonography is the imaging modality of choice. BK-polyoma viral infection can cause ARF from tubulonephritis in 3% to 5% of kidney transplant patients and has been documented in persons with AIDS as well. Its presence has less relevance to the emergency physician, who should still look for correctable etiologies. Chronic rejection develops over 4 to 6 months and is not the explanation for this presentation. Increases in blood pressure, serum creatinine, and proteinuria progress much more slowly. Cyclosporine and tacrolimus are agents frequently used for post–renal transplant immunosuppression. They are known to be nephrotoxic at higher serum levels, which can result from drug interactions. Toxicity should be evaluated by measuring serum drug levels to help differentiate from acute or chronic rejection. Toxic levels commonly cause renal insufficiency and hypertension associated with symptoms of tremor, headache, and gastrointestinal tract disturbances but rarely cause anuria. Urine leak is an uncommon complication of transplant that occurs within the first month with a disruption in the ureter connection. Patients have symptoms of abdominal pain and swelling with fever and can have worsening renal function.

268. The answer is B, Central retinal vein occlusion.

(Marx, 871; Tintinalli, 1545)

The blood-and-thunder appearance of this retina (diffuse hemorrhages and dilated vessels) is consistent with a central retinal vein occlusion. Ischemia of the retina is the result of a lack of blood flow through the engorged vessels. A central retinal artery occlusion, in contrast, results in decreased blood flow into the retina and a pale retina with a normal-colored macula, described as a cherry red macula. Both conditions tend to be rapid onset and unilateral and result in significant vision loss. Hypertensive and diabetic retinopathy are more gradual in onset and occur in both eyes to a similar degree. Vitreous hemorrhage fills the vitreous humor with blood and makes the retina very difficult to see. It can be sudden and unilateral and result in significant vision loss, but the appearance on ophthalmoscopic examination distinguishes it from artery or vein occlusion.

A central retinal vein occlusion occurs in patients with hypertension, hyperlipidemia, or vasculitis and in patients with hypercoagulable states. There is no specific therapy; emergency department management includes administering aspirin and arranging ophthalmologic followup care.

269. The answer is B, Hydrochlorothiazide.

(Geetha; Marx, 916, 2210; Tintinalli, 867-868)

The patient in this question has acute poststreptococcal glomerulonephritis. Although this sequela of streptococcal infection is most common in children 3 to 7 years old, it can also present in adults. Treatment in the early phase is supportive and usually involves restricting salt and water intake. Outpatient management with close followup is adequate. Edema and hypertension are best treated with diuretics, avoiding loop diuretics (furosemide). Other antihypertension medications (lisinopril, metoprolol) are reserved for patients who do not respond to diuretics (malignant hypertension). Patients presenting with pulmonary edema and heart failure require aggressive treatment and hospitalization. There is a latent period of about 2 weeks between the onset of infection and physical findings such as facial swelling (poor renal excretion of fluid), dark urine (hemolysis of red blood cells), and at times, nausea and vomiting.

270. The answer is A, *Borrelia burgdorferi.*

(Marx, 1382-1383; Wolfson, 784-786)

The most common known cause of bilateral peripheral or seventh cranial nerve (the facial nerve) palsy is infection with *Borrelia burgdorferi,* the organism that causes Lyme disease. Patients who present with idiopathic facial nerve paralysis, also known as Bell palsy, should be asked about risk factors for Lyme disease. In particular, patients who present with bilateral peripheral seventh nerve palsy should be evaluated with serologic testing. Human immunodeficiency virus, infectious mononucleosis, and sarcoidosis are other known etiologies of bilateral facial nerve palsy. The most common etiology of Bell palsy, which typically presents with unilateral facial nerve palsy, is herpesvirus. Other etiologies include Lyme disease; other viral etiologies; bacterial etiologies such as *Pseudomonas aeruginosa* (the most common bacteria present in malignant otitis externa); trauma (the facial nerve is the most commonly injured cranial nerve); and tumor (typically a more insidious or relapsing/remitting onset). *Rickettsia rickettsii* is the bacteria known to cause Rocky Mountain spotted fever, which does not commonly cause cranial nerve abnormalities. Patients with Bell palsy typically present with symptoms of complete facial paralysis (which does not spare the forehead). Additional symptoms can include ear pain, hyperacusis (acute and often painful hearing), increased or decreased tearing, decreased sensation in the affected area, and an alteration in taste. Because motor function is impaired in Bell palsy (including the ability to fully close the eye on the affected side, often in conjunction with decreased tearing), patients are at risk for corneal abrasions. They should be evaluated for such and treated with patching and lubrication as needed to prevent abrasions at high-risk times, such as while sleeping. Currently accepted treatments include steroids such as prednisone and antiviral agents for presumptive herpes infection.

271. **The answer is C, No anesthesia is needed for local pain control with full-thickness burns.**

(Marx, 765; Roberts, 712-714; Wolfson, 314)

Escharotomy is the incision into a full-thickness burn on either the torso or an extremity. Full-thickness burns are insensate to pain, so local anesthesia is not needed for incisions. Superficial blood vessels are typically coagulated as well, so bleeding is not usually a concern. Escharotomy typically extends only through the eschar into the subcutaneous fat and is therefore more superficial than a fasciotomy; this limits the associated bleeding as well. Compartment pressures greater than 30 mm Hg indicate a need for decompression, but patients can be symptomatic and have other indications for escharotomy before pressures rise this high. Pulselessness of the involved extremity is a less common finding, even if significant compromise of the tissues exists. Escharotomy is performed by making a longitudinal incision down to the fat through the eschar. Nerves and vessels should be avoided, but the most common mistake is not performing a deep enough incision. Cautery should be considered to reduce bleeding during the procedure.

272. **The answer is B, Lung cancer.**

(Marx, 1507, 1592-1594; Tintinalli, 1509-1512)

Superior vena cava (SVC) syndrome occurs when venous flow in the SVC is obstructed. It is associated with malignancy in more than half of cases, the majority of which are lung cancer. Superior vena cava syndrome occurs from obstruction of blood flow from extrinsic compression of the vessel, intrinsic clot formation, or a combination of both. Increasingly, pacemaker leads and intravascular catheters are leading to thrombosis and SVC syndrome. Symptoms of SVC syndrome include headache, jugular venous distention, and plethora (facial swelling). The diagnosis is made using chest CT. Treatment should be targeted to the underlying cause. For external compression caused by a tumor, treatments targeting the cancer include steroids, radiation, and chemotherapy. Diuretics can be helpful in the setting of cerebral edema. More recently, endovascular shunts and stents have been used to relieve the obstruction. Heparin should be initiated for thrombosis. Goodpasture syndrome is a hypersensitivity autoimmune disease. It is caused by antiglomerular basement antibodies that damage the lungs and kidneys. Symptoms are often gradual but include fatigue, weight loss, and shortness of breath. Patients often do not notice the symptoms until they develop hemoptysis and pulmonary hemorrhage. Although the initial symptoms of Goodpasture syndrome are similar to lung cancer, the condition itself does not cause compression of the SVC. Pregnancy is associated with an increased risk of pulmonary embolism and deep vein thrombosis, which does not obstruct the SVC. Although pneumonia can lead to mediastinal lymphadenopathy, it also does not often cause central venous obstruction.

273.   The answer is A, Admit for 24 hours for serial abdominal examinations.

(Marx, 430-433; Wolfson, 229-231)

When a patient presents after suffering blunt abdominal trauma and has a concerning abdominal examination but a negative workup, decisions about appropriate management can be challenging. In this particular patient, the negative CT scan and FAST results are reassuring in terms of solid organ injury, but there is potential for other serious injuries, such as hollow viscus injury or pancreatic injury. The seatbelt sign (ecchymosis on the abdomen) suggests that the patient could have these injuries, so a period of observation in the hospital is warranted. Discharging the patient without a period of observation either in the hospital or in the emergency department creates the potential for the patient to suffer significant complications from undiagnosed intraabdominal injury. Diagnostic peritoneal lavage would be helpful in this patient if grossly positive but might not otherwise definitively determine the indication for surgical management. The formal abdominal ultrasound examination done in the radiology department is no more accurate than a FAST examination done by an experienced provider for identifying hollow viscus injury or acute pancreatic injury.

274.   The answer is C, Onset with heavy lifting.

(Marx, 204-210; Tintinalli, 1889-1893)

The onset of back pain associated with heavy lifting or any other specific task suggests a mechanical cause, of which the vast majority of episodes are self-limiting. In the evaluation of a patient with back pain, some historical features point toward serious causes. Red flags that are more likely to be associated with a serious underlying pathology include the following: pain that is unrelieved by rest or analgesia; pain that keeps the patient awake at night; pain associated with nausea or diaphoresis; and pain that has a gradual onset. Abnormal vital signs in a patient with back pain are particularly concerning, especially in older patients. Additional red flags that point to significant underlying pathology include age older than 70 and history of cancer, immunosuppression, parenteral drug use, or recent trauma. Broadly, the serious pathologies that can present as back pain include occult fractures, congenital anomalies, tumors, vascular catastrophes, infections of the vertebral disc or spinal cord meninges, and space-occupying lesions within the canal that lead to spinal cord or nerve root compression.

275. The answer is B, Right lower quadrant pain.

(American College of Emergency Physicians [appendicitis], 71-116; Marx, 1194-1197)

According to a January 2010 ACEP Clinical Policy designed to determine which findings can be used to guide clinical decision-making, right lower quadrant abdominal pain significantly increases the pretest probability of acute appendicitis. Classically, the presentation of appendicitis is periumbilical pain that migrates to the right lower quadrant associated with anorexia, fever, elevated WBC count, and tenderness with guarding at McBurney point on examination. Using likelihood ratios (LRs), the symptom of right lower quadrant pain raises the pretest probability of appendicitis more than any other single finding. A positive LR is calculated by dividing the sensitivity of a finding by 1 minus the specificity. A positive LR of 1 has no effect, while an LR of 10 significantly increases the pretest probability. The positive LR of right lower quadrant pain is approximately 8. Anorexia and guarding are neither sensitive nor specific for appendicitis. Fever has a very low sensitivity, and elevated WBC count has a very low specificity. Further calculations reveal that anorexia, guarding, fever, and WBC count greater than 10,000/mcL all have positive LRs between 1 and 3. Therefore, each finding individually has relatively little effect on the pretest probability of appendicitis.

276. The answer is B, Insufficient caloric intake.

(Fleisher, 643-648; Strange, 1115; Wolfson, 1147-1149)

Failure to thrive is a condition in which a patient experiences chronic weight loss or inadequate weight gain. This is often diagnosed before a child is 3 years old and can be related to not only physiologic causes but also psychosocial issues. The most common cause of failure to thrive is insufficient caloric intake (malnutrition). Difficult social circumstances place infants at risk for neglect, particularly with respect to appropriate nutritional intake. With inappropriate priorities, inadequate education, and inadequate resources, a caregiver might not provide adequate caloric intake to an infant. Diluting formula to make it last longer is one example of a cost-saving measure that seemingly inadvertently leads to malnutrition. Clinical clues to issues of neglect in this case include the state of the patient's clothing and signs of poor nutrition, including thin legs, skin folds, and the inability to sit up. These are indicators of dehydration, weight loss, or even muscular atrophy. The maintenance of his head circumference in the scenario of falling or proportional loss of weight and height is a classic example of constitutional growth delay, which can often be reversed with increased nutrition. A trial of adequate nutrition and serial weight measurements will likely confirm this diagnosis. Inborn errors of metabolism can lead to inadequate weight gain and are not typically associated with dysmorphism. However, inborn errors of metabolism are rare compared with malnutrition as a cause of failure to thrive. Intracranial neoplasms can present with inadequate weight gain but are also associated with increased head size in infants. Intestinal atresia usually presents in early infancy with bilious vomiting and rapid deterioration unless emergent surgery is performed. Intestinal atresia is not considered a cause of failure to thrive.

277. The answer is C, Start thrombolytic therapy and unfractionated heparin; obtain thoracic surgery consultation.

(Konstantinides, 2804-2813; Quinlan, 175-183; Tintinalli, 430-441)

This patient has pulmonary embolism (PE) with hypotension. The image shows a large filling defect in the right main pulmonary artery and a filling defect in a distal branch of the left pulmonary artery. Anticoagulation and thrombolytic therapy are indicated in a patient with confirmed PE, a sustained systolic blood pressure of less than 100 mm Hg, and no contraindications to thrombolytic therapy. Thrombolytic agents have been shown to rapidly resolve thromboembolic obstruction and lead to favorable hemodynamic effects in those with hemodynamic instability. Heparin should be discontinued only while the fibrinolytic drug is being infused. Surgical embolectomy can be a lifesaving intervention in a patient with PE when there is arterial hypotension or shock and thrombolysis has failed or is absolutely contraindicated. Getting a thoracic surgery consultation early, if available, is prudent in the management of hemodynamically compromised patients with PE. There is no benefit to giving aspirin in a patient with a pulmonary embolism. Because the patient in the question is hypotensive despite fluid resuscitation, further risk stratification with transthoracic echocardiography and cardiac troponin testing will not add further to the risk assessment of a confirmed PE. Although troponin testing does help in risk assessment of death associated with PE, it does not influence risk stratification or treatment in hemodynamically compromised patients. Anticoagulation and thrombolytic therapy should not be delayed for these patients. For those patients with PE who are hemodynamically stable, thrombolytics are not indicated, as the risk of bleeding probably outweighs any benefits. There are currently no studies that document a significant benefit of thrombolysis in patients with PE and normal blood pressure. In patients with nonmassive PE, a meta-analysis has shown that low-molecular-weight heparin can be used to treat patients with stable conditions who have PE.

278. The answer is C, Oxygen administration will fail to correct the cyanosis.

(Marx, 215-216, 772-773; Wolfson, 1484-1487)

Cyanosis induced by methemoglobinemia cannot be corrected by oxygen administration. Methemoglobinemia is a dyshemoglobinemia in which an oxidant stress converts the ferrous iron moiety in Hgb to the ferric form termed MetHb. Oxidant stresses can be caused by benzocaine, dapsone, metoclopramide, and phenazopyridine (marketed under many brand names, including Azo, Pyridium, Uristat) and substances high in nitrites, such as well water. Sodium nitrite can be used to treat cyanide poisoning and actually induces MetHb, which can then bind cyanide. MetHb is unable to bind oxygen, and additionally there is a shift of the oxygen dissociation curve to the left, so that at a given partial pressure of oxygen, the Hgb more avidly binds the bound oxygen and is less willing to release it. This combination leads to tissue hypoxia. Symptoms are determined by the percentage of methemoglobinemia present, baseline Hgb, and underlying conditions such as coronary artery disease. When MetHb concentrations reach approximately 1.5 g/dL, cyanosis occurs and is not the result of deoxygenated Hgb, which causes cyanosis at approximately 5 g/dL. Unlike cyanosis from deoxygenated Hgb, which can correct with oxygen administration, cyanosis from methemoglobinemia does not correct with oxygen administration. Oxygen should be administered to symptomatic patients, however, to ensure maximum oxygenation. Because cyanosis is determined by Hgb concentration multiplied by the percentage of Hgb that is in the form of MetHb (Hb × % MetHb), in anemia, cyanosis occurs with a higher (not lower) percentage of MetHb. A MetHb level determined by co-oximetry, accurate from either venous or arterial blood, confirms the diagnosis. Clinically significant methemoglobinemia is treated with the antidote methylene blue (a blue drug to treat a blue patient).

279. **The answer is D, Sudden onset of fever, malaise, and cough followed by fulminant pneumonia, hemoptysis, respiratory failure, disseminated intravascular coagulation, circulatory collapse, and death within 24 hours.**

(Marx, 2495-2504; Tintinalli, 43-56; Wolfson, 1667-1670)

Presenting signs and symptoms of the plague include sudden-onset fever, chills, malaise, and nonproductive cough followed by fulminant pneumonia, hemoptysis, respiratory failure, circulatory collapse, and death usually within 24 hours of symptom onset. Treatment options include ciprofloxacin, doxycycline, chloramphenicol, and gentamicin. Called black death in the Middle Ages, plague causes a coagulopathy that results in disseminated intravascular coagulation and acral (extremity) gangrene. There is concern that attacks by terrorist groups using weapons of mass destruction, including biologic agents that cause illnesses such as plague, are imminent. In the event of chemical, biologic, radiologic, nuclear, and explosive (CBRNE) attacks, emergency physicians will likely be the first health care providers to come into contact with victims and might not be aware that an attack has occurred. The military uses the term CBRNE to refer to the different types of agents or weapons that could be used. Of the biologic agents likely to be used in an attack, anthrax, smallpox, and plague seem to be most likely. The most effective way to expose a large population to these agents is through aerosol dispersal, and victims would likely present with vague upper respiratory tract signs and symptoms associated with flulike illness.

Of particular concern would be a large number of patients presenting with flulike symptoms during a season that is not typical for the flu to be common. Typical presenting signs and symptoms of anthrax exposure are flulike illness beginning with malaise, fever, and nonproductive cough with progression to sepsis, shock, hemorrhagic mediastinitis, dyspnea, stridor, and hemorrhagic meningitis. Chest radiographs classically show enlarged hilar nodes. Treatment options include ciprofloxacin, doxycycline, and penicillin G. Of the chemical agents that can be used in an attack, mustard and nerve agents such as sarin, soman, tabun, and VX seem to be the most likely. Victims of chemical attack present with symptoms immediately to only a few hours after exposure, and the larger challenge associated with these exposures is decontamination and treatment. Mustard agent exposure presents as conjunctivitis with skin blisters progressing from second-degree to full-thickness burns, pulmonary irritation progressing to hemorrhagic pulmonary necrosis, followed in 3 to 5 days by bone marrow suppression and death from secondary infection. Treatment is supportive therapy and decontamination. Nerve agent exposure presents with rhinorrhea and miosis followed by increased secretions, wheezing and dyspnea, muscle fasciculations, nausea, and vomiting, which proceeds to apnea, seizures, loss of consciousness, flaccid paralysis, and death. Treatment includes atropine, pralidoxime chloride (2-PAM), and diazepam.

280. The answer is C, *Histoplasma capsulatum*.

(Adams, 1882-1885; Wolfson, 926)

This is a typical presentation of histoplasmosis, an infectious disease caused by the fungus *Histoplasma capsulatum*. It is most common in the Ohio and Mississippi River valleys. The clinical picture is very similar to that caused by *Coccidioides immitis*, a fungus assocated with soil in the southwestern United States. Both diseases are associated with erythema nodosum, an autoimmune reaction resulting in painful red nodules on extensor surfaces, usually the anterior lower leg. Patients with pneumonia from histoplasmosis are very likely to also complain of a headache. *Cryptosporidium parvum* is a protozoan that causes a protracted diarrheal illness. Although it is self-limited in most patients, those with suppressed immune systems (from HIV infection for example), can suffer from it indefinitely. *Cryptococcus neoformans* is a common cause of meningitis in patients with HIV infection. It usually presents with an indolent course, with headache, fever, and altered mental status. Lumbar puncture demonstrates an elevated opening pressure, and the organism can be seen with India ink staining of the CSF. *Mycobacterium tuberculosis* is always a possibility in patients with subacute pulmonary symptoms. This patient does not describe having night sweats, hemoptysis, and weight loss typical of tuberculosis.

281. The answer is B, Intracranial bleeding.

(Kittner, 767-769; Marx, 2286-2289; Tintinalli, 444-445, 697-698)

Severe pre-eclampsia is apparent in a patient with elevated blood pressure, generalized nonpitting edema, and evidence of end-organ involvement such as new headache, blurry vision, thrombocytopenia, and elevated serum transaminase levels. Complications of severe pre-eclampsia stem from vasospasms leading to necrosis and hemorrhage of organs, including intracranial hemorrhage, hepatic and splenic hemorrhage, placental abruption, and death of the fetus. Intracranial hemorrhage can occur in the peripartum period and up to 6 weeks after delivery. A head CT should be obtained if the patient has persistent seizures, altered mental status, localizing neurologic findings, or concerns for an intracranial process. The risk of exposure to ionizing radiation and fetal birth defect is low. All patients with severe pre-eclampsia should undergo emergency obstetric consultation and consideration for hospitalization. Treatment of severe pre-eclampsia is the same as that of pre-eclampsia, with magnesium sulfate, antihypertensive drugs, and delivery of the fetus. In this particular patient, the elevated transaminase levels warrant consideration of HELLP syndrome, but she has normal coagulation studies, and proteinuria and hypertension are more consistent with pre-eclampsia. The HELLP syndrome consists of hemolysis (H), elevated liver enzymes (EL), and low platelets (LP). Cholecystitis and pancreatitis are not complications of severe pre-eclampsia and are unlikely in this patient given that her abdomen is nontender. Placenta previa presents with painless vaginal bleeding and is not a complication of pre-eclampsia.

282. The answer is B, Osteoarthritis.

(Harrington, 389-412; Marx, 1482-1485)

Osteoarthritis is a degenerative joint disease and the most common cause of arthritis in older patients. The most commonly affected joints are the proximal and distal interphalangeal joints, base of the thumb, knees, and cervical and lumbar spine. Patients with osteoarthritis usually complain of pain that is worse after use of the joint. They do not have fever or other signs of systemic toxicity. The joint might be enlarged and warm but typically is not erythematous. First-line treatment is acetaminophen or NSAIDs for pain, or both. There has been no good study showing a better effect with NSAIDs in patients with arthritis pain. Gout is a condition in which sodium urate crystals are deposited into the joint and cause pain, swelling, and restriction of movement. These symptoms are typically acute in onset. The most commonly affected joint is the first metatarsal; this is the initial presentation in almost half of patients. Rheumatoid arthritis is an autoimmune arthritis that produces a symmetric polyarthritis. Patients are most commonly affected in their hands, wrists, and elbows and complain of morning stiffness. Septic arthritis is an acute infection of the synovial space and is an immediate threat to the joint. Patients typically have erythema and warmth and severe restriction of range of motion. Diagnosis is made using arthrocentesis and analysis of the synovial fluid, which typically reveals an elevated synovial WBC count. Typically, WBC counts are greater than 100,000/mcL and mostly PMNs. Osteoarthritis joint fluid typically has less than 2,000/mcL WBCs. Counts in the middle can be the result of either a septic or an inflammatory (gout, rheumatoid) process; these fluid samples should be sent for analysis crystals and Gram stain and culture.

283. The answer is A, Axillary.

(Roberts, 872; Wolfson, 260)

A substantial percentage of patients who have anterior shoulder dislocations have injury to the axillary nerve, although most recover without intervention. The axillary nerve comes off of the superior trunk of the brachial plexus at the level of the axilla, carrying nerve fibers from C5 and C6. The axillary nerve travels with the posterior circumflex humeral artery and vein. It supplies the deltoid, teres minor, and long head of the triceps. It also carries sensory information from the shoulder joint, as well as the skin covering the inferior region of the deltoid muscle. The sensory function of the nerve should be tested over the lateral deltoid—sensory loss in the deltoid region is described as the shoulder badge or regimental badge distribution and can be inconsistent. Unfortunately, testing the motor portion of the axillary nerve can be difficult because of the injury, but the axillary nerve is tested by abducting the arm at the shoulder. The brachial plexus, although less commonly injured, is the next most commonly injured nerve. It is usually injured by a stretch mechanism, and injury to it results in variable deficits. Radial and ulnar injuries can occur but are much less common. Radial motor function is tested by having the patient extend the wrist against resistance; the ulnar nerve is tested by having the patient attempt to pinch a piece of paper between the thumb and index finger. A full motor and sensory examination should be performed after a dislocation, as any nerve can be injured. In anterior dislocations, many of the nerve injuries are neuropraxies, and patients do well.

284. The answer is D, Remove him from the ventilator and allow him to exhale.

(Marx, 23-28, 900-901; Tintinalli, 510)

Breath-stacking or autopeep is a condition that develops in intubated patients who are unable to exhale adequately. This is likely the case in the patient in this question because of his underlying asthma, so the correct action is to take him off of the ventilator and allow for a prolonged expiration. Intubated asthmatic patients can be extremely challenging to manage. Some patients with asthma fail to respond to initial medical therapy, including inhaled beta-agonists and anticholinergics, corticosteroids, and systemic beta-agonists. Controversy exists over adjuvant therapies such as magnesium, heliox, and ketamine. Indications for intubation in asthma include worsening hypercapnia, hypoxia, and acidosis. Mental status changes can be an ominous sign. Once intubated, an asthmatic patient can be difficult to ventilate as a result of the high airway pressures and bronchoconstriction. Exhaling is particularly difficult; as a result of excess residual volume, the next breath is delivered to a partially filled lung. As this occurs repeatedly, the volume and pressure build up in the chest. If the resulting autopeep reaches a critical level, the patient can become hypotensive and hypoxic as a result of increased intrathoracic pressure, leading to decreased venous return. To prolong the expiratory phase, the respiratory rate might need to be slowed. This technique of ventilation is known as permissive hypercapnia: the patient's oxygen saturation is maintained, but the carbon dioxide level is allowed to rise to allow for improved pulmonary mechanics. Asthmatic patients are at risk of pneumothorax; hypotension and hypoxia are signs of tension pneumothorax, as are tracheal deviation, decreased breath sounds on one side, and jugular venous distention. The treatment of tension pneumothorax is needle decompression with a 14-gauge catheter at the second intercostal space just over the rib. This should be done with unilateral symptoms consistent with pneumothorax. Chest radiography might be helpful, but it is not the first action in this critical situation.

285. The answer is D, Urgent outpatient orthopedic referral is required.

(Marx, 570-573; Wolfson, 258-259)

Of all clavicle fractures, about 80% are middle third fractures. Most of these fractures heal well with pain control and immobilization with either a simple sling or a figure-of-eight harness. Healing is usually uneventful, and most middle third clavicle fractures do not require surgery. Urgent orthopedic referral within 72 hours is indicated for patients with displaced or shortened clavicle fractures with greater than 2 cm of displacement secondary to the higher incidence of nonunion, poor cosmesis, and neurovascular compromise. A figure-of-eight harness has not been proved to be superior to a simple sling. It can be preferable for a patient who needs the use of both hands for activities of daily living, but it can cause skin irritation and compression of the axillary neurovascular bundle. Passive range of motion (ROM) exercises of the shoulder should be encouraged immediately after injury, but active ROM should be discouraged for the first month in adults. Unless the fracture is open or markedly displaced and causing neurovascular compromise, emergent orthopedic consultation is rarely necessary in the emergency department for a clavicle fracture.

286. The answer is C, Metabolic acidosis.

(Marx, 124-131; Wolfson, 91-94)

Metabolic acidosis produces a compensatory respiratory alkalosis, which can manifest as dyspnea and tachypnea, and occasionally, respiratory distress. Metabolic alkalosis, in contrast, produces a compensatory respiratory acidosis with hypoventilation. However, hypoxia limits the extent to which hypoventilation and respiratory acidosis can compensate for metabolic alkalosis. Dyspnea, or shortness of breath, is uncomfortable or labored breathing. It is a symptom experienced subjectively by the patient, and the severity might not be related to the severity of the underlying condition. The pathophysiology of dyspnea is thought to relate to a mismatch between signals from the afferent neurons in the lungs, chest wall, and carotid bodies; the efferent neurons to the muscles of the diaphragm and chest wall; and between the respiratory centers of the brain. Individually, hyperglycemia and hyperkalemia are not associated with respiratory symptoms. In diabetic ketoacidosis, metabolic acidosis might be associated with hyperkalemia and hyperglycemia, but it leads to the sensation of dyspnea. This is seen classically as Kussmaul breathing in patients with diabetic ketoacidosis and can occur in other patients with severe metabolic acidosis.

287. The answer is B, Obtain surgery or obstetrics consultation.

(Marx, 1194-1198; Tintinalli, 574-578)

Appendicitis is the most commonly encountered nonobstetric surgical emergency during pregnancy. Among pregnant patients with appendicitis, more than one third of cases result in fetal demise when the diagnosis is not made before rupture. The clinical presentation is often similar to that in a nonpregnant patient, but diagnosis can be delayed if symptoms are inappropriately attributed to the pregnancy. If ultrasound examination does not visualize the appendix, the appropriate action is to obtain a consultation from obstetrics or surgery depending on hospital practice. When readily available, MRI can be used as a second-line diagnostic test. But before ordering a CT scan, the risks of radiation to the fetus, as well as the risk of rupture to the mother and fetus, must be seriously considered and discussed with the patient and consultants. Although the patient requires parenteral antibiotics, admission without surgical and/or obstetric consultation first would further delay management. Likewise, admission to an observation unit for serial abdominal examinations is not appropriate for a pregnant patient who likely requires surgery. Discharge with close followup is appropriate only if clinical suspicion for appendicitis or some other acute abdominal pathology is very low following a brief period of observation in the emergency department.

288. **The answer is D, Chest radiography, ECG, and D-dimer.**

(Kline, 772-780; Konstantinides, 2804-2813; van Belle, 172-179)

In this question, the patient has a low pretest probability of pulmonary embolism (PE) and cardiac disease. Thus, obtaining only an ECG, chest radiograph, and D-dimer measurement is appropriate for the initial diagnostic management. According to the simplified Wells criteria for PE, which have performed well in prospective validation studies, this patient scores only 1.5 points for tachycardia and is considered low enough risk to be safe for D-dimer testing (<4 points). Thus, a negative D-dimer test would be appropriate to rule out PE. Other Wells criteria for PE include the following: clinically suspected deep vein thrombosis (DVT), 3 points; heart rate greater than 100, 1.5 points; surgery/immobilization within 4 weeks, 1.5 points; previous DVT or PE, 1.5 points; hemoptysis, 1 point; malignancy, 1 point; PE most likely diagnosis, 3 points. In this case, obtaining a chest radiograph and/or ECG might not be adequate. According to the PE Rule-out Criteria (PERC), patients who have a low pretest probability of PE (based on Gestalt or use of a decision rule such as the Wells criteria) and absence of any positive PERC are in a group that has a very low probability of PE and require no further diagnostic testing. The PERC rule includes the following: age younger than 50 years; heart rate lower than 10 beats/min; oxygen saturation greater than or equal to 95%; no unilateral leg swelling; no hemoptysis; no recent surgery; no history of venous thromboembolism; and no oral hormone use. This patient should undergo D-dimer testing because she is low risk for PE but positive for one of the PERC (tachycardia).

289. **The answer is A, Administration of an iodinated contrast material is a precipitating factor.**

(Marx, 1663-1666; Wolfson, 1023-1024)

The iodine in iodinated contrast material can precipitate thyroid storm in patients with untreated or poorly controlled thyrotoxicosis. Searching for and treating a precipitating etiology (particularly infectious) is essential to optimize management of thyroid storm. Thyroid storm refers to the extreme manifestations of elevated circulating thyroid hormones; it is a severe form of thyrotoxicosis that can be distinguished by the presence of CNS dysfunction, hyperthermia, and exaggerated tachycardia. The presence of an elevated free T4 level is expected in the vast majority of cases (small minority have T3 toxicosis). Thyroxine-stimulating hormone, released from the pituitary, is in a feedback loop with circulating thyroid hormone and is expected to be extremely low in thyrotoxicosis and thyroid storm. Both general supportive care and specific treatment are required to optimally manage thyroid storm. Supportive care involves intravenous fluid administration to replace potentially significant deficits (caution in patients with heart failure). Specific treatment includes the administration of beta-blockers to counteract peripheral effects (propranolol has the added benefit of inhibiting conversion of T4 to T3). Propylthiouracil (PTU) inhibits synthesis of thyroid hormone and the conversion of T4 to the active T3 (methimazole does only the former). Treatment with PTU should precede (by at least 1 hour) the administration of iodine. Iodine administration, by a feedback loop mechanism, helps to inhibit the release of preformed thyroid hormone. Administration prior to PTU, however, leads to its incorporation into new thyroid hormone. Similar to PTU, corticosteroid (dexamethasone or hydrocortisone) administration inhibits further thyroid hormone release and also inhibits peripheral conversion of T4 to T3. Corticosteroids also can help with coexisting adrenal suppression and have been found to improve survival rates in patients with thyroid storm.

290. The answer is C, Morphine.

(Grissom, 461-465; Hackett, 980-986; Honigman, 587-592; Levine, 1707-1713; Marx, 1917-1928; Tintinalli, 1405-1407)

Narcotic analgesic agents such as morphine impair hypoxic ventilatory response (HVR) and depress the respiratory drive during sleep. In a patient such as the one in the question, whose history of recent ascent to high altitude and pattern of illness indicate acute mountain sickness (AMS), those effects would make the condition worse. Symptomatic treatments of AMS are useful as long as they do not impair acclimatization or initial HVR resulting from exposure to high altitude. Ibuprofen and antiemetic agents are helpful, with prochlorperazine providing the added benefit of stimulating HVR. Numerous studies have demonstrated the effectiveness of acetazolamide in preventing and treating AMS. Although typically reserved for more serious forms of high-altitude illness such as high-altitude cerebral edema, dexamethasone has been shown to improve symptoms among adults suffering from AMS. In mild AMS, stopping further ascent for 1 to 4 days to wait for acclimatization with medical therapy and observation might be appropriate. However, if symptoms do not improve over time, or if the patient develops signs or symptoms concerning for progression to pulmonary or cerebral edema, immediate descent is required.

291. The answer is B, Lateral gaze palsy of the left eye.

(Duong, 137-180, vii; Marx, 1385-1386; Tintinalli, 1575)

This question describes a patient with a cavernous sinus thrombosis (CST) secondary to a dental abscess and a lateral gaze palsy on the ipsilateral side, as the facial pain is an expected finding. Cranial nerves II, III, IV, and VI all run through the cavernous sinus. Cranial nerve VI, the abducens, floats freely within the sinus; the other nerves lie along the lateral walls, so the abducens is the first to be affected. Left-sided ptosis, caused by compression of cranial nerve III, can occur, but it is associated with a mydriatic pupil, not miosis. Ptosis, miosis, and anhidrosis (loss of sweating) are the classic triad indicating a Horner syndrome, or loss of sympathetic inputs to that side of the face. One potential cause of Horner syndrome is a mass in the apex of the lung, referred to as a Pancoast tumor. On the right side, this can also compress the superior vena cava, resulting in facial swelling. Cranial nerve VII does not pass through the cavernous sinus, so facial paresis is not observed in CST. Although cranial nerve II, the optic nerve, lies within the cavernous sinus, blindness and afferent pupil defect are unusual in CST. Papilledema can develop in chronic cases but is not seen in acute cases. Proptosis, chemosis, and eye pain are more common. Chemosis results from occlusion of the ophthalmic vein that drains into the sinus.

292. The answer is D, Initial treatment of an unconjugated (indirect) hyperbilirubinemia is phototherapy.

(Marx, 2168-2171; Strange, 83-89)

Phototherapy is the initial treatment of most neonatal patients who have an unconjugated (indirect) hyperbilirubinemia and require treatment. Emergency physicians should be familiar with the indication for phototherapy because it is commonly prescribed as outpatient therapy. Guidelines for phototherapy have been published and include a graph that can be used to identify infants at low, medium, or high risk for complications of hyperbilirubinemia. The thresholds for greater risk are inversely related to age in hours up to about 5 days. In other words, younger infants have lower thresholds for high risk. Therefore, a 2-day-old infant cannot tolerate a higher bilirubin level than a 5-day-old infant can. ABO incompatibility causes an unconjugated (indirect) hyperbilirubinemia. However, unconjugated (indirect) hyperbilirubinemia is most likely because of the benign causes of physiologic jaundice or breast milk jaundice. It is recommended that infants with breast milk jaundice continue breastfeeding because oral intake increases enterohepatic circulation and, therefore, should decrease the infant's bilirubin levels.

293. The answer is A, Antidepressant.

(Marx, 2200-2201, 2217; Tintinalli, 648-649)

Priapism is an erection due to engorgement of the corpora cavernosa lasting 6 hours or longer. A careful history and examination can lead to clues as to the etiology. Included in the differential diagnosis for priapism are use of medications (selective serotonin reuptake inhibitor antidepressants, antipsychotics, and those for erectile dysfunction), drugs of abuse, and intracavernous injections of certain agents. Antihistamines like diphenhydramine are associated more with impotence or erectile dysfunction. Other causes are direct trauma to the penis, spinal cord injury, sickle cell disease, thalassemia, leukemia, and Peyronie disease. Peyronie disease (penile fibromatosis involving the corpus cavernosum) is a chronic progressive disorder and is unlikely to present as described in the question. Compulsive sexual arousal would cause an erection, but when manual arousal ceases, the penis should not remain erect. Treatment of priapism is the same regardless of the cause. Initial management includes intravenous hydration, pain medication, and oxygen. A dorsal penile nerve block with lidocaine 1% without epinephrine can be helpful in pain control. Aspiration of the cavernosa and irrigation with saline containing alpha$_1$-adrenergic agonists can be effective if done within the first hour. Parenteral vasodilators might also be helpful.

294. The answer is B, Nimodipine should be started to prevent cerebral ischemia.

(Edlow, 237-250; Tintinalli, 1118-1121, 1129)

The CT image of the head in this question reveals diffuse hyperdense subarachnoid blood surrounding the basal cisterns and extending into the sylvian fissures bilaterally. This finding, in conjunction with the history, is consistent with a diagnosis of subarachnoid hemorrhage (SAH). Vasospasm is a major complication following SAH and can lead to cerebral infarction. Nimodipine 60 mg given orally every 6 hours improves outcomes and reduces the incidence of vasospasm. Up to 20% of patients have a seizure during or soon after SAH. Elevations in intracranial pressure can occur during a seizure; this can result in rebleeding, a major complication in SAH. Prophylactic phenytoin loading is controversial but is clearly indicated in patients who have a postevent seizure to prevent future seizures. Sedation is indicated for agitated patients, as are antiemetic agents to prevent nausea and vomiting. Although the target blood pressure for patients with SAH remains controversial, lowering blood pressure is associated with a lower risk of rebleeding. Nitroprusside should be avoided because of its tendency to increase intracranial pressure. Labetalol, nicardipine, and esmolol are commonly used intravenous agents. Lumbar puncture is not required if a noncontrast CT scan shows SAH. Lumbar puncture is recommended for patients with suspected SAH after a negative noncontrast head CT. Studies using third-generation scanners demonstrate sensitivities in the range of 90% to 98% within the first 24 hours; therefore, a CT scan alone will miss some subarachnoid bleeds. Regardless of the indication for anticoagulation, reversal of anticoagulation is recommended in patients with intracranial bleeding because the risk of death from this is much higher than the risk of thrombosis in the acute setting.

295. The answer is C, Pass a guidewire into the balloon port.

(Roberts, 1024-1026; Tintinalli, 659)

The most common cause of a nondeflating balloon on a catheter is trouble with the flap valve. A thin angiographic or central venous catheter can be inserted into the balloon port lumen to clear the flaplike defect in the canal. This procedure is effective and unlikely to result in balloon fragmentation. Cutting the inflation port might allow the balloon to deflate, but this is a less common site of obstruction. Another method to consider is instilling 50 to 100 mL of saline solution into the balloon, thereby increasing its size, which allows the balloon to be punctured using a suprapubic approach. Ultrasound guidance is very helpful in this approach. The thin needle may be passed suprapubically, transvaginally, transperineally, or transrectally. It is rare for fragmentation to occur with this method. Injection of a caustic material such as toluene, ether, acetone, or mineral oil ruptures the balloon but can allow it to fragment, requiring subsequent cystoscopic inspection of the bladder; this also can lead to a chemical cystitis. Overinflation of the balloon by injecting up to 200 mL of fluid or air is often successful but leads to balloon fragmentation as well.

296. The answer is A, Azithromycin.

(Fine, 243-250; Mandell, S27-S72; Tintinalli, 479-491)

The treatment of community-acquired pneumonia (CAP) should be targeted at the likely causative organisms. The most common cause of CAP is infection with *Streptococcus pneumoniae,* but coverage should include atypical pathogens, especially *Mycoplasma pneumoniae.* Azithromycin is an excellent choice because of its high oral bioavailability, efficacy against typical and atypical pathogens, and ease of administration. Doxycycline is a good choice for the same reasons, but it has to be taken twice a day and for a longer course, so patient compliance is decreased. Ceftriaxone has excellent coverage for typical pathogens but little activity against atypical pathogens. Ceftriaxone is available only intravenously, limiting its role in outpatient therapy. It is an excellent choice for inpatient management of CAP when combined with a macrolide. A respiratory fluoroquinolone like levofloxacin can also be used as single agent; however, ciprofloxacin specifically does not provide good coverage for *S. pneumoniae.* Penicillin does not provide coverage against atypical pathogens, and *S. pneumoniae* resistance is a problem as well. Vancomycin is not absorbed orally and mainly has activity against *Staphylococcus aureus.* Severity of illness scores such as the CURB-65 criteria or the pneumonia severity index can be used to help identify patients at low risk for complications who can be safely treated as outpatients. The CURB-65 acronym stands for confusion, uremia (BUN >19), respiratory rate greater than 30, blood pressure less than 90 systolic or less than 60 mm Hg diastolic, and age older than 65 years. Patients with three or more CURB-65 risk factors should be considered for ICU admission; those with two risk factors should be admitted, and those with zero or one risk factor may be considered for outpatient therapy. The pneumonia severity index or PORT score is a two-step process in which patients are assigned to a risk class between I and V. Patients in lower risk groups who are candidates for outpatient management include the following: age younger than 50 years; no significant comorbidities (cancer, heart failure, stroke, renal, liver); normal mental status; pulse less than 125 or respiratory rate greater than 30; and systolic blood pressure less than 90. Placement of patients into risk classes

II through V is determined by a complex scoring system that includes demographics, comorbidities, physical examination findings, and essential laboratory findings.

297. The answer is C, 7,020 mL.

(Marx, 762-763; Wolfson, 313)

The Parkland formula is used to calculate the total amount of crystalloid solution that needs to be administered over the first 24 hours in patients with second- or third-degree burns, with the first half being administered over the first 8 hours and the remainder over the next 16 hours. The volume is calculated using this formula: 4 mL/body weight in kg/% body surface area (BSA) burned. In this case, it is 4 mL × 65 kg × 27% body surface area = 7,020 mL. Although this seems like a large amount, the burn produces microvascular injury that leads to increased vascular permeability and edema formation, depleting intravascular volume and leading to the need for this amount of crystalloid solution to maintain plasma volume. The BSA can be calculated in many different ways, but a good estimate can be made using the rule of nines, in which the head is 9%, each arm is 9%, the front and back of the thorax are each 18%, and the legs are each 18%. The perineum is 1%. This patient has involvement of the posterior half of each arm at 4.5% each, and the back, 18%, for a total of 27%.

298. The answer is D, Hemoptysis is bright red and alkaline.

(Marx, 223-225; Tintinalli, 473-476)

Blood from a pulmonary source (hemoptysis) is bright red and alkaline. Distinguishing hemoptysis from hematemesis based on history is usually straightforward, as the patient can usually distinguish coughing from vomiting. Occasionally, the history is unclear or the patient is unsure. Simple inspection of the blood can be helpful. Blood from the lungs and pulmonary tree appears dark red. In the absence of massive upper gastrointestinal tract bleeding, the blood sits in the stomach for a period of time, and exposure to the stomach acid turns the blood from bright red to brown or black with fragmentation. This is referred to as coffee-grounds emesis. Blood from the stomach contains stomach acid and is acidic on pH testing (with litmus paper). Blood from a pulmonary source remains alkaline. Both hematemesis and hemoptysis can be accompanied by mucus from the nose, oropharynx, lungs, or stomach, so the presence of mucus is not useful in differentiating between the two. The presence of bile in hematemesis is rare and is usually associated with bleeding within the biliary tract. Small-volume or mild hemoptysis is described as less than 20 mL per day, but the volume of blood lost does not identify the etiology or predict death. Hemoptysis is considered massive if it is more than 600 mL in 24 hours.

299. The answer is C, Necrotizing enterocolitis.

(Marx, 2174-2176; Tintinalli, 740)

The diagnosis of necrotizing enterocolitis (NEC) is confirmed by radiographs demonstrating pneumatosis coli, air within the bowel wall, air in the biliary tree, or free air in the abdomen. Emergent surgical intervention is required. Nonspecific irritability and vomiting, followed by gastrointestinal tract bleeding, abdominal distention, and shock in a 3-week-old premature infant suggest NEC. Most cases of NEC are diagnosed before newborns initially leave the hospital, but up to 10% are diagnosed within a few weeks after discharge. Early nonspecific symptoms such as emesis and irritability can lead to an initial misdiagnosis. As NEC progresses, patients typically develop hematemesis, hematochezia, and abdominal distention. Rigidity is seen with perforation. Gastroesophageal reflux disease presents with varying degrees of vomiting, and plain radiographs are usually normal. Hirschsprung disease results from congenital absence of colonic ganglion cells. It presents in early infancy with obstructive symptoms without overt shock. Radiographs reveal dilation of the colon and proximal bowel due to stool buildup. Malrotation with midgut volvulus also presents in the neonatal period. The history and physical examination can be similar to those in NEC, and radiographs help distinguish between the two. Radiographs of malrotation demonstrate air-fluid levels and occasionally a double bubble sign. The upper gastrointestinal series confirms the diagnosis by revealing the abnormal location of the duodenum. Pyloric stenosis presents with progressive, nonbilious, often times projectile vomiting. An olive-shaped mass in the right upper abdomen might be palpated, especially when the patient is under general anesthesia. Diagnosis is confirmed with visualization of a thickened pylorus on ultrasound examination. Plain radiographs are typically not ordered for suspected pyloric stenosis, but an upper gastrointestinal series might reveal a collection of contrast in the dilated prepyloric antrum.

300. The answer is D, Noninvasive positive-pressure ventilatory support.

(Marx, 1045-1053; Vital, CD005351)

Treatment of acute cardiogenic pulmonary edema with noninvasive positive-pressure ventilation in addition to standard medical therapy results in significantly decreased endotracheal intubation rates and in-hospital mortality rates compared with standard medical therapy alone. Although the majority of patients with acute pulmonary edema respond to medical therapy, some patients require noninvasive ventilation with either continuous positive airway pressure (CPAP) or bilevel positive airway pressure (BiPAP). Both CPAP and BiPAP improve oxygenation, reduce work of breathing, and decrease left ventricular afterload, thereby reducing the need for intubation, length of hospital stay, and possibly the number of in-hospital deaths. Medical therapy for pulmonary edema includes nitrates to decrease preload and myocardial oxygen demand, morphine sulfate to decrease systemic catecholamines and preload, and loop diuretics to decrease preload and increase water excretion. Nebulized ipratropium is unlikely to help this patient, and the anticholinergic effect could theoretically worsen the tachycardia of a patient who is already sympathomimetically activated. Endotracheal intubation is indicated for apnea, acute respiratory distress, mental status change, and hypoxemia not responsive to supplemental oxygen. Aspirin may be given to patients in whom cardiac ischemia might be the precipitating event, but it is not an acute treatment of pulmonary edema. Finally, inotropic agents such as dopamine or milrinone are typically administered to patients with heart failure and cardiogenic shock with a low blood pressure. In addition, milrinone is typically used in patients with chronic heart failure awaiting heart transplantation.

301. The answer is C, Purpura – any skin eruption resulting from extravasated blood.

(Marx, 1530; Tintinalli, 1601-1610; Wolfson, 840)

Correctly diagnosing dermatologic conditions requires knowledge of how to accurately identify and describe skin lesions. Purpura describes any skin eruption, including petechiae (<3 mm), resulting from extravasated blood. Purpura can be various shades of color consistent with hemorrhage. Since the blood is extravascular, a particular defining characteristic is that the lesions do not blanch. This is in contrast to many blanchable erythematous lesions resulting from blood vessel vasodilation in which the mobile intravascular red blood cells move with compression. Bullae are fluid-filled circumscribed lesions, but they are larger than 0.5 cm (vesicles are <0.5 cm). Similarly, nodules are superficial, elevated, solid lesions larger than 0.5 cm (papules are <0.5 cm). Macules are nonpalpable circumscribed areas of skin color change. A wheal refers to a papule or plaque of dermal edema; cales are flakes of stratum corneum. Skin lesion descriptors and definitions are as follows:

- Bulla – fluid-filled circumscribed lesion larger than 0.5 cm in diameter
- Crusts – dried blood, serum, or purulent exudate on skin surface
- Ecchymosis – purpura (eruption resulting from extravasated blood) larger than 1 cm
- Erosion – defect in epidermis only (dermis not involved, will not scar); occurs from physical abrasions, rupture of vesicles and bullae
- Erythema – red skin appearance due to vasodilation of dermal blood vessels, blanchable
- Induration – dermal thickening that is palpably thick and firm
- Lichenification – visible and palpable epidermal thickening with accentuated skin markings
- Macule – nonpalpable circumscribed area of skin color change
- Nodule – superficial, elevated, solid lesion larger than 0.5 cm in diameter
- Papule – superficial, elevated, solid lesion smaller than 0.5 cm in diameter
- Patch – a barely elevated plaque (lesion between a macule and a plaque)

- Petechiae – purpura (eruption resulting from extravasated blood) smaller than 3 mm
- Plaque – plateaulike elevation above the skin surface occupying a large surface area compared with its height
- Purpura – any skin eruption resulting from extravasated blood; nonblanchable
- Pustule – vesicle filled with purulent material
- Scales – flakes of stratum corneum
- Telangiectasia – small, blanchable superficial capillaries
- Ulcer – defect that extends into dermis or deeper (heals with scarring)
- Vesicle – fluid-filled circumscribed lesion smaller than 0.5 cm in diameter
- Wheal – papule or plaque of dermal edema

302. The answer is C, Migratory polyarthritis.

(Gerber, 1541-1551; Marx, 2164-2165; Tintinalli, 909)

The most common clinical manifestation of acute rheumatic fever (ARF) is a migratory polyarthritis that predominantly involves larger joints. It is seen in up to 75% of cases. Wrists, elbows, ankles, and knees are the joints typically involved. As with most cases of arthritis, the pain is often out of proportion to the examination. An immune-mediated illness, ARF occurs 2 to 6 weeks after a group A beta-hemolytic streptococcal (GABHS) pharyngitis. In the earlier half of the 1900s, it was the leading cause of death in children and heart disease in young adults. After a dramatic decline resulting from the use of antibiotics, rheumatic fever has recently shown a resurgence caused by resistant strains of GABHS. To establish the diagnosis, the Jones criteria require one major and two minor *or* two major criteria with evidence of antecedent streptococcal infection. The Jones criteria are as follows:

- Major – carditis, chorea, erythema marginatum, migratory polyarthritis, subcutaneous nodules
- Minor – arthralgias, fever, increased ESR or C-reactive protein level, prolonged PR interval

Throat cultures are often negative, but antistreptococcal antibody titers remain positive for 4 to 6 weeks. Treatment includes penicillin, salicylates, and evaluation for cardiac complications. (Pan)carditis is present in 30% to 40% of new cases of ARF. It can present with cardiomegaly, pericardial effusions, valvular dysfunction, or heart failure. The mitral valve is most frequently implicated, often resulting in a new murmur. Erythema marginatum is a painless and nonpruritic rash found in less than 10% of patients with ARF. It commonly involves the proximal extremities and trunk and is highly suggestive of the diagnosis. Subcutaneous nodules are small, nontender nodules found primarily over the extensor surfaces of the upper and lower extremities. They are present in less than 10% of cases.

303. **The answer is A, Blood smear.**

(House, 499-516; Tintinalli, 1056-1062)

A blood smear is required to make the definitive diagnosis of malaria, which is characterized by high fever, ill appearance, tachypnea, and tachycardia. Hepatomegaly, anemia, and mildly elevated liver transaminase levels are not unusual. A thick-and-thin blood smear is used for testing; the thick smear is used to identify the presence of any malarial parasite in general, and the thin smear is used to identify the species, either Plasmodium falciparum or non-*Plasmodium falciparum*. In this question, malaria should be considered because the patient is from an endemic area (Haiti). Viral hepatitis is possible, but high fever and acute illness are unlikely; also transaminase levels in viral hepatitis often exceed 1,000. The presence of stool ova and parasites can be used to diagnose several gastrointestinal parasites, including *Entamoeba histolytica*, which causes amoebic abscess. Liver abscesses rarely cause an elevation of liver transaminase levels, and only about 10% of cases result in elevated bilirubin levels. Absence of petechial rash and joint pain suggests diagnoses other than leptospirosis. Bleeding symptoms, pleural effusion, and ascites can also be associated with dengue.

304. **The answer is B, Placenta previa.**

(Ma, 324-326; Tintinalli, 698-700)

Vaginal bleeding in the second and third trimesters affects 5% of pregnancies. Placental abruption is the cause 13% of the time, and placenta previa 7% of the time. The primary focus of ordering an ultrasound examination in the evaluation of third trimester bleeding is to rule out placenta previa. The sensitivity of ultrasound for detecting placenta previa is 92% to 98%. Although cervical effacement can be identified with ultrasonography, it is not the primary focus in the setting of third trimester bleeding. The sensitivity and specificity of ultrasonography for diagnosing placental abruption are about 50%. Once placenta previa is ruled out, the diagnosis of placental abruption is made clinically with history, physical examination, and fetal heart monitoring showing fetal distress and uterine irritability. Uterine rupture presents as a complication of labor and is described as a sharp, tearing pain associated with maternal shock. The patient in this question is not in labor, has no pain, and has normal vital signs, making uterine rupture unlikely.

305. **The answer is B, Patients have earlier relief of pain with surgical discectomy.**

(Harrington, 389-412; Marx, 593-599)

Patients with herniated lumbar discs often present with recurrent back pain. Surgical discectomy has been shown to provide earlier pain relief compared to conservative medical treatment, although long-term studies show no difference in pain recurrence. Most patients with lumbar disc herniations are between 30 and 50 years old. Radicular symptoms occur when the nucleus pulposus of the disc protrudes through the annulus fibrosis and causes local nerve root inflammation. Sciatica, or pain in a radicular distribution, is present in up to 95% of patients with lumbar disc herniation. Patients with atraumatic mechanisms (heavy lifting is not considered traumatic) do not need to be imaged in the immediate period unless there are red flags present indicating more serious disease. Red flags include extremes of age (younger than 18, older than 50), fever or immunocompromise, history of cancer or systemic symptoms suggestive of cancer, or duration of symptoms longer than 6 weeks. In the emergency department, patients with red flags can be imaged with lumbrosacral radiography, which might reveal bony abnormalities such as fractures or significant changes in alignment. Patients with symptoms that persist for more than 6 weeks should undergo nonurgent outpatient MRI. A CT scan is not adequate to evaluate the soft tissue structures of the spine. Bed rest is no longer thought to be helpful in patients with back pain, and patients should be encouraged to carry out activities of daily living. Pain management should include anti-inflammatory medications and narcotic pain medications as needed. Steroids, either locally injected or taken systemically, have not been shown to decrease the eventual need for surgery.

306. The answer is B, Decreasing the number of shocks needed to defibrillate.

(Link, S708-S709; Roberts, 220, 229; Wolfson, 32)

The advent of newer, biphasic defibrillators has resulted in an increased first shock success rate, less electrical current required, and reduced damage to cardiac cells. The biphasic waveforms are used to deliver current through the heart, reverse polarity, and return through the myocardium. Therefore, less energy is needed with biphasic technology to convert arrhythmias. Because the patient is in ventricular fibrillation for a shorter period of time, a decreased rate of postfibrillation rhythm disturbances can be expected. Biphasic defibrillators produce a waveform that flows back and forth between the electrodes as either a BTE (biphasic truncated exponential) waveform or biphasic rectilinear waveform. It is important for emergency physicians to be knowledgeable about the defibrillators available for their use, as the device-specific effective waveform determines the starting energy level for defibrillation. With a biphasic rectilinear waveform, 120 joules is appropriate; with a BTE waveform, 150 joules is a starting energy to terminate ventricular fibrillation. When the type is not known, the recommended starting energy is 200 joules.

307. The answer is C, T-cell lymphoma.

(Schwartz, 52-55, 105-112; Townsend, 1185-1204)

T-cell lymphoma causes an anterior mediastinal mass that can easily be seen on AP or PA chest radiography. The tracheal air column is laterally displaced because of the mass. A lateral radiograph can help locate the mass in the anterior mediastinum. Other causes of anterior mediastinal mass include thymoma, teratoma, thyroid, and bronchogenic carcinoma. Anterior mediastinal masses appear as distinct masses on chest radiograph with sharp edges. Anterior mediastinal masses should be distinguished from more life-threatening causes of widened mediastinum. Esophageal rupture causes a widening of the mediastinum seen on a chest radiograph. The classic radiographic finding of esophageal rupture is pneumomediastinum. The classic radiographic finding of tuberculosis is cavitary lesion in the upper lobe in the lung parenchyma, but often the only finding on chest radiograph is hilar adenopathy. A round pneumonia also presents with worrisome round density on chest radiograph. However, the density generally involves the parenchyma and not the mediastinum. Round pneumonias are not always round and can vary in density. Chest radiography should be repeated after treatment with antibiotics to ensure resolution.

308. The answer is A, Admit to the hospital for surgery.

(Marx, 337-342; Wolfson, 194-197)

The patient in this question sustained a flexion injury of the cervical spine that resulted in a flexion teardrop fracture. The CT scan finding for this injury is described as a wedge-shaped fragment off of the inferior, anterior portion of the vertebral body. This is an extremely unstable injury and is likely to involve ligament disruption. In addition, because of the mechanism of injury, the patient is at risk for spinal cord injury despite normal findings on neurologic examination. Therefore, further workup is required, possibly MRI and emergent consultation with a spine specialist; surgical stabilization of this injury is required. Cervical spine precautions are required; she should be admitted to the hospital or transferred to a trauma center if the level of care needed is not available. Flexion and extension radiographs are not appropriate; discharge either with or without a cervical spine collar is not appropriate given the unstable nature of the fracture and risk of spinal cord injury.

309. The answer is D, Nonbilious vomiting.

(Fleisher, 1524-1526; Marx, 2171-2172; Wolfson, 1309-1310)

Nonbilious vomiting is the hallmark of pyloric stenosis and is present in nearly all infants with the condition. Pyloric hypertrophy results in an obstruction proximal to the duodenum. The resultant vomiting is expected to be nonbilious: the contents of the duodenum are not expected to pass through the obstruction. Although young, dehydrated infants can have jaundice, this jaundice would be indirect. Hypochloremic hypokalemic metabolic alkalosis is seen with hypertrophic pyloric stenosis (HPS), but only in severe cases (<15%). The classic presentation of HPS is in the first-born male between 2 and 5 weeks old. The male predominance is 4:1; there seems to be a higher incidence if there is a family history of HPS, especially if the mother had HPS. The exact cause is unknown. Classic symptoms include emesis within 30 minutes of feeding, with increasing force leading to projectile emesis. Abdominal examination can be remarkable for an olive-like mass found in the midepigastrium, whereas the abdomen is soft and nondistended. There can be a peristaltic wave noted on examination when the infant is fed small amounts of sugar water. Diagnosis often requires radiographic visualization of the pylorus, for which ultrasonography has been used. An upper gastrointestinal series can be used, but ultrasonography is preferred because of its simplicity, availability, and minimal invasiveness.

310. The answer is C, Lumbar puncture.

(Marx, 149-158, 1356-1366; Tintinalli, 1116, 1547)

Neuroimaging is appropriate in the evaluation of a patient who complains of vomiting with headache. However, in this situation, because of the history, a diagnosis of idiopathic intracranial hypertension (also referred to as benign intracranial hypertension and pseudotumor cerebri) is likely, and measurement of CSF pressure would be diagnostic. The differential diagnosis for elevated intracranial pressure includes but is not limited to space-occupying lesions, both neoplastic and hemorrhagic, and other etiologies of cerebral edema such as venous sinus thrombosis. Idiopathic intracranial hypertension has strict diagnostic criteria that include headache with either a normal neurologic examination or neurologic abnormalities that are limited to papilledema, an enlarged blind spot, or a visual field defect (this might be progressive if the intracranial hypertension is untreated). Additional diagnostic criteria include increased CSF pressure (>250 mm H_2O) measured by lumbar puncture with the patient in the recumbent position, normal CSF analysis, no hormonal or metabolic cause for intracranial hypertension, and no structural intracranial pathology. When evaluating a patient with vomiting, the history and physical examination should guide any investigations. When vomiting has been present for 1 month, it is referred to as chronic. Plain abdominal radiographs are of limited utility in patients with vomiting and have largely been superseded by abdominal CT scans, except in the assessment of suspected bowel obstruction. An abdominal CT scan is indicated if an acute surgical condition or an inflammatory or infectious process is suspected. In a patient who has had headache and vomiting for 1 month without abdominal pain, an intra-abdominal process is not likely the underlying cause. Abdominal ultrasonography is extremely useful in the evaluation of suspected biliary pathology or pelvic pathology but is unlikely to have any utility in the evaluation of this patient.

311. The answer is A, Analgesics and sucralfate.

(Marx, 1240-1241, 1252-1256; Wolfson, 608-612)

Prostate cancer patients undergoing radiation therapy commonly develop acute radiation proctocolitis, which is best managed with analgesics and, according to some studies, sucralfate. Intensive radiation causes sloughing of intestinal epithelial cells faster than they can be replaced, resulting in mucosal ulcerations. Patients present with varying degrees of diarrhea, rectal bleeding, tenesmus, abdominal pain, and incontinence. Diagnosis is often made clinically without further testing. Most cases promptly resolve with adjustment or termination of radiation therapy. Chronic radiation proctocolitis is a distinct entity from the acute form. Radiation induces endarteritis in the bowel wall, leading to ischemic changes anywhere from months to years after therapy. Complications include luminal narrowing, fistulae, necrosis, and perforation. Radiographs and CT scans identify most complications. Empiric ceftriaxone, doxycycline, and acyclovir are used to treat proctitis from venereal diseases, which often present with bloody and mucoid rectal discharge. Oral steroids and mesalamine are used for treatment of ulcerative colitis flares. Surgical consultation for incision and drainage is often indicated for deep perirectal abscesses, but they do not typically present with bloody diarrhea and incontinence.

312. The answer is A, Cardiomegaly, Kerley B lines, and pulmonary venous redistribution.

(Tintinalli, 405-415; Wang, 1944-1956)

Pulmonary venous redistribution, Kerley B lines, and cardiomegaly are all radiographic findings of heart failure. The normal cardiac silhouette in an upright PA chest radiograph should span no more than half the thorax; an enlarged cardiac silhouette (cardiomegaly) suggests heart failure. Pleural effusion is also a radiographic finding in heart failure. Small effusions can be seen as blunted costophrenic angle on upright chest radiograph, and larger ones should have a meniscal appearance unless there is underlying pleural scarring. Fluid can also collect in the fissure from the same mechanism and appear as long, strained lines running the width or length of the pleural cavity. Pulmonary venous congestion, also known as cephalization, can be seen on an upright view and is characterized by distention of the pulmonary veins and redistribution to the apices. Normally, the vasculature in the upper lung fields is narrower than in the lower lung fields due to the influence of gravity, resulting in greater flow to the lower fields. As the pulmonary venous pressure rises, the additional pressure is accommodated by more flow to the upper field vasculature. When the upper vasculature is the same or larger diameter than the lower field vasculature at a similar distance from the hilum, cephalization is said to be present. Kerley lines are thin linear pulmonary opacities caused by fluid in the lung interstitium in diseases such as heart failure. Kerley A lines are short, straight lines, 2 cm or less in length, angling diagonally from hila to the periphery and located close to the hilum. Kerley B lines are short horizontal lines less than 1 cm in length at lung periphery. Peribronchial cuffing is another radiographic finding in heart failure. It represents thickening of the bronchial walls. Normally, the bronchial walls are unnoticeable or hairline thin. Conditions that cause fluid accumulation in the bronchial walls, such as pulmonary venous hypertension or inflammation of the bronchial walls, such as infection, lead to small, thick-walled circles. Interstitial pulmonary edema is said to occur when hydrostatic pressure is greater than 10 mm Hg, equal to a left atrial pressure of 20 to 25 mm Hg. It manifests as increased opacity of the lung markings and inability to visualize crisp vascular markings. Alveolar edema is said to occur at left atrial pressures greater than 24 mm Hg and presents with a bat-wing appearance. In a systematic review of radiographic findings in heart failure, pulmonary venous redistribution and interstitial pulmonary edema had the highest positive likelihood ratios. Air bronchograms, lucent lines running through opacified lung, can occur but are more commonly due to consolidation from pneumonia. The Westermark sign is dilation of the pulmonary hilum with oligemia of the vasculature distal to that. It is found in pulmonary embolism due to a large proximal clot and represents a finding with low sensitivity but reportedly high specificity. Hampton hump is a peripheral wedge-shaped density representing a pulmonary infarct that extends to the pleura from pulmonary embolism. A widened mediastinum and large aortic knob are findings that can be seen with aortic dissection.

313. The answer is D, Pseudoephedrine.

(Nelson, 1029-1031; Wolfson, 1504-1509)

Linezolid (marketed in the United States as Zyvox) is an antibiotic that can be used orally to treat methicillin-resistant *Staphylococcus aureus* infections. It has monoamine oxidase inhibitor (MAOI) activity, so the addition of pseudoephedrine could potentially lead to a life-threatening drug-drug interaction of catecholamine excess. Patients who are prescribed linezolid should be warned that eating foods rich in tyramine, such as aged, mature cheeses and red wines, can trigger significant stored norepinephrine release and a severe hyperadrenergic crisis. The current use of MAOIs for depression is uncommon due to newer, safer drugs. However, occasionally patients are still prescribed MAOIs for depression, and drugs used for other purposes, such as selegiline for Parkinson disease and linezolid, have MAOI activity. The major problems with MAOIs include overdose and adverse food-drug and drug-drug interactions. The MAOIs inhibit the breakdown of the monoamines dopamine, norepinephrine, and serotonin and lead to their accumulation in nerve terminals. Amphetamines, including over-the-counter pseudoephedrine, act by releasing preformed norepinephrine, which in the setting of MAOI use can be excessive and dangerous. Another significant adverse MAOI drug-drug interaction is serotonin toxicity that can occur with the coadministration of a serotonergic drug and other medications such as meperidine and dextromethorphan. Treatment of catecholamine excess associated with all of the various MAOI interactions is supportive and also involves the use of agents such as nitroprusside or phentolamine to counteract the potentially severe hypertension. The other drugs listed do not need to be avoided in patients on MAOIs and have not been found to interact significantly with linezolid. Diphenhydramine and chlorpheniramine are antihistamines with antimuscarinic activity. Benzonatate (found in Tessalon Perles) acts as an oropharyngeal anesthetic.

314. The answer is B, It will have few false-negative results.

(Marx, 2517-2520; Straus, 67-99)

Specificity and sensitivity are two commonly reported measures of diagnostic test accuracy. The sensitivity of a test is often defined as the probability of a positive test given the presence of the target disorder (a positive test with disease). A test that is highly sensitive will have few false-negative results. Thus, a negative result of a highly sensitive test allows the emergency physician to exclude or rule out the disorder in question. The mnemonic "SnNout" is useful to describe this: a high sensitivity (Sn), negative (N) result rules out (out) the diagnosis. The specificity of a test is often defined as the proportion of patients who are disease free and have a negative or normal result (negative test without disease). A test that is highly specific will have few false-positive results. Thus, a positive result of a highly specific test allows the emergency physician to include or rule in the given disorder. The mnemonic "SpPin" is a helpful way to describe this: high specificity (Sp), positive result (P), rules in (in) the diagnosis. Although diagnostic tests are typically thought of in the context of laboratory data or imaging modalities, any feature of the history and physical examination may also be considered as a diagnostic test. Sensitivity and specificity are independent of the disease prevalence and are inherent properties of the test. Negative predictive value, or NPV, places sensitivity into the context of disease prevalence; positive predictive value, or PPV, does the same for specificity. The rarer the disease is, the more specific a test must be to be helpful clinically. Diagnostic tests that make significant changes from the pretest probability of disease to the post-test probability of disease are most likely to be clinically useful in patient care.

315. The answer is C, Oxymetazoline applied by aerosol significantly reduces bleeding.

(Marx, 883-885; Tintinalli, 1565)

Epistaxis, or nose bleeding, is usually controlled with direct pressure alone. By the time a patient comes to the emergency department for treatment, direct pressure has probably failed; oxymetazoline (marketed as Afrin, Allerest, Duramist, and many other names) is the next reasonable step. It is an alpha-agonist vasoconstrictor, and it will significantly reduce the bleeding. If it does not stop the bleeding, it will facilitate visualizing and localizing the source of bleeding, which can then be cauterized. Ninety percent of bleeds originate from the anterior nare in the Kiesselbach plexus. These vessels are more accessible and amenable to direct pressure, so bleeding from this area is rarely severe or life-threatening. Posterior bleeding, however, originates from the posterior branch of the sphenopalatine artery, which is not directly compressible. Posterior bleeding requires the placement of a posterior nasal pack, by way of a commercial device or a Foley catheter. Anterior nasal packs are effective for the management of persistent nasal bleeding. Any patient with a nasal pack should be given antibiotic prophylaxis to prevent streptococcal infection and, therefore, toxic shock syndrome. Beta-lactam antibiotics are usually sufficient, but ciprofloxacin does not have sufficient coverage against *Streptococcus*.

316. The answer is D, Levofloxacin.

(Centers for Disease Control and Prevention [sexually transmitted diseases], 67-69; Marx, 1318-1319)

The patient in this question has orchitis. The bacterial etiology can be *Neisseria gonorrhoeae, Chlamydia trachomatis, Escherichia coli, Klebsiella,* or *Pseudomonas.* In this case, there is no indication of a sexually transmitted disease. In an elderly male patient, especially one with benign prostatic hypertrophy, the gram-negative organism is predominant. The best antibiotic is levofloxacin, which covers gram-negative bacteria. Cephalexin and amoxicillin do not provide adequate coverage for *Pseudomonas.* In younger male patients (35 years old and younger) whose infections are presumed to be sexually acquired, ceftriaxone is the appropriate choice as a single-dose agent followed by either doxycycline or tetracycline for 10 days. Ceftriaxone as a single agent for any age group does not adequately cover the other organisms. In the younger patient, testicular torsion can be considered. Torsion peaks during the first year of life and again at puberty but can occur in adults. It results from twisting of the spermatic cord.

317. The answer is B, Perform needle decompression of the chest.

(Roberts, 179; Wolfson, 82, 129)

Once the diagnosis of a tension pneumothorax with hypotension is suspected, immediate needle decompression should occur. One study found auscultation to be sensitive in 84% of patients and to have a diagnostic accuracy of only 89% despite a hemothorax or pneumothorax. It is possible for a patient to have a false-negative of symmetrical breath sounds despite having a tension pneumothorax. Insertion of a large-bore catheter is the immediate action. This procedure should not be delayed for a chest radiography or CT. Tube thoracostomy is time consuming and is done later as a followup intervention. Intravenous fluid administration can transiently improve the hypotension caused by a tension pneumothorax but will do nothing to address the tension pneumothorax. The emergency physician should immediately consider and treat without delay apnea, hypotension, or cardiac arrest in an injured patient. The diagnosis is confirmed when the vital signs improve after placement of the needle.

318. The answer is B, Lateral decubitus.

(Marx, 393-396, 943-946; Roberts, 161-164; Tintinalli, 471-473)

Small pleural effusions are best visualized as small stripes on the lateral decubitus chest radiography view, with the affected side down. A lateral decubitus radiograph in an AP or PA projection is taken with the patient lying on either the right or left side. The side that the patient is lying on determines whether the radiograph is named left or right. Lateral decubitus radiographs allow fluid to travel and collect in the lowest points. The side with the suspected effusion should be placed down. For example, in a patient with suspected right pleural effusion on an upright chest radiograph, a right lateral decubitus radiograph can be taken while the patient is lying on his or her right side. If there is more than 1 cm of fluid on this view, it indicates a large enough effusion to perform a diagnostic tap. It takes between 250 and 500 mL of fluid to visualize pleural effusions on upright chest radiograph. The classic finding is blunting of the costophrenic angle. On the lateral upright chest radiograph, fluid can be seen in the posterior costophrenic gutter. Large effusions can obscure the hemidiaphragm or even the entire hemithorax. The fluid tends to form a meniscus that curves up to the lateral wall. Effusions are harder to identify on supine radiographs because, in the supine position, the effusion forms a thin layer across the entire hemithorax, which creates a slight increased haziness on the supine view. Supine radiographs are generally used for patients who are unable to sit up, such as trauma patients on backboards or patients with hypotension. Stable intubated patients may be angled upward for semiupright chest radiographs. Chest radiographs are normally taken on inspiration to allow maximal expansion of the chest and better visualization. End-expiratory radiographs, which are taken at the end of expiration to allow for maximal collapse of lung parenchyma, can be useful in detecting small pneumothoraces by accentuating the space between the chest wall and lung parenchyma. Expiratory radiographs limit the evaluation of lung parenchyma and are more useful in detecting small pneumothoraces when compared with standard inspiratory views. Bedside ultrasonography can also be helpful in identifying small effusions and pneumothoraces.

319. The answer is C, Pain control, intravenous penicillin, and admission to the hospital with oral surgery consultation.

(Marx, 328-329; Wolfson, 170-171)

Treatment of open mandibular fractures warrants intravenous administration of antibiotics and usually requires admission to the hospital. An open mandibular fracture is likely in this patient given the mechanism of injury and the pain, malocclusion, and inability to bite down on the affected side.

There can also be anesthesia of the lower lip if the inferior dental nerve is injured. Injuries of the mandibular neck, coronoid process, or ramus can lead to trismus. Many of these injuries require surgery, arch bar placement, and interdental fixation, or "wiring the jaw shut" for a period of time. Panoramic radiography can detect most mandibular fractures; although CT is slightly more sensitive, either of these studies can be obtained to determine the location and extent of the fracture. This patient in particular should undergo imaging (4-view plain radiography of the mandible, panoramic radiography, or CT) and should receive intravenous antibiotic therapy, pain control, and oral surgery consultation either in the emergency department or as an inpatient. He will most likely require surgery.

320. The answer is C, Impaired thirst drive.

(Marx, 1617-1618; Tintinalli, 120-121)

Thirst is the body's main defense against hypernatremia, defined as a serum sodium level greater than 150 mEq/L. The most common presentation of hypernatremia in the emergency department is in patients who are unable to take in enough water. Patients who are unable to obtain or swallow water, patients with an impaired thirst drive (such as those with illness or altered mental status), and patients with increased insensible losses can all present with hypernatremia. Broadly speaking, hypernatremia is caused by a decrease in total body water or from increased sodium (either increased intake or decreased excretion). Overall, a decrease in total body water is by far the most common cause. Among emergency department patients, hypernatremia is most commonly the result of significant hypovolemia. In these patients, the kidneys are maximally concentrating the urine to preserve free water and circulating volume. The overall volume of urine is often so low that enough sodium cannot be excreted.

321. The answer is D, Mallory-Weiss syndrome.

(Marx, 151, 1137-1152; Tintinalli, 543-545; Wolfson, 548)

The patient in this question has experienced a typical episode of Mallory-Weiss syndrome, protracted vomiting and subsequent hematemesis. Forceful retching and vomiting result in an upper gastrointestinal bleed from a longitudinal mucosal laceration (Mallory-Weiss tear) at the junction of the distal esophagus and proximal stomach. Mallory-Weiss syndrome occurs more frequently in adults, representing 5% to 15% of all upper gastrointestinal bleeds. The laceration results from an increase in the pressure gradient between the stomach and the thorax. Bleeding is generally mild and self-limited. Surgical intervention is rarely required. In contrast, Boerhaave syndrome is a complete esophageal perforation and a surgical emergency. It has a high mortality rate, mandating prompt surgical repair. Patients classically present with vomiting, acute severe chest pain, and subcutaneous emphysema and often a wide mediastinum on chest radiograph. Esophageal perforation from vomiting (Boerhaave syndrome) commonly occurs in the distal esophagus, but iatrogenic injuries (from endoscopy) are now more common and occur at the proximal esophagus. In the emergency department, treatment includes broad-spectrum antibiotics (aminoglycoside and second-generation cephalosporin), fluid resuscitation, and emergent surgical consultation. Esophageal varices occur as a result of sustained portal hypertension in patients with chronic liver disease and cirrhosis. This patient has no history to support a suspicion of variceal bleeding. Gastritis and peptic ulcer disease result from infection with *Helicobacter pylori* or from chronic alcohol abuse or NSAID use. Symptoms include nausea, vomiting, and upper gastrointestinal bleeding without diarrhea.

322. The answer is C, Small bolus of normal saline.

(Marx, 1045-1053; Silvers, 627-669)

The initial treatment goal in patients with systemic hypotension should be to maintain or restore coronary perfusion pressure, including restoration of intravascular volume and vasopressor therapy. In this clinical scenario, patients either have true cardiogenic shock from pump dysfunction or intravascular volume depletion. It is difficult to distinguish between these two states clinically because both have signs of systemic hypoperfusion. If bedside ultrasonography is available, a measurement of the inferior vena cava may be used to distinguish cardiogenic shock from intravascular volume depletion, guide fluid resuscitation, and rule out cardiac tamponade due to pericardial effusion as an etiology of the shock. In half of these cases, a judicious fluid challenge alone can restore hemodynamic stability if respiratory failure is not imminent. If the patient with cardiogenic shock does not respond to an adequate fluid challenge or develops worsening hypoxia, then inotropic and vasopressor therapy, endotracheal intubation, and emergency coronary revascularization for cardiac ischemia are indicated. Norepinephrine is the vasopressor of choice in patients with cardiogenic shock because it raises blood pressure and coronary perfusion pressure. Inotropic agents with vasodilator effects such as dobutamine can cause more profound hypotension and hemodynamic compromise unless given with other vasopressor agents. Intravenous furosemide and sublingual nitroglycerin are commonly used to treat heart failure but can worsen hypotension. Digitalis is a cardiac glycoside with modest inotropic effect but has minimal potency in improving hemodynamics compared to other inotropics; therefore, it has very little role in acute heart failure.

323. The answer is D, Rectal decompression.

(Fleisher, 828, 1527-1528; Marx, 2179; Strange, 67-68; Wolfson, 1117-1120)

Rectal decompression is generally recommended in the management of classic presentations of Hirschprung disease. Hirschprung disease is also known as congenital megacolon and is characterized by congenital aganglionosis of the colon. The absence of ganglions typically starts distally at the anus and is present for a variable distance proximally. In general, the greater the length of the colon involved, the earlier and more critical the patient's presentation. Although definitive therapy is surgical resection of the aganglionic segment, some temporizing measures are indicated in the emergency department. These include gastric and rectal decompression, broad-spectrum antibiotics, and fluid and electrolyte replacement. Abdominal ultrasonography is not likely to be helpful in this case, as the abdominal distention is caused by gaseous colonic distention, and ultrasound waves travel poorly through air. Esophagogastroduodenoscopy (EGD) can be useful for evaluating upper gastrointestinal bleeding in infants, but this infant is exhibiting what is most likely to be lower gastrointestinal bleeding. It is used primarily in children with chronic (>3 months) abdominal pain, those with suspected peptic ulcer disease or concerns of *Helicobacter pylori*, or those with acute upper gastrointestinal bleeding. It is the most accurate way to diagnose peptic ulcer disease because it can visualize the tissue and facilitate biopsy of suspicious areas. Exchange transfusion is indicated for severe neonatal jaundice and is not indicated in this case. In infants, the causes of diarrhea are predominantly related to infectious etiologies. Rare but clinically important scenarios include hemolytic uremic syndrome or pseudomembranous colitis, but these are associated with bloody diarrhea. Malabsorption diarrhea is related to other disorders, including cystic fibrosis and celiac disease, even certain cancers not generally seen in children this age.

324. The answer is A, Active rewarming can precipitate hypotension.

(Marx, 1668-1671; Wolfson, 1028-1029)

Active rewarming measures such as electric blankets in the setting of myxedema coma can in fact precipitate hypotension. This can occur as a result of reversal of peripheral vasoconstriction that coexists with both significant volume depletion and diminished cardiac output. For this reason, at least initially, passive rewarming is favored. Myxedema coma is a life-threatening manifestation of longstanding hypothyroidism that requires early diagnosis and appropriate management to prevent death. Despite the name, patients can present with neither myxedema (nonpitting edema due to accumulation of mucopolysaccharides from decreased metabolism) nor coma. A depressed level of consciousness, rather than agitation, is common. However, an unusual but well-described variant referred to as myxedema madness can manifest with agitation, delirium, and psychosis. Hyponatremia is common in both hypothyroidism and myxedema coma. Unless severe and associated with convulsions, it should correct with treatment of the underlying thyroid disorder. Due to decreased gluconeogenesis, decreased insulin clearance, and potentially coincident adrenal suppression, hypoglycemia, rather than hyperglycemia, can occur. Searching for and treating the precipitant (particularly infectious) of myxedema is essential, as are meticulous supportive care, intravenous fluids, and hydrocortisone. Thyroid hormone replacement is obviously critical. Intravenous administration of T3 has been associated with cardiac dysrhythmias and death. For this reason, many advocate administering exclusively T4, a combination of T3 and T4, and only considering T3 alone in younger patients with healthy hearts in whom rapid correction is desired.

325. The answer is B, Descent.

(Grissom, 461-465; Hackett, 980-986; Honigman, 587-592; Levine, 1707-1713; Marx, 1917-1928; Tintinalli, 1406-1408)

In the management of severe altitude illness, the cornerstone of treatment is reversal of the pathophysiologic processes through immediate descent. Descents of 1,500 to 3,000 ft often provide complete resolution of symptoms in the early stages of both high-altitude cerebral edema (HACE) and high-altitude pulmonary edema (HAPE). Portable hyperbaric oxygen chambers such as the Gamow bag are useful for simulating descent when transport to lower altitudes is not possible. Supplemental oxygen also facilitates reversal of the hypoxic state that drives much of the pathophysiologic responses to high altitude. The administration of furosemide and nifedipine to persons suffering from HAPE is considered to be adjunctive treatment to descent and supplemental oxygen. Likewise, the use of dexamethasone, mannitol, and diuretics in persons suffering from HACE is merely adjunctive to descent to a lower altitude.

326. The answer is D, Pyrimethamine and sulfadiazine plus folinic acid.

(Marx, 1740-1742, 1767; Tintinalli, 498, 1034-1036)

Toxoplasmosis, caused by the protozoan parasite *Toxoplasma gondii,* is the most common ring-enhancing lesion in the CNS of patients with AIDS. It usually presents with fever, headache, seizures, altered mental status, and coma. It is treated with pyrimethamine and sulfadiazine. Folinic acid is added to prevent folate deficiency because pyrimethamine is a folate antagonist. Steroids such as decadron are usually required to reduce the surrounding cerebral edema. Ring-enhancing lesions in the brain in patients with AIDS are most likely to be toxoplasmosis but might also be lymphoma or cerebral tuberculosis. Lymphoma tends to present with solitary lesions, usually in the periventricular white matter. Primary CNS lymphoma is very unusual in patients who do not have HIV infection. The treatment options are varied but generally involve chemotherapy plus radiation. Surgical excision is rarely indicated. Tuberculosis does not typically present with multiple ring-enhancing lesions. In patients who have cerebral tuberculosis, CT results are usually normal but might show a fluid collection in the basal cisterns. Tuberculosis is treated with long-term anti-tuberculosis therapy. *Cryptococcus neoformans* is a common cause of meningitis in patients with HIV infection.

It usually presents with an indolent course, with headache, fever, and altered mental status. Lumbar puncture demonstrates an elevated opening pressure, and the organism can be seen with India ink staining of the CSF. It is treated with antifungal medications such as liposomal amphotericin B. Cytomegalovirus causes a sight-threatening retinitis in severely immunocompromised patients. Intravenous gancyclovir is a treatment option.

327.   The answer is D, Expectant management.

(Kenyon, 979-988; Marx, 2335-2338; Mercer, 989-995; Tintinalli, 703-711)

The patient in this question presents with premature labor, defined as onset of labor prior to 37 weeks' gestation. Beyond 34 weeks' gestation, a fetus should be mature enough to do well without steroids or tocolytic agents; in this patient, then, given that there are no apparent complications, the most appropriate plan is expectant management. Antibiotics are indicated if a patient has a positive test result for group B *Streptococcus* infection or if she has preterm premature rupture of membranes and is being managed expectantly. Steroids (betamethasone, dexamethasone) are indicated in premature labor that occurs before 34 weeks' gestation to speed fetal lung maturity. Typical dosing is betamethasone 12 mg IM every 24 hours for two doses or dexamethasone 6 mg IM every 6 hours for four doses and weekly after. Tocolysis is indicated in patients in premature labor between 24 and 34 weeks' gestation. Prior to 23 weeks, the probability of fetal survival is very low. Terbutaline is administered subcutaneously as an initial dose of 0.25 mg and then a maintenance dose of 0.25 mg every 20 minutes up to 3 hours or until contractions stop. Other tocolytic agents include magnesium sulfate, ritodrine, nifedipine, and indomethacin. Oxytocin is administered to aid in uterine contractions and control uterine bleeding by increasing uterine tone. It should not be administered prior to delivery of the placenta because it can cause placenta fragmenting or retention.

328.   The answer is B, Respiratory failure.

(Tintinalli, 1170-1171; Wolfson, 798-800)

The most common cause of death in patients with severe Parkinson disease is respiratory failure. Parkinson disease is characterized by one or more of four classic findings: resting tremor, cogwheel rigidity, bradykinesia (slowed movement) or akinesia (absence of movement), and altered posture and equilibrium. The pathophysiology of the disease involves a loss of functional dopaminergic receptors due to alterations at the cellular level. Patients are at risk for respiratory distress and pneumonia, especially during off periods. On and off periods are characteristic of patients with Parkinson disease. During off periods, patients lack available dopamine needed to initiate movement and can experience freezing episodes or significant slowing of movements. Medications used to treat Parkinson disease (levodopa) can become less effective over time. Side effects related to increasing doses of dopaminergic agents include nausea, vomiting, orthostatic, dysrhythmias, and acute psychosis. A trial of a drug holiday, during which the dopaminergic agent is withdrawn and reintroduced in a week, can increase the sensitivity of the drug. During the holiday time, patients might experience a worsening of their symptoms. Patients with Parkinson disease are at high risk for injuries related to falls, and this is a major reason for these patients to present to emergency departments. Patients with Parkinson disease have a high incidence of depression; however, suicide is not a common cause of death among them.

329. The answer is C, Pulseless electrical activity.

(Marx, 1278; Roberts, 287-307)

Pulseless electrical activity (PEA) is the most common clinical scenario in which truly emergent pericardiocentesis is needed, as cardiac tamponade can be the cause. In one study, three out of 20 patients with PEA had tamponade requiring emergency pericardiocentesis. Penetrating wounds to the chest, back, and upper abdomen can also lead to cardiac injury. Stab wounds are the most common cause of injuries that result in tamponade. Penetrating trauma leading to tamponade is less common and is best treated using open thoracotomy. Iatrogenic causes of pericardial hemorrhage occur but are unusual. They include pacemaker insertion, cardiac catheterization, cardiac surgery, and central venous catheter placement. Cardiac tamponade should be included in the differential for a patient who rapidly decompensates after an invasive procedure. Other causes of pericardial effusion (such as severe hypothyroidism and uremia from chronic renal failure) cause a slower incidence of fluid accumulation and give time for the pericardium to stretch and accommodate the fluid, leading to a less emergent presentation.

330. The answer is B, Flulike illness.

(Marx, 1719-1720; Tintinalli, 1070-1077)

Symptoms of hantavirus include fever, fatigue, and myalgias in a flulike illness. Hantavirus pulmonary syndrome (HPS) is the most common presentation in the United States, although it is still a relatively rare disease. Hantavirus causes more than 100,000 cases of hemorrhagic fever with renal syndrome (HFRS) in Asia and Europe. Both diseases start with a febrile illness. After the initial flulike prodromal illness of 3 to 4 days' duration, HPS rapidly progresses to pulmonary edema, hypoxia, hypotension, tachycardia, and metabolic acidosis. It has a high mortality rate of greater than 50%. In comparison, HFRS often presents with febrile illness as well as gastrointestinal symptoms (abdominal pain, nausea, vomiting, diarrhea). It progresses to thrombocytopenia and renal failure and has a mortality rate of about 6%. Humans become infected by coming in contact with infected rodents or urine or feces of infected rodents (rats and mice). The virus can become aerosolized if contaminated urine or feces is stirred up, such as might happen with cleaning. Human-to-human transmission does not occur. Hantavirus mainly occurs in the southwestern United States. Initial symptoms can develop weeks after exposure. Hantavirus treatment is mostly supportive. Ribavirin is considered an experimental therapy. Hantavirus can cause a hemorrhagic fever, which can lead to thrombocytopenia, which can cause petechiae and ocular bleeding, but it does not cause conjunctivitis or rashes. Many other zoonotic diseases cause hepatitis, encephalitis, and myocarditis. Hepatitis is seen in *Ehrlichia* and tularemia. Meningitis (and occasionally encephalitis) is seen in many zoonotic diseases but is not characteristic for hantavirus.

331. The answer is B, Blunt abdominal trauma, dome rupture, gross hematuria.

(Marx, 440-446; Wolfson, 238-239)

Intraperitoneal bladder rupture tends to occur when a patient with a full bladder sustains a traumatic injury from a compressive force that causes the bladder to burst at its dome, thus rupturing into the intraperitoneal cavity. Gross hematuria is present in 98% of patients with bladder rupture. Diagnosis is made using conventional or CT cystogram. Extraperitoneal rupture is thought to be caused by lacerations from adjacent sharp pelvic fragments, which can be present in a patient with a full bladder who sustains a pelvic fracture. Leakage of urine occurs into the perivesicular space extraperitoneally. A patient with extraperitoneal bladder rupture can present with or without pelvic fractures and gross hematuria. Diagnosis is made using conventional or CT cystogram. Patients with urethral injuries present with scrotal or perineal hematoma, blood at the urethral meatus, a high-riding prostate, and an inability to void. Diagnosis is made using retrograde urethrogram.

332. The answer is A, Bradycardia with a fever can occur in Lyme disease.

(Marx, 83-86; Tintinalli, 1042-1044, 1082-1088)

Although an elevated body temperature is typically associated with tachycardia, there are certain disease processes that produce a relative bradycardia, such as the concomitant use of beta-blockers, or even an overt bradycardia. Overt bradycardia in association with a fever is classically described with infection and inflammation of the cardiac structures themselves, including Lyme disease, endocarditis, and rheumatic fever. Rectal temperatures are often 0.7 to 1°C higher than oral temperatures. Axillary and tympanic temperatures are quite variable and cannot be reliably related to a core temperature measurement. In adult patients, the heart rate can increase by 10 beats/min for each 0.55°C rise in temperature; the respiratory rate can increase by 2 to 4 breaths/min per 1°C rise in temperature. Chills occur when a fever causes the hypothalamus to reset the thermostatic normal to a higher temperature. Since the body temperature is low, the patient shivers or has chills until the body temperature is raised to this new febrile level as set by the hypothalamus. Sweating occurs as the patient's fever declines.

333. The answer is B, Emergent surgery consultation.

(Marx, 151, 156, 1139-1140; Tintinalli, 363-364, 550-551)

Boerhaave syndrome is an esophageal rupture caused by vomiting. In this question, the patient's history of vomiting, followed by severe, persistent pain and systemic toxicity, combined with the widened mediastinum on chest radiograph, strongly suggests the diagnosis. Boerhaave syndrome is a surgical emergency; the mortality rate is 50% without rapid, aggressive treatment and definitive surgical repair within 24 hours. The rupture occurs when forceful vomiting causes a sudden rise in intraesophageal pressure. The result is a transmucosal esophageal tear, and then perforation. Rupture leads to leakage of luminal contents into the mediastinum and thorax, with subsequent necrotizing mediastinitis. Classically, patients present with vomiting, chest pain, and subcutaneous emphysema with progression to sepsis and cardiovascular collapse. The pain is typically acute, severe, and constant, often radiating to the back or shoulders and worsened by swallowing. The Hamman sign, or crunch, is another feature of Boerhaave syndrome. It is a crunching and crackling noise heard over the precordium with each heartbeat resulting from free air within the mediastinum. Radiographic findings include a wide mediastinum, pleural effusion, pneumothorax, and subcutaneous emphysema. Other common causes of esophageal rupture include sneezing, seizures, childbirth, heavy lifting, defecation, and coughing. Upper endoscopy is an increasingly common cause of more proximal esophageal iatrogenic perforation. Definitive management of esophageal rupture consists of aggressive resuscitation with intravenous fluids and hemodynamic support, intravenous broad-spectrum antibiotics, and emergent surgical consultation for definitive repair. Endoscopy, CT scan, or an esophagram with water-soluble contrast can establish the diagnosis but should not delay the definitive surgical repair.

334. The answer is B, Beta-blockers – acute MI.

(Jones, 1-3; Marx, 1082-1084, Tintinalli, 441-450)

Beta-blockers have been shown to lower blood pressure and reduce anginal symptoms, cardiac output, and mortality rates in patients after acute MI (AMI). Treatment with oral beta-blockers is recommended within 24 hours of admission for all AMI patients without contraindications. Treatment with beta-blockers on discharge is also a Joint Commission measure of the quality of patient care for hospitals. Contraindications include findings of heart failure or low output state, known left ventricular systolic dysfunction, conduction blocks, active asthma, or reactive airway disease. Both ACE inhibitors and angiotensin II receptor blockers (ARBs) are contraindicated in pregnant women due to reported fetal toxicity and fetal demise. In contrast, methyldopa does not compromise uteroplacental blood flow or have long-term adverse effects on a child's development and, therefore, is considered safe in pregnancy. Labetalol is also considered to be safe in pregnancy, although the data supporting its use are limited. Hydralazine has also been used extensively in pregnancy. Short-acting dihydropyridine calcium-channel blockers have the potential to increase mortality rates in the setting of AMI. In addition, they are considered second-line therapy for treatment of aortic dissection. Both ACE inhibitors and ARBs are more effective in slowing the progression of chronic kidney disease than other antihypertensive agents. These, in combination with a loop diuretic (rather than thiazide diuretics), are more effective in treating hypertension in these patients.

335. The answer is A, Hydroxocobalamin.

(Marx, 2383-2384; Nelson, 783, 1678-1683; Wolfson, 1470-1472)

Hydroxocobalamin is a vitamin B_{12} precursor that has recently been approved by the U.S. Food and Drug Administration for use in cyanide poisoning. Hydroxocobalamin binds to cyanide to form cyanocobalamin (vitamin B_{12}). Potential etiologies of cyanide toxicity include ingestion of cyanogenic compounds (apricot pits, cassava); ingestion of cyanide salts (potassium cyanide); inhalation of smoke from fires that involve burning of nitrocellulose, rubber, silk, and wool; and iatrogenic causes (excessive use of cyanide containing nitroprusside). Cyanide binds to cytochrome oxidase in the electron transport chain and inhibits oxidative phosphorylation. The resulting inability of cells to use oxygen manifests clinically quickly in large oxygen-requiring organs such as the brain (convulsions, coma) and the heart (hypotension, dysrhythmias). Anaerobic metabolism leads to significant lactic acidosis. The diagnosis of cyanide poisoning is made clinically, and treatment must be initiated without delay for confirmatory testing. Pyridoxine (vitamin B_6) is the treatment for isoniazid (INH)-induced convulsions. By various mechanisms, including pyridoxine depletion, INH inhibits the vitamin B_6-dependent conversion of the excitatory neurotransmitter glutamate to the inhibitory neurotransmitter GABA. Vitamin K is used to antagonize the effects of warfarin and superwarfarin (such as those used in rodenticides). Thiamine (vitamin B_1) is used in the treatment of thiamine deficiency, which can lead to Wernicke encephalopathy.

336. The answer is A, 14-year-old with a facial laceration after an assault.

(Marx, 2582, 2593-2594; Tintinalli, 2023-2024; Wolfson, 1677)

In general, if a minor presents to the emergency department for care and does not have an emergency medical condition (EMC) and does not meet the criteria for mature minor or emancipated minor status, proper consent must be obtained before treatment. The mature minor and emancipated minor designations are exceptions that state laws and courts have applied to allow minors to seek treatment on their own without parental consent. The mature minor is defined as a minor, usually between 15 and 17 years old, who is clearly able to understand the nature of his or her illness or injury as well as appreciate the risks and benefits of the proposed treatment. A mature minor's feelings and choices should be taken into account when making treatment decisions, as long as he or she has the ability to understand the effects of those decisions. Emancipated minor is a different legal status. In general, the emancipated minor is capable of making his or her own medical decisions if he or she is a member of the U.S. Armed Forces; married, divorced, separated, or widowed; a parent; pregnant; believes he or she has a disease that is a public health threat, such as a sexually transmitted infection; or financially independent. Although state laws vary regarding consent in the care of minors, the Emergency Medical Treatment and Labor Act, known as EMTALA, is a federal law and takes precedence over any state consent laws. Therefore, any minor who presents to an emergency department should be evaluated for an EMC without delay. If stabilization and treatment for the EMC (with or without transfer) are needed, they should be provided without delay.

337. The answer is B, Parent-applied mouth-to-mouth blowing.

(Botma, 598-600; Roberts, 719)

Nasal foreign bodies are a common problem in young children. Fortunately, having a parent provide positive pressure into the oral cavity can expel the object. Most techniques for removing the foreign body (catheter, forceps, probe) require remarkable patience and cooperation from the child. Since this is not a reasonable expectation of young children, restraints or procedural sedation is usually required. The application of positive pressure into the mouth to expel a nasal foreign body has been described in the literature. An older child can simply be asked to close one nostril and blow out. The physician can also blow air into the mouth with a bag-valve-mask device. But to reduce the child's fear and anxiety, the parent can be asked to blow in the child's mouth, with the clear nostril held closed. The parent is told to blow "like giving mouth-to-mouth," and the child is told the parent is going to "give you a big kiss." Fifteen of 19 children were successfully treated with this technique in the case series by Botma. None of the children required restraint or sedation, and all of the parents were satisfied with the approach.

338. The answer is A, Admit with urology consultation.

(Evans, 379-384; Tintinalli, 656)

The ultrasound image in this question is consistent with hydronephrosis, and the patient's symptoms are consistent with a kidney stone. In a pregnant patient, admission and surgical intervention are considered if conservative treatment fails or if the patient has infected hydronephrosis, obstruction of a solitary kidney, or bilateral ureteric obstruction. The urinalysis in this patient appears to indicate infection, so surgical intervention is needed. Gynecologic evaluation might also be needed, but the urologic consultation takes precedence so that the obstructed collecting system can be drained. Although kidney stones are uncommon in pregnancy, they do occur and should be considered in the differential diagnosis of abdominal or flank pain and hematuria. Pregnant patients are treated the same as nonpregnant patients, with hydration, analgesia, and imaging. The imaging modality of choice in pregnant patients with kidney stones is ultrasonography because of the lack of ionizing radiation. It lacks the ability to consistently diagnose the stone and ureteric obstruction, but it is painless and requires no preparation or contrast material.

339. The answer is A, Order head CT, shunt series, and shunt tap.

(Duhaime, 705-713; Tintinalli, 1180-1183)

The most common complications of ventriculoperitoneal (VP) shunts are shunt malfunction and infection. They frequently present with nonspecific symptoms such as headache, nausea, vomiting, abdominal pain, irritability, and lethargy and can progress to coma and death. Although the patient in this question might have a viral illness, given the symptoms and exposure to influenza A, the more serious consideration of a shunt obstruction or infection should be addressed first. Shunt infections might not present classically with fever and meningismus. Difficulty compressing the ventricular chamber can indicate a distal obstruction, and a refill time greater than 3 seconds can indicate a proximal obstruction. However, up to 40% of obstructions can feel normal with palpation over the chamber. The appropriate initial workup for suspected VP shunt obstruction or infection includes head CT to evaluate for obstruction or ventriculitis, a shunt series to detect kinks or breaks in the shunt tubing, and a shunt tap to test fluid for infection. An emergent neurosurgery consultation is essential for admission, replacement of the shunt, and administration of intravenous or intrathecal antibiotics if an infection is found. Lumbar puncture is not accurate for diagnosing shunt infection. Antiemetics and rehydration are appropriate management for a viral syndrome. Again, treatment with an antiviral medication and followup care provided by the pediatrician are appropriate if influenza is subsequently diagnosed, but this should not be the first course of action when a more serious etiology is suspected. Acetazolamide, serial lumbar punctures, and fibrinolytic agents are appropriate nonsurgical management for children with critical hydrocephalus who are too unstable for surgical shunt placement.

340. **The answer is D, Myocarditis can present with difficulty breathing, retractions, and wheezing as the dominant features.**

(Marx, 2160; Strange, 439-442)

Respiratory distress that includes difficulty breathing, retractions, and wheezing is the most common complaint in children with myocarditis. The main features of the clinical presentation of myocarditis are variable and nonspecific. Although most common, respiratory distress is the dominant symptom complex in only about two-thirds of children with myocarditis. Other symptom complexes associated with myocarditis include vomiting, diarrhea, and abdominal pain; chest pain, palpitations, and heart failure; and lethargy, syncope, and shock. The erythrocyte sedimentation rate is likely to be elevated in children with myocarditis, but this is a nonspecific finding and does not differentiate myocarditis from other conditions. Beta-blockers are contraindicated in children with myocarditis, as heart block can present or subsequently develop. The ECG findings in children with myocarditis are generally nonspecific and include nonspecific ST-segment changes, low-voltage complexes, inverted T waves, AV blocks, and other dysrhythmias. High voltage is an unlikely finding in ECGs of children with myocarditis.

341. **The answer is B, Remove all of the patient's clothing.**

(Marx, 768; Roberts, 771-772)

Hospital personnel should first protect themselves in this situation, and then attend to the patient. The emergency physician's first step should be to apply personal protective equipment (PPE), to include a respirator, protective clothing, face shield, and two layers of gloves. When at all possible, decontamination of the patient should occur next, with removal of clothing and removal of the offending substance and collection to avoid further contamination. All clothing should be removed; it is important to cut the clothing off instead of pulling it off. The next step is to brush off as much of the dry material as possible, then wash the patient with copious amounts of warm water. Large amounts of low-pressure saline or water should be used to minimize splashing and skin irritation.

342. **The answer is C, *Mycoplasma pneumoniae*.**

(Marx, 929-937; Tintinalli, 479-489)

Mycoplasma pneumoniae is the most common cause of atypical pneumonia in adults and the most common cause of all types of pneumonia in adults younger than 40 years. In addition to causing pneumonia, *Mycoplasma* can also cause bullae of tympanic membrane. *M. pneumoniae* generally causes a mild pneumonia with severe cough and mild sputum production. It is also associated with extrapulmonary manifestations, including dermatologic, cardiac, hematologic, and neurologic. The rash varies from a morbilliform pattern to, in rare cases, Stevens-Johnson syndrome. Cardiac complications include conduction defects and myocarditis or pericarditis. Neurologic complications include Guillain-Barré syndrome and aseptic meningitis. The radiographic appearance is a diffuse interstitial pattern or cobweb-like infiltrates. The treatment of choice is a macrolide such as azithromycin. In contrast, atypical pneumonia caused by *Legionella pneumophila* accounts for a very small percentage (about 5%) of pneumonias but has a higher mortality rate. *Legionella* tends to affect the elderly or immunocompromised. It is often spread by contaminated water supplies or ventilation systems. *Legionella* also has extrapulmonary manifestations that include altered mental status, relative bradycardia, abdominal pain, vomiting and diarrhea, abnormal liver function test results, hematuria, hyponatremia, and renal insufficiency. *Legionella* is treated with a macrolide or respiratory fluoroquinolone. *Bordetella pertussis* causes whooping cough and should be suspected when a patient has had a cough for more than 2 weeks. Up to 25% of patients with a prolonged cough can have pertussis. Treatment is with a macrolide, but antibiotics do not appear to have a significant impact on duration or severity of illness. *Yersinia pestis* is the bacterium that causes bubonic plague. It can cause pneumonia, septicemia, or plague. Symptoms include fever, headache, and lymphadenopathy (buboes). Streptomycin or gentamicin is considered first-line treatment. Unlike *Chlamydophilia pneumoniae*, which causes pneumonia, *Chlamydia psittaci* causes an infection known as psittacosis.

343. The answer is A, Calcification of the laryngeal cartilages is incomplete in pediatric patients.

(Marx, 382-383; Wolfson, 186-188)

Computed tomography is the primary imaging modality used to diagnose laryngeal injuries. However, calcification of the laryngeal cartilages does not occur until the teenage years, which makes the diagnosis of trauma to these structures difficult in pediatric patients. The laryngeal structures include the incomplete tracheal rings and the cricoid cartilage, which is the only complete ring in the larynx. Trauma to the cricoid cartilage can lead to complete airway obstruction. Direct laryngoscopy, flexible laryngoscopy, or direct visualization of laryngeal trauma through a penetrating neck injury can also be used to make the diagnosis. Most laryngotracheal injuries occur as a result of motor vehicle crashes, in particular, from the blunt trauma involved with striking the neck on a fixed structure such as the steering wheel or dashboard. Assaults, clothesline-type injuries, injuries caused by improperly fitting shoulder belts, and athletic injuries can also cause laryngeal trauma, but none is the most common etiology. Pain with tongue movement can be seen with injuries to the hyoid bone, epiglottis, or larynx; it does not localize trauma to the larynx alone. A patient with laryngeal trauma can present with immediate airway compromise, or the impact on the airway can be more subtle and present in a delayed manner depending on the severity of injury.

344. The answer is B, Postural hypotension.

(Marx, 2191-2199, 2348-2352; Tintinalli, 402, 971-972)

Postural hypotension is commonly seen in elderly patients with relatively minor volume loss. Frank hypotension can be seen at lower levels of volume loss in elderly patients compared to younger patients; elderly patients are unable to increase their heart rates sufficiently to compensate for volume loss and have loss of autonomic reflexes through physiologic changes of aging, disease processes, and medications. In pediatric patients with dehydration, tachycardia typically predominates until the volume loss is extreme, so hypotension in a pediatric patient implies major volume loss. Postural hypotension is not commonly seen in pediatric patients, most likely because they have very brisk autonomic reflexes and very responsive cardiovascular systems. The clinical signs of extreme dehydration are well characterized in the pediatric population. Many of these clinical signs are shared across age groups and include reduced skin turgor, dry mucus membranes, sunken eyes, and tachycardia. The assessment of fluid status in elderly patients is often more difficult than in pediatric patients, and good evidence is lacking as to what specific clinical signs help guide management. In the elderly, dehydration is also commonly associated with confusion, which is unusual in younger adults and pediatric patients. Skin turgor can be poor in elderly patients at baseline, and it has been suggested that assessing skin turgor over the sternum might be helpful in older patients.

345. The answer is A, Broad-spectrum antibiotics.

(Chau, 446-447; Marx, 1148; Wu, e5-e7)

In a patient who presents with sudden pain after vomiting, a history of hiatal hernia, and signs of shock, along with radiographic findings of a distended stomach above the diaphragm, the diagnosis of a strangulated paraesophageal hernia with subsequent gastric volvulus is likely. Aggressive fluid resuscitation, broad-spectrum antibiotics, and an emergent surgical consultation are required. A hiatal hernia can be sliding, with only a small portion of the stomach below the gastroesophageal junction prolapsed through the diaphragm into the chest, or paraesophageal, with the entire fundus of the stomach prolapsed into the chest. Gastric volvulus occurs most commonly in patients with paraesophageal hernias who are between 40 and 50 years old. The combination of abdominal or chest pain, retching or vomiting, and the inability to pass a nasogastric tube defines the Borchardt triad of gastric volvulus. Initially, nasogastric decompression should be attempted to reduce the volvulus. However, endoscopic reduction should not be performed if late signs of ischemia or infarction are present; the patient in the question, for example, is critically ill and has an elevated lactate level, so endoscopy is not appropriate. Although the patient is hypotensive and tachycardic, the hemoglobin level does not mandate transfusion of blood products. The underlying etiology of the lactic acidosis is gastric ischemia, which cannot be corrected with sodium bicarbonate.

346. The answer is B, Short, soft diastolic murmur – aortic regurgitation.

(Marx, 1072-1074; Tintinalli, 415-423)

Murmurs are described based on the following features:
- Intensity – from barely audible in a quiet room (= 1) to heard without the stethoscope (= 6)
- Timing – systole or diastole
- Location on the chest at which best heard
- Shape – crescendo or decrescendo, and so on
- Pitch – harsh, blowing, or rumbling, and so on
- Presence or absence of radiation

Mitral stenosis classically presents with a loud S_1 and an opening snap in early diastole (just after S_2), with a low-pitched, rumbling mid-diastolic apical murmur. Aortic regurgitation is described as a soft early diastolic, decrescendo murmur heard best at the left upper sternal border with the patient leaning forward. It is often associated with a widened pulse pressure and can be associated with a rapidly rising and falling carotid pulse, spontaneous nail bed pulsations, and a to-and-fro murmur over the femoral artery. Mitral regurgitation classically presents as a blowing holosystolic murmur that radiates to the axilla. It is best heard with the bell when the patient is in the left lateral decubitus position. Patients with aortic stenosis classically have a harsh crescendo-decrescendo systolic murmur heard best at the right second intercostal space that radiates to the carotids and is associated with an S_4 gallop. In comparison, ventricular septal defects have a characteristic loud, harsh, blowing holosystolic murmur heard best over the lower left sternal border (third or fourth intercostal spaces); when large, they can be accompanied by a displaced point of maximal impulse and a palpable thrill.

347. The answer is C, Potassium chloride.

(Marx, 1620; Wolfson, 1046-1047, 1052)

The ECG indicates signs of hypokalemia (QT-interval prolongation and U waves), which fits with the clinical picture of the autosomal dominantly inherited hypokalemic periodic paralysis that can be induced by a large carbohydrate meal. Administration of small doses of potassium is the appropriate initial management. Periodic paralyses include both familial periodic paralysis, of which there are both hypokalemic (more common) and hyperkalemic variants, and thyrotoxic periodic paralysis. The latter is similar to the hypokalemic variant but is associated with hyperthyroidism (treatment includes propranolol, not thyroxine). Thyrotoxic periodic paralysis is most common in persons of Asian descent. Thyroid studies should be sent in patients with a first episode of hypokalemic paralysis and those without a family history of it. In periodic paralysis, weakness typically affects the lower extremities more than the upper extremities and results from a greatly exaggerated rapid transient transcellular shifting of potassium that might occur in response to certain triggers such as a large carbohydrate meal (induces insulin release). Importantly, although in the hypokalemic variant serum potassium concentrations are low during the event, total body stores are normal. Therefore, as in the case described, administration of only small amounts of potassium with close monitoring to avoid overshooting is essential. Hypomagnesemia and hypocalcemia can both cause a QT-interval prolongation similar to that seen with hypokalemia. Significant depletion typically manifests with neuromuscular excitation, including hyperreflexia and tetany, and, after identification, repletion should occur. Magnesium depletion can coexist in situations of significant total body potassium depletion (not present with periodic paralysis) and hinder hypokalemia correction without magnesium administration.

348. The answer is C, Rewarming of the part should continue despite painful sensation.

(Jurkovich, 247-267; Marx, 1861-1867; Tintinalli, 1332-1335)

In the management of frostbite, generous analgesia is required during rewarming, as reperfusion can be intensely painful. A common pitfall is the premature termination of rewarming secondary to return of sensation (in the setting of intense pain), resulting in a partially thawed part. Rewarming is complete when the part feels pliable and appears erythematous, typically requiring 10 to 30 minutes of submersion in 40°C to 42°C water. More than 75% of patients present complaining of numbness and some initial sensory deficit. Initial presenting signs include a hard, cold, white, and anesthetic body part. The severity of the frostbite determines the extent of the injury: in more severe cases, victims have an early black, dry eschar prior to mummification. In the most severe cases (fourth degree), victims have tissue necrosis and gangrene. The pathophysiology of frostbite includes ice crystal formation on a cellular level, cellular dehydration secondary to changes in water balance, and microthrombi and vasospasm from endothelial injury, resulting in thrombotic injury. Further thrombotic occlusion occurs after thawing due to the arachidonic acid cascade that results in vasoconstriction and platelet aggregation. The coagulopathy associated with hypothermic trauma does not prevent this cascade. Prehospital care is an important component and should include removal of wet or constrictive clothing. Friction massage should be avoided to prevent further damage, and rewarming should never be initiated if there is any risk for interrupted or incomplete thawing. Post-thaw injuries include severe edema from vascular permeability resulting in compartment syndrome, gangrene, and superinfection with tetanus, *Staphylococcus*, and *Streptococcus*. Hyperbaric oxygen therapy has not been shown to have any benefit in the treatment of frostbite at any stage of disease. Current research suggests that the use of digital angiography and thrombolytic drugs might have a place as part of the immediate post-thaw management of frostbite.

349. The answer is B, Commonly associated with leukopenia.

(Marx, 1788-1789; Tintinalli, 1070-1074)

Ehrlichiosis is an infectious disease caused by *Ehrlichia*, a gram-negative obligate intracellular bacteria. It is transmitted by the bite of *Ixodes* or *Amblyomma* ticks. Most cases are reported from the southeastern United States, but forms of the disease occur throughout the country. Ehrlichiosis is a prolonged febrile, flulike illness, and the clinical picture is similar to that of Rocky Mountain spotted fever (RMSF). Patients experience myalgias, malaise, and headache. Gastrointestinal symptoms are also common, including nausea, vomiting, anorexia, and abdominal pain. A point of difference between ehrlichiosis and RMSF is that rash is unusual in ehrlichiosis; when it does exist, it spares the palms and soles. The laboratory findings in ehrlichiosis include leukopenia, thrombocytopenia, and elevated liver enzymes. The leukopenia is partially due to its propensity to infect white blood cells. Ehrlichiosis is treated with doxycycline 100 mg twice daily for 1 to 2 weeks. Other diseases transmitted by ticks include Colorado tick fever, a viral illness transmitted by *Dermacentor* ticks; it requires only supportive care. *Borrelia burgdorferi* is the causative agent of Lyme disease. *Anopheles* mosquitoes are the vector for malaria.

350. The answer is A, Endometritis.

(Marx, 2346; Tintinalli, 702-703)

Pelvic infection is the most common serious complication postpartum. The presentation described in the question is consistent with endometritis. Classic findings are fever, foul-smelling, profuse, bloody discharge, uterine and adnexal tenderness, and abdominal pain. The single most significant risk factor for endometritis is cesarean delivery (5% of all vaginal deliveries, 10% of all cesarean deliveries). Other risk factors include lower socioeconomic level, multiple gestations, younger maternal age, and longer duration of labor and membrane rupture. Most patients with postsurgical endometritis require admission. This patient is at increased risk for pyelonephritis because of Foley catheter placement during the cesarean delivery, so urinalysis is warranted. However, pyelonephritis does not explain the foul-smelling vaginal discharge. Mastitis usually presents with a unilateral, tender, warm, swollen breast. When a patient experiences hemorrhage during cesarean delivery, uterine packing with gauze is sometimes used to provide tamponade. This increases the risk of infection, but since the patient reports no complications related to the delivery, packing is not likely present. With the fever and foul-smelling discharge, a wound hematoma is unlikely.

351. **The answer is D, 60-year-old woman with a history of brain tumor and resection 6 months earlier, symptom onset 90 minutes earlier; blood pressure 175/90, NIH stroke scale score 18, head CT negative.**

(Albers, 483S-490S; Jauch, S823; Marx, 1333-1345)

Intravenous administration of tPA is the only therapy approved for acute ischemic stroke. The criteria are lengthy; of the patients described, only the 60-year-old woman is a candidate. She is older than 18 with symptom onset less than 180 minutes, blood pressure less than 185/110 mm Hg, and a stroke scale score lower than 20. She has had intracranial surgery, but it was more than 3 months earlier, and her head CT does not show any evidence of hemorrhage or infarction. The literature has shown that patients with NIH stroke scores higher than 20 have a higher risk of intracranial hemorrhage (ICH). The 60-year-old man is not a candidate because his blood pressure is higher than 185/110. Labetalol (1-2 doses of 10-20 mg IV) can be started to bring it to within the acceptable range, but only then would he be eligible for thrombolytic therapy. The 45-year-old man is not eligible for tPA because of his stroke scale score and platelet count. The 45-year-old woman is not eligible because of the seizure at symptom onset. One other notable exception to those eligible for thrombolytic therapy is sickle cell patients: those with acute ischemic stroke are treated with exchange transfusion. Inclusion criteria for tPA in acute ischemic stroke are as follows:

- Age 18 years and older
- Clinical diagnosis of ischemic stroke causing a measureable neurologic deficit
- Time of symptom onset well established to be less than 180 minutes before treatment would begin

Exclusion criteria are as follows:

- Evidence of intracranial hemorrhage on noncontrast head CT
- Only minor or rapidly resolving stroke symptoms
- High clinical suspicion of subarachnoid hemorrhage even with normal CT findings
- Active internal bleeding within the past 21 days
- Known bleeding diathesis, including but not limited to: platelet count less than 100,000/mcL; heparin within 48 hours and elevated activated PTT; recent use of anticoagulant and elevated PT greater than 15 seconds or INR greater than 1.7
- Within 3 months of intracranial surgery, serious head trauma, or previous stroke
- Within 14 days of major surgery or serious trauma
- Recent arterial puncture at noncompressible site
- Lumbar puncture within 7 days
- History of intracranial hemorrhage, arteriovenous malformation, or aneurysm
- Witnessed seizure at stroke onset
- Recent acute MI

- On repeated measurements, systolic pressure greater than 185 mm Hg or diastolic pressure greater than 110 mm Hg at time of treatment requiring aggressive treatment to reduce blood pressure to within these limits

352. The answer is A, Abduction and external rotation.

(Marx, 581; Roberts, 877-881)

The Milch technique is described as gentle, well tolerated, and highly successful for reducing shoulder dislocations. The technique includes abduction, external rotation, and gentle traction of the arm, as if having the patient reach for an apple. The goal is to have the arm abducted in an arm-over-the-head position. The patient might be able to help initiate the procedure by raising the arm and placing the hand behind the head. Once in this position, gentle traction and external rotation are applied; the emergency physician might need to gently push the humeral head into the glenoid fossa. If the patient is subsequently able to place the palm on the opposite shoulder, reduction is complete. The external rotation method occurs when the arm is in adduction and gently and slowly fully externally rotated until the forearm is nearly in the coronal plane. The traction-countertraction method is a familiar and frequently used reduction technique. An assistant uses a sheet to apply countertraction, then the emergency physician applies traction and, if needed, gentle, limited external rotation. Postreduction radiographs should be reviewed to assess for occult fracture and displacement of fracture fragments and to confirm the reduction. The patient should be immediately placed in a shoulder immobilizer or sling.

353. The answer is B, *Klebsiella pneumoniae.*

(Marx, 929-937; Tintinalli, 479-489)

Klebsiella pneumoniae is a gram-negative bacillus that is considered a rare cause of community-acquired pneumonia (CAP). The characteristic sputum is described as currant jelly because it is a mixture of blood and sputum, giving it a translucent appearance. It is often associated with aspiration. *Klebsiella* rarely causes disease in a normal host and is more commonly seen in patients with COPD and in alcoholic and elderly patients. Radiographic findings include a lobar pneumonia with a bulging fissure on chest radiograph. *Klebsiella* can lead to lung necrosis. Resistance patterns vary widely, but third-generation cephalosporins are first-line agents. However, treatment for CAP should cover all common pathogens, which include typical and atypical organisms. All of the organisms listed are causes of CAP. *Streptococcus pneumoniae* is the most common cause of pneumonia in adults. The classic description of the sputum in *S. pneumoniae* infection is rusty colored. *Haemophilus influenzae* is the second most common cause of CAP. *Mycoplasma pneumoniae* is considered an atypical cause of CAP but is associated with complications, including Guillain-Barré and transverse myelitis.

354. The answer is D, The most common cause of immediate death is exsanguination.

(Marx, 383-385; Wolfson, 189-194)

Penetrating trauma to the neck most commonly occurs in zone 2, between the cricoid cartilage and the angle of the mandible. Vascular injury is common and occurs in up to 25% of penetrating neck wounds because of the superficial location of the vessels anteriorly. The internal jugular vein is the most commonly injured vessel overall, and the carotid artery is the most commonly injured artery. Therefore, exsanguination is the most common cause of immediate death with these injuries. The vertebral artery has a relatively deep and posterior location, which is why injury occurs in only 1.3% of penetrating traumatic neck injuries. Angiography remains the gold standard of diagnostic workup in penetrating neck injuries that involve vascular trauma; it can improve detection of zone 1 (base of the neck, below the cricoid cartilage) and zone 3 (upper neck, above the angle of the mandible) injuries that are occult clinically. Computed tomography angiography has been a useful adjunct as well in these patients. Zone 3 vascular injuries can be difficult to access surgically, so many surgeons prefer routine imaging. But because zone 2 injuries are so surgically accessible, there is some controversy regarding routine imaging of injuries in this area because it can delay definitive management. Duplex ultrasonography can be useful for identifying vascular dissection and hematoma. Its usefulness can be limited in zone 1 and zone 3 injuries; it can miss distal carotid and vertebral artery injuries. Therefore, many surgeons still believe that angiography is the gold standard for the evaluation of vascular trauma in the neck.

355. The answer is A, Chronic kidney disease.

(Marx, 1554; Mathur, 1410-1419)

Pruritus is associated with many systemic conditions, and, in many, there are no visible skin lesions, only the scratch marks and complications such as infections. Pruritus is frequently associated with chronic kidney disease and is most often seen in patients who are being treated with hemodialysis, where it can be quite disabling. The exact mechanism is not understood. It is rarely seen in patients with acute renal failure and is not thought to be caused by accumulations of urea or creatinine. The broad groups of systemic illnesses associated with pruritus are renal disease, cholestatic disease, hematologic disease (especially iron deficiency and polycythemia), endocrine disorders, pruritus related to malignancy (especially lymphoma), and idiopathic generalized pruritus. Pruritus is not associated with heart failure unless there is associated hepatic congestion. Pruritus might be seen as a side effect of thiazide or loop-acting diuretics. Pruritus is not typically described in association with adrenal diseases. It is frequently described in association with hyperthyroidism (possibly due to skin blood flow) and with hypothyroidism (dry skin). The association of diabetes mellitus with pruritus is typically only seen in the presence of a diabetic neuropathy.

356. The answer is A, Admission to a basic pediatric unit for the initiation of corticosteroid therapy.

(Marx, 2210-2211; Wolfson, 1250-1252)

The patient in this question presents with nephrotic syndrome and is best cared for by being admitted to a basic pediatric unit for workup and to have a pediatric nephrologist evaluate for any contraindications for high-dose steroid therapy. Although the mainstay of treatment for nephrotic syndrome is oral corticosteroid therapy (prednisone 2 mg/kg/day), this can wait for contraindications to be carefully ruled out. This often includes a tuberculin skin test. Although some children can have substantial intravascular fluid losses leading to shock, the child in this scenario is not in shock. Therefore, admission to an ICU for invasive blood pressure monitoring is unwarranted. Renal failure is rare in children with nephrotic syndrome and is not present in the child in this scenario based on the normal BUN and creatinine levels and the continued production of urine. Therefore, hemodialysis is not indicated in the emergency department and is unlikely to be needed during hospitalization. Diuresis is typically indicated for children who have respiratory distress with or without pleural effusions and those with substantial ascites. Thus, diuresis is not indicated, but workup and observation for these complications make discharge home not a good option. Children with nephrotic syndrome are hypercoagulable, but anticoagulation is indicated only for those children manifesting clinically appreciable vascular thromboses given the risks associated with anticoagulation.

357. The answer is C, Esophageal endoscopy.

(Marx, 410-413; Tintinalli, 551)

Iatrogenic injury accounts for about three-fourths of all esophageal perforations. Overall, endoscopy is the most common cause of esophageal perforation. The risk is higher with rigid endoscopes than with flexible endoscopes. Esophageal dilation of strictures is the next most common iatrogenic etiology of perforation. Too rapid a dilatation of the stricture can result in perforation. Nasogastric intubation is the most common cause of esophageal perforation in the emergency department. Spontaneous rupture of the esophagus, otherwise known as Boerhaave syndrome, classically occurs in men 40 to 50 years old, often after excessive alcohol or food intake and forceful emesis. It accounts for 10% to 15% of esophageal perforations. Foreign bodies can cause esophageal perforation by direct injury, chemical injury, or pressure on the endothelial wall causing necrosis. They account for roughly 10% of esophageal perforations. Trauma can result in esophageal injury and occurs in 5% to 10% of patients with neck injuries. Esophageal injury and perforation occur in penetrating trauma more frequently than in blunt trauma. Caustic burns occur after ingestion of acidic or basic substances and occur most commonly as accidental ingestions in patients 1 to 5 years old or as intentional ingestions (suicide attempts) in older patients. Generally, larger amounts of the substances are ingested during suicide gestures. Pediatric patients are likely to ingest only small amounts because of the taste. Perforation of the esophagus is a true emergency and has a high mortality rate even with effective treatment, especially if the diagnosis is delayed for more than 24 hours. Treatment involves airway management, fluid resuscitation, broad-spectrum antibiotics, and emergent surgery consultation.

358. The answer is D, Ventricular fibrillation.

(Maron, 917-927; Tintinalli, 1759)

Commotio cordis is ventricular fibrillation that occurs after a blunt blow to the chest in a patient who does not have any structural heart disease. Most victims of commotio cordis are previously healthy athletes who sustain the injury during a sporting event. It is thought that the location of the blow must be directly over the heart, as there is no evidence in humans or experimental models that a blow outside the precordium can cause sudden death. The timing of this blow must occur during the upstroke of the T wave to cause ventricular fibrillation. Commotio cordis leads to sudden cardiac death; because interventions to address ventricular fibrillation are frequently delayed, resuscitation is rare. Appropriate treatment consists of standard CPR according to basic life support/advanced cardiovascular life support guidelines, including defibrillation. Asystole, atrial fibrillation, and pulseless electrical activity are not pathophysiologic rhythms associated with commotio cordis.

359. The answer is B, Lorazepam.

(Marx, 1964-1969; Nelson, 1056; Wolfson, 1498-1510)

Lorazepam or another benzodiazepine is the preferred initial agent to treat convulsions associated with tricyclic antidepressant (TCA) poisoning. Sodium bicarbonate is a reasonable choice to prevent worsened acidosis, but it is not effective for the treatment of the convulsions themselves. Various properties of TCAs that manifest in poisoning include sodium-channel blockade, antimuscarinic activity, peripheral alpha$_1$ blockade, and GABA antagonism. The QRS prolongation from sodium-channel blockade is treated predominantly with intravenous administration of sodium bicarbonate, with the goal of preventing further prolongation and deterioration into dysrhythmias. The etiology of TCA-induced convulsions is probably multifactorial. Although status epilepticus can occur, even isolated convulsions represent significant toxicity after a TCA overdose and should be treated aggressively. Benzodiazepines, by causing GABA agonism, can stop convulsions and are considered first-line therapy. Rapid chemical paralysis to avoid worsening acidosis and subsequent exacerbation of sodium-channel blockade effect on the heart is prudent if benzodiazepines fail to work immediately. For convulsions refractory to benzodiazepines, propofol or barbiturates can be considered, although they are often challenging to administer in a hypotensive patient. Physostigmine, a reversible acetylcholinesterase inhibitor, can be used both diagnostically and therapeutically in various antimuscarinic poisonings. However, administration of physostigmine to patients with TCA poisoning (QRS-interval prolongation, convulsions) has resulted in asystole and is contraindicated. Flumazenil is also contraindicated for TCA poisoning. Although it does not cause seizures, it will temporarily reverse a coingested benzodiazepine, and, in the presence of a proconvulsant coingestant such as a TCA, this could lead to status epilepticus. The anticonvulsive properties of phenytoin are distinct from how TCAs induce convulsions. It has not been demonstrated to be of benefit in TCA-induced convulsions (or any other drug-induced convulsions), and it is not recommended.

360. The answer is D, Examination for an emergency medical condition.

(Adams, 2195-2196; Bitterman, 23, 40-41, 46-47, 98-99; Marx, 2582-2590; Wolfson, 1684-1685)

The Emergency Medical Treatment and Labor Act (EMTALA) is a federal law that has had significant impact on the way patients are evaluated in emergency departments nationwide. It has generated a large number of regulations and much debate, but the purpose of the law itself is straightforward: to ensure that people who come to emergency departments to see if they have emergency medical conditions (EMCs) are examined and stabilized as needed regardless of whether they can pay for those services. Of all EMTALA mandates, those regarding the medical screening examination (MSE) are the most complex. Hospitals must provide an appropriate MSE to any individual who comes to the emergency department and a request is made on that person's behalf for examination or treatment for a medical condition. The purpose of the MSE is to determine whether the individual has an EMC, and it must be performed using whatever resources are routinely available to the emergency department, including ancillary services and on-call physicians. And because the MSE and required stabilizing treatment must be provided without regard for the individual's ability to pay, the hospital must be careful regarding the documentation of insurance and medical information: obtaining this information must not delay examination or treatment. This step is not required or prohibited, but delaying care to complete it or denying care if an individual does not have it is a violation of federal regulations. The law does not specify which type of health care provider must perform the MSE, but the regulations are clear on the role of triage, stating that triage is not the equivalent of the MSE. The treatment of pain as it relates to EMTALA-mandated care has been controversial. Severe pain constitutes an EMC if it places the individual's health in jeopardy or if it is causing the individual to have serious impairment or dysfunction of body functions or parts. However, this does not mean that an emergency physician must provide a patient with the pain medication he or she requests, especially if the patient's EMC is stabilized. Followup care has also been controversial. Hospitals are required to provide stabilizing treatment for patients' EMCs; this includes specialty care provided by on-call physicians. Hospitals are required to maintain on-call panels so that specialty care can be provided in the hospital, but these regulations apply only to patients with EMCs as diagnosed in the MSE. A patient who does not have an EMC and is stable for discharge can be referred for followup care, but the hospital is not required to make these arrangements as part of the EMTALA mandates.

361. The answer is B, Approach the nerve from the contralateral side of the mouth (approximate 30-degree angle), about 1 cm above the occlusive surface of the teeth and parallel to the teeth, and advance the needle until it is in direct contact with the mandible.

(Auerbach, 642; Roberts, 502)

The correct approach as described allows the inferior alveolar nerve to be anesthetized with decreased risk of injecting the wrong nerve, causing nerve or vascular injury, or depositing anesthesia over bone rather than nerve. Injecting directly into the nerve can result in prolonged inferior alveolar paresthesias and the possibility of a permanently numb lip. The target for this procedure is the nerve that runs along the medial surface of the mandible; injecting the buccal mucosa results in depositing anesthetic in the V_2 sensory branches of the face, resulting in a numb cheek. Using too high an approach anesthetizes maxillary teeth and might result in an intra-arterial injection. Finally, advancing the needle directly posteriorly likely results in anesthetic being deposited in the parotid gland, which can result in temporary facial nerve paralysis and anesthesia. This approach also has a high risk of intra-arterial injection.

362. The answer is C, Perform perimortem cesarean delivery.

(Katz, 571-576; Roberts, 1058-1059; Tintinalli, 94-96; Vanden Hoek, S833-S838)

Perimortem cesarean delivery is rarely indicated and involves complex medical, ethical, and emotional considerations. According to the literature, infant survival is excellent if delivery takes place within 5 minutes of maternal death and might improve maternal outcome. Survival is unlikely if delivery occurs after 20 minutes of maternal arrest. Survival of the infant is also related to the performance of CPR on the mother, maturity of the fetus, and the availability of a neonatal ICU. Perimortem cesarean delivery is indicated only if the fetus is more than 24 weeks' gestation. Fundal height can be used to predict gestational age if unknown. The procedure involves using a No. 10 scalpel and making a mid-vertical incision through the abdominal wall, extending from the pubic symphysis to the umbilicus.

The incision should penetrate all abdominal layers to the peritoneal cavity. Retractors are used to expose the anterior surface of the uterus. The bladder should be reflected inferiorly to provide better access to uterus. Then, a 5-cm vertical incision is made through the lower uterine segment until amniotic fluid is obtained. The index and middle fingers should be inserted into the incision to separate the uterine wall from the fetus and the incision extended vertically up to the fundus using bandage scissors. The final steps involve delivering the fetus through the incision, suctioning the mouth and nose, and clamping and cutting the umbilical cord. The baby should be monitored in the neonatal ICU after birth. The 2010 advanced cardiovascular life support guidelines do not recommend intubation during the initial stages of resuscitation. Magnesium is used for hypertensive emergencies in pregnant females but is considered a second-line therapy for patients in ventricular fibrillation. There is no indication for thoracotomy in a patient with ventricular fibrillation with no history of trauma.

363. **The answer is D, Request neurosurgery consultation for urgent laminectomy and start cefepime and vancomycin.**

(Darouiche, 2012-2020; Marx, 207, 600-601)

Anterior epidural abscess (in addition to osteomyelitis and discitis, in this case) is most appropriately treated with urgent decompressive laminectomy and intravenous antibiotics. The most common organisms are staphylococci, including methicillin-resistant *Staphylococcus aureus*, as well as gram-negative bacilli (often from urinary sources). The most appropriate antibiotic choice is vancomycin and an extended-spectrum cephalosporin such as cefepime or ceftazidime. Patients who are considered to be at high risk for developing this condition include those with underlying immunocompromised disease states (diabetes, alcoholism, HIV), spine abnormalities or procedures, local infections or sepsis states, indwelling catheters, or a history of intravenous drug abuse. Impairment of neurologic function can progress rapidly; a baseline neurologic examination is essential and is highly predictive of ultimate outcome. Conservative (nonsurgical) therapy may be considered for patients who refuse surgery or are poor candidates for it. Additional situations for which surgical intervention is delayed or decided against include signs of paralysis for more than 24 hours and infections that extend through most of the spinal canal. The literature reflects controversy on this topic. For patients in whom surgery is not planned, antibiotics should be chosen based on positive blood cultures or on organisms cultured by radiology-guided aspiration of the abscess fluid. Lumbar puncture is not indicated for this patient; it is not an acceptable way to obtain abscess fluid and can disseminate infection further by introducing bacteria into the spinal canal. There is no role for urgent electromyography in this patient, whose urgent need is abscess decompression and antibiotic treatment.

364. **The answer is D, Temporarily stops the AICD response to a tachydysrhythmia.**

(Roberts, 245-246; Wolfson, 492-496)

When a magnet is applied over an AICD, it temporarily turns off the defibrillation action; thus, the AICD will not respond to a tachydysrhythmia and will not fire the defibrillator. When a magnet is placed over a pacemaker or AICD, the pacing function is not disabled; rather, the pacer reverts to an established rate and mode of operation. The response to the magnet does indeed vary by manufacturer, and also by model and mode of operation. In obese patients and in those with heavily developed chest wall musculature, more than one magnet might be required to elicit the desired effect on the implanted device. This can be accomplished by stacking the magnets on top of each other. The magnet does not turn the pacemaker off: it temporarily reprograms the pacer into asynchronous mode. Although there are several types of magnets, in general, any pacemaker magnet can be used. In any patient who presents with ventricular fibrillation, the device must be assumed to be nonfunctioning; the use of a magnet has no role in this situation, and, instead, standard ACLS protocols should be followed. The only impact of the presence of an AICD on a cardiac arrest situation is on the positioning of the paddles (anteroposterior) and avoiding shocks over the device.

365. **The answer is D, Vancomycin and levofloxacin.**

(Marx, 928-937; Tintinalli, 479-486)

The classic presentation of *Staphylococcus aureus* pneumonia is post–viral pneumonia that progresses to formation of a lung abscess that creates a cavitary lesion (pneumatoceles) on chest radiograph leading to bronchopleural fistulas and empyema. *S. aureus* is also associated with intravenous drug use and cystic fibrosis. Antibiotic choice should include vancomycin as well as coverage for community-acquired pneumonia such as levofloxacin. The choice of empiric antibiotics needs to be made based on epidemiologic factors of likely organisms. Coverage needs to be directed at both typical and atypical pathogens. Community-acquired pneumonia (CAP) was historically divided into typical and atypical patterns. Typical pneumonias were thought to be caused by pyogenic bacteria like *Streptococcus pneumoniae* or *Haemophilus influenzae* and presented with fever, productive cough, and lobar pneumonias. Atypical pneumonias were classically thought to present with fever, headache, and myalgias in addition to respiratory symptoms. They often do not take a lobar form. Atypical organisms include *Mycoplasma, Legionella,* and *Chlamydia.* Initially, the atypical pneumonias were thought to be viral because they were hard to identify and culture. This historical distinction between typical and atypical causes is not clinically useful as it is hard to distinguish between them based on clinical presentation. It is more important to identify specific organisms based on clinical features. All patients with CAP should be treated with coverage for both typical and atypical causes of pneumonia. Common initial antibiotic choices for CAP include second- or third-generation cephalosporins (ceftriaxone) for the typical pathogens plus either a macrolide (azithromycin) or doxycycline for better coverage of atypical pathogens. A respiratory fluoroquinolone (levofloxacin) can be used as a single agent for CAP because it covers both typical and atypical pathogens. Ampicillin and gentamicin have good activity against *Streptococcus* and *Escherichia coli* infections but provide weak coverage against *Staphylococcus* and atypical pathogens. Tuberculosis also causes cavitary lesions seen on chest radiographs. The presentation of tuberculosis is more indolent with fever, night sweats, hemoptysis, and weight loss. Isoniazid, rifampicin, and ethambutol are used to treat tuberculosis, but the diagnosis should be confirmed in most cases before the initiation of antibiotics.

366. The answer is D, Wood.

(Marx, 864-866; Wolfson, 184-185)

Penetrating intraocular injuries, regardless of what substance is involved, require ophthalmologic consultation. Wood, as an organic material, is particularly concerning because it can cause infection and lead to an inflammatory reaction. The decision to remove an intraocular foreign body is best determined by the ophthalmologist. Depending on the type of material and the amount of penetration, some inert materials are best left in place, and the rest are best removed surgically. Computed tomography is the most reliable study to evaluate the eye for intraocular foreign body in cases of penetrating globe injury. Many materials are magnetic, making MRI an unsafe choice unless the material is known not to be magnetic and plain radiography is unreliable. The materials causing the highest degree of inflammation are organic materials such as wood, copper, iron, and steel. Aluminum, mercury, nickel, and zinc can also produce an inflammatory reaction, but it is less severe. Glass, lead, plastic, and porcelain are inert and do not generally produce an inflammatory reaction.

367. The answer is C, Nystagmus.

(Marx, 95-99; Tintinalli, 1551)

The presence of nystagmus is generally associated with benign etiologies of tinnitus. Tinnitus and nystagmus are commonly associated with Ménière disease. However, if other neurologic abnormalities are found on history or physical examination in addition to tinnitus (and/or nystagmus), a more serious and potentially life-threatening etiology should be considered. If tinnitus is pulsatile or unilateral in nature, the concern is a tumor or vascular abnormality at the cerebellopontine angle. Tumors can produce pulsatile symptoms through the additional blood supply to the tumor. Approximately 80% of cerebellopontine angle tumors are caused by an acoustic neuroma (also known as a vestibular schwannoma). Acoustic neuromas are intracranial and extraaxial tumors that eventually expand to compress major structures within the cerebellopontine angle. Patients typically present with headaches, tinnitus, hearing loss, and/or balance issues; in later stages, patients might also present with facial numbness (cranial nerve V, trigeminal nerve), facial nerve weakness (cranial nerve VII, facial nerve), and eventually lower cranial nerve palsies. The finding of a bruit in the neck (or anywhere above the clavicles) is concerning for an arteriovenous malformation, tortuous carotid artery, or jugular vein and rarely for a carotid dissection. Patients might describe the tinnitus associated with vascular malformations as a low-pitched venous hum.

368. The answer is D, Start intravenous antibiotics and obtain a surgery consultation.

(Marx, 1168-1169; Tintinalli, 562-566)

The ultrasound image reveals gallstones, gallbladder wall thickening, and pericholecystic fluid. These findings, along with the presenting symptoms of biliary disease, confirm the diagnosis of acute cholecystitis. The appropriate next steps are intravenous antibiotics and surgical evaluation. Patients with acute cholecystitis typically present with constant right upper quadrant abdominal pain, nausea, and vomiting but are frequently afebrile. In one study of elderly patients with confirmed acute cholecystitis, about half were afebrile, and 40% had a normal WBC count. To make the diagnosis of acute cholecystitis, clinical and laboratory examinations must be supported by diagnostic imaging. Ultrasound is the most effective imaging modality in the emergency department. Sonographic findings suggestive of acute cholecystitis include gallstones, gallbladder wall thickening more than 3 mm, pericholecystic fluid, and a sonographic Murphy sign, which is tenderness on compression of the gallbladder under direct visualization with the ultrasound probe. Gallstone obstruction of the biliary outflow tract is the main cause of acute cholecystitis. Obstruction raises intraluminal pressures, which leads to mucosal ischemia. This, in turn, initiates the release of inflammatory mediators, causing further mucosal injury, gallbladder wall thickening, and possible leakage of pericholecystic fluid. Invasion by enteric bacteria complicates 50% to 80% of cases, with *Escherichia coli* and *Klebsiella* being the most common pathogens. Endoscopic retrograde cholangiopancreatography, or ERCP, is appropriate only when common bile duct obstruction is suspected. The diameter of this patient's common bile duct is normal (<6 mm). Although it is more sensitive and specific than ultrasound, a hepatobiliary iminodiacetic acid, HIDA, scan adds nothing when cholecystitis is already diagnosed using ultrasonography. This patient has acute cholecystitis and should be admitted for treatment with antibiotics and cholecystectomy. Outpatient management is inappropriate.

369. The answer is B, Admit the patient for cardiac monitoring and consultation for defibrillator placement.

(Marx, 1023; Tintinalli, 63-64, 151-152)

The ECG shows the characteristic Brugada syndrome pattern. This presentation can be distinguished from ST-segment elevation MI (STEMI) because the patient is relatively young and his symptoms are not characteristic of acute MI. But in the setting of appropriate symptoms and lack of consideration for Brugada syndrome, the pattern could easily be mistaken for STEMI. Patients with syncope (or cardiac arrest) and suspected or confirmed Brugada syndrome must be admitted with continuous cardiac monitoring for implantable cardiac defibrillator (ICD) placement. In this condition, an ICD is currently the only intervention to prevent future sudden cardiac death. Brugada syndrome is a genetic condition affecting a gene encoding a cardiac sodium channel. It is transmitted with an autosomal dominant pattern of inheritance. The clinical expression of the phenotype is influenced by sex, as 90% of affected individuals identified by ECG are male. Typically, the resulting cardiac effects of Brugada syndrome (syncope or cardiac arrest) manifest in the third and fourth decades of life. Sudden cardiac death is caused by rapid polymorphic ventricular tachycardia or fibrillation. There are three recognized patterns of Brugada syndrome, distinguished by their precordial ST-segment and T-wave morphologies. Characteristically, there is an incomplete right bundle branch block pattern and J-point segment and ST-segment elevation in leads V_1 through V_3. There are three patterns of ST-segment elevation, the most typical being saddlebacked or coved in appearance. These abnormalities might be confused with the ST-segment elevations seen in ST-segment elevation myocardial infarction (STEMI). The ST-segment elevation pattern of Brugada syndrome can be intermittently present, requiring administration of sodium-channel blockers to uncover the typical ECG pattern. This is not a case of STEMI, and cardiac catheterization is not indicated. Likewise, because the ECG is concerning for Brugada syndrome and the presentation is not consistent with a seizure, consultation with neurology is not the next best step in management. Cardiac markers do not have a role in diagnosing Brugada syndrome. Brugada syndrome is not associated with structural heart disease, so echocardiography would not be an appropriate next step. In a patient incidentally found to have a Brugada pattern on ECG, a thorough history should determine whether there have been past symptoms such as syncope attributable to arrhythmia. If not, most such patients are considered safe for discharge and an accelerated outpatient evaluation.

370. The answer is B, Mortality rate is higher than that for diabetic ketoacidosis.

(Kitabchi, 2739-2748; Wolfson, 1009-1011)

Diabetic ketoacidosis (DKA) and hyperosmolar hyperglycemic state (HHS) are the most serious acute metabolic complications of diabetes. Death in either condition usually results from the underlying precipitating illness rather than the metabolic state itself and is, in fact, significantly higher in HHS than in DKA. Currently, HHS is the term used by the American Diabetes Association for the condition of severe hyperglycemia (>600 mg/dL), hyperosmolarity (calculated effective osmolarity [urea excluded from osmolarity equation] >320 mg/dL), pH greater than 7.3, and serum bicarbonate greater than 15 mEq/L. Terms formerly used to describe the condition have included hyperosmolar nonketotic state and hyperosmolar coma. The current term more accurately reflects that, indeed, a mild ketosis is typically present, and coma occurs in less than 30% (not the majority) of patients. Both DKA and HHS result from a reduction in the net effective action of insulin in combination with elevation in counterregulatory hormones. In HHS, although there is sufficient insulin to prevent significant lipolysis, there is an insufficient amount for tissue glucose utilization. Of the two, DKA is more common than HHS and often occurs in insulin-dependent diabetic patients who are noncompliant with their insulin regimens or in patients presenting with new-onset insulin-dependent diabetes. In contrast, HHS typically occurs in diabetic patients in whom an underlying medical illness provokes the condition. Although precipitating or coincident medical illnesses such as infections and MI should be sought in both, the higher incidence in HHS explains why mortality rates are higher. The onset of HHS is in fact typically more insidious than that of DKA, partly accounting for the significant fluid deficits found that can be greater than those found in many patients with DKA. Treatment of both disorders is similar, including fluid resuscitation, insulin, and potassium replacement therapy.

371. The answer is A, ABG analysis should not be temperature corrected prior to interpretation.

(Jurkovich, 247-267; Marx, 1868-1881; Tintinalli, 1336-1338)

Arterial blood gas samples are warmed to 37°C (98.6°F) before they are analyzed in the laboratory. This increases the partial pressures of dissolved gases, which results in the reporting of higher carbon dioxide and oxygen levels with lower pH than a hypothermic patient actually has. Correction for temperature is unnecessary, though, as attempts to maintain physiologic values at hypothermic temperatures have led to decreased cerebral and coronary blood flow with higher risk of ventricular fibrillation. A goal of an uncorrected pH of 7.4 and $Paco_2$ of 40 mm Hg is ideal. Hypothermic patients are at increased risk for arrhythmia. Prolonged intervals, atrial fibrillation, ventricular fibrillation, and ventricular tachycardia present through the progression to severe hypothermia. Patients must be handled carefully to prevent irritations that can precipitate these arrhythmias, such as premature ventricular contractions from central line access through an internal jugular or subclavian line. Similarly, an arrhythmia such as atrial fibrillation should resolve with rewarming and obviate the need for cardioversion. Numerous laboratory abnormalities exist in hypothermic patients. Hyperglycemia can be present, as hypothermia stimulates catecholamine-induced glycogenolysis, inhibits insulin release, and inhibits insulin uptake by membranes below temperatures of 30°C (86°F). Rebound hypoglycemia can occur with exogenous insulin administration during rewarming. In severe hypothermia, all reflexes can be lost, including the corneal reflex. The last deep tendon reflex to be lost (and first regained) is the knee jerk. Successful rewarming and resuscitation of patients with no reflexes do occur, so the absence of corneal reflexes is not a reliable predictor for death.

372. The answer is A, Bilateral facial palsy and atrioventricular block.

(Marx, 1770-1779; Tintinalli, 1072-1073, 1662-1663)

An erythematous patch with central clearing is a characteristic finding for erythema migrans, the pathognomonic rash of Lyme disease. This rash appears at the site of the inoculation in the first stage of the illness. The patient in this question has a healing bite wound at the center of the rash. An additional clue is the exposure on a camping trip to Wisconsin, a highly endemic region for Lyme disease (along with the northeastern United States). The second stage of the disease occurs with the dissemination of the *Borrelia* spirochetes, resulting in fever, adenopathy, and multiple annular lesions. Neurologic abnormalities, most commonly bilateral facial palsy, and cardiac abnormalities, including atrioventricular block, can occur in this stage. If it continues to be untreated, tertiary Lyme disease results in chronic arthritis, myocarditis, subacute encephalopathy, and axonal polyneuropathy. Lyme disease can be readily treated in the first stage, and patients usually respond to therapy in the second stage. But tertiary disease is notoriously difficult to treat. Relapsing fever is also a tick-borne disease associated with *Borrelia* species, but it results in a pruritic eschar followed by relapsing fever alternating with afebrile periods. Regional suppurative lymphadenopathy should prompt the consideration of plague, infection from *Yersinia pestis* transmitted by the bite of a flea that had been feeding on infected rodents, usually rats. Left untreated, overwhelming sepsis and death can occur within 24 hours.

373. The answer is C, Anemia, high creatinine, low platelets.

(Marx, 1206-1207; Strange, 696; Wolfson, 972)

Hemolytic uremic syndrome, more common in children, is characterized by the following: a microangiopathic hemolytic anemia; nephropathy, including an elevation of creatinine rapidly progressing to renal failure; and thrombocytopenia. Hemolytic uremic syndrome is typically seen in young children and often follows a nonspecific early course manifesting as a minor respiratory illness or gastroenteritis. Although the etiology remains obscure in many cases, there is a known association with *Escherichia coli* O157:H7 infections. Hemolytic uremic syndrome has a wide range of severity and myriad associated signs, symptoms, and laboratory abnormalities. At the mild end of the severity spectrum, a mild elevation of BUN level, a relatively mild anemia, and moderate thrombocytopenia are seen. At the most severe end of the severity spectrum, complete renal failure with anuria, severe anemia, and profound thrombocytopenia are seen. Associated findings include hypertension, irritability, seizures, abdominal pain, bloody diarrhea, toxic megacolon, intussusception, and coma. Associated laboratory abnormalities include hyponatremia, hypocalcemia, elevated BUN, creatinine, and C-reactive protein levels, low hemoglobin, and a platelet count below 50,000/mcL. Purpura, swollen joints, and abdominal pain are symptoms found mostly in patients with Henoch-Schönlein purpura. Abdominal distention, headache, and hypertension are more consistent with nephrotic syndrome. Cyanosis and low back pain are not characteristically seen in hemolytic uremic syndrome and are not part of the defining triad.

374. The answer is B, Menorrhagia.

(Acien, 41-51; Tintinalli, 668; Wallach, 393-406)

Fibroids (leiomyomas) are benign tumors of muscle cell origin in the uterus. They occur in 20% to 40% of women during their reproductive years. Fibroids are estrogen-dependent tumors; most patients present with menorrhagia (more than 80 mL of blood/cycle or more than 1 maxi pad in 1 hour, prolonged menses more than 7 days). Fibroids are named after their location and are categorized as intramural (within the myometrium), submucosal (beneath the endometrium), or subserosal (beneath the uterine serosa). Acute pelvic pain is rare but can be associated with torsion of a pedunculated subserosal fibroid or degeneration of a fibroid. Treatment depends on the size of the fibroid and symptoms. Medical management includes NSAIDs, gonadotropin-releasing hormone agonist, and/or progestational agents. Unfortunately, fibroids usually recur after medications are stopped. Other treatment options include hysterectomy, myomectomy, and uterine artery embolization. Indications for surgical removal include abnormal uterine bleeding that causes anemia, severe pelvic pain, uterine size (greater than 12-week size), urinary symptoms (frequency, retention, hydronephrosis), uterine growth after menopause, recurrent miscarriage or infertility, and rapid increase in size. Hysterectomy is the definitive treatment option for fibroids. The disadvantages of myomectomy are fibroid recurrence in 50% of women and adhesions causing pelvic pain and possible infertility. Amenorrhea (the absence of a menstrual cycle) is not associated with fibroid tumors, but nulliparity (having no children) is associated with an increased risk for fibroids.

375. **The answer is C, Oral gabapentin.**

(Marx, 73; Wolfson, 1550)

Postherpetic neuralgia, the most common neuropathic pain, is a difficult-to-treat complication of herpes zoster that occurs in about 10% of patients. Commonly used medications include the anticonvulsants gabapentin, pregabalin, and carbamazepine. Lidocaine or other anesthetic agents have been used in intravenous forms, topical preparations, and peripheral nerve blocks. Acyclovir, valacyclovir, and famciclovir, the antiviral agents used to treat herpes zoster, are not effective in treating postherpetic neuralgia once it has already developed. There is some evidence to support the effect of acyclovir in decreasing the development of postherpetic neuralgia if given within 72 hours after the lesions appear. There is also evidence that supports the use of antiviral agents to decrease the duration of viral shedding while lesions are present. Topical steroids and topical antiviral preparations are not effective. Topical agents that have some utility include anesthetics (lidocaine patch, EMLA) and capsaicin.

376. **The answer is A, Iron oxidation over 1 to 2 days kills surrounding epithelial cells and allows the ring to be removed in one piece.**

(Marx, 862; Roberts, 1157-1159)

When a metallic foreign body is embedded in the cornea, the iron begins to oxidize, and a rust ring begins to form immediately. It can be visualized on the cornea within a few hours. As the cornea softens over the first 1 to 2 days, the rust material migrates toward the surface, making removal much easier after 24 hours. This facilitates rust ring removal in followup, including when the ring cannot be completely removed during the initial emergency department visit. Large rust rings can impair visual acuity when they lie in the line of site, and they can delay corneal healing from the initial foreign body and abrasion. The preferred method of removal in the emergency department is with a rotating drill device. This can be done safely by the emergency physician. If the preferred burr or commercial eye spud is unavailable, a 25-gauge needle on a 1- to 3-mL syringe as a handle is recommended in several emergency medicine texts. When using a needle for foreign body or rust ring removal, the needle should be held parallel to the surface of the cornea to avoid puncturing the cornea.

377. The answer is C, Right lower.

(Marx, 720-724; Tintinalli, 789, 792-793)

Aspiration can affect any lobe of the lung, but it most commonly involves the right lower lobe. The left mainstem bronchus makes a sharper angle when it comes off the trachea, so material is less likely to go there. The right mainstem bronchus has a more vertical orientation, which creates a straight path for aspirated particulate. Most cases involve children younger than 4 years, with a peak incidence between 1 and 3 years old. In young children, there is less of a difference in the angles of the bronchus, and both lungs tend to be affected equally. Diagnosis is often made based on history and requires a high index of suspicion. Most foreign bodies that are aspirated are translucent on radiographs. Bilateral decubitus radiographs can be helpful. A foreign object can prevent normal pulmonary collapse when the involved hemithorax is dependent (or on the down side on the radiography table), leading to unilateral hyperinflation on radiograph. Foreign body aspiration should be suspected in all children with unilateral wheezing. Bronchoscopy can be used for both diagnosis and treatment. Aspirated organic or vegetable matter can cause a severe pneumonitis and lead to a subsequent pneumonia.

378. The answer is D, Oblique, partial-thickness laceration of the upper eyelid.

(Marx, 865; Wolfson, 180-182)

Emergency physicians can manage simple eyelid lacerations safely when they are partial thickness and horizontal or oblique and are not at high risk for complications, such as poor cosmesis or function. In general, these simple eyelid lacerations can be closed using 6-0 or 7-0 interrupted nonabsorbable sutures. Care should be taken to avoid any traction on the eyelid that might prevent incomplete closure during blinking or sleeping to prevent exposure keratitis. Sutures can be removed after 5 days. There are several types of complex lid lacerations that should be closed primarily by an ophthalmologist. Lacerations involving the lid margin are complex and require meticulous attention to the exact approximation to avoid poor cosmesis and function of the lid. Lacerations of the medial canthus have a high likelihood of involving the canalicular system, and care must be taken to avoid scarring in this area; treatment sometimes involves stenting. Any eyelid laceration with exposed fat protruding violates the orbital septum, which indicates a high likelihood of foreign body or globe penetration. Again, evaluation by the ophthalmologist is required. Eyelids themselves do not contain subcutaneous fat. Eyelid lacerations with avulsed tissue are difficult to close. These wounds are at high risk for poor cosmesis and lid function.

379. The answer is C, Lymphedema.

(Marx, 1836-1837; Tintinalli, 1015-1016)

Cellulitis is an infection of the skin and soft tissue caused by blood or lymph system dissemination or more commonly by direct inoculation of bacteria through skin trauma. Recent studies have shown that the clinical risk factors for the development of cellulitis include lymphedema, portal of entry, venous insufficiency, and obesity. The portal of entry can include chronic fungal infection of the feet, particularly between the toes. Remarkably, studies have not supported that cancer, tobacco use, and diabetes mellitus are risk factors for cellulitis. Interestingly, bacteria are often cleared from the site of the infection within 12 hours, and the remainder of the symptoms are the result of infiltration of inflammatory cells and the production of cytokines. Arterial insufficiency is not an independent risk factor for the development of cellulitis. Typical signs and symptoms of cellulitis include local erythema, increased warmth, localized swelling, and pain. Skin flora (*Staphylococcus aureus, Streptococcus pyogenes*) are the most common bacterial organisms.

380. The answer is D, Intubation.

(Marx, 1172-1180; Tintinalli, 558-566)

Patients with severe pancreatitis accompanied by respiratory failure require intubation for ARDS. The patient in this question, given her abdominal symptoms and elevated lipase level, likely has pancreatitis. With pancreatitis, there is a release of inflammatory mediators that might set up a systemic inflammatory response and multiorgan failure; ARDS occurs when these secretions and inflammatory mediators reach the thoracic cavity. Pancreatitis is typically caused by gallstone ductal obstruction or alcohol abuse. The net effect is premature activation of trypsinogen and zymogen in the pancreatic ducts or acinar cells, resulting in autodigestion of the pancreas. Pancreatic enzymes can also spread locally, causing digestion and necrosis of nearby structures. Pancreatitis typically presents with epigastric abdominal pain that radiates to the back along with nausea and vomiting. A serum lipase level two times the upper limit of normal has a higher sensitivity and specificity than amylase levels. Emergent imaging is indicated when the diagnosis is in doubt or when there is clinical deterioration. Otherwise, ultrasonography is typically performed within 24 hours of admission. Treatment is supportive and includes aggressive fluid resuscitation and pain control for mild to moderate pancreatitis. In severe pancreatitis presenting with multiorgan failure, advanced airway management, fluid resuscitation, vasopressors, and dialysis might be required. Abdominal ultrasonography and CT are indicated once the patient is stabilized. Early cholecystectomy in pancreatitis carries a high risk of death. Endoscopic retrograde cholangiopancreatography (ERCP) with sphincterotomy might relieve pancreatic duct obstruction, with less risk.

381. The answer is C, Do not delay transport.

(Mattu, 30-32; Tintinalli, 148-149)

The rhythm strip shows a first-degree AV block in the setting of an acute inferior MI. All types of AV block can occur with MI. First-degree and Mobitz type I (Wenckebach) AV block are transient in this setting, and prophylactic pacing is not required. This patient should go directly to the cardiac catheterization laboratory without further delay. However, Mobitz type II and third-degree AV block are concerning rhythms peri-MI, and preparations for prophylactic pacing should be undertaken. In an unstable patient, administration of atropine should be considered as a temporizing measure while external pacing is being set up. There is no indication for amiodarone in this setting. First-degree AV block involves a constant prolongation of the PR interval with all P waves conducted into QRS complexes. There are no cardiovascular consequences. There are two types of second-degree AV block. The first is Mobitz type I (Wenckebach), which is characterized by cycles of intermittently dropped QRS complexes that are preceded by increasing PR intervals. Mobitz type II AV block is a serious form of AV block characterized by sudden blockage of AV conduction without prolongation of the PR interval. Although Mobitz type I (Wenckebach) AV block can occur in normal individuals and have no clinical significance, Mobitz type II AV block is never a normal variant and occurs only in a diseased conduction system. Mobitz type II AV block can degenerate into third-degree AV block. In a third-degree AV block, an escape pacemaker usually takes over at the level of the AV junction or lower. If an escape pacemaker originates at the AV junction, the escape rhythm beats (with a narrow QRS complex) at a rate of 40 to 55 beats/min. If the AV junction pacemaker fails, then an idioventricular escape rhythm originating more distally can take over. However, this escape rhythm has a widened QRS complex, beats at a rate of 20 to 40 beats/min, and is at considerable risk of abruptly failing. These rhythms generally need an external pacemaker. In patients with third-degree block and narrow QRS complex who have a pulse, atropine can be used as a temporizing measure while preparing for pacing. Third-degree blocks resulting from acute inferior MI are usually temporary but can persist for up to several days.

382. The answer is B, Jimsonweed.

(Marx, 2062-2064; Wolfson, 1514-1516)

Tachycardia, mild hyperthermia, dry skin, delirium, and mydriasis are classic signs of antimuscarinic or anticholinergic poisoning consistent with poisoning with jimsonweed (*Datura stramonium*). All parts of jimsonweed contain the antimuscarinic agents atropine, hyoscyamine, and scopolamine. Significant toxicity typically occurs in teenagers seeking hallucinogenic effects who will ingest, smoke, or make a tea from the plant. Other antimuscarinic or anticholinergic manifestations include picking behavior, diminished bowel sounds, and urinary retention. Treatment is supportive, although the short-acting acetylcholinesterase inhibitor physostigmine can be used both diagnostically and therapeutically. Oleander (*Nerium oleander*) is one of multiple plants that contain cardiac glycosides. Although small accidental exposures by children are typically without consequence, larger exposures such as from a suicide attempt from an oleander tea can be fatal. Manifestations and treatment are similar to those for digoxin poisoning. *Dieffenbachia*, also known as dumb cane, is a common household plant that causes local oral pain and swelling when ingested. The plant contains calcium oxalate crystals that cause this local reaction, which typically prevents further ingestion. *Nicotiana tabacum* is a plant used to make cigarette and cigar tobacco and contains nicotine. Most exposures to nicotine are from accidental ingestions of cigarette or cigar butts in children and are fortunately mostly benign, likely from vomiting that prevents absorption. Poisoning from nicotine can be confusing, as both sympathetic (tachycardia, hypertension, diaphoresis) and parasympathetic (salivation, lacrimation, vomiting, diarrhea) manifestations can occur. Muscular fasciculations and diaphragmatic paralysis can result from the agonism of nicotinic receptors on the neuromuscular junction. Seizures can also occur with significant toxicity. Management is supportive.

383. The answer is C, Child abuse.

(Adams, 2205; Marx, 2599; Tintinalli, 1978-1980, 2026)

All 50 states have reporting requirements for child abuse. These state statutes override patients' rights of confidentiality, and physicians are typically immune from civil or criminal liability if the reporting is done in good faith. Elder abuse is also a reporting requirement in all 50 states. Assault, which is any wound, injury, or illness resulting from a criminal act of violence, must also be reported and includes sexual assault, spousal abuse, and domestic violence. Suspicious injuries and suspected child or elder abuse must also be reported. All deaths must be reported; additionally, deaths that must be reported to the county medical examiner include the following: deaths from violence, poisoning, or suicide; any unexpected death in an otherwise healthy person; any death occurring in a correctional institution or under police custody; and any death occurring under unnatural or suspicious circumstances. A few states, including Hawaii, Indiana, Illinois, Pennsylvania, Rhode Island, and Utah, have mandatory reporting of alcohol-related motor vehicle crashes. Several other states have laws that permit reporting but do not require it, and this tends to be controversial. Most, but not all, states require reporting of animal bites such as dog and cat bites as well as bites from animals known to be possible carriers of rabies, including bats, cattle, foxes, raccoons, and skunks. Pediatric near-drowning is not a reportable illness or event.

384. The answer is B, Notify operating room staff and prepare for a surgical airway.

(Marx, 920; Tintinalli, 1586-1587)

The patient in this question has Ludwig angina, an infection of the floor of the mouth that spreads into the submental, submandibular, and sublingual spaces, pushing the tongue superiorly and posteriorly and closing off the airway. Patients exhibiting stridor, drooling (inability to handle secretions), and tachypnea have an impending airway collapse, and definitive airway management is essential. Because of the posterior and superior displacement of the tongue, standard endotracheal intubation is likely impossible. Because the infection extends into the anterior neck, a cricothyrotomy is technically difficult but might be the only option in a crashing patient. Fiberoptic or nasotracheal intubation is a reasonable approach. Ideally, airway management should occur in the operating room, where an otolaryngologist can perform an immediate tracheotomy. Blood cultures are not likely to be useful for the management of this condition, as oral anaerobes and *Streptococcus* species are the presumed etiology. Besides, airway management takes priority. Antibiotic regimens for Ludwig angina include high-dose penicillin, ampicillin-sulbactam, and clindamycin. Cefazolin does not have sufficient anaerobic coverage to be the primary agent. Incision and drainage of the sublingual abscess is a complicated process that should be left to a head and neck surgeon. In a stable patient with suspected Ludwig angina, a CT scan might help establish the diagnosis and guide surgical therapy. The CT scanning should be done with contrast to identify the fluid collections in the neck.

385. The answer is C, Focal seizure.

(Marx, 1417-1429; Wolfson, 884-887)

Encephalitis is infection of the brain parenchyma. Meningitis is infection of the membranes of the brain and spinal cord (meninges). They present with similar signs and symptoms, but focal neurologic findings (seizure, hallucinations, aphasia, motor weakness) are seen more commonly in encephalitis. There are many etiologies of meningitis, with *Streptococcus pneumoniae* being the most common bacterial etiology in adults and *Neisseria meningitidis* in children and adolescents. *Listeria monocytogenes* must be considered in elderly and immunocompromised patients. Viral etiologies typically present with a self-limited complex of similar symptoms. The most commonly implicated virus is the Enterovirus. The most common cause of encephalitis is the herpes simplex virus. Patients who are at the highest risk of developing bacterial meningitis include those at the extremes of age, those with ENT infections, the chronically ill and immunosuppressed, and those who use alcohol and cigarettes. Outbreaks have been found among persons in crowded living conditions such as dorms and barracks and in poverty-stricken areas. Diagnosis of both entities is based on CSF analysis from lumbar puncture; bacterial meningitis is more likely to have a neutrophilic predominance of the white blood cells. The cell count in viral or aseptic meningitis and encephalitis tends to be lower (<500 mm³) and predominantly mononuclear. Other indicators of bacterial meningitis include a CSF-to-serum glucose ratio of less than 0.5 and CSF protein level greater than 150 mg/dL. Both meningitis and encephalitis present with symptoms that prompt brain imaging. In patients with meningitis, most unenhanced CT scan results are normal. Contrast-enhanced CT might show enhancement of the meninges, which is a nonspecific finding. Magnetic resonance imaging is more sensitive and might show leptomeningeal enhancement with distention of the subarachnoid space (a finding more common in patients with severe disease.) Patients with encephalitis are more likely to have findings on CT, although MRI is still more sensitive. As herpes is the most common etiology of viral encephalitis, findings of hypodense areas on CT or hyperintensity on MRI will most likely be found in the temporal lobes. More advanced disease can manifest as hemorrhage on either imaging modality.

386. The answer is B, Dog bite to the face.

(Marx, 703-704; Roberts, 575-578)

Certain wounds are almost never managed with primary closure, including wounds with heavy contamination from soil, organic matter, feces, or freshwater streams or lakes and wounds involving heavy tissue damage. Additional exclusions are large stellate lacerations to the foot and human and dog bite wounds on the hand. Human bite wounds should never be closed and are typically extended for exploration and debridement. Dog bites to the face, dog bites involving other cosmetic concerns, and bite wounds that can be excised completely are often closed primarily with good results. Delayed primary closure is a safe alternative to be considered for dirty or high-impact or crush wounds. The overall healing is comparable, and the infection rate is markedly improved with proper care. The wound must be inspected, cleaned, debrided, and irrigated as it would be with a primary closure, but the wound is then packed and dressed. The wound is reinspected at 24 hours, and the dressing is changed. If it remains clean, the delayed closure occurs at 96 hours.

387. The answer is C, Ceftriaxone and levofloxacin.

(Mandell, S27-S72; Tintinalli, 479-486)

Severe community-acquired pneumonia requiring ICU admission requires broad antibiotic coverage against *Streptococcus pneumoniae* and *Legionella*. Double antipneumococcal coverage in severe pneumonia has been shown to improve outcome. The use of a beta-lactam (ceftriaxone) and a respiratory fluoroquinolone (levofloxacin) meets this goal. Selection of appropriate antibiotic coverage is part of the Centers for Medicare % Medicaid Services (CMS) core measures designed to improve patient care. Vancomycin provides excellent coverage against *Staphylococcus* and *Streptococcus* but does not cover *Legionella* or *Pseudomonas*. The addition of vancomycin is suggested if methicillin-resistant *Staphylococcus aureus* is a concern as part of good clinical care, but it is not part of the 2010 CMS guidelines. Azithromycin and levofloxacin cover atypical pathogens like *Legionella*, but azithromycin, which is a macrolide, does not provide the same antipneumococcal coverage that a beta-lactam does. Common beta-lactams include ceftriaxone, cefotaxime, ampicillin-sulbactam, and ertapenem. Levofloxacin also has the advantage of providing coverage against *Pseudomonas* as well as *Legionella* and *Pneumococcus*. If *Pseudomonas* is suspected, an antipseudomonal beta-lactam like cefepime, imipenem, meropenem, or piperacillin-tazobactam should be used in combination with levofloxacin.

388. The answer is B, Arteriovenous fistula.

(Marx, 456-460; Wolfson, 243-246)

In a patient with penetrating trauma to the axilla, expanding hematoma, palpable thrill, decreased pulse, and decreased blood pressure in the afflicted extremity, the most likely underlying complication is arteriovenous fistula. The distinguishing feature among the symptoms is the palpable thrill. A fistula is formed when adjacent vessels are injured, and when one is arterial and one is venous. A tract between the two vessels is formed, and the higher pressure blood in the artery flows into the lower pressure vein. The turbulence of this flow leads to the palpable thrill. The steal phenomenon can lead to distal ischemia in the affected extremity. Arteriovenous fistulas can present immediately or very late after blunt trauma, after time has allowed the fistula to grow large enough to be detected. Intimal tears can present with normal pulses or decreased pulses, or with ischemia if thrombosis has occurred, but palpable thrill is not common. Pseudoaneurysm can occur when a tear of the vessel wall is incomplete, thus allowing the surrounding fascia and fibrous tissue to contain the resultant hematoma. These patients usually present later, months to years after the injury, with a firm, slowly expanding mass that can compress adjacent structures and lead to thrombosis, embolism of thrombus, or bleeding from wall rupture. A thrill might or might not be present. Complete transection of an artery leads to ischemia, and, if the vessel does not spasm, to expanding hematoma or compartment syndrome from the hematoma as well. But, a thrill is not present with complete transection.

389. The answer is D, 78-year-old woman with urinary tract infection.

(Centers for Disease Control and Prevention [catheter-associated UTI], 8-48; Marx, 1301; Tintinalli, 642)

Isolated urinary tract infections take longer to clear, even with appropriate antibiotic use, when a urinary catheter is left in place. Recently, there has been an increased recognition of the effect of urinary catheters in the risk of urinary tract infections, particularly in hospitalized or institutionalized patients. These infections are referred to as catheter-associated urinary tract infections (CA-UTI or CAUTI). There is significant evidence that many patients are catheterized for the convenience of staff and not for any therapeutic benefit. National guidelines have emerged as to which patients potentially benefit from the placement of a urinary catheter (the risk of infection notwithstanding) and in which patients the risks of a CAUTI outweigh the benefits of urinary catheterization. Urinary catheterization continues to be indicated in patients with acute urinary retention, critically ill patients who require measurements of urine output (cardiogenic shock), and in patients with multiple pelvic injuries or proximal femur injuries requiring immobilization (neck of femur fracture and multiple pelvic fractures). If a patient is able to void on his or her own, then the use of in-and-out catheters to collect a urine specimen is associated with an increased rate of infection and should be avoided when possible.

390. The answer is A, Intravenous erythromycin.

(Marx, 1679-1681; Wolfson, 1297-1299)

The presentation described in this question is classic for pertussis. Although pertussis is also known as whooping cough because of the loud inspiratory sound made during paroxysms of coughing, young infants do not demonstrate this characteristic feature, probably because they lack the inspiratory strength to generate the sound. Antibiotics have no effect on the course of the illness once paroxysmal coughing begins. Nonetheless, intravenous administration of a macrolide antibiotic such as erythromycin is recommended to minimize spread of the causative agent, *Bordetella pertussis*, to others. All young infants with suspected pertussis should be admitted to the hospital because of a relatively high risk for apnea. Nebulized albuterol is not indicated, especially since this infant does not demonstrate wheezing or respiratory distress. Parenteral corticosteroids are controversial in even the most severe cases and are not indicated in moderate cases such as this one. Subcutaneous epinephrine has no role in the treatment of young infants with a cough regardless of severity.

391. The answer is B, ICU.

(Marx, 1172-1180; Tintinalli, 558-562)

Using the Ranson criteria, a patient with a WBC count of 20,000 cells/mcL, blood glucose level of 450 mg/dL, and AST 375 IU/L is classified as having severe pancreatitis, with a predicted mortality rate of at least 15%, necessitating admission to an ICU. The Ranson criteria are used to predict death associated with pancreatitis. At the time of admission, points are given for age older than 55, WBC count greater than 16,000 cells/mcL, glucose greater than 200 mg/dL, LDH greater than 350 IU/L, and AST greater than 250 U/L. Additional points are calculated during the first 48 hours of admission and then tabulated. A score of 3 or more is associated with at least a 15% mortality rate and indicates the need for admission to the ICU. This patient already has a Ranson score of 4. A general medical admission, surgical floor admission, or observation unit admission is inappropriate in light of the high risk of death. Monitoring in an ICU is indicated in most patients with severe pancreatitis who have no indication for surgical management. Pancreatitis is typically caused by gallstone ductal obstruction or alcohol abuse. Pancreatic ductal obstruction increases the pressure on pancreatic enzymes, whereas alcohol abuse has a direct toxic effect. Both result in premature activation of trypsinogen and zymogen within the pancreas and subsequent autodigestion. Patients typically present with epigastric pain that radiates to the back along with nausea and vomiting; they are often afebrile. Serum lipase level has a higher sensitivity and specificity than serum amylase when diagnosing pancreatitis but has no correlation with morbidity or mortality rates.

392. The answer is D, When paroxysmal supraventricular tachycardia occurs with this condition in a stable patient, adenosine is an appropriate therapy.

(Delacretaz, 1039-1051; Mattu, 156-159; Tintinalli, 136-141)

This ECG demonstrates Wolff-Parkinson-White (WPW) syndrome. It is the most common preexcitation syndrome, affecting 0.15% to 0.25% of the general population. Adenosine is an appropriate agent to address a narrow-complex, regular paroxysmal supraventricular tachycardia (SVT) associated with WPW. In WPW syndrome, an accessory pathway is present between the atria and ventricles, circumventing the AV nodal pathway and causing earlier ventricular activation. The classic ECG findings include a short PR interval (less than 0.12 second), a prolonged QRS duration, a delta wave (initial slurring of the QRS complex representing preexcitation of the ventricular depolarization), and secondary ST-segment-T wave repolarization changes. However, this ECG pattern can be absent or appear intermittently depending on the degree of conduction down the accessory pathway at any given time. Patients with WPW are predisposed to tachyarrhythmias such as paroxysmal SVTs and atrial fibrillation. The most common arrhythmia is reentry tachycardia, also called paroxysmal SVT (70%-80%). In a narrow-complex QRS regular tachycardia such as AVRT, the impulses travel antegrade (orthodromic) through the AV node and retrograde through the accessory pathway in a continuing (circus) fashion. The delta wave is absent, and the P wave is buried within the ST-T segment. In antidromic reentry, impulses travel down the accessory pathway and retrograde through the AV node, causing a wide QRS complex. It is often not possible to distinguish such an antidromic AV reentry tachycardia from ventricular tachycardia on ECG. The treatment goal of paroxysmal SVT in patients with WPW is to interrupt the reentry circuit. Electrical cardioversion should be used for patients who are hemodynamically unstable. In hemodynamically stable patients, vagal maneuvers may be attempted. If they fail, pharmacologic agents should be used. For reentry SVT with a narrow QRS complex in WPW syndrome, treatment is the same as other cases of reentry SVT. This entails slowing conduction through the AV node with agents such as calcium-channel or beta-adrenergic blockers (if there is no hypotension or heart failure) or adenosine. Procainamide is indicated for the treatment of SVT or ventricular tachycardia; it is an appropriate treatment for a patient with WPW and a wide-complex regular tachycardia, which might be due to SVT with antidromic conduction or ventricular tachycardia.

393. The answer is D, Venlafaxine.

(Nelson, 1041, 1043-1044; Wolfson, 1510)

Venlafaxine (marketed as Effexor) is a serotonin-norepinephrine reuptake inhibitor that, unlike many of the newer antidepressants, has sodium-channel blockade properties. Significant overdoses can manifest with QRS interval prolongation and convulsions. The presentation is similar to that of tricyclic antidepressant overdose, as is the treatment, with sodium bicarbonate and benzodiazepines, respectively. A variety of nonmonoamine oxidase inhibitor, nontricyclic antidepressant agents exist. They are referred to as newer antidepressants and have varying mechanisms of action. Some have selective serotonin reuptake activity (SSRIs), some with serotonin reuptake activity (SRIs) with other activity, and others with distinct mechanisms of action. The SSRIs (with brand names in parentheses for ease of reference) include citalopram (Celexa), escitalopram (Lexapro), fluoxetine (Prozac, Rapiflux, Sarafem, and others), fluvoxamine (Luvox), paroxetine (Paxil, Pexeva), and sertraline (Zoloft). Atypical (non-SSRI) antidepressants include bupropion (Aplenzin, Wellbutrin and marketed as Buproban and Zyban for smoking cessation), duloxetine (Cymbalta), mirtazapine (Remeron), trazodone (Desyrel, Oleptro), and venlafaxine (Effexor). Fortunately, most SSRIs and atypical antidepressants in overdose are not associated with significant toxicity. Exceptions include rare massive overdoses of almost all of the agents. Additionally, certain agents can occasionally cause certain manifestations that, although uncommon, must be kept in mind when managing an overdose with them. Citalopram is associated with convulsions and QT-interval prolongation. The main complication of bupropion overdoses that emergency physicians should be aware of is convulsions, which also occur with therapeutic use. With extended-release preparations, significant time delay in onset of convulsions is possible. Trazodone has alpha$_1$ antagonist activity, and overdoses can manifest with peripheral vasodilation and resulting hypotension that typically responds to fluid administration. Both therapeutic use and overdose are also associated with priapism.

394. The answer is B, Breach of duty.

(Adams, 2199-2213; Amoco; Gillette; Wolfson, 1679-1680)

In a professional liability action against an emergency physician, the plaintiff, in order to prevail, must prove that:

- The physician had a duty to provide reasonable care and breached that duty,
- Actual injury or harm occurred, and
- The physician's actions were the proximate cause.

Duty of reasonable care is better defined as meeting the standard of care in the specialty. It was originally described as the "average degree of skill, care, and diligence exercised by members of the same profession, practicing in the same or similar locality in light of the present state of medical and surgical science." This definition has since expanded from local to national standards. Breach of the duty of reasonable care is also known as negligence, which can be defined legally as the "failure to use such care as a reasonably prudent and careful person would use under similar circumstances; it is the doing of some act which a person of ordinary prudence would not have done under similar circumstances or failure to do what a person of ordinary prudence would have done under similar circumstances." Injury or harm is the adverse outcome that occurred with the patient; the possibility of harm without harm actually occurring is not enough to prove negligence in a medical liability case. Causation is the presumption that an action caused the resulting medical harm, but since causation could theoretically be traced to the beginning of time, courts have determined that the action must have occurred close enough to the resultant harm, within the "chain of events," in order to find a person to be the legally culpable cause of the harm (the proximate cause). Proximate cause is the relationship between the breach of duty and the resultant harm. The goal of the plaintiff is to show that a particular action or inaction on the part of the physician led to the injury or harm to the patient. Further, for proximate cause to be found, the resultant harm must have been a foreseeable consequence of the physician's conduct. This tends to be the most difficult and complicated part of the case to prove because adverse outcomes frequently occur with serious disease processes in the absence of negligence. There are many forms of ethical misconduct in medicine. These and other professional misconduct incidents are usually dealt with by hospital governing bodies and state medical societies; ethical misconduct is not a legal term, although it can be used in determining the scope of a physician's "duty."

395. The answer is C, Doxycycline.

(Marx, 1782-1787; Tintinalli, 1070-1074)

The patient in this question has contracted Rocky Mountain spotted fever (RMSF), a zoonotic infection caused by the obligate intracellular bacteria *Rickettsia rickettsii*. It is transmitted by *Dermacentor* ticks, most commonly found in the southeastern United States. Only half of patients with disease recall their tick exposure. Its characteristic rash proceeds centripetally; it begins on the hands and feet (including the palms and soles) and spreads centrally to the trunk. The rash appears in the first 2 weeks of the illness but can be absent in about 20% of patients. Especially in children, it can result in severe illness, including encephalitis, renal failure, myocarditis, pulmonary infiltrates, and respiratory failure. The treatment of choice is doxycyline 100 mg twice daily for 7 to 10 days. Chloramphenicol is also an acceptable treatment, but its risk of toxicity, including myelosuppression, limits its use. Tetracycline, although likely effective, is contraindicated in children because it stains the teeth. Ciprofloxacin is relatively contraindicated in young children, and it is not indicated for the treatment of RMSF.

396. The answer is A, Between 30% and 50% of patients have long-term sequelae.

(Marx, 1417-1429; Wolfson, 888-889)

The head CT scan reveals that this patient has a left frontal lobe abscess with surrounding mass effect and effacement of the sulci. Intracranial abscesses are a significant cause of illness and death, with between 30% and 50% of patients having long-term sequelae that can include seizures (both focal and general), motor deficits, and cognitive delay or behavioral change. The mortality rate in patients with impending herniation is close to 50%. When signs of herniation are present, as evident in this patient by his obtundation, sluggish pupils, bradycardia, bradypnea, and hypertension, aggressive treatment to decrease the intracerebral pressure should be undertaken. This can include hyperventilation, administration of mannitol, and use of corticosteroids to decrease swelling. This is the only situation in which corticosteroids should be used in patients with intracranial abscesses, as they have been shown to increase mortality rates by decreasing antibiotic penetration in the abscess cavity. The definitive treatment for these patients is surgical decompression. Use of antibiotics should not delay surgery. Empiric antibiotic coverage should be started, which for this patient (and most patients with ENT or oral sources) should include a combination of a cephalosporin and metronidazole. In patients with nosocomial infections, specifically postsurgical patients, vancomycin should be added to cover methicillin-resistant *Staphylococcus aureus*.

397. The answer is C, If one rotation of 180 degrees does not relieve the pain completely, further efforts at detorsion should be continued by rotating an additional turn.

(Marx, 1314-1316; Roberts, 1010-1012)

In testicular torsion, the affected testis can be torsed up to 1080 degrees, and successful manual detorsion can require several turns. Success can be confirmed by relief of pain and by Doppler measurement of return of blood flow to the testis. Even with complete detorsion, the scrotum should be explored surgically and the problem definitively addressed. Torsion that has been present for several hours is associated with significant edema to the testis, scrotum, and epididymis, which can mimic cancer. Detorsion relieves these symptoms as well over a similar length of time when flow is reestablished. The successfully detorsed testis readily resumes its normal anatomic position. In two-thirds of cases, the torsion occurs in a medial direction, and detorsion is achieved as if opening a book and twisting laterally. This means one-third of cases involve torsion in the opposite direction; if pain is increased by the detorsion efforts, rotating in the opposite direction should be attempted.

398. The answer is D, Plain radiographs.

(Marx, 720-724, 1137-1138; Tintinalli, 552-554)

Radiographs are indicated in every patient with a history suggestive of foreign body ingestion. The sensitivity varies with the type of foreign body and location. Radiographs are primarily helpful to identify radiopaque objects, and indirect signs such as soft tissue swelling can be seen. In this case, a fish bone might be seen on a radiograph. If radiographs are nondiagnostic, further workup is required, as inconclusive plain radiographs do not eliminate the possibility of a foreign body. Options for visualization include direct laryngoscopy, indirect laryngoscopy with a mirror, or use of a fiberoptic nasopharyngeal scope. Removal can be accomplished using these techniques as well. Computed tomography of the neck has also been used to identify foreign bodies not seen on plain radiographs. Contrast swallow studies can be helpful if the foreign body is in the esophagus but have limited utility in upper airway foreign bodies. Barium is contraindicated in cases in which esophageal perforation is suspected. Water-soluble iodinated contrast material (brand names Gastrografin, MD-Gastroview) may be used if a study is needed. Patients may be discharged home only after a thorough evaluation. Many of these foreign bodies end up being swallowed but irritate the pharyngeal mucosa, leading to a foreign body sensation.

399. The answer is D, Painful range of motion.

(Marx, 481-482; Wolfson, 246-247)

Sprains are ligamentous injuries that occur as a result of abnormal movement of a joint. Sprains are divided into three categories. A second-degree sprain is characterized by a partial tear of a ligament with moderate soft tissue swelling and hemorrhage, tenderness to palpation of the ligament, painful range of motion of the joint, and some loss of function of the joint but not gross instability. A first-degree sprain is a tearing of only a few of the ligamentous fibers. Minimal soft tissue swelling and hemorrhage are present, along with minimal point tenderness of the ligament. Placing stress on the joint does not result in abnormal joint opening or instability. A third-degree sprain results from complete disruption of a ligament. A large amount of soft tissue swelling and hemorrhage occur, and hemarthrosis is possible. The joint is unstable; when stress is placed on the joint, motion is abnormal. There is no real end-point of joint movement when the ligament is stressed. If these injuries do not heal properly, chronic joint instability can occur. First-degree sprains are best treated with early mobilization, which can help the patient return to work and athletic activities. Second-degree sprains are treated similarly but with a slower increase in activity than first-degree sprains. Third-degree sprains are best treated with immobilization, non–weight-bearing, and urgent orthopedic referral. Due to the relatively avascular nature of the ligament, healing can be prolonged. Patients might experience delays in return to function and need physical therapy.

400. The answer is C, Start ceftriaxone.

(Marx, 1162; Thomsen, e21; Tintinalli, 569-572)

Patients presenting with signs of spontaneous bacterial peritonitis (SBP) require intravenous ceftriaxone for empiric antibiotic coverage. Spontaneous bacterial peritonitis is an idiopathic bacterial infection of ascitic fluid. It usually occurs in cirrhotic patients with ascites. Portal hypertension created by a cirrhotic liver creates bowel edema and facilitates transmural migration of enteric flora into the immunocompromised peritoneal cavity. The majority of the flora consists of gram-negative Enterobacteriaceae (*Escherichia coli, Salmonella, Klebsiella*; 63%) and *Streptococcus pneumoniae* (15%). Patients can present with a variety of signs and symptoms but typically present with abdominal pain. Up to 50%, however, are afebrile. Diagnostic workup includes a paracentesis and ascitic fluid analysis with cell count and culture. A polymorphonuclear (PMN) count greater than 250 per cubic millimeter of ascitic fluid correlates with a high incidence of SBP. Definitive diagnosis is achieved by a positive ascitic fluid culture. Patients with SBP require early parenteral antibiotics covering gram-negative organisms. Third-generation cephalosporins such as ceftriaxone are the antibiotics of choice for SBP. Withholding or delaying treatment for culture results increases the risk of worsened disease and death. These patients require medical management with intravenous antibiotics. There is no urgent indication for surgical intervention.

401. The answer is D, Recommended for ventricular fibrillation unresponsive to shock delivery, CPR, and vasopressor treatment.

(Neumar, S729-S767; Tintinalli, 158)

The 2010 advanced cardiovascular life support guidelines published by the American Heart Association recommend administration of amiodarone for ventricular fibrillation or pulseless ventricular tachycardia unresponsive to CPR, shock, and a vasopressor. In this case, it is given as a 300 mg IV bolus that may be repeated as a 150 mg IV bolus. No antiarrhythmic agents have been shown to increase survival to hospital discharge in cardiac arrest patients. However, amiodarone has been shown to increase short-term survival to hospital admission when compared to placebo or lidocaine. Amiodarone has multiple mechanisms of action, including sodium, potassium, and calcium-channel blockade, as well as alpha- and beta-adrenergic blocking effects. It delays repolarization by prolonging the action potential duration and effective refractory period. Through this mechanism, amiodarone slows SA nodal function and AV nodal conduction and prolongs the refractory period in accessory pathways. Adverse effects from intravenous administration include hypotension and bradycardia. For dysrhythmias not associated with cardiac arrest, amiodarone is given at a loading dose of 150 mg over 10 minutes, followed by an infusion of 1 mg/min for 6 hours, and then 0.5 mg/min thereafter. Although long-term oral therapy is associated with thyroid disorders and pulmonary fibrosis, this is not the case for short-term intravenous therapy.

402. The answer is B, Observation and measurement of serial salicylate concentrations.

(Marx, 1954-1956; Wolfson, 1387-1391)

The patient in this question is presenting soon after the ingestion of an unknown quantity of aspirin, so the course of illness is unpredictable. Observation and measurement of serial salicylate concentrations are the most appropriate management. Significant aspirin poisonings, particularly but not exclusively with extended-release or enteric-coated preparations, are characterized by prolonged absorption; it is impossible to make a definitive disposition recommendation this early by a single point in time. Close observation and repeated measurement of salicylate concentrations, typically with serial blood gases and chemistry measurements, are appropriate to ensure that peak toxicity has clearly resolved. In poisoning, salicylates can uncouple oxidative phosphorylation and cause a primary respiratory alkalosis, a metabolic acidosis, and capillary leak, which can lead to noncardiogenic pulmonary edema. Urinary alkalinization (not acidification, which is not used in any poisoning) can help eliminate salicylate by ion trapping salicylate and preventing renal reabsorption. Ensuring that serum pH is at least normal is probably more crucial for outcome to help prevent the lipid soluble form of salicylate from entering the CNS. Hemodialysis should be available; when performed at the appropriate time, it is the definitive treatment to prevent death. Indications for hemodialysis include altered level of consciousness, significant acidosis, noncardiogenic pulmonary edema, worsening clinical condition, and renal failure. Texts list indications for hemodialysis based on serum concentrations of 100 mg/dL in acute cases and 40 mg/dL in chronic cases. These are reasonable recommendations, but hemodialysis must not be withheld if the patient meets other indications despite not having concentrations this high. In the scenario described, the patient does not meet criteria for hemodialysis but certainly might later. The Rumack-Matthew nomogram is used to guide therapy in acute acetaminophen poisonings. Another nomogram (Done nomogram) was attempted to help determine management of salicylate poisoning, but it was flawed, and its use has been abandoned.

403. The answer is D, Sialolithiasis.

(Marx, 885; Tintinalli, 1561)

Salivary gland stone, or sialolithiasis, is the likely underlying condition in this patient. In 80% of cases, the stone is in the submandibular gland because the duct that drains it (Wharton duct) tends to have more viscous secretions and has a course running against gravity. The diagnosis is made clinically, suggested by the location of the pain and swelling and the key history of enlargement with eating. Salivary gland stones can also be seen on CT scans. Any neck mass raises the concern of a neoplasm, but the change in size with eating is not characteristic of a tumor. A young adult with a neck mass from a neoplasm is most likely to have lymphoma and might have symptoms of fever, night sweats, and weight loss, but generally a nontender node. Squamous cell cancer of the oral cavity is more common in patients who use tobacco products, either by smoking or chewing, and drink alcohol. It is generally painless. Ludwig angina is a life-threatening infection of the floor of the mouth that involves the submental, submandibular, and sublingual spaces. It is characterized by an elevation of the tongue and induration of the neck under the chin. Acute necrotizing ulcerative gingivitis (ANUG), also known as Vincent angina and trench mouth, is a severe polymicrobial infection of the gingiva. Patients with ANUG will have bright red gingiva that bleed easily and halitosis.

404. The answer is C, Myoclonic atonic.

(Marx, 2225; Wolfson, 770-772)

Myoclonic atonic seizures are characterized by a sudden myoclonic jerk, typically affecting the axial muscles and manifesting as a sudden propelling forward of the torso, followed immediately by loss of focal muscle or postural muscle tone. The result is that the patient slumps to the ground, in this case, face forward. This type of seizure occurs typically in children and is a type of atonic seizure commonly known as a drop attack. In a typical drop attack, the head falls forward and the victim collapses to the ground buttocks first. Unfortunately, in a myoclonic atonic seizure, the myoclonic jerk can propel the patient forward, which, in combination with loss of muscle tone, can lead to significant facial injury. These patients typically do not lose consciousness and recover immediately. Atonic seizures are in the larger category of nonconvulsive seizures, which also includes absence seizures. Absence seizures typically last seconds to minutes and are of sudden onset without preceding aura. Patients typically are staring off, often with tic-type movements (eye twitching or blinking, lip smacking). There is no postictal period, and patients tend to resume exactly what they were doing when the seizure began, even conversation. The other major category of seizures is convulsive seizures, the most commonly known of which is the grand mal or tonic-clonic seizure. These generalized seizures might be preceded by a short feeling of unease after which the patient suffers a loss of consciousness, a period of stiffening from severe muscle clonus (tonic phase), followed by bilateral rhythmic contraction of the muscles (clonic phase). This typically lasts for 1 to 2 minutes and is followed by a postictal phase. Patients often complain of fatigue and headache as well. The final group of convulsive seizures is focal seizures. Focal seizures can be either simple partial or complex partial. Simple partial seizures affect only one hemisphere and, therefore, do not affect consciousness. These patients have a focal clonic movement, a focal sensory change with paresthesias or sensory hallucination (visual or olfactory), onset of fear, or even sweating. Complex partial seizures do affect consciousness, and patients are amnestic to the event; they often describe an aura and are postictal. Some demonstrate automatisms such as repeating a word or phrase, lip or tongue smacking, or a repetitive movement. Complex partial seizures are more likely to generalize to full tonic-clonic seizures.

405. The answer is D, The risk of sinusitis with short-term anterior nasal packing is minimal.

(Marx, 883-885; Roberts, 1197-1209; Schlosser, 784-789)

Although there is no proof that antibiotic prophylaxis is needed or effective with short-term anterior nasal packing, some practitioners still prescribe oral antibiotics routinely in the management of epistaxis. The risk of infection and other significant complications, including bradycardia, hypertension, arrhythmias, and death, is much greater with posterior nasal packing, so hospital admission and observation are recommended for the majority of these patients, especially the elderly. Elevated blood pressure in most cases of epistaxis is related to stress and anxiety, and, unless there are signs of a hypertensive emergency, hemorrhage control should precede blood pressure treatment, with success also addressing the blood pressure elevation. Epistaxis by itself is not a sign of end-organ injury or a hypertensive crisis. Vasoconstrictive agents are frequently helpful in slowing down or stopping bleeding when profuse bleeding obscures the source. Cocaine is still identified as a preferred agent to perform both local anesthesia and vasoconstriction, but most emergency departments more readily supply oxymetazalone for this purpose. Blood coming from the nasolacrimal duct occasionally occurs following packing and backward flow. This can be a source of further anxiety for the patient but is not an indication of packing problems.

406. The answer is D, Serum glucose level measurement.

(Fleisher, 565-567, 765; Marx, 2228-2231)

Hypoglycemia in children is defined as a serum glucose level lower than 50 mg/dL, with or without any symptoms. The clinical manifestations range from mild malaise to severe neurologic alteration. The causes, in nondiabetic patients, often relate to fasting or inadequate intake. Other factors include toxins, especially alcohols and oral hypoglycemia agents. Hypoglycemia is an easily identified and treated cause of seizures and in infants is related to limited glycogen stores. Approximately 4% to 6% of all children younger than 16 years have at least 1 seizure. Treatment of hypoglycemia in a pediatric patient is determined based on patient age and the type or size of intravenous access established. The general approach is to provide 0.5 to 1 g/kg of glucose. A quick mnemonic for this is "5, 2, 1": to provide 0.5 g/kg, administer 5 mL/kg of D10, 2 mL/kg of D25, or 1 mL/kg of D50. Because the peripheral veins in children cannot withstand significant osmolar stressors, it is not advised to give D50 through the peripheral route, but it can be infused using an intraosseous line. In a neonatal patient, this amount of fluid can cause significant hemodynamic shifts, so the patient's physiologic state must be considered before the D10 (5 mL/kg) is used. Arterial blood gas and CSF analyses and measurement of serum bicarbonate level are important in the evaluation of a sick pediatric patient but, in this case, are not as important as a bedside dextrose stick; this patient might continue to seize because of persistent hypoglycemia if it is not immediately addressed.

407. The answer is A, Admit him to the hospital.

(Marx, 517-518; Wolfson, 285)

A high-pressure injection injury from a paint gun can cause a large inflammatory reaction and ultimately require amputation. Discharge without imaging is not appropriate. The paint gun operates at pressures high enough to inject material through a digit and into the forearm. Early on, the patient can have an unimpressive physical examination, with only minimal pain and swelling. But these injuries progress to cause a large inflammatory reaction that leads to amputation of the digit in up to 60% to 80% of patients. In such a case, the patient usually develops severe pain, swelling, and tenderness over the following 6 hours, and there is a high risk of ischemia to the digit and tissue necrosis. Paint causes a particularly large and early inflammatory response. Radiography can help determine the extent of the injected material. Digital block as a pain control measure is contraindicated because it can make tissue distention and ischemia worse. A patient with this injury must be evaluated emergently by a hand surgeon. The mainstay of treatment is prompt detection followed by early surgical debridement and irrigation. The patient should not be discharged, even if the examination is unremarkable, until radiographs have been obtained and a hand surgery evaluation has taken place. A delay in definitive care increases the risk that amputation will be needed, so outpatient hand surgery evaluation is not the appropriate management.

408. The answer is A, Ethylene glycol.

(Nelson, 250, 511, 1403; Wolfson, 1388)

Ethylene glycol is an intoxicating alcohol (accounting in this case for the depressed level of consciousness) that is metabolized to toxic metabolites capable of causing a profound anion gap acidosis. The acidosis is not caused by hypoperfusion, and blood pressure and heart rate are often unremarkable. A depressed level of consciousness, tachypnea, and ABG measurements that reveal acidemia from a metabolic acidosis with normal respiratory compensation are most consistent with ethylene glycol poisoning. In a compensated metabolic acidosis, arterial PCO_2 is usually the same as the last two digits of the arterial pH (23 and 0.23). The Winters equation ($PCO_2 = 1.5 (HCO_3^-) + 8$ +/- 2) can also be used to interpret the blood gas, as it predicts what the PCO_2 will be in an acute metabolic acidosis with normal respiratory compensation. In this case, the equation predicts the PCO_2 of 23 that was in fact observed, consistent with ethylene glycol poisoning. Using the Winters equation, if the PCO_2 is much lower than predicted, an additional respiratory alkalosis is likely present. Such a combination of a metabolic acidosis and respiratory alkalosis is classic for salicylate poisoning. A pure metabolic acidosis with normal respiratory compensation, as in this case, would be very unusual for salicylate poisoning. A normal pulse would be very unusual in a patient with a severe acidosis from salicylate poisoning, as tachycardia would be expected. The metabolites of isopropanol, or rubbing alcohol, cause a ketosis but no acidosis. Although it can produce intoxication and coma, it does not cause acidemia. Both barbiturates and opioids in poisoning can cause a depressed level of consciousness, but decreased minute ventilation and respiratory acidosis would be expected.

409. The answer is C, Varicella.

(Marx, 1708; Tintinalli, 1027-1029)

Herpes zoster infection, or shingles, is caused by the varicella zoster virus (VZV). It has a characteristic vesicular, dermatonal pattern, as shown in this question. This virus first manifests as chickenpox, a febrile illness associated with a primarily truncal vesicular rash with the lesions appearing in various stages of development, or "crops." Patients who contract chickenpox are at risk of reactivation years later, usually during periods of stress, resulting in zoster or shingles. It manifests as a burning pain isolated to the affected dermatome, preceding a vesicular eruption in that dermatome. The patient in this question has a particularly severe reactivation, likely complicated by a superinfection, usually with *Staphylococcus aureus*. Since 1995, children have been vaccinated against VZV, so the prevalence of zoster will likely decrease over time. In 2006, the U.S. Food and Drug Administration licensed a vaccine for older adults targeting shingles. Herpes simplex virus also causes a vesicular eruption and is closely related to VZV. At least eight types of herpes viruses are known, including VZV. Herpes simplex 1 is associated with predominantly oral and labial lesions, and herpes simplex 2 manifests predominantly as genital lesions. Variola is the smallpox virus, and it presents with vesicular lesions primarily on the arms and face. The lesions are in the same stage of development and crusting, or "synchronized." Vaccinia is the cowpox virus, used in the smallpox vaccine. Rubeola is the measles virus, presenting with the three Cs: cough, conjunctivitis, and coryza. Its pathognomonic finding is Koplik spots, white spots on the buccal mucosa.

410. The answer is A, Ankylosing spondylitis.

(Marx, 1485-1487; Tintinalli, 1932)

All four conditions listed have symptoms of peripheral inflammatory arthropathy, most associated with a genetic component associated with the HLA-B27 antigen. Ankylosing spondylitis frequently manifests as chronic back pain of months' duration as a result of inflammation of the axial skeleton later developing the classic bamboo spine. The most common extra-articular manifestation of anklysosing spondylitis is uveitis with symptoms of photophobia, conjunctival redness, and eye pain in up to 30% of patients. Reactive arthritis, also a peripheral inflammatory arthropathy that was formerly known as Reiter syndrome, presents with the classic triad of symptoms—uveitis, urethritis, arthritis ("can't see, can't pee, can't climb a tree")—only one-third of the time. The syndrome is predominantly asymmetric and typically involves multiple weight-bearing joints. Arthropathy of inflammatory bowel disease occurs in 20% of affected patients during flareups. Patients develop acute migratory and polyarticular inflammation of the large lower extremity joints. Systemic juvenile rheumatoid arthritis, or Still disease, represents 10% to 20% of all cases of juvenile rheumatoid arthritis and presents with a salmon-pink rash at onset. Very rarely does a patient with this condition have a positive rheumatoid factor; the changing nomenclature of juvenile rheumatoid arthritis to juvenile idiopathic arthritis implies an unknown etiology. Patients with psoriatic arthritis have many of the same symptoms as those with reactive arthritis but have fewer constitutional symptoms, and the joint symptoms are preceded by psoriasis.

411. The answer is D, Using a pencil-point needle.

(Marx, 1363-1365; Wolfson, 756)

Using a pencil-point or atraumatic tip needle has been shown to decrease the incidence of postdural puncture headache following lumbar puncture. This is presumably the result of spreading the dural fibers (atraumatic insertion) rather than cutting them, which occurs with the beveled needles. Other approaches to prevent postdural puncture headache include using a smaller diameter needle and orienting the bevel pointing up (up to the ceiling) when the patient is lying on his or her side; the bevel causes less trauma if it is parallel to the fibers of the dura. There is no supporting literature to suggest that leaving the patient in a recumbent position after lumbar puncture decreases the incidence of headache. Most postdural puncture headaches are self-limited and resolve as the CSF leak from the puncture site resolves. Persistent symptoms (headache worsened with upright position and any Valsalva maneuver) should be treated with bed rest and hydration. More persistent symptoms might require caffeine or theophylline administration. In severe and unremitting cases lasting longer than 24 hours, a blood patch over the puncture site might be indicated.

412. The answer is A, If the postextraction examination is normal and there is no evidence of perforation, the patient may be discharged.

(Roberts, 803-807; Wolfson, 613-615)

Rectal foreign bodies are the source of much emergency department humor and lore, but they can create difficult problems. Some patients with chronic rectal stimulation and lax rectal tone can be treated with just viscous lidocaine and removal with examination. Other patients require local, spinal, or general anesthesia for foreign body removal. Both conscious sedation and local anesthesia are suggested as required adjuncts to allow the patient and the anal sphincter to relax and facilitate removal. Lidocaine 1% with epinephrine can be injected submucosally around the circumference of the anus. Glass foreign bodies, in particular, can create a vacuum in the rectum, making removal more difficult. A Foley catheter can be inserted around the object and passed more proximally to break the vacuum seal and allow removal, or a rigid sigmoidoscope can be used to insufflate air and accomplish the same effect. Cathartics and enemas should not be used because they can cause the foreign body to move higher in the colon or become impacted. Any time rectal perforation is suspected, surgical consultation should be obtained for removal. Patients who undergo successful extraction in the emergency department and have normal examinations can be safely discharged home. Prolonged presence of a foreign body can cause local edema and rectal bleeding. Any postprocedural pain, fever, or significant bleeding warrants a surgical consultation.

413. The answer is C, Multiple-level amputations.

(Marx, 518-519; Wolfson, 315-317)

When a digit is amputated at multiple levels or is in many pieces, crushed, contaminated, or otherwise compromised, replantation is generally contraindicated: the chances of later viability of the digit are minimal. Even in the best circumstances, replanted fingers might not function normally, or multiple surgical procedures and prolonged recovery time might be required. Proximal amputations can tolerate less ischemia time than distal amputations, so replantation of a distal amputation, such as between the distal interphalangeal and proximal interphalangeal joints, has a better chance of recovery than one proximal to the flexor digitorum superficialis insertion. Attempts to replant an amputated thumb are warranted because the function of opposition is so important in everyday life. The same is true for multiple-digit amputations because of the high morbidity rates associated with multiple-digit amputations and the chance for preservation of some function if these digits are replanted. Children tend to have good outcomes with replantation; every effort should be made to replant digits in children, regardless of which digit is involved or level of amputation.

414. The answer is C, Activated charcoal is generally contraindicated.

(Nelson, 1364-1370, 1374; Wolfson, 1466-1470)

Caustic agents include both acids and alkalis that are capable of causing tissue damage on contact. With very rare exceptions, activated charcoal administration is contraindicated; zinc chloride and mercuric chloride are exceptions in which risks of systemic absorption outweigh caustic risks, so charcoal should be given. Charcoal does not adsorb well to most caustic agents; its administration interferes with endoscopic visualization and hence determination of injury and might cause the patient to vomit and reexpose the upper gastrointestinal tract and airway to the caustic agent. Acids cause coagulative necrosis, whereas alkalis cause liquefactive necrosis. Both are capable of causing significant burns. Degree of injury depends on a variety of factors, including the pH of the agent, volume ingested, and contact time. Identifying the agent ingested can be helpful, as can measuring its pH if unknown. Absorption of certain agents can cause systemic toxicity in addition to local burns. Systemic fluoride toxicity occurs with ingestion of hydrofluoric acid; in fact, ingestions are nearly uniformly fatal. Initial management includes attention to the airway, as significant ingestions can produce significant airway compromise. Early intubation should be strongly considered for patients with stridor or voice change, as airway edema can progress quickly. Gastrointestinal perforation can be an early consequence of significant ingestions and mandates immediate aggressive resuscitation and surgical intervention. Systemic absorption of agents can also have severe consequences. The presence or absence of oropharyngeal burns unfortunately has very poor predictive value for identifying patients who have more distal burns. Endoscopy is helpful in determining the degree of burn injury and predicting what, if any, future complications are expected. As with caustic injury to the surface of the body, pain is expected. Assessment for this symptom can be challenging in children. However, in adults, particularly those with unintentional ingestions, the asymptomatic patient does not require endoscopy, as significant injuries will not be found.

415. The answer is C, 55%.

(Centor, 239-246; Tintinalli, 1583-1584)

This patient has all four clinical criteria that are associated with predicting a positive group A *Streptococcus* throat culture, indicating a 56% likelihood of a positive culture. The Centor criteria were established in 1981 from a study of 286 consecutive adult patients (older than 15 years) who presented to an emergency department in Virginia with pharyngitis. In that study, patients with all four (tonsillar exudates, swollen tender anterior cervical nodes, lack of a cough, history of a fever) had positive cultures 56% of the time. When patients had three criteria, the percentage dropped to 32%. With two criteria, it was 15%. Only 6.5% of patients with one of the four criteria had a positive culture, and 2.5% of patients with none of the criteria developed a positive culture. The actual likelihood of a positive culture varies tremendously and is highly dependent on the local prevalence of the disease. Another criterion sometimes used to gauge the pretest likelihood of strep throat is appropriate epidemiologic setting. This includes patients who might be at risk for the disease because of exposures: family members or roommates of patients with documented strep throat, day care workers, college students living in dormitories, and soldiers living in barracks. The Centor criteria were established in adult patients and have not been validated for use in children. Children have a higher pretest likelihood of disease as a result of epidemiologic exposures. They also have a wider variation in clinical presentation and are more likely to develop complications from the disease. Therefore, rapid antigen and throat culture testing should generally be used more often in children rather than relying solely on clinical diagnosis.

416. The answer is C, An RBC count greater than 10,000/mcL is consistent with a radiographically detectable hemorrhage.

(Edlow, 237-251; Roberts, 1120-1121; Wolfson, 75)

Studies have found up to 15% of patients with subarachnoid hemorrhage (SAH) have a normal head CT scan, and emergency physicians have historically used the finding of red blood cells in the CSF obtained during lumbar puncture to determine if a patient has a SAH. One study has found that an RBC count greater than 10,000/mcL is consistent with a radiologically detectable hemorrhage. Subarachnoid bleeds will reliably produce more red blood cells than a traumatic tap. A decrease of 30% or more is more likely compatible with a traumatic tap but not specific; the last tube RBC count should approach zero. An RBC count less than 500/mcL in tube 4 favor a traumatic tap; greater than 1,000 RBCs/mcL has been suggested as criteria for SAH. Red blood cell counts can decrease in SAH from tubes 1 to 4, but this will normally not be greater than a 9% decrease; the cause is thought to be layering of cells in a patient who is recumbent. The rate of RBC clearance can be variable. Counts ranging between 500 and 10,000 warrant further study to eliminate subarachnoid bleed as a possibility. The development of xanthochromia from hemolysis of red blood cells and the release of the pink or yellow heme pigment in the CSF is typically delayed for several hours after the hemorrhage, although the precise time that this occurs cannot be reliably stated. Emergency medicine texts state xanthochromia typically appears by 4 to 6 hours. The presence of any clotting in the samples favors a traumatic tap, as in SAH the blood is defibrinated at the site of the bleed, and clots, therefore, should not appear in the CSF. Lumbar puncture remains an important procedure to determine if there is a subarachnoid hemorrhage because extravasated blood can be isodense to the surrounding tissue, meaning CT might not detect small or sentinel bleeds.

417. The answer is C, Pain with pinching and loss of pinch strength.

(Marx, 511-516; Wolfson, 282-283)

Skier's thumb, also known as gamekeeper's thumb, is an injury to the ulnar collateral ligament at the base of the thumb on the ulnar aspect of the metacarpophalangeal (MCP) joint. Usually, a patient presents after falling while holding a ski pole and has pain, swelling, and perhaps ecchymosis at the MCP joint. Key findings are loss of pinch strength and pain with the pinching movement. The patient should be able to abduct the thumb without difficulty. Radiographs might demonstrate a bony avulsion fracture from the insertion of the ulnar collateral ligament into the proximal phalanx. Radiographs might also demonstrate volar subluxation and radial deviation of the proximal phalanx, which indicates complete rupture of the ligament. There is tenderness at the ulnar aspect of the MCP joint of the thumb but not at the interphalangeal joint unless there is another injury. Treatment consists of immobilization in a thumb spica splint or cast for 4 weeks. Some patients require surgical repair to prevent instability of the joint, chronic pain, and chronic weakness of pinch strength.

418. The answer is D, Serotonin syndrome.

(Marx, 1629, 1661; Nelson, 238-239, 1041-1043)

Hyperreflexia is an expected but obviously not specific finding in serotonin syndrome (also referred to as serotonin toxicity) and is not present in the other conditions listed. A physical examination finding characteristic of serotonin toxicity is clonus, which represents an extreme manifestation of hyperreflexia. It refers to a rhythmic unidirectional reflex muscle contraction in which each beat is caused by renewed stretch of the muscle during relaxation from a previously contracted state. It is typically tested for by dorsiflexion of the ankle. Serotonin toxicity is an iatrogenic disorder that occurs from agonism of serotonin receptors. It can occur after an overdose of a single serotonergic drug such as a selective serotonin reuptake inhibitor (SSRI) or a combination of two drugs that contribute to serotonergic agonism. Similar to neuroleptic malignant syndrome, serotonin toxicity is characterized by a triad of autonomic instability, mental status changes, and neuromuscular changes. Neuroleptic malignant syndrome is often an idiosyncratic reaction precipitated by either the administration of a dopamine antagonist such as haloperidol or withdrawal from a dopamine agonist such as L-dopa. It is characterized by much more muscular rigidity (often described as lead pipe) than serotonin toxicity and bradykinesia. Hyperreflexia is one of many physical examination findings found in hyperthyroidism, not hypothyroidism. Hypermagnesemia is associated with muscular weakness and hyporeflexia. Serial reflex measurements are used to help guide magnesium therapy in treating pre-eclampsia.

419. The answer is A, Efavirenz – psychosis.

(Tintinalli, 1110; Venkat, 274-285)

Efavirenz is a non-nucleoside reverse transcriptase inhibitor used with other medications to treat HIV infection in patients with or without AIDS. It is known to cause psychosis and depression, usually in the first 4 weeks of therapy. A patient might also experience nightmares and irritability. The advent of highly active antiretroviral therapy, or HAART, has transformed HIV into a chronic, manageable disease. As patients live longer, they become more at risk for cardiovascular disease. The metabolic syndrome associated with the use of protease inhibitors—hyperlipidemia, hypergylcemia, and truncal obesity—makes this cardiovascular risk even greater. These patients are at 25% to 75% higher risk than a person of the same age who is not taking these medications. Nevirapine, rather than ritonavir, is notorious for its risk of hepatic failure, leading to a change in recommendations for postexposure prophylaxis. Ritonavir, as with any protease inhibitor, is associated with the metabolic syndrome and hyperlipidemia. Indinavir is well known to cause nephrolithiasis, and patients taking it are advised to drink additional glasses of water each day. Most of the nucleoside reverse transcriptase inhibitors (NRTIs) pose a risk for lactic acidosis, including zidovudine (AZT), didanosine (DDI), and lamivudine (3TC). The most common adverse reaction to AZT is bone marrow suppression, characteristically resulting in a macrocytic anemia.

420. The answer is C, Fluoroquinolone use.

(Marx, 679-680; Wolfson, 307)

There are several risk factors for Achilles tendon rupture, including age older than 40 years, male sex, previous Achilles tendinitis, previous steroid injection, fluoroquinolone use, systemic steroid therapy, and comorbid diseases such as renal failure, hyperparathyroidism, lupus, gout, and rheumatoid arthritis. Achilles tendon rupture occurs after sudden, unexpected, forced dorsiflexion or forceful plantar flexion during sports such as basketball or running. It can also occur as a result of direct trauma. The patient presents with pain and swelling over the Achilles tendon, and the tendon is not firmly palpable. The Thompson test can be useful in making the diagnosis. With the patient prone, the examiner squeezes the calf and observes the foot for passive plantar flexion. If this does not occur, there should be high suspicion for complete rupture of the Achilles tendon. Treatment of this injury is primarily surgical repair, so a patient with Achilles tendon rupture should undergo orthopedic consultation in the emergency department or as arranged as an outpatient if done in a timely manner.

421. The answer is C, Scombroid poisoning.

(Marx, 1211-1212; Nelson, 669, 671, 677; Wolfson, 1590-1593)

Facial flushing and throbbing headache are classic symptoms of scombroid poisoning. Improper preservation or refrigeration of a wide variety of histidine-rich dark meat fish allows for bacterial conversion of histidine to histamine and histamine-like substances. Other symptoms include diarrhea, abdominal cramping, and rarely hypotension. The implicated fish is occasionally described as having a peppery taste. Emergency department treatment includes antihistamines (H1 and H2 blockers) and intravenous fluids if necessary. If a patient is seen soon after ingestion, charcoal administration is not unreasonable. Symptoms usually resolve quickly, and most patients can be discharged. The poisoning is not an allergic reaction, and the location of flushing (face, neck, upper torso) is quite characteristic. Scombroid poisoning can also be distinguished from an allergic reaction if multiple individuals with the same signs and symptoms are involved. Ciguatera and tetrodotoxin poisoning can also result from ingestion of fish. Ciguatera poisoning results from the ingestion of ciguatoxin, found in mostly reef fish. Ciguatoxin acts on sodium channels, and signs and symptoms are gastrointestinal, cardiac (bradycardia), and neurologic. Paresthesias are common; hot and cold reversal is characteristic but not common. Tetrodotoxin is found in the puffer fish served as the delicacy fugu and also in certain newts and the blue-ringed octopus. Tetrodotoxin is a sodium-channel blocker and can cause paresthesias and, in severe cases, respiratory paralysis. The local or state health department should be notified in cases of suspected seafood poisoning such as scombroid to help prevent additional exposures.

422. The answer is C, Dacrocystitis.

(Fleisher, 240-244, 956; Marx, 226-240; Tintinalli, 764)

Dacrocystitis is an inflammation of the nasolacrimal duct with subsequent obstruction or discharge of mucus or exudate from the conjunctiva. The lacrimal system helps drain tears into the nasal passages; it is lined with bacteria-colonized membranes of the nasal and conjunctival mucosa. The bacteria involved in the infectious process are the same as those associated with conjunctival flora, commonly *Streptococcus pneumoniae, Staphylococcus aureus, S. epidermidis, Haemophilus influenzae,* and *S. agalactiae.* The possibility of infection from *Neisseria gonorrhoeae* or *Chlamydia* must be considered, but since the mother was cared for throughout the pregnancy and the baby was delivered in a hospital, the likelihood of this is decreased. *Chlamydia* is the most common cause of neonatal conjunctivitis. The clinical presentation for chlamydial conjunctivitis is often noted after 2 weeks of life with a mucopurulent discharge. Gonorrheal infection is seen when the infant is 5 to 7 days old, with a Gram stain showing gram-negative intracellular diplococci. Dacrocystitis can lead to significant complications, including the following: extension into the bony orbit, leading to abscess formation; development of orbital cellulitis, which can lead to blindness, cavernous sinus thrombosis, and ultimately death; and fistula formation from the sac to the skin. Blepharitis is inflammation of all four eyelid margins associated with crusting on awakening. It is related to diminished tear production. A hordeolum, or sty, is an abscess in the eyelash at the lid margin. It is denoted as external or internal depending on which side of the lid the abscess is pointing to.

423. The answer is A, Obtain vascular surgery consultation.

(Marx, 1095-1100; Tintinalli, 543, 545-547)

In an unstable patient with gastrointestinal bleeding who has a history of abdominal aortic aneurysm (AAA) repair, the appropriate action is to get an emergent surgery evaluation for operative intervention. An aortoenteric fistula (AEF) can be a primary complication of AAA before repair or, more commonly, a secondary complication occurring anytime after repair. The AEF typically begins to develop when the bowel is eroded by the aneurysm, resulting in local infection, abscess, or occasionally, a sentinel bleed from a local vessel in the bowel wall. Typically, massive bleeding from a duodenal fistula follows. However, bleeding can be acute or chronic, upper or lower, depending on the exact site and source. Aortoenteric fistula must be ruled out in any patient presenting with a newly diagnosed or repaired AAA and upper or lower gastrointestinal bleeding. Management depends on the patient's hemodynamic stability. With overt shock, emergent surgical diagnosis and definitive repair are required. In patients whose conditions are stable, CT scanning often does not reveal the AEF directly but can identify the local infection accompanying fistula formation, as well as other possible diagnoses such as diverticular disease. Angiography can be used in patients whose conditions are stable, to diagnose AAA and AEF but has largely been replaced by ultrasonography and CT. Nasogastric lavage is helpful in identifying the location of bleeding and need for intervention with gastrointestinal bleeding but only delays definitive management in an unstable patient with AEF. Proton pump inhibitors and octreotide drips are important for suspected variceal bleeding but are not indicated for AEF.

424. **The answer is D, Evacuation of auricular hematoma is necessary because the cartilage is avascular.**

(Roberts, 620; Wolfson, 156)

Auricular cartilage is inherently avascular and relies on the vascular supply of the overlying skin. If the cartilage does not remain approximated to the skin, as is the case with auricular hematoma or denuded cartilage, then a cauliflower deformity or erosive chondritis can result. Evacuation of auricular hematomas helps prevent erosive chondritis. If performed in a sterile manner, evacuation should not increase the risk of infection. A pressure dressing should be applied to the ear after aspiration of auricular hematoma and after ear laceration repair to prevent reaccumulation or development of auricular hematomas. When repairing lacerations of the ear and when performing aspiration of an auricular hematoma, anesthesia is best achieved by performing a field block at the base of the ear to avoid distending the tissue around the laceration. Auricular cartilage should be repaired with absorbable sutures and should be approximated in the case of through-and-through lacerations. The wound should also be covered in cases of denuded cartilage, because of its avascular nature, to avoid infection and necrosis. The overlying skin should be approximated using nonabsorbable sutures both anteriorly and posteriorly.

425. **The answer is D, Reassure and discharge with NSAIDs.**

(Grimes, CD006134; Tintinalli, 675)

The patient in this question has a functional ovarian cyst with hemorrhagic rupture. Findings that are consistent with this diagnosis are the acute onset of one-sided pelvic pain with ultrasound examination findings of ovarian cyst and free fluid in the peritoneal cavity. Ovarian cysts that are less than 8 cm, unilocular, and unilateral can be managed expectantly. These patients do not need to be admitted for pain control if they are not in extremis; they can follow up in the emergency department or with a gynecologist. Cyst resolution usually occurs within 2 to 3 months and can be confirmed with another ultrasound examination. Current literature shows that oral contraceptives offer no benefit to ovarian cyst resolution. There is no indication for ordering a CT scan of the abdomen and pelvis because the pain is most likely the result of the ruptured ovarian cyst. The patient's discomfort can be managed with NSAIDs, but she should follow up for reassessment and repeat ultrasonography. Urgent consultation is not needed in the emergency department because there is no evidence of torsion, and she is hemodynamically stable. If the ovarian cyst persists and the pain does not resolve, the patient might need outpatient surgery to remove the cyst.

426. The answer is A, Discharge home with reassurance.

(Fleisher, 1178-1180, 1194; Marx, 1989)

Household bleach is commonly a dilute (5.25%) sodium hypochlorite solution, and ingestion rarely leads to illness or complications. Poison centers recommend discharge home without emergency department observation for simple household bleach ingestions. However, industrial-strength bleach or other cleaners can cause significant damage as a result of the higher concentration of alkali. Pediatric ingestions usually involve a single agent and a smaller quantity than an adult ingestion because the pediatric ingestion is often unintentional. Activated charcoal (AC) should not be used in an acid/alkali ingestion because it does not provide any mitigation; it can actually worsen the clinical scenario because this vomiting can lead to an aspiration pneumonitis, not only from the caustic agent but also from the AC. Activated charcoal provides limited, if any, absorption of toxin and should not be used in ingestions of caustic substances, pesticides, hydrocarbons, alcohols, iron, lithium, or solvents. Whole bowel irrigation is often considered when an ingested toxin might be a sustained-release preparation, a heavy metal, or an overwhelming ingestion that AC might not bind completely or when evacuation of the substance (cocaine or heroin packets, lead) must be accomplished quickly.

427. The answer is C, C6.

(Marx, 352-354; Tintinalli, 1716-1717; Wolfson, 194-197)

The patient in this question presents with a complete neurologic lesion, defined as "the absence of sensory and motor function below the level of injury." He is breathing spontaneously and can shrug his shoulders but cannot flex at the elbow or move his arms, which indicates a lesion at C6. He also has a sensory level of C6, which is loss of sensation below the clavicle but sensation along the arm including the thumb. A lesion at C3 would result in inability to breathe because C3, C4, and C5 innervate the diaphragm. A lesion at C3 also results in loss of sensation at the level of the thyroid cartilage. A lesion at C5 results in loss of sensation below the clavicle but not on the arms. A lesion at C7 results in loss of elbow extension but intact elbow flexion. A lesion at C8/T1 results in loss of flexion of the fingers but intact elbow extension. A lesion at C8 results in loss of sensation of the fourth and fifth digits and ulnar aspect of the forearm.

428. The answer is C, History of urethral strictures.

(Tintinalli, 651; Vilke, 193-198)

A common reason for failed Foley catheter placement in older male patients is enlarged prostate. In this situation, the Coudé catheter is the best solution. However, because the Coudé catheter has a rigid tip, care should be taken in patients who have failed Foley catheter placement and have a history of urethral strictures because false tracts can be created and worsened. The procedure for placing the Coudé is similar to that used for the Foley, except that the curved tip should be pointing upward (toward the dorsal surface of the penis). Hematuria and infections are not contraindications to catheter placement but can be complications. In women, the most common error of inability to pass a catheter is attempting clitoral intubation.

429. The answer is A, Community-level outbreaks of a novel virus in at least two regions.

(World Health Organization [influenza], 6-9)

In 2005, the World Health Organization (WHO) revised its 1999 preparedness plan for dealing with a new influenza pandemic. In these guidelines, the WHO describes six phases of a pandemic development. A full pandemic is occurring when stage 6 is reached, the documentation of community-level outbreaks of the disease in at least two WHO regions, which are Africa, the Eastern Mediterranean, Europe, the Americas, Southeast Asia, and the Western Pacific. Phase 1 is the period before any new influenza subtypes have been detected in animals, a stage that is unlikely to occur as new subtypes are discovered every year. Phase 2 begins when one of these new animal viruses is shown to be able to infect humans. Phase 3 occurs when sporadic cases of the new animal virus appear in humans throughout the world. This is the current phase for the H5N1 virus, or avian flu, a disease that humans can catch from birds but does not easily spread between humans. Phase 4 indicates that such a virus can easily transmit between humans; this results in community-level outbreaks in the areas where the virus first developed the ability to spread between humans. In phase 5, the disease spreads across a continent or one WHO region. At this point, a true pandemic is essentially inevitable, as international travel and commerce spread the virus to other continents. Finally, in phase 6, it has been documented on multiple continents, or two WHO regions.

430. The answer is A, Avulsion fracture of the greater tuberosity of the humerus occurs in 10% to 15% of dislocations.

(Marx, 579-582; Wolfson, 260-261)

Anterior shoulder dislocations are very common. Associated fractures are also common, occurring in 25% to 40% of cases. Avulsion fractures of the greater tuberosity of the humerus can be seen on plain radiographs obtained in patients with shoulder dislocations 10% to 15% of the time. The most common fracture seen with anterior shoulder dislocations is a Hill-Sachs deformity, which is a compression fracture of the posterolateral humeral head, and this can occur in 40% of cases. A Bankart fracture is a fracture of the anterior glenoid rim, which occurs in approximately 5% of cases. The most common neurologic injury associated with an anterior shoulder dislocation is an axillary nerve injury. Injury to the nerve is assessed by testing sensation over the lateral deltoid muscle, or weakness of the deltoid muscle and teres minor muscle. Motor assessment of nerve function is more reliable than sensory assessment but can be difficult because of the pain the patient is experiencing. Injury to the axillary nerve heals spontaneously in most patients with good recovery of function.

431. The answer is C, Lung cancer.

(Adams, 399-400; Marx, 1156)

The most common cause of liver cancer is metastasis from another primary cancer. When liver lesions suspicious for malignancy are found on ultrasound or CT, a search must be made for a primary pulmonary, gastrointestinal, or breast cancer. The most common primary hepatic cancer is hepatocellular carcinoma. Eighty percent of primary hepatocellular carcinomas result from hepatitis B virus (HBV) or hepatitis C virus (HCV). Hepatitis B virus is a double-stranded DNA virus that is typically transmitted through sexual contact or blood exposure. The transmission rate of HBV is higher than those of HCV and HIV but is significantly reduced with vaccination. Persons infected with HBV are at risk for developing cirrhosis and hepatocellular carcinoma. Hepatitis C virus is an RNA virus that is also transmitted through sexual contact or blood exposure. Up to 5% of these patients develop hepatocellular carcinoma. Unlike HBV, there are no vaccinations against HCV. Chronic alcohol abuse, primary biliary cirrhosis, hemochromatosis, and several other causative agents also predispose patients to developing hepatocellular carcinoma. Symptoms are nonspecific and include weight loss, nausea, vomiting, right upper quadrant abdominal pain, and jaundice. Although typically abnormal, liver function test results and alpha-fetoprotein levels are nonspecific. Ultrasonography and CT are helpful initial imaging modalities in the emergency department, with definitive diagnosis confirmed with subsequent biopsy.

432. The answer is C, Preparation, notification, grief response, viewing of the body, concluding process.

(Marx, 2574-2578; Tintinalli, 2017-2021)

The appropriate sequence of events used when communicating bad news, such as notifying family members when a patient dies, is preparation, notification, grief response, viewing of the body, and concluding process. Ideally, preparation involves finding a private room where family members can be gathered and advised of ongoing events if there are any, usually with the aid of social services, a designated nurse, and a chaplain. The notification phase starts with the physician introducing himself or herself and identifying who the family members are. The physician should then sit down with the family members and give them a brief synopsis of the events that occurred, including the care provided by EMS personnel, if involved, and then tell them the patient has died. Terms that can be misleading such as "passed on" or "no longer with us" should not be used. During the family's grief response, the emergency physician should give physical comfort if comfortable doing so and not move away. After some time, the emergency physician should ask a question about the patient; if appropriate, the family should be assured that no suffering was involved. Finally, the emergency physician should advise the family that he or she will contact the family physician and coroner, then leave the room. Before the viewing phase, the body should be covered with sheets, leaving the hands and face exposed, and the room cleaned. A staff member should accompany the family members and allow them to view the body if they want to, but they should not be forced to. During the concluding process, the emergency physician should express condolences and ask family members if they have any questions. This is the point in the process to inquire about autopsy and organ donation and sign appropriate papers. Family members who are at risk for pathologic grief should be identified and appropriate followup arranged. Finally, family members should be told when they can leave the emergency department.

433. The answer is B, Complications of scalp wound infection include osteomyelitis and brain abscess.

(Laughlin, 126-128; Marx, 703-711; Roberts, 623-625)

When scalp lacerations involve the galea aponeurotica, bacteria can penetrate the layer of loose connective tissue beneath it, gaining access to the venous sinuses of the brain. A wound infection can, therefore, cause osteomyelitis, meningitis, or brain abscess. It is of utmost importance to make sure that all foreign bodies are removed and that cautious and conservative debridement is performed prior to closure of the galea and superficial layers of the wound to avoid this complication. It is controversial whether the galea should be closed as a separate layer or whether it can be closed along with the superficial layers of the wound. Blindly clamping bleeding vessels is unlikely to be helpful in gaining control of bleeding. Using Raney clips and administering an anesthetic agent with added epinephrine are helpful in controlling active bleeding. Hair may be washed a few hours after closure; the patient does not need to wait 24 to 48 hours to remove remaining blood and debris. Although care should be taken to avoid getting hair in the wound, in most cases, shaving is unnecessary. Hair can be removed by clipping around the wound or moved out of the way using a petroleum-based antibiotic ointment or tape.

434. The answer is C, Oral dicloxacillin.

(Adams, 1400-1402; Tintinalli, 721-722; Wolfson, 702-703)

Acute puerperal mastitis occurs in nursing mothers who develop inflammation and cracking of the nipples that leads to localized infection of a ductal system. Signs and symptoms include a focal area of tenderness and erythema of the breast, in addition to systemic symptoms of fever and myalgias. The correct treatment is antibiotics that cover *Staphylococcus* and other skin bacteria, such as dicloxacillin. Up to one-third of nursing mothers develop mastitis, most commonly in the first few months postpartum. The nipples often develop colonization of *Candida,* which can be controlled by topical nystatin on the mother's nipples and breast in conjunction with oral nystatin for the infant. Continuation of breastfeeding with mastitis seems to help increase the movement of the milk through the ducts to empty the breast, improving healing. If left untreated, an abscess can form in the ducts, requiring incision and drainage. Abscess should be suspected if simple mastitis does not improve 2 days after antibiotics are started. If suspected, an abscess can be diagnosed using ultrasonography. Discontinuation of breastfeeding is often suggested if incision and drainage is required.

435. The answer is B, Elevated advancing margin of infection.

(Marx, 1838-1839; Tintinalli, 1014-1018)

An elevated advancing margin of infection helps distinguish erysipelas (a rapidly advancing superficial cellulitis often caused by group A *Streptococcus* infection) from simple skin infections and other types of cellulitis. This erythematous rash is most often seen on the lower extremities, and signs and symptoms include a localized burning sensation and a bright red, shiny rash with a well-demarcated elevated edge. Patients often appear toxic from infection and might have typical systemic symptoms such as fever and malaise. *Haemophilus influenzae* cellulitis, now rare since most infants receive the Hib vaccination, also causes a very ill appearance in infants and a purple-red rash. Erysipelas does not routinely lead to abscess formation, which is much more common in cellulitis from Staphylococcus aureus infection. An MRSA infection causes a more invasive cellulitis that is more likely to cause an abscess, and, although most are more localized, some MRSA cellulitis can progress rapidly to a progressive and systemic infection. Most cases of cellulitis are caused by local bacterial invasion of the skin with the rash primarily from a significant localized inflammatory response. This explains why only 10% of cultures from aspiration of the leading edge of the rash are positive for a specific organism.

436. The answer is B, Malrotation with midgut volvulus.

(Marx, 2117, 2171-2175; Strange, 57-63, 66-67; Tintinalli, 740, 830-832)

Malrotation with midgut volvulus occurs predominantly in newborn infants younger than 1 month and is associated with bilious vomiting. The symptoms begin after the congenitally malrotated bowel twists on the mesentery near the duodenum; this causes an acute obstruction that can lead to compression of the superior mesenteric artery and vascular compromise. Most infants present with acute symptoms and rapidly develop shock. Another concern in this neonatal period is necrotizing enterocolitis (NEC), which generally presents with abdominal distention and nonbilious vomiting from the resultant ileus. Necrotizing enterocolitis is seen predominantly in preterm infants with feeding difficulty and vomiting. On plain radiographs, malrotation is associated with paucity of small bowel air, and NEC is characterized by diffusely dilated loops of small bowel. Duodenal atresia generally manifests less than 24 hours after birth with vomiting, and up to one-third of patients have trisomy 21 (Down syndrome). The vomitus can be either bilious or nonbilious depending on the exact location of the atresia. Tracheoesophageal fistula is a rare disorder. It can cause vomiting in the early infancy period, but it is more often also associated with respiratory symptoms such as choking, coughing, and cyanosis with feeding. Pyloric stenosis might also be a consideration with this presentation, but most patients have gradually increasing emesis after the age of 2 to 3 weeks. All four conditions require emergent surgical consultation, and, in ill-appearing infants, consultation is indicated even before the completion of diagnostic studies.

437. The answer is B, CT angiography is the best diagnostic study.

(Adams, 697-699; Marx, 1104-1110; Tintinalli, 459-462)

Acute vascular occlusion is most commonly caused by an embolus, especially in patients with atrial fibrillation who are not appropriately anticoagulated. Historically, traditional arteriography was considered the gold standard, but now CT angiography (CTA) is being used more commonly because it is less invasive and more readily available. Some studies show that CTA results and traditional angiography results are the same 100% of the time. Duplex ultrasonography is very sensitive for proximal occlusions (95%), but the sensitivity decreases in the distal extremities such as the calf. This noninvasive study might be used to make the diagnosis of arterial occlusion, but most vascular surgeons require that a contrast study be performed before surgery to better define the vasculature. Ankle-brachial index (ABI) is the ratio of the systolic blood pressure of the ankle (using the posterior tibial or dorsalis pedis pulse) to the systolic blood pressure of the brachial artery on the arm using Doppler to accurately hear the measurements. If this ratio is normal, it is between 0.91 and 1.30; anything below 0.90 indicates some type of peripheral vascular disease. The region of acute occlusion can be identified using Doppler to determine the systolic pressure of the lower leg, lower thigh, and upper thigh: any change by 30 points indicates significant obstruction. Decreased sensation can be an early neurologic sign of occlusion, but the first physical finding is generally pallor of the distal extremity. Other symptoms include pain, pulselessness, paresthesia, and paralysis; the last two are signs of significant limb ischemia.

438. The answer is C, Epinephrine 0.3 to 0.5 mg IM is appropriate pharmacotherapy.

(Marx, 750-752; Tintinalli, 1344-1346)

The clinical manifestations of bee stings include local, toxic, anaphylactic, delayed, and unusual reactions. The cornerstone of therapy for the patient in this question involves removal of the stingers and administration of 0.3 to 0.5 mg epinephrine 1:1,000 dilution IM. Other first-line therapy in patients with ongoing hypotension includes placing the patient in a recumbent position and providing intravenous fluid replacement with normal saline. Shortness of breath and bronchospasm can also be treated with a nebulized beta-agonist (albuterol). Other treatments include the administration of parenteral antihistamines (diphenhydramine) and H2-receptor antagonists (ranitidine). Using H1 and H2 medications together is more efficacious, but, because the onset of action is slow, this approach is considered second-line therapy. Systemic steroid therapy might help with prolonged or recurrent anaphylaxis, although there is little direct evidence to support this approach and the effect is not seen for several hours. Local reactions to bee stings include pain, erythema, edema, and pruritus at the site of the sting; treatment for this patient should include washing the sting sites with soap and water and applying ice packs to lessen associated edema. Most anaphylactic reactions occur within 6 hours after the sting and can include vertigo, chest pain, dyspnea, and cyanosis. Toxic reactions to bee stings include nausea, vomiting, and headache. Delayed reactions occur 5 to 14 days after a sting and can include fever, malaise, and headache. Unusual reactions have included encephalopathy, vasculitis, and nephrosis. Africanized honeybees, or killer bees, are found across Southern regions of the United States; they are hybrids of African bees. In comparison to American honeybees, they are very aggressive but have similar venom toxicity. Antivenoms for bee stings, although studied, are not commercially available.

439. The answer is C, Hypotension.

(Fleisher, 1157-1164; Marx, 2161-2164; Tintinalli, 827-828, 922-923)

Kawasaki disease (KD) is a multisystem vasculitis that characteristically causes prolonged fever, conjunctivitis, and lymphadenopathy. The definitive treatment is administration of intravenous immunoglobulin (IVIG). Vomiting, hypotension, and seizures are among the side effects of IVIG therapy. When given early in the course of the disease, the combination therapy of IVIG and high-dose aspirin reduces the incidence of cardiac complications. Aspirin alone has not been shown to decrease the development of coronary artery aneurysms. Although rare, there have been cases of Reye syndrome with use of aspirin in KD. Currently, administration of corticosteroids is reserved for refractory cases; in comparison to conventional therapy, earlier administration of corticosteroids has not been shown to improve clinical outcomes. Hyperglycemia is a common finding in patients who are taking corticosteroids. Kawasaki disease most commonly occurs in children younger than 5 years old and is classified as either classic or incomplete (atypical) disease. The diagnostic criteria for classic disease include fever for 5 days plus four of the following symptoms: bilateral nonexudative conjunctivitis, mucous membrane changes, skin changes of the extremities, cervical lymphadenopathy, and rash. The diagnostic criteria for incomplete or atypical presentation of KD include fever for 5 days plus two to three of the clinical criteria of classic disease, plus elevated C-reactive protein level or ESR, plus three or more of the following supplemental laboratory test results: low albumin level, anemia, thrombocytosis, leukocytosis, elevated ALT level; and pyuria. Of note is that both classifications of KD include fever of at least 5 days' duration. The main treatment goals are to prevent coronary artery aneurysm formation and decrease myocardial inflammation. Risk factors for coronary artery aneurysm include age younger than 1 year, male, prolonged fever, and cardiomegaly on presentation. The height of the fever is not an associated risk factor for coronary artery aneurysm formation.

440. The answer is D, Splenomegaly is common.

(Fleisher, 936-937; Marx, 1710; Tintinalli, 1029-1030, 1583-1584)

The list of microbial causes of acute pharyngitis is extensive; however, the clinical scenario presented in this question makes the probability of infectious mononucleosis very likely. Splenomegaly or hepatosplenomegaly is found in up to 60% of patients and is most commonly present during the second week of illness. Splenic rupture is a rare complication but should be considered when the patient's presenting symptoms include abdominal pain. The disease is characterized by malaise, exudative pharyngitis, fever, and lymphadenopathy. The lymphadenopathy is most often prominent in the posterior aspect of the neck. Petechiae can be seen on the soft palate in patients with pharyngitis from several causes and does not distinguish one etiology from another. Infectious mononucleosis commonly presents either in early childhood or in young adulthood and is caused by the Epstein-Barr virus (EBV). The length of the illness is usually 2 to 4 weeks, but malaise and fatigue can persist for months. Laboratory findings often include lymphocytosis with greater than 50% lymphocytes and the presence of atypical lymphocytes on a blood smear. However, atypical lymphocytes are not pathognomonic for infectious mononucleosis and can be seen with cytomegalovirus infection, HIV infection, and viral hepatitis. The monospot test has a high sensitivity and specificity for infectious mononucleosis but can be negative early in the course of the disease (the first week of illness). Although rare, a persistently negative monospot test result can occur in some patients with infectious mononucleosis. A generalized rash is occasionally seen in patients with EBV, but a maculopapular rash develops only if a patient with an acute EBV infection is inadvertently treated with ampicillin or amoxicillin. Treatment is mainly supportive. Corticosteroids are advocated only with severe disease when there is evidence of organ dysfunction or airway compromise.

441. The answer is B, Belonging to the Goth subculture increases the risk of attempted suicide.

(Marx, 1463-1471; Tintinalli, 969-970, 1943-1946)

Suicides are the third leading cause of death among adolescents and young adults. Threatened suicide is a commonly encountered pediatric psychiatric emergency. Adolescents belonging to the Goth subculture are at increased risk of self-harm and attempted suicide. Adolescents with a history of panic attack are also at a higher risk of attempting suicide compared to those without panic attacks. Investigations have revealed that 1 in 5 high school students has considered suicide. Of these, approximately 20% have made plans and 10% have attempted suicide. When comparing boys to girls, suicide attempts are more prevalent in girls, often with various substance ingestions. These acts often do not result in death. In contrast, boys who do attempt suicide often carry the attempt to completion with the use of firearms. The ratio of attempted to completed suicides is 25:1 for adolescent girls and 3:1 for adolescent boys. Most adolescents with thoughts or acts of suicide often have one or more underlying psychiatric disorders such as depression, bipolar disorder, anxiety disorder, and antisocial disorder. Alcohol and substance abuse are often contributory factors. Eating disorders also place adolescents at risk for suicide attempts.

442. The answer is C, Scalene muscle contractions are more suggestive of severe obstruction than are subcostal and intercostal muscle retractions.

(Marx, 2115-2122; Tintinalli, 801-810)

Physical examination findings of hypoxemia, poor air entry, and retractions indicate that the patient in this question has a severe asthma exacerbation. In determining the severity of asthma, progressive use of accessory muscles for respiration occurs in a caudal-to-cephalad direction; scalene muscle contractions are more suggestive of severe obstruction than are subcostal and intercostal muscle retractions. Objective assessment of airflow obstruction with spirometry is advocated by the National Asthma Education and Prevention Program. However, PEFR or forced expiratory volume measurements with spirometry are often hard to obtain in children, especially children younger than 6 years. As a result, assessment of asthma severity in children is often based on the clinical presentation and physical findings. Scoring systems have been advocated for use in an attempt to standardize the clinical assessment. One such scoring system is the 12-point Pediatric Respiratory Assessment Measure. Variables that have been included within this scoring system include signs such as the presence or absence of suprasternal retractions and scalene muscle contractions, the amount of decrease in air entry, wheezing, and oxygen saturation. It can be used for both the assessment of severity and response to treatment. An increase of 3 or more points is considered clinically meaningful improvement.

Increased heart rate and respiratory rate are associated with decreased percentage of forced expiratory volume in 1 second (%FEV$_1$). Although the presence of wheezing indicates an obstructive process, its absence should not deter the physician from excluding asthma. In a severe asthma exacerbation, limited airflow will not result in significant wheezing. This patient should be treated immediately with oxygen, nebulized, short-acting beta$_2$ agonists with ipratropium bromide, and systemic corticosteroids.

443. The answer is B, Metoprolol.

(Nelson, 1096; Tintinalli, 441-448, 1234-1237)

Sedation with agents such as benzodiazepines is the primary initial management needed to control the agitation associated with cocaine and other sympathomimetic agent intoxications. Adequate sedation and hydration also effectively treat the associated hypertension and tachycardia. In the uncommon situation in which sedation does not effectively control the hypertension, direct-acting vasodilators such as nitroglycerin, nitroprusside, possibly nicardipine, and the alpha-antagonist phentolamine can all be used. The administration of beta-blockers such as metoprolol can lead to unopposed alpha agonism leading to vasospasm, worsened hypertension, and resultant complications. Although labetalol has some alpha$_1$ antagonism in addition to beta antagonism, it has not been demonstrated to reverse potential coronary vasoconstriction. Some individuals have recently questioned the potential harm of beta-blocker administration in patients with MI and a history of cocaine use. However, hypertension from acute cocaine intoxication can certainly be exacerbated by beta-blocker administration, so it remains absolutely contraindicated.

444. The answer is D, Pelvic ultrasonography is indicated.

(Marx, 193-198, 1294-1296; Tintinalli, 524, 674, 716-720)

The diagnosis of pelvic inflammatory disease (PID) is primarily based on history and physical examination; this patient was treated appropriately on her initial visit. Complications of PID include tubo-ovarian abscess (as is likely in this question) and Fitz-Hugh–Curtis syndrome. Pelvic ultrasonography is the most appropriate next step to evaluate a patient who has returned with worsening symptoms. Although CT might be better for diagnosing acute appendicitis, in most cases, pelvic pathology is more clearly identified using ultrasonography. This includes the most likely and most concerning diagnoses in this patient of tubo-ovarian abscess, ovarian cysts, and torsion of the ovary. On a CT scan, a tubo-ovarian abscess is seen as a nonspecific mass and is hard to distinguish from a hemorrhagic cyst or pelvic mass. Exposing a young female patient to radiation also makes CT less ideal. The most common presenting signs and symptoms of PID include lower abdominal pain and abnormal vaginal discharge. The presence of mucopurulent discharge, cervical motion tenderness, and adnexal tenderness all increase the likelihood of PID. There is no specific laboratory finding that is diagnostic of PID. Wet mount often reveals white blood cells, and, in their absence, the possibility of PID becomes less likely. Pelvic cultures that are positive for gonorrhea and *Chlamydia* provide a public health service for followup if the patient has already been treated presumptively with appropriate antibiotics (ceftriaxone and doxycycline in this case). Blood cultures are often negative and are not helpful in the management of PID. The absence of fever does not exclude the possibility of tubo-ovarian abscess. Diagnosis is most often made using pelvic ultrasonography, which can more clearly define pelvic infections and abscesses than a CT scan. Most patients respond well to antimicrobial therapy alone, and surgical intervention is often not needed. However, the presence of tubo-ovarian abscess is considered an indication for hospital admission and initiation of intravenous antibiotics. Fitz-Hugh–Curtis syndrome is an extension of infection to the right upper quadrant area causing perihepatitis. It often responds well to the same antimicrobial therapy used to treat PID. Although a patient who returns to the emergency department within 72 hours of an initial visit is at greater risk for a serious problem, hospitalization is not necessary in every case.

445. The answer is A, Abdominal CT angiography.

(Cangemi, 527-540; Tekwani, 747-765; Tintinalli, 522-523, 546)

A patient presentation of atrial fibrillation and abdominal pain out of proportion with physical examination findings is consistent with acute mesenteric ischemia. In this setting, multidetector CT angiography (CTA) is the diagnostic imaging modality of choice. It allows for visualization of either arterial or venous occlusion and can detect bowel wall abnormalities specific for mesenteric ischemia. The sensitivity and specificity of CTA are reported to be 92% to 96% and 64% to 94%, respectively. Mesenteric ischemia should be suspected in a patient with atrial fibrillation and acute onset of severe abdominal pain, especially if it is out of proportion to the tenderness on physical examination. This most commonly occurs in an embolic manner, with an acute embolus in the superior mesenteric artery, although mesenteric venous thrombosis or ischemia can cause similar symptoms. Plain radiographs of the abdomen can identify free air from a bowel perforation (which can cause similar symptoms) or late signs of bowel ischemia, including thumbprinting caused by bowel wall edema, portal vein gas, and pneumatosis intestinalis (air in the bowel wall). Plain radiographs provide less useful information than CTA, so CTA should not be delayed to obtain plain radiographs unless it is not readily available. There are no laboratory tests that are sensitive or specific for mesenteric ischemia. An elevated serum lactate level appears later in the course of the disease, usually after the onset of infarction. Ultrasonography is minimally helpful in the diagnosis of mesenteric ischemia, although recent studies have shown attempts to diagnose this disease using Doppler ultrasonography to measure flow through the superior mesenteric and celiac arteries.

446. **The answer is A, Associated radial nerve injury is common.**

(Marx, 468-469, 541-542; Tintinalli, 901-902, 1830)

The combination of a proximal ulnar fracture and an associated radial head dislocation is referred to as a Monteggia fracture. The deep branch of the radial nerve can be injured in up to 70% of cases as a result of the hematoma associated with the ulnar fracture. This leads to weakness of the extensors of the hand, although it commonly improves over time with the resolution of the hematoma and injury. Treatment of this fracture in adults is always surgical open reduction and internal fixation of the ulna, with repair of the annular ligament of the radial head when needed to prevent recurrent radial head dislocations or subluxations. If the patient is not going immediately to the operating room, a long arm splint is used to place the elbow joint in flexion and the arm in supination. Children can be treated with a splint only if good alignment and radial head reduction can occur through closed reduction.

447. **The answer is D, Outpatient elective arthroscopy 2 weeks earlier.**

(Adams, 483-485; American Thoracic Society, 388-416; Wolfson, 422-424)

The American Thoracic Society and the Infectious Diseases Society of America have identified the following risk factors for the development of health-care–associated pneumonia (HCAP): hospitalization for 2 or more days within the past 90 days; an extended care facility patient; any patient within the past month who received either intravenous antibiotics, chemotherapy, wound care, or chronic hemodialysis; and treatment with antibiotics within the past 90 days. Outpatient elective surgery is not among these criteria if the patient received no prophylactic antibiotics, which would be the case with arthroscopy: no antibiotics are recommended preoperatively in a site that is unlikely to be contaminated or have a high risk of infection. Community-acquired pneumonia (CAP) is most commonly caused by *Streptococcus pneumoniae, Haemophilus influenzae,* and *Mycoplasma pneumoniae.* A patient with CAP should be treated with ceftriaxone or an advanced fluoroquinolone. In contrast, HCAP is caused predominantly by gram-negative bacteria and *Staphylococcus aureus.* If a patient has HCAP and is at risk for multidrug-resistant organisms, the recommended antibiotics are an antipseudomonal cephalosporin or carbipenem, or antipseudomonal fluoroquinolone plus piperacillin-tazobactam.

448. **The answer is C, Normal saline bolus.**

(Kleinman, S889-S890; Marx, 1006-1016; Mattu, 45-52)

This patient's ECG reveals sinus tachycardia with a rate of 195. This finding is most commonly seen in children with hypovolemia, sepsis, or hypoxemia. Given the child's history of vomiting and diarrhea, a normal saline fluid bolus (20 mL/kg) is the most appropriate treatment. Sinus tachycardia can be identified by the consistent, uniform, and always present P waves that are found before every QRS interval and are upright in all limb leads except aVR. The P-P and PR distances should be consistent across the ECG if the rate remains stable. In infants and young children, heart rates as high as 220 beats/min can be seen in sinus tachycardia. In contrast, in adults, rates above approximately 170 beats/min are generally seen in supraventricular tachycardia or tachycardia from preexcitation and accessory pathways. Because this is a sinus rhythm, synchronized cardioversion will not change the rhythm and should not be performed. The increased heart rate provides the increase in cardiac output when a patient's stroke volume does not adequately adapt to the cardiovascular stress. Slowing this patient's heart rate down with medication such as digoxin could lead to hypotension. Adenosine would not affect the rhythm and cause harm but would also not treat this patient's underlying condition.

449. The answer is D, von Willebrand disease.

(Marx, 1206-1207, 1581-1589; Tintinalli, 1464-1466)

In a patient who has von Willebrand disease, the number of platelets is normal, but the adhesion properties are decreased, making them less functional. A lack of factor VIII (hemophilia A) and/or von Willebrand factor can cause abnormal platelet adhesion, resulting in the classic findings of bleeding with minimal trauma. There are three general causes of thrombocytopenia or decreased platelets: increased destruction of platelets, decreased production of platelets, and splenic sequestration. Thrombocytopenia from destruction can be caused by collagen vascular diseases, many medications (of which heparin is a specific concern), viral infections, and overwhelming sepsis. Destruction of platelets is seen in hemolytic uremic syndrome, which causes low platelet counts; thrombotic thrombocytopenia purpura complicates 2% to 3% of cases. Disseminated intravascular coagulation results in mechanical destruction of platelets when the clotting cascade is inappropriately activated. Excessive hemorrhage causes a low platelet count as a result of the loss of platelets from bleeding as well as the dilutional effect of fluid and packed red blood cells used in the resuscitation of a patient with massive bleeding.

450. The answer is C, She is at risk for adverse events and should be admitted for cardiac monitoring.

(American College of Emergency Physicians [syncope], 431-444; Marx, 142-146)

Given her history and presentation, the patient in this question potentially has a cardiovascular etiology for her syncope and is at risk for adverse events. According to current guidelines, she should be admitted for cardiac monitoring. Once immediately evident causes of sudden loss of consciousness have been excluded, the next step in the evaluation of syncope is to risk stratify the patient for cardiovascular disorders (cardiac ischemia, dysrhythmia, structural cardiac lesion, aortic dissection) and CNS disorders (subarachnoid hemorrhage). Patients who have a history of coronary artery disease, cerebrovascular disease, diabetes, hypertension, or other chronic diseases have an increased risk of death after a syncopal episode. Classic symptoms of neurocardiogenic syncope, also known as vasovagal syncope, include a prodrome of lightheadedness, nausea, and blurry vision while standing upright with rapid recovery when supine. Emotion and pain are common triggers. The ACEP Clinical Policy describes the following factors to predict increased risk of adverse outcome: older age, structural heart disease, or a history of coronary artery disease. The policy describes low-risk factors to be nonexertional syncope in younger patients, no history or signs of cardiovascular disease, no family history of sudden death, and no comorbidities. According to the San Francisco Syncope Rule, the absence of an abnormal ECG, shortness of breath, hypotension (systolic <90 mm Hg), anemia (Hct <30%), or a history of heart failure defines a low-risk group of patients who may be referred for outpatient evaluation. The San Francisco Syncope Rule does not include age as a risk factor, but some studies have concluded that hospitalization may be considered for older patients or those with comorbidities similar to those in the ACEP Clinical Policy. Patients with an abnormal ECG, prior ventricular dysrhythmia, history of heart failure, and age older than 45 years have a higher risk of dysrhythmia or death at 1 year (up to 58% adverse event rate). Orthostatic hypotension is present in up to 40% of asymptomatic patients older than 70 years and should be cautiously used to risk stratify otherwise high-risk patients. Although cardiac dysrhythmias are a cause of syncope, an implantable cardioverter-defibrillator is not needed without evidence of a life-threatening dysrhythmia.

Bibliography

Abraham M, Ahlman JT, Boudreau AJ, et al. *2011 Current Procedural Terminology (CPT)*. Chicago, IL: American Medical Association; 2010.

ACEP Task Force Report on Boarding. Emergency department crowding: high-impact solutions. ACEP Web site. http://www.acep.org/crowding/. Accessed January 18, 2010.

Acién P, Quereda F. Abdominal myomectomy: results of a simple operative technique. *Fertil Steril*. 1996;65(1):41-51.

Adams JG, Barton ED, Collings J, et al, eds. *Emergency Medicine*. Philadelphia, PA: Saunders; 2008.

Aguilar C, Vichinsky E, Neumayr L. Bone and joint disease in sickle cell disease. *Hematol Oncol Clin North Am*. 2005;19(5):929-941.

Albers GW, Amarenco P, Easton JD, et al. Antithrombotic and thrombolytic therapy for ischemic stroke: the Seventh ACCP Conference on Antithrombotic and Thrombolytic Therapy. *Chest*. 2004;126(3 Suppl):483S-512S.

American College of Emergency Physicians. 1995 Documentation guidelines for evaluation and management services. ACEP Web site. http://www.acep.org/content.aspx?id=32168&list=1&fid=912. Accessed February 24, 2011.

American College of Emergency Physicians. Clinical policy: critical issues in the evaluation and management of adult patients presenting to the emergency department with seizures. *Ann Emerg Med*. 2004;43:605-625.

American Thoracic Society, Infectious Diseases Society of America. Guidelines for the management of adults with hospital-acquired, ventilator-associated, and healthcare-associated pneumonia. *Am J Respir Crit Care Med*. 2005;171:388-416.

Amoco Chemical Corp v Hill, 318 A2d 614 (Del Super Ct 1974).

Anderson JL, Adams CD, Antman EM, et al. ACC/AHA 2007 guidelines for the management of patients with unstable angina/non ST-elevation myocardial infarction. *Circulation*. 2007;116(7):e148-e304.

Anderson JL, Adams CD, Antman EM, et al. ACC/AHA 2007 guidelines for the management of patients with unstable angina/non-ST-elevation myocardial infarction: a report of the American College of Cardiology/American Heart Association Task Force on Practice Guidelines (Writing Committee to Revise the 2002 Guidelines for the Management of Patients With Unstable Angina/Non-ST-Elevation Myocardial Infarction) developed in collaboration with the American College of Emergency Physicians, the Society for Cardiovascular Angiography and Interventions, and the Society of Thoracic Surgeons endorsed by the American Association of Cardiovascular and Pulmonary Rehabilitation and the Society for Academic Emergency Medicine. *J Am Coll Cardiol*. 2007;50(7):e1-e157.

Antman EM, Anbe DT, Armstrong PW, et al. ACC/AHA guidelines for the management of patients with ST-elevation myocardial infarction. *Circulation*. 2004;110(5):588-636.

Auerbach PS. *Wilderness Medicine*. 5th ed. Philadelphia, PA: Mosby, Inc.; 2007.

Barretti P, Montelli AC, Batalha JE, et al. The role of virulence factors in the outcome of staphylococcal peritonitis in CAPD patients. *BMC Infect Dis*. 2009;9:212.

Bates SM, Ginsberg JS. Clinical practice. Treatment of deep-vein thrombosis. *N Engl J Med*. 2004;351(3):268-277.

Bitterman RA. *Providing Emergency Care Under Federal Law: EMTALA*. Dallas, TX: American College of Emergency Physicians; 2001, 2004.

Bonow RO, Carabello BA, Chatterjee K, et al. 2008 Focused update incorporated into the ACC/AHA 2006 guidelines for the management of patients with valvular heart disease. *Circulation*. 2008;118(15):e523-e661.

Bosch X, Poch E, Grau JM. Rhabdomyolysis and acute kidney injury. *N Engl J Med*. 2009;361(1):62-72.

Botma M, Bader R, Kubba H. 'A parent's kiss': evaluating an unusual method for removing nasal foreign bodies in children. *J Laryngol Otol*. 2000;114:598-600.

Brenner BM. *Brenner and Rector's The Kidney*. 8th ed. Philadelphia, PA: Saunders; 2008.

Cainzos M, Gonzalez-Rodriguez FJ. Necrotizing soft tissue infections. *Curr Opin Crit Care*. 2007;13(4):433-439.

Cangemi JR, Picco MF. Intestinal ischemia in the elderly. *Gastroenterol Clin North Am*. 2009;38(3):527-540.

Centers for Disease Control and Prevention. Anthrax. CDC Web site. http://www.bt.cdc.gov/agent/anthrax/. Accessed November 15, 2010.

Centers for Disease Control and Prevention. Guideline for prevention of catheter-associated urinary tract infections 2009. CDC Web site. www.cdc.gov/hicpac/pdf/CAUTI/CAUTIguideline2009final.pdf. Accessed January 2, 2011.

Centers for Disease Control and Prevention. Preventing tetanus, diphtheria, and pertussis among adolescents: use of tetanus toxoid, reduced diphtheria toxoid, and acellular pertussis vaccines. *MMWR Morb Mortal Wkly Rep*. 2006;55(3):1-34. http://www.cdc.gov/mmwr/preview/mmwrhtml/rr5503a1.htm. Accessed January 19, 2011.

Centers for Disease Control and Prevention. Sexually transmitted diseases treatment guidelines 2010. *MMWR Morb Mortal Wkly Rep.* 2010;59(12):1-110. http://www.cdc.gov/std/treatment/2010/STD-Treatment-2010-RR5912. pdf. Accessed January 19, 2011. With erratum for pages 50, 51, 57.

Centers for Disease Control and Prevention. Updated U.S. Public Health Service guidelines for the management of occupational exposures to HIV and recommendations for postexposure prophylaxis. *MMWR Morb Mortal Wkly Rep.* 2005;54(RR-9):1-17. http://www.cdc.gov/mmwr/PDF/rr/rr5409.pdf. Accessed January 4, 2011.

Centor RM, Witherspoon JM, Dalton HP, et al. The diagnosis of strep throat in adults in the emergency room. *Med Decis Making.* 1981;1(3):239-246.

Chau B, Dufel S. Gastric volvulus. *Emerg Med J.* 2007;24(6):446-447.

Chiu YH, Chen JD, Tiu CM, et al. Reappraisal of radiographic signs of pneumoperitoneum at emergency department. *Am J Emerg Med.* 2009;27(3):320-327.

Cucchiara B, Ross M. Transient ischemic attack: risk stratification and treatment. *Ann Emerg Med.* 2008;52(2):S27-S39.

Darouiche RO. Spinal epidural abscess. *N Engl J Med.* 2006;355(19):2012-2020.

Delacrétaz E. Clinical practice. Supraventricular tachycardia. *N Engl J Med.* 2006;354(10):1039-1051.

Duhaime AC. Evaluation and management of shunt infections in children with hydrocephalus. *Clin Pediatr (Phila).* 2006;45(8):705-713.

Duong DK, Leo MM, Mitchell EL. Neuro-ophthalmology. *Emerg Med Clin North Am.* 2008;26(1):137-180, vii.

Edlow JA, Malek AM, Ogilvy CS. Aneurysmal subarachnoid hemorrhage: update for emergency physicians. *J Emerg Med.* 2008;34(3):237-251.

Edlow JA, Panagos PD, Godwin SA, et al. American College of Emergency Physicians. Clinical policy: critical issues in the evaluation and management of adult patients presenting to the emergency department with acute headache. *Ann Emerg Med.* 2008;52(4):407-436.

Eren S, Kantarci M, Okur A. Imaging of diaphragmatic rupture after trauma. *Clin Radiol.* 2006;61(6):467-477.

Evans HJ, Wollin TA. The management of urinary calculi in pregnancy. *Curr Opin Urol.* 2001;11(4):379-384.

Fesmire FM, Decker WW, Diercks DB, et al. ACEP Clinical Policies Subcommittee (Writing Committee) on non–ST-segment elevation acute coronary syndromes. Clinical policy: critical issues in the evaluation and management of adult patients with non–ST-segment elevation acute coronary syndromes. *Ann Emerg Med.* 2006;48(3):270-301.

Fine MJ, Auble TE, Yealy DM, et al. A prediction rule to identify low-risk patients with community-acquired pneumonia. *N Engl J Med.* 1997;336(4):243-250.

Fleisher GR, Ludwig S, eds. *Textbook of Pediatric Emergency Medicine.* 6th ed. Philadelphia, PA: Lippincott Williams & Wilkins; 2010.

Geetha D. Glomerulonephritis, poststreptococcal. eMedicine Web site. http://emedicine.medscape.com/article/240337-overview. Accessed February 17, 2011.

Gerber MA, Baltimore RS, Eaton CB, et al. Prevention of rheumatic fever and diagnosis and treatment of acute streptococcal pharyngitis: a scientific statement from the American Heart Association Rheumatic Fever, Endocarditis, and Kawasaki Disease Committee of the Council on Cardiovascular Disease in the Young, the Interdisciplinary Council on Functional Genomics and Translational Biology, and the Interdisciplinary Council on Quality of Care and Outcomes Research: endorsed by the American Academy of Pediatrics. *Circulation.* 2009;119(11):1541-1551.

Gillette v Tucker, 65 NE 865 (1972).

Godwin SA, Caro DA, Wolf SJ, et al. American College of Emergency Physicians. Clinical policy: procedural sedation and analgesia in the emergency department. *Ann Emerg Med.* 2005;45(2):177-196.

Goldman L, Ausiello DA. *Cecil Medicine.* 23rd ed. Philadelphia, PA: Saunders; 2008.

Grimes DA, Jones LB, Lopez LM, et al. Oral contraceptives for functional ovarian cysts. *Cochrane Database Syst Rev.* 2009;(2):CD006134.

Grissom CK, Roach RC, Sarnquist FH, et al. Acetazolamide in the treatment of acute mountain sickness: clinical efficacy and effect on gas exchange. *Ann Intern Med.* 1992;116(6):461-465.

Hackett PH, Roach RC. Medical therapy of altitude illness. *Ann Emerg Med.* 1987;16(9):980-986.

Hall JB, Schmidt GA, Wood LDH, eds. *Principles of Critical Care.* New York, NY: McGraw-Hill; 2005.

Han JH, Zimmerman EE, Cutler N, et al. Delirium in older emergency department patients: recognition, risk factors, and psychomotor subtypes. *Acad Emerg Med.* 2009;16(3):193-200.

Harrington L, Schneider JI. Atraumatic joint and limb pain in the elderly. *Emerg Med Clin North Am.* 2006;24(2):389-412, vii.

Hirtz D, Ashwal S, Berg A, et al. Practice parameter: evaluating a first nonfebrile seizure in children: report of the Quality Standards Subcommittee of the American Academy of Neurology, The Child Neurology Society, and The American Epilepsy Society. *Neurology.* 2000;55(5):616-623.

Honigman B, Theis MK, Koziol-McLain J, et al. Acute mountain sickness in a general tourist population at moderate altitudes. *Ann Intern Med.* 1993;118(8):587-592.

Howell JM, Eddy OL, Lukens TW, et al. American College of Emergency Physicians. Clinical policy: critical issues in the evaluation and management of emergency department patients with suspected appendicitis. *Ann Emerg Med.* 2010;55(1):71-116.

Huff JS, Decker WW, Quinn JV, et al. American College of Emergency Physicians Clinical Policies Subcommittee (Writing Committee) on Syncope. Clinical policy: critical issues in the evaluation and management of adult patients presenting to the emergency department with syncope. *Ann Emerg Med.* 2007;49(4):431-444.

Hustey FM, Meldon SW. The prevalence and documentation of impaired mental status in elderly emergency department patients. *Ann Emerg Med.* 2002;39(3):248-253.

James AH, Jamison MG, Biswas MS, et al. Acute myocardial infarction in pregnancy: a United States population-based study. *Circulation.* 2006;113(12):1564-1571.

Jones DW, Hall JE. Seventh report of the Joint National Committee on Prevention, Detection, Evaluation, and Treatment of High Blood Pressure and evidence from new hypertension trials. *Hypertension.* 2004;43(1):1-3.

Jurkovich GJ. Environmental cold-induced injury. *Surg Clin North Am.* 2007;87(1):247-267, viii.

Katz VL, Dotters DJ, Droegemueller W. Perimortem cesarean delivery. *Obstet Gynecol.* 1986;68(4):571-576.

Kenyon SL, Taylor DJ, Tarnow-Mordi W, et al. Broad-spectrum antibiotics for preterm, prelabour rupture of fetal membranes: the ORACLE I randomised trial. ORACLE Collaborative Group. *Lancet.* 2001;357(9261):979-988.

Kitabchi AE, Umpierrez GE, Murphy MB, et al. Hyperglycemic crisis in adult patients with diabetes: a consensus statement from the American Diabetes Association. *Diabetes Care.* 2006;29(12):2739-2748.

Kittner SJ, Stern BJ, Feeser BR, et al. Pregnancy and the risk of stroke. *N Engl J Med.* 1996;335(11):767-769.

Kleinman ME, Chameides L, Schexnayder SM, et al. Part 14: pediatric advanced life support: 2010 American Heart Association Guidelines for Cardiopulmonary Resuscitation and Emergency Cardiovascular Care. *Circulation.* 2010;122(18 suppl 3):S876-S908.

Kline JA, Courtney DM, Kabrhel C, et al. Prospective multicenter evaluation of the pulmonary embolism rule-out criteria. *J Thromb Haemost.* 2008;6(5):772-780.

Knoop KJ, Stack LB, Storrow AB, et al. *Atlas of Emergency Medicine.* 3rd ed. New York, NY: McGraw-Hill; 2010.

Koenig KL, Schultz CH, eds. *Koenig and Schultz's Disaster Medicine: Comprehensive Principles and Practices.* New York, NY: Cambridge University Press; 2010.

Kohn LT, Corrigan JM, Donaldson MS, eds. *To Err Is Human: Building a Safer Health System.* Washington, DC; The National Academies Press; 2000. http://books.nap.edu/openbook.php?record_id=9728. Accessed February 9, 2011.

Konstantinides S. Clinical practice. Acute pulmonary embolism. *N Engl J Med.* 2008;359(26):2804-2813.

Laughlin TJ, Armstrong DG, Caporusso J, et al. Soft tissue and bone infections from puncture wounds in children. *West J Med.* 1997;166(2):126-128.

Levine BD, Yoshimura K, Kobayashi T, et al. Dexamethasone in the treatment of acute mountain sickness. *N Engl J Med.* 1989;321(25):1707-1713.

Levine MS, Scheiner JD, Rubesin SE, et al. Diagnosis of pneumoperitoneum on supine abdominal radiographs. *AJR Am J Roentgenol.* 1991;156(4):731-735.

Lin MG. Umbilical cord prolapse. *Obstet Gynecol Surv.* 2006;61(4):269-277.

Link MS, Atkins DL, Passman RS, et al. Part 6: electrical therapies: automated external defibrillators, defibrillation, cardioversion, and pacing: 2010 American Heart Association Guidelines for Cardiopulmonary Resuscitation and Emergency Cardiovascular Care. *Circulation.* 2010;122(18 Suppl 3):S706-S719.

Liu C, Bayer A, Cosgrove SE, et al. Clinical practice guidelines by the Infectious Diseases Society of America for the treatment of methicillin-resistant *Staphylococcus aureus* infections in adults and children. *Clin Infect Dis.* 2011;52(3):e18-e55. http://cid.oxfordjournals.org/content/early/2011/01/04/cid.ciq146.full.pdf+html. Accessed April 21, 2011.

Ma OJ, Mateer JR, Blaivas M, eds. *Emergency Ultrasound.* New York, NY: McGraw-Hill; 2008.

MacFarlane C, Benn C. Evaluation of emergency medical services systems: a classification to assist in determination of indicators. *Emerg Med J.* 2003;20(2):188-191.

Mahmood AR, Narang AT. Diagnosis and management of the acute red eye. *Emerg Med Clin North Am.* 2008;26(1):35-55,vi.

Mandell LA, Wunderink RG, Anzueto A, et al. Infectious Diseases Society of America/American Thoracic Society consensus guidelines on the management of community-acquired pneumonia in adults. *Clin Infect Dis.* 2007;44 Suppl 2:S27-S72.

Marco CA, Schoenfeld CN, Hansen KN, et al. Fever in geriatric emergency patients: clinical features associated with serious illness. *Ann Emerg Med.* 1995;26(1):18-24.

Marik PE, Plante LA. Venous thromboembolic disease and pregnancy. *N Engl J Med.* 2008;359(19):2025-2033.

Maron BJ, Estes NA 3rd. Commotio cordis. *N Engl J Med.* 2010;362(10):917-927.

Marx JA, Hockberger RS, Walls RM, eds. *Rosen's Emergency Medicine: Concepts and Clinical Practice*. 7th ed. St. Louis, MO: Elsevier; 2009.

Mathur VS, Lindberg J, Germain M, et al. A longitudinal study of uremic pruritus in hemodialysis patients. *Clin J Am Soc Nephrol*. 2010;5(8):1410-1419.

Mattu A, Barish RA, Tabas JA, eds. *Electrocardiography in Emergency Medicine*. Dallas, TX: American College of Emergency Physicians; 2007.

McMullan J, Valento M, Attari M, et al. Care of the pacemaker/implantable cardioverter defibrillator patient in the ED. *Am J Emerg Med*. 2007;25(7):812-822.

Medeiros I, Saconato H. Antibiotic prophylaxis for mammalian bites. *Cochrane Database Syst Rev*. 2001;(2):CD001738.

Mercer BM, Miodovnik M, Thurnau GR, et al. Antibiotic therapy for reduction of infant morbidity after preterm premature rupture of the membranes. A randomized controlled trial. *JAMA*. 1997;278(12):989-995.

Miner JR, Burton JH. Clinical practice advisory: emergency department procedural sedation with propofol. *Ann Emerg Med*. 2007;50(2):182-187.

Moran GJ, Krishnadasan A, Gorwitz RJ, et al. Methicillin-resistant *S. aureus* infections among patients in the emergency department. *N Engl J Med*. 2006;355(7):666-674.

Nabel EG, Federman DD, eds. *ACP Medicine*. New York, NY: BC Decker; 2010.

National Highway Traffic Safety Administration (NHTSA), Emergency Medical Services. NHTSA EMS Web site. http://www.ems.gov/. Accessed January 25, 2010.

Nelson LS, Lewin NA, Howland MA, et al, eds. *Goldfrank's Toxicologic Emergencies*. 9th ed. New York, NY: McGraw-Hill; 2010.

Neumar RW, Otto CW, Link MS, et al. Part 8: adult advanced cardiovascular life support: 2010 American Heart Association Guidelines for Cardiopulmonary Resuscitation and Emergency Cardiovascular Care. *Circulation*. 2010;122(18 Suppl 3):S729-S767.

Nishimura RA, Carabello BA, Faxon DP, et al. ACC/AHA 2008 Guideline update on valvular heart disease: focused update on infective endocarditis. *J Am Coll Cardiol*. 2008;52(8):676-685.

O'Connor RE, Brady W, Brooks SC, et al. Part 10: acute coronary syndromes: 2010 American Heart Association Guidelines for Cardiopulmonary Resuscitation and Emergency Cardiovascular Care. *Circulation*. 2010;122(18 Suppl 3):S787-S817.

Quinlan DJ, McQuillan A, Eikelboom JW. Low-molecular-weight heparin compared with intravenous unfractionated heparin for treatment of pulmonary embolism, a meta-analysis of randomized, controlled trials. *Ann Intern Med*. 2004;140(3):175-183.

Roberts JR, Hedges JR, eds. *Clinical Procedures in Emergency Medicine*. 5th ed. St. Louis, MO: WB Saunders; 2010.

Roy CL, Minor MA, Brookhart MA, et al. Does this patient with a pericardial effusion have cardiac tamponade? *JAMA*. 2007;297(16):1810-1818.

Santora TA, Rukstalis DB. Fournier gangrene. eMedicine Web site. http://emedicine.medscape.com/article/438994-overview. Accessed February 15, 2011.

Schlosser RJ. Clinical practice. Epistaxis. *N Engl J Med*. 2009;360(8):784-789.

Schwartz DT. *Emergency Radiology Case Studies*. New York, NY: McGraw-Hill; 2008.

Sgarbossa EB, Pinski SL, Barbagelata A, et al. Electrocardiographic diagnosis of evolving acute myocardial infarction in the presence of left bundle-branch block. GUSTO-1 (Global Utilization of Streptokinase and Tissue Plasminogen Activator for Occluded Coronary Arteries) Investigators. *N Engl J Med*. 1996;334(8):481-487.

Shah R, Sabanathan S, Mearns AJ, et al. Traumatic rupture of diaphragm. *Ann Thorac Surg*. 1995;60(5):1444-1449.

Silvers SM, Howell JM, Kosowsky JM, et al. American College of Emergency Physicians Clinical Policies Subcommittee (Writing Committee) on Acute Heart Failure Syndromes. Clinical policy: critical issues in the evaluation and management of adult patients presenting to the emergency department with acute heart failure syndromes. *Ann Emerg Med*. 2007;49(5):627-669.

Simon RP, Greenberg DA, Aminoff MJ, et al. *Clinical Neurology*. 7th ed. New York, NY: McGraw-Hill; 2008.

Singh A, Alter HJ, Littlepage A. A systematic review of medical therapy to facilitate passage of ureteral calculi. *Ann Emerg Med*. 2007;50(5):552-563.

Slovis CM, Reddi AS. Increased blood pressure without evidence of acute end organ damage. *Ann Emerg Med*. 2008;51(3 Suppl):S7-S9.

Spiro DM, Tay KY, Arnold DH, et al. Wait-and-see prescription for the treatment of acute otitis media: a randomized controlled trail. *JAMA*. 2006;296(10):1235-1241.

Statement on sarcoidosis. Joint Statement of the American Thoracic Society (ATS), the European Respiratory Society (ERS) and the World Association of Sarcoidosis and Other Granulomatous Disorders (WASOG) adopted by the ATS Board of Directors and by the ERS Executive Committee, February 1999. *Am J Respir Crit Care Med*. 1999;160(2):736-755.

Stein PD, Fowler SE, Goodman LR, et al. Multidetector computed tomography for acute pulmonary embolism. *N Engl J Med.* 2006;354(22):2317-2327.

Strange GR, Ahrens WR, Schafermeyer RW, et al, eds. *Pediatric Emergency Medicine.* 3rd ed. New York, NY: McGraw-Hill; 2009.

Straus SE, Richardson WS, Glasziou P, et al. *Evidence-Based Medicine: How to Practice and Teach EBM.* 3rd ed. London, England: BMJ Publishing Group; 2003.

Straus SE, Thorpe KE, Holroyd-Leduc J. How do I perform a lumbar puncture and analyze the results to diagnose bacterial meningitis? *JAMA.* 2006;296(16):2012-2022.

Stringer JR, Beard CB, Miller RF. Spelling *Pneumocystis jirovecii* [letter]. *Emerg Infect Dis* [serial online]. 2009. http://www.cdc.gov/EID/content/15/3/506a.htm. Accessed May 6, 2011.

Stringer JR, Beard CB, Miller RF, et al. A new name *(Pneumocystis jiroveci)* for *Pneumocystis* from humans. *Emerg Infect Dis.* 2002;8(9):891-896.

Tabas JA, Rodriguez RM, Seligman HK, et al. Electrocardiographic criteria for detecting acute myocardial infarction in patients with left bundle branch block: a meta-analysis. *Ann Emerg Med.* 2008;52(4):329-336.e1.

Tekwani K, Sikka R. High-risk chief complaints III: abdomen and extremities. *Emerg Med Clin North Am.* 2009;27(4):747-765, x.

Thomsen TW, Shaffer RW, White B, et al. Videos in clinical medicine. Paracentesis. *N Engl J Med.* 2006;355(19):e21.

Tintinalli JE, Stapczynski JS, Ma OJ, et al, eds. *Tintinalli's Emergency Medicine: A Comprehensive Study Guide.* 7th ed. New York, NY: McGraw-Hill; 2010.

Townsend CM, Beauchamp RD, Evers BM, et al. *Sabiston Textbook of Surgery.* 18th ed. Philadelphia, PA: Saunders Elsevier; 2008.

van Beeck EF, Branche CM, Szpilman D, et al. A new definition of drowning: towards documentation and prevention of a global public health problem. *Bull World Health Organ.* 2005;83(11):853-856.

van Belle A, Büller HR, Huisman MV, et al. Effectiveness of managing suspected pulmonary embolism using an algorithm combining clinical probability, D-dimer testing, and computed tomography. *JAMA* 2006;295(2):172-179.

Vanden Hoek TL, Morrison LJ, Shuster M, et al. Part 12: cardiac arrest in special situations: 2010 American Heart Association guidelines for cardiopulmonary resuscitation and emergency cardiovascular care. *Circulation.* 2010;122(suppl 3):S829-S861.

Venkat A, Piontkowsky DM, Cooney RR, et al. Care of the HIV-positive patient in the emergency department in the era of highly active antiretroviral therapy. *Ann Emerg Med.* 2008;52(3):274-285.

Venkat KK, Venkat A. Care of the renal transplant recipient in the emergency department. *Ann Emerg Med.* 2004;44(4):330-341.

Vilke GM, Ufberg JW, Harrigan RA, et al. Evaluation and treatment of acute urinary retention. *J Emerg Med.* 2008;35(2):193-198.

Vital FM, Saconato H, Ladeira MT, et al. Non-invasive positive pressure ventilation (CPAP or bilevel NPPV) for cardiogenic pulmonary edema. *Cochrane Database Syst Rev.* 2008;(3):CD005351.

Wallach EE, Vlahos NF. Uterine myomas: an overview of development, clinical features, and management. *Obstet Gynecol.* 2004;104(2):393-406.

Wang CS, FitzGerald JM, Schulzer M, et al. Does this dyspneic patient in the emergency department have congestive heart failure? *JAMA.* 2005;294(15):1944-1956.

Wenzel RP, Fowler AA 3rd. Clinical practice. Acute bronchitis. *N Engl J Med.* 2006;355(20):2125-2130.

World Health Organization. WHO global influenza preparedness plan: The role of WHO and recommendations for national measures before and during pandemics. Switzerland, World Health Organization, 2005. WHO Web site. http://www.who.int/csr/resources/publications/influenza/WHO_CDS_CSR_GIP_2005_5.pdf. Accessed January 2, 2011.

Wolff K, Johnson R, eds. *Fitzpatrick's Color Atlas & Synopsis of Clinical Dermatology.* 6th ed. New York, NY: McGraw-Hill; 2009.

Wolfson AB, Hendey GW, Ling LJ, et al, eds. *Harwood-Nuss' Clinical Practice of Emergency Medicine.* 5th ed. Philadelphia, PA: Lippincott, Williams & Wilkins; 2010.

Wood JP, Shufeldt JJ, Rapp MT, eds. *Contract Issues for Emergency Physicians.* Irving, TX: Emergency Medicine Residents' Association; 2007.

Wu MH, Chang YC, Wu CH, et al. Acute gastric volvulus: a rare but real surgical emergency. *Am J Emerg Med.* 2010;28(1):118.e5-e7.

Index

congenital megacolon. *see* Hirschprung disease
conjunctivitis, 75, 242
contact vulvovaginitis, 116
continuous positive airway pressure (CPAP), 171
contrast media, iodinated, 165–166
conus medullaris syndrome, 7
conversion disorders, 67
convulsions. *see* seizures
cooling, evaporative, 64–65
COPD
  noninvasive ventilation and, 43
  NPPV indications, 82
cornea
  abrasions, visualization, 70–71
  abrasions in infants, 149
  examination of, 70–71
  herpes simplex infection, 74
  perforation, 101
coronary artery disease (CAD), 52
coronary artery emboli, 108
cortisporin otic, 5
Coudé catheters, 244–245
COWS mnemonic, 41
Coxiella burnetii, 10
cranial nerve (CN III), 53–54
cranial nerves, routes of, 166
creatinine, serum, 66
cricothyrotomy, 220
Crohn disease
  abscess formation, 131–132
  bowel wall in, 126
  complication of, 131–132
croup, presentation, 115
crowding, boarding and, 56
crusts, skin, 172
crutches, 83
Cryptococcus neoformans, 18, 160, 186–187
Cryptosporidium parvum, 160
crystalloid resuscitation
  hypotension and, 93
  Parkland formula, 170
cultures, throat, 173, 238
CURB-65 criteria, 169
currant-jelly stool, 106
Current Procedural Terminology (CPT) codes, 24
cyanide, 191
cyanide poisoning, 159
cyanosis
  methemoglobinemia and, 158–159
  peripheral, 125
  tetralogy of Fallot and, 81
cyclobenzaprine, 129
cyclosporine, 153
cystic fibrosis (CF), 97–98
cysticercosis, 19
cytochrome oxidase, 191
cytomegalovirus (CMV), 119, 251
cytomegalovirus (CMV) retinitis, 18

D
D-dimer assay
  levels in DIC, 5–6
  in pregnancy, 73
  screening, 43
dacrocystitis, 241–242
dapsone
  oxidant stress and, 158
  use of, 134
decompression sickness (DCS), 128
decompressive laminectomy, 207
decubitus ulcers, 13
deep tendon reflexes, 88
deep vein thrombosis (DVT)
  diagnosis of, 73–74
  pulmonary emboli and, 151–152
defibrillation, 175
dehydration
  in infants, 177
  postural hypotension and, 196
  rehydration after, 150–151
delirium, 82, 112
dementias
  definition of, 82
  primary, 82
  secondary, 82
dental avulsions, 118
Dermacentor ticks, 226–227
dermatitis, allergic phytocontact, 3
dermatographism, 71
dermatomyositis, 137–138
developmental dysplasia of the hip (DDH), 90–91
diabetic autonomic neuropathy, 24
diabetic ketoacidosis
  hyperosmolar hyperglycemic state and, 211
  Kussmaul breathing in, 164
  potassium deficits, 146
diabetic neuropathies, 53–54
dialysis, peritoneal, 9–10
diaphragm rupture, 150
diarrhea, rehydration after, 150–151
diazepam, 34
diazoxide, 11
dicloxacillin, 247–248
didanosine (DDI), 240
Dieffenbachia poisoning, 219
digitalis, 184
digits. *see also* fingers
  amputations, 236–237
  replantation, 237
diltiazem, 1, 2
diphenhydramine
  mechanism of action, 180
  poisoning by, 55
  for transfusion reactions, 80
diplopia, 53–54, 147
disseminated intravascular coagulation (DIC), 5–6, 256